The Treasury of Precious Instructions: Essential Teachings of the Eight Practice Lineages of Tibet

Volume 6: Sakya
Part 2

The Tsadra Foundation Series

published by Snow Lion, an imprint of Shambhala Publications

Tsadra Foundation is a U.S.-based nonprofit organization that contributes to the ongoing development of wisdom and compassion in Western minds by advancing the combined study and practice of Tibetan Buddhism.

Taking its inspiration from the nineteenth-century nonsectarian Tibetan Buddhist scholar and meditation master Jamgön Kongtrul Lodrö Taye, Tsadra Foundation is named after his hermitage in eastern Tibet, Tsadra Rinchen Drak. The Foundation's various program areas reflect his values of excellence in both scholarship and contemplative practice, and the recognition of their mutual complementarity.

Tsadra Foundation envisions a flourishing community of Western contemplatives and scholar-practitioners who are fully trained in the traditions of Tibetan Buddhism. It is our conviction that, grounded in wisdom and compassion, these individuals will actively enrich the world through their openness and excellence.

This publication is a part of Tsadra Foundation's Translation Program, which aims to make authentic and authoritative texts from the Tibetan traditions available in English. The Foundation is honored to present the work of its fellows and grantees, individuals of confirmed contemplative and intellectual integrity; however, their views do not necessarily reflect those of the Foundation.

Tsadra Foundation is delighted to collaborate with Shambhala Publications in making these important texts available in the English language.

Sakya

The Path with Its Result

Part 2

THE TREASURY OF PRECIOUS INSTRUCTIONS:
ESSENTIAL TEACHINGS OF THE EIGHT PRACTICE
LINEAGES OF TIBET
VOLUME 6

Compiled by Jamgön Kongtrul Lodrö Taye

TRANSLATED BY
Malcolm Smith

SNOW LION

Snow Lion
An imprint of Shambhala Publications, Inc.
2129 13th Street
Boulder, Colorado 80302
www.shambhala.com

Cover art: Detail from thangka "The Sakya Practice Lineage of Tibetan Buddhism." Collection Eric Colombel. Photo: Rafael Ortet, 2018. © Eric Colombel, New York.

9 8 7 6 5 4 3 2 1

First Edition
Printed in the United States of America

Shambhala Publications makes every effort to print on acid-free, recycled paper. For more information please visit www.shambhala.com. Snow Lion is distributed worldwide by Penguin Random House, Inc., and its subsidiaries.

LIBRARY OF CONGRESS CATALOGING-IN-PUBLICATION DATA

Names: Kong-sprul Blo-gros-mtha'-yas, 1813–1899, author. |
Smith, Malcolm (Buddhism practitioner), translator.
Title: Sakya. / compiled by Jamgön Kongtrul Lodrö Taye; translated by Malcolm Smith.
Description: Boulder: Shambhala, 2022– | Includes bibliographical references and index.
Identifiers: LCCN 2021011443
ISBN 9781611809664 (hardback, part one)
ISBN 9781611809671 (hardback, part two)
Subjects: LCSH: Lam-'bras (Sa-skya-pa) | Sa-skya-pa (Sect)—Doctrines. |
Tripiṭaka. Sūtrapiṭaka. Tantra. Hevajratantrarāja—Commentaries.
Classification: LCC BQ7672.4 .K66 2022 | DDC 294.3/420423—dc23
LC record available at https://lccn.loc.gov/2021011443

Contents

Foreword by the Seventeenth Karmapa xi

Series Introduction xiii

Translator's Introduction xvii

Technical Note xxiii

Part One: The Eight Ancillary Path Cycles

1. Supplication to the Lineage of the Eight Ancillary Path Cycles 3
by Ngorchen Kunga Zangpo

2. *Accomplishment of the Connate* Composed by Ḍombi Heruka 11
by Drakpa Gyaltsen

3. Ācārya Padmavajra's *Creation Stage Adorned with the Nine Profound Methods* and *Completion Stage Instruction Resembling the Tip of a Lamp Flame* 21

Ācārya Padmavajra's *Creation Stage Adorned with the Nine Profound Methods* 25
by Drakpa Gyaltsen

Ācārya Padmavajra's *Completion Stage Instruction Resembling the Tip of a Lamp Flame* 41
by Padmavajra

4. *Completing the Whole Path with Caṇḍālī* Composed by Ācārya Kṛṣṇācārya 45
by Drakpa Gyaltsen

5. The *Instruction for Straightening the Crooked* Composed by Kṛṣṇa Acyuta 57
by Drakpa Gyaltsen

6. *Obtained in Front of a Stupa* Composed by Ācārya Nāgārjuna 61
by Drakpa Gyaltsen

7. *Mahāmudrā without Syllables* Composed by Ācārya Vāgīśvarakīrti 69
by Drakpa Gyaltsen

8. Śrī Koṭalipa's *Instruction on the Inconceivable* 83

Intimate Instructions on the Stages of the Inconceivable 85
by Koṭalipa

The Chronicle of Ācārya Koṭalipa's Path, the Five Inconceivabilities 103
by Drakpa Gyaltsen

The Clarification of the Instruction on the Inconceivable Composed by Ācārya Koṭalipa 107
by Drakpa Gyaltsen

9. *The Path Cycle of the Mudra* Composed by Ācārya Indrabhūti 121
by Drakpa Gyaltsen

Part Two: Jamgön Kongtrul's Commentary on the Eight Ancillary Path Cycles

Introduction 139

10. Medicinal Elixir of the Fortunate Bezoar: The Manual of Ḍombi Heruka's *Accomplishing the Connate* 141
by Jamgön Kongtrul

11. Fortunate Mustard Seedpod: The Manual of the *Nine Profound Methods* of Padmavajra 155
by Jamgön Kongtrul

12. Essence of Fortunate Curd: The Manual of *Straightening the Crooked* by Kṛṣṇa Acyuta 181
by Jamgön Kongtrul

13. Excellent Tree of Fortunate Bilva: Ārya Nāgārjuna's Manual *Obtained in Front of a Stupa* 187
by Jamgön Kongtrul

14. Fortunate Shoot of Dūrva Grass: The Manual of *Mahāmudrā without Syllables* Composed by Ācārya Vāgīśvarakīrti 207
by Jamgön Kongtrul

15. Fortunate Pure Crystal Mirror: The Instruction Manual of Śrī Koṭalipa's *Inconceivable* 223
by Jamgön Kongtrul

16. Fortunate Right-Turning White Conch: The Manual of Indrabhūti's *Path of the Mudra* 243
by Jamgön Kongtrul

17. Fortunate Vermilion Ornament: Kṛṣṇācārya's Manual of *Completing the Whole Path with Caṇḍālī* 257
by Jamgön Kongtrul

Part Three: Ancillary Instructions and Rites

18. The Manual Known as *The Dharma Connection with the Six Gatekeepers* Received by Drokmi Lotsāwa from the Six Paṇḍita Gatekeepers 273

Merging Sutra and Tantra 277
by Drokmi Lotsāwa

The Trio for Removing Obstructions by Prajñākaragupta, Jñānaśrī, and Ratnavajra 281
by Drokmi Lotsāwa

Clear Mindfulness of the Innate 285
by Drokmi Lotsāwa

Mahāmudrā That Removes the Three Sufferings 291
by Drokmi Lotsāwa

19. Lineage Supplication of *Parting from the Four Attachments* 295
by Kunga Zangpo and Khyentse Wangpo

20. The Mind Training Titled *The Cycle of Parting from the Four Attachments* 299

Parting from the Four Attachments 301
by Sachen Kunga Nyingpo and Drakpa Gyaltsen

Commentary on *Parting from the Four Attachments* 303
by Drakpa Gyaltsen

Instruction on *Parting from the Four Attachments* 307
by Sakya Paṇḍita

Parting from the Four Attachments 309
by Nupa Rikzin Drak

The Words of the Lord Guru Ānandabhadra: The Manual of *Parting from the Four Attachments* 313
by Kunga Lekpai Rinchen

The Necklace of Ketaka Gems: The Explanatory Method for the Manual of *Parting from the Four Attachments* Mind Training Composed by the Bodhisattva Kunga Lekrin 339
by Ngawang Lekdrup

21. Increasing the Two Accumulations: A Systematic Arrangement of the Offering Rite to the Gurus of the Path with Its Result 355
by Kunga Chöphel

22. Procedure for Preparing Barley Liquor from the *Śrī Samvarodaya Tantra* 389
by Kunga Lodrö

23. Blazing Brilliance and Strength: The Sādhana and Permission of the Eight Deities of Śrī Vajramahākāla Pañjaranātha 403
by Jamgön Kongtrul

Abbreviations 425

Notes 427

Bibliography 467

Index 481

Foreword

In his vast work *The Treasury of Precious Instructions* (*gDams ngag rin po che'i mdzod*), Jamgön Kongtrul Lodrö Taye, that most eminent of Tibetan Buddhist masters, collected all the empowerments, instructions, and practices of the eight great chariots of the practice lineages. Not only that, but he himself received the complete transmissions for all the practices, accomplished them including the retreats, and preserved them in his own mind stream. He then passed on the transmissions to his own students and all who requested them.

The Treasury of Precious Instructions exemplifies how Jamgön Kongtrul Lodrö Taye's whole life was dedicated to teaching and spreading the dharma, whether it be sutra or mantra, *kama* or *terma*, old or new translation school, free of sectarian bias. Without his supreme efforts, many traditions of Tibetan Buddhism would have been lost.

The teachings of the Buddha have now spread throughout the Western world, and there is a growing need for major texts to be translated into English so that Western dharma students and scholars have access to these essential teachings. I was, therefore, delighted to hear that having successfully published a translation in ten volumes of Jamgön Kongtrul Lodrö Taye's *The Treasury of Knowledge* (*Shes bya kun khyab mdzod*), the Tsadra Foundation has embarked on a second major project, the translation of *The Treasury of Precious Instructions*, and I would like to express my gratitude to them.

May their work be of benefit to countless sentient beings.

His Holiness the Seventeenth Karmapa, Ogyen Trinley Dorje
Bodhgaya
February 21, 2016

Series Introduction

The *Treasury of Precious Instructions* (*gDams ngag rin po che'i mdzod*) is the fourth of the five great treasuries compiled or composed by Jamgön Kongtrul Lodrö Taye (1813–1900), also known as Karma Ngawang Yönten Gyatso, among many other names. Kongtrul was one of the greatest Buddhist masters of Tibet. His accomplishments were so vast and varied that it is impossible to do them justice here. The reader is referred to an excellent short biography in the introduction to the first translated volume of another of his great works, *The Treasury of Knowledge*, or the lengthy *Autobiography of Jamgön Kongtrul*. Even if his achievements had consisted solely of his literary output represented in these five treasuries, it would be difficult to comprehend his level of scholarship.

Unlike *The Treasury of Knowledge*, which is Kongtrul's own composition, his other four treasuries may be considered anthologies. Kongtrul's stated mission was to collect and preserve without bias the teachings and practices of all the lineages of Tibetan Buddhism, particularly those that were in danger of disappearing. The English publication of *The Treasury of Knowledge* in ten volumes and the forthcoming translations of this *Treasury of Precious Instructions* in some eighteen volumes can attest to the success of his endeavor, perhaps even beyond what he had imagined.

The Treasury of Precious Instructions is, in some ways, the epitome of Kongtrul's intention. He first conceived of the project around 1870, as always in close consultation with his spiritual friend and mentor Jamyang Khyentse Wangpo (1820–1892). The two of them, along with other great masters, such as Chokgyur Dechen Lingpa, Mipam Gyatso, and Ponlop Loter Wangpo, were active in an eclectic trend in which the preservation of the texts of Tibetan Buddhism was paramount.[1] It was with Khyentse's encouragement and collaboration that Kongtrul had created *The Treasury of Knowledge*—his incredible summation of all that was to be known—and compiled the anthologies of *The Treasury of Kagyu Mantra* and *The Treasury of Precious Hidden Teachings*. This next treasury expanded the scope by aiming to collect in one place the most important instructions of *all* the main practice lineages.

Kongtrul employed a scheme for organizing the vast array of teachings that flourished, or floundered, in Tibet during his time into the Eight Great Chariots of the practice lineages (*sgrub brgyud shing rta chen po brgyad*), or eight lineages that are vehicles of attainment. He based this on a much earlier text by Sherap Özer (Skt. Prajñārasmi, 1518–1584).[2] The structure and contents of that early text indicate that the seeds of the so-called nonsectarian movement (*ris med*) of the nineteenth century in eastern Tibet had already been planted and just needed cultivation. The organizing principle of the scheme was to trace the lineages of the instructions for religious practice that had come into Tibet from India. This boiled down to eight "charioteers"—individuals who could be identified as the conduits between India and Tibet and who were therefore the sources of the practice lineages, all equally valid in terms of origin and comparable in terms of practice. This scheme of eight practice lineages became a kind of paradigm for the nonsectarian approach championed by Kongtrul and his colleagues.[3]

The Treasury of Precious Instructions implements this scheme in a tangible way by collecting the crucial texts and organizing them around those eight lineages. These may be summarized as follows:

1. The Nyingma tradition derives from the transmissions of Padmasambhava and Vimalamitra during the eighth century, along with the former's illustrious twenty-five disciples (*rje 'bangs nyer lnga*) headed by the sovereign Trisong Detsen.
2. The Kadam tradition derives from Atiśa (982–1054) and his Tibetan disciples headed by Dromtön Gyalwai Jungne (1004–1063).
3. The Sakya tradition, emphasizing the system known as the "Path with Its Result," derives from Virūpa, Ḍombi Heruka, and other mahāsiddhas, and passes through Gayadhara and his Tibetan disciple Drokmi Lotsāwa Śākya Yeshe (992–1072).
4. The Marpa Kagyu tradition derives from the Indian masters Saraha, Tilopa, Nāropa, and Maitrīpa, as well as the Tibetan Marpa Chökyi Lodrö (1000?–1081?).
5. The Shangpa Kagyu tradition derives from the ḍākinī Niguma

and her Tibetan disciple Khyungpo Naljor Tsultrim Gönpo of Shang.

6. Pacification and Severance derive from Padampa Sangye (d. 1117) and his Tibetan successor, Machik Lapkyi Drönma (ca. 1055–1143).
7. The Six-Branch Yoga of the *Kālacakra Tantra* derives from Somanātha and his Tibetan disciple Gyijo Lotsāwa Dawai Özer during the eleventh century and was maintained preeminently through the lineages associated with Zhalu and Jonang.
8. The Approach and Attainment of the Three Vajras derives from the revelations of the deity Vajrayoginī, compiled by the Tibetan master Orgyenpa Rinchen Pal (1230–1309) during his travels in Oḍḍiyāna.

The very structure of *The Treasury* thus stands as a statement of the nonsectarian approach. With all these teachings gathered together and set side by side—and each one authenticated by its identification with a direct lineage traced back to the source of Buddhism (India)—maintaining a sectarian attitude would be next to impossible. Or at least that must have been Kongtrul's hope. In explaining his purpose for the collection, he states:

> Generally speaking, in each of the eight great mainstream lineages of accomplishment there exists such a profound and vast range of authentic sources from the sutra and tantra traditions, and such limitless cycles of scriptures and pith instructions, that no one could compile everything.[4]

Nevertheless, he made a good start in *The Treasury of Precious Instructions*, which he kept expanding over the years until at least 1887. The woodblocks for the original printing—carved at Palpung monastery, where Kongtrul resided in his nearby retreat center—took up ten volumes. An edition of this is currently available in twelve volumes as the Kundeling printing, published in 1971–1972.[5] With the addition of several missing texts, an expanded and altered version was published in eighteen volumes in 1979–1981 by Dilgo Khyentse Rinpoche. Finally, in 1999 the most complete version became available in the edition published by Shechen monastery, which is the basis for the current translations.[6] The structure of this enhanced edition, of course, still centers on the eight lineages, as follows:

1. Nyingma (Ancient Tradition), volumes 1 and 2;
2. Kadampa (Transmitted Precepts and Instructions Lineage), volumes 3 and 4;
3. Sakya, or Lamdre (Path with Its Result), volumes 5 and 6;
4. Marpa Kagyu (Precept Lineage of Marpa), volumes 7 through 10;
5. Shangpa Kagyu (Precept Lineage of Shang), volumes 11 and 12;
6. Zhije (Pacification), volume 13, and Chöd (Severance), volume 14;
7. Jordruk (Six Yogas [of Kālacakra]), volume 15; and
8. Dorje Sumgyi Nyendrup (Approach and Attainment of the Three Vajras, also called after its founder "Orgyenpa"), volume 15.

Volumes 16 and 17 are devoted to various other cycles of instruction. Volume 18 mainly consists of the *One Hundred and Eight Teaching Manuals of Jonang*, a prototype and inspiration for Kongtrul's eclectic anthology, and also includes his catalog to the whole *Treasury*.

Translator's Introduction

This second part of *Sakya: The Path with Its Result* principally concerns the remaining eight path cycles from among the nine path cycles (*lam skor dgu*) of the Sakya school, of which the Path with Its Result[1] teaching is the first, presented in volume 5 of *The Treasury of Precious Instructions*. These remaining path cycles are termed "the eight ancillary path cycles" (*lam skor phyi ma brgyad*), which are oral instructions transmitted to Drokmi Lotsāwa by the early eleventh-century Indian masters—Ācārya Vīravajra, Mahāsiddha Amoghavajra, Paṇḍita Prajñāgupta of Oḍḍiyāna, and Paṇḍita Gayadhara. In Tibet, Drokmi imparted these to Setön Kunrik (1029–1116), who transmitted them to Zhangtön Chöbar (1053–1135), who in turn transmitted them to Sachen Kunga Nyingpo (1098–1158). Sachen then gave these teachings to two of his sons, Sönam Tsemo (1142–1182) and Drakpa Gyaltsen (1147–1216). Two of these transmissions include translations of Indian texts: Padmavajra's *Instruction Resembling the Tip of a Lamp Flame* (in chapter 3) and Koṭalipa's *Stages of the Inconceivable* (in chapter 8). The remaining six consist of oral instructions committed to writing by Drakpa Gyaltsen.

While the eight ancillary path cycles were regularly taught in Sakya monasteries, we have only one example of a comprehensive Sakya commentary on the eight ancillary path cycles, *Effortless Accomplishment of the Two Benefits*, composed in the seventeenth century by the twenty-seventh Sakya throne holder, Amezhap Ngawang Kunga Sönam. This text also serves as a teaching manual for the eight ancillary path cycles. The only other source for the eight ancillary path cycles is the *One Hundred and Eight Manuals of Jonang*,[2] compiled by the Sakya master Kunga Drölchok, the twenty-fourth abbot of Jonang.

After Drakpa Gyaltsen, the first person to write comprehensive, independent commentaries on each cycle was Jamgön Kongtrul under the guidance of Jamyang Khyentse Wangpo. Many of Kongtrul's commentaries reorganize the original material written by Drakpa Gyaltsen to make the subject matter easier to comprehend. When considering Kongtrul's commentaries on the eight ancillary path cycles, it is important for the reader to note that the order of both the original texts and Kongtrul's commentaries presented in this volume is neither the traditional order nor the order in which his commentaries were composed. The traditional order may be found in the lineage prayer in chapter 1. I suggest that the reader follow the order given there.

The scheme for the order of the eight ancillary path cycles and Kongtrul's commentaries presented in this volume is found in Kongtrul's introduction to the cycle found in chapter 15, *Fortunate Pure Crystal Mirror*:

> Now, when these renowned eight ancillary path cycles are precisely divided, six are for the completion stages of Cakrasaṃvara, Hevajra, and Guhyasamāja, and two are connected with the general divisions of tantra. Ḍombi Heruka's *Accomplishing the Connate* and Saroruha's *Nine Profound Methods* are systems commenting on Hevajra. The latter is the actual completion stage of the Saroruha system. *Completing the Whole Path with Caṇḍālī* and *Straightening the Crooked* are related to Cakrasaṃvara. *Obtained in Front of a Stupa* is related to Akṣobhya Guhyasamāja, and *Mahāmudrā without Syllables* is related to the Buddhajñānapāda system [of Guhyasamāja]. *Inconceivable* and Indrabhūti's path cycles are for the completion stage of unsurpassed tantras in general.

This reflects the order in which Kunga Drölchok presents his summaries in the *One Hundred and Eight Teaching Manuals*. The introduction for all eight of Kongtrul's commentaries is found in chapter 15, *Fortunate Pure Crystal Mirror*, while the colophon to these commentaries is found in chapter 16, *Fortunate Right-Turning White Conch*. Also, chapter 17, *Fortunate Vermilion Ornament*, is presented last, not in the order supplied by Kongtrul in his introduction to the cycle. In addition, while each text is titled individually, Kongtrul himself refers to them as sections (*le tshan*), indicating that he conceived of these eight commentaries as sections of one integral work. Here they are presented as independent chapters, following the table of contents in the *Treasury of Precious Instructions* block print.

With respect to the relationship between the main Path with Its Result cycle and these eight ancillary path cycles, Amezhap remarks that a student who has received the entire Path with Its Result teaching is authorized to receive the transmissions of the eight ancillary path cycles. This is also the case for anyone who has received one of the following four major empowerments: the Hevajra Empowerment of the Intimate Instruction tradition (the Path with Its Result); the Nairātmyā Empowerment; the Hevajra Empowerment of the Commentarial tradition (also known as the Ḍombi Heruka tradition); and the Hevajra Empowerment of the Saroruhavajra tradition. Amezhap makes the point that the student *must* obtain an empowerment that is from the transmission lineage of Drokmi Lotsāwa. He also makes the point that these teachings *must* be received from a guru who has obtained the empowerments for the meditation of guru yoga, the creation stage, and the completion stage, in accordance with Sakya Paṇḍita's numerous arguments and in accordance with the traditional approach of the Sakya school. Most of the teachings to be found in the eight ancillary path cycles focus on completion stage teachings, and all have the realization of mahāmudrā as their goal. With this in mind, the interested reader is reminded that they should make an effort to receive the proper transmissions related to these texts from a lineage holder who is able to bestow the correct empowerments from the lineage of Drokmi Lotsāwa. Kongtrul also remarks on the import of receiving the special transmission from Drokmi's lineage:

> It appears that the tantras [mentioned above] are connected through their general ripening transmissions to each text; however, because of the power of the transmission of the special lineage, the empowerment of the Intimate Instruction system of Hevajra is sufficient to ripen [a student] for all. Also, the eight path cycles are defined as dependent upon the *Precious Oral Intimate Instructions*.

The introduction to each chapter of the eight ancillary path cycles contains specific remarks about each text or texts in the eight ancillary path cycles and their commentaries. The introduction to Kongtrul's eight commentaries is an overview of the eight cycles, underscoring his unique contributions.

There are two texts that exercise the most influence in the three tantras literature: *Obtained in Front of a Stupa* in chapter 6 and *Accomplishment of the Connate* in chapter 2. In the concise explanation of the inseparability of samsara and nirvana in the general outline of the three tantras literature, the treatment of the meditation of the inseparability of clarity and emptiness is drawn directly from *Obtained in Front of a Stupa*, while the treatment of the connate dharmas is drawn directly from *Accomplishment of the Connate*. In addition, the approach to meditating on the creation stage is derived from Padmavajra's *Creation Stage Adorned with the Nine Profound Methods*.

Another important doctrinal feature found in the eight ancillary path cycles and in Kongtrul's commentaries, treated a total of sixteen times, is the presentation of the three kāyas called "the seven limbs of the three kāyas" (*sku gsum yan lag bdun pa*) or "the seven limbs of union" (*kha sbyor yan lag bdun pa*). This unique Vajrayāna treatment of the three kāyas is connected to the realization of mahāmudrā. The limbs attributed to the dharmakāya and nirmāṇakāya are not completely consistent in the eight ancillary path cycles. While it is maintained that the three kāyas are inseparable, in some places the dharmakāya is presented as having three limbs, and in other places the nirmāṇakāya is presented as having three limbs. There is very little extended discussion of the seven limbs of the three kāyas in Indian treatises other than Vāgīśvarakīrti's *Seven Limbs.*[3] The significance of this author and his text for the early Tibetan reception of Indian traditions of mahāmudrā is discussed briefly in the introduction to chapter 7.

These sixteen texts broaden our understanding of how mahāmudrā itself is understood and practiced in the Sakya school. The Sakya reception of Indian mahāmudrā traditions has not been comprehensively explored beyond a narrow focus upon the various polemical exchanges of scholars in the Sakya and Kagyu schools between the thirteenth and sixteenth centuries.

The next major section of this volume is chapter 18, the *Dharma Connection with the Six Gatekeepers.* This is a cycle of six brief instructions requested of six paṇḍitas residing at Vikramaśīla at the time of Drokmi's departure to Tibet. These six instructions are also summarized by Kunga Drölchok in volume 18 of this series, *Jonang: The One Hundred and Eight Teaching Manuals.*[4]

Chapter 20 contains the cycle on *Parting from the Four Attachments.* These seminal Sakyapa mind training texts have been translated numerous times by others, most recently by Thubten Jinpa in *Mind Training: The Great Collection.*[5] There is only one text included in this cycle that has not been translated elsewhere, the *Necklace of Ketaka Gems*, which presents an explanatory method that ties together the preceding texts in the collection for the purpose of presenting them to an assembly.

Chapter 21 is a guru offering rite. Chapter 22 details the method of preparing ritual alcohol based on the *Saṃvarodaya Tantra*. Chapter 23 is a permission ritual for the main protectors of the Sakya tradition, the Eight-Deity Mahākāla sādhana.

Acknowledgments

First, I would like to acknowledge my root guru, His Holiness Sakya Trichen Rinpoche, the forty-first Sakya throne holder, from whom I had the good fortune of receiving the teachings and transmissions of the Path with Its Result, as well as many other cycles of Sakya teachings. I would also like to recall the memory of the late His Holiness Dagchen Rinpoche, from whom I received the same. I owe a debt of gratitude to Khenpo Migmar Tseten, who guided me through my three-year retreat on the Path with Its Result cycle, who has continually tutored me in Tibetan since 1990, from whom I received the ācārya title in 2004 as a result of my studies at Sakya Institute in Cambridge, Massachusetts, and who patiently answered my questions concerning the obscure terms in the colloquial language of his native Tsang province that occasionally make an appearance in these manuals. I would like to express my appreciation to all the translators of Sakya works who have tread before me in this area of study. My work here has been made easier because of their trailblazing efforts. I would like to thank Osa Karen Manell, who worked with me through all phases of this project and whose exacting attention to detail improved the manuscript inestimably. I would also like to thank Anna Wolcott Johnson, our editor at Shambhala, whose advice was invaluable in polishing and preparing the manuscript for print. Finally, I would like to thank Eric Colombel and the staff of Tsadra Foundation for the opportunity to work on these texts that are essential to the Sakya tradition.

Technical Note

The basic edition followed here is the Shechen edition of the Palpung block prints; the page numbers in brackets reflect the pagination of that edition. However, because of the poor quality of the carving of the Sakya texts in the Palpung block prints, I have principally relied on the versions found in *The Explanation of the Path with Its Result for Disciples* (L) and *The Collection of All Tantras* (G). All canonical works are identified throughout with their Tohoku catalog numbers. There is one work that is not found in the Tohoku catalog, which is taken from the Narthang Tengyur (N). Titles of identified Sanskrit and Tibetan works that appear in the body of the texts have been translated into English, apart from a few well-known titles—Hevajra, Vajrapañjara, and so on—that have been left untranslated.

Sanskrit personal names and place names—as well as the names of Indian Buddhist schools and nonhuman beings, such as *yakṣas*—have been left in Sanskrit, with translations in parentheses where needed. A few technical terms that do not have uniform or satisfactory English translations have been left in Sanskrit. I have opted to back-translate the anatomical terms *tsa* (*rtsa*), *lung* (*rlung*), *tikle* (*thig le*), and *khorlo* (*'khor lo*) to their corresponding Sanskrit terms *nāḍī*, *vāyu*, *bindu*, and *cakra*.

In all cases Sanskrit words and names have been rendered with full diacritics, with the exception of some words that have entered the English lexicon, such as samsara, nirvana, and so on. Tibetan personal names and place names have been phoneticized following Tsadra Foundation's conventions. Textual annotations in the block prints are indicated in the endnotes by "NOTE" in small caps, while a translator's interpolation is indicated in notes by "TN."

PART ONE

The Eight Ancillary Path Cycles

1. Supplication to the Lineage of the Eight Ancillary Path Cycles[1]

Ngorchen Kunga Zangpo

{2} The lineage of the *Inconceivable*:

oṃ svasti
I offer a supplication to Mahāvajradhara, the Jñānaḍākinī,
Ācārya Paramāśva, Vīṇa,
Indrabhūtipāda, Lakṣmīkara,
Lalitavajra, and Gundhiri.

I offer a supplication to Padmavajra,
Śrī Dharmasena, Bhadrapāda,
Lord Koṭalipa, Bhusanapa,
Dharmakarṇapa, and Vīravajra.

I offer a supplication to the great guru Drokmi,
Setön Kunrik, Zhangtön Chöbar,
Palden Sakyapa, and the Lord Brothers,
Dharma Lord Sakya Paṇḍita and Chögyal Phakpa.

I offer a supplication to Könchok Pal,
Dharma Lord Sönam Pal,
Sönam Gyaltsen, Palden Tsultrim Zhap,
the incomparably kind Mahāsiddha Buddhaśrī,
and the glorious gurus.

May those who obscure their minds with clouds of concepts that grasp duality, which from the start are free of proliferation like the expanse of space,
be blessed with the blaze of nondual gnosis
through the yoga of inconceivable nonarising.

The lineage of *Accomplishing the Connate*:

I offer a supplication to Vajradhara,
Nairātmyā,
Virūpa,
Amazing Ḍombi, Dorje Naktrö,[2]
Garbharipa, Piṇḍapa,
Durjayacandra, and Vīravajra.

I offer a supplication to the great guru Drokmi, {3}
Setön Kunrik, Zhangtön Chöbar,
Palden Sakyapa, and the Lord Brothers,
Dharma Lord Sakya Paṇḍita and Chögyal Phakpa.

I offer a supplication to Könchok Pal,
Dharma lord Sönam Pal,
Sönam Gyaltsen, Palden Tsultrim Zhap,
the incomparably kind Mahāsiddha Buddhaśrī,
and the glorious gurus.

The connate of the cause is the nonarising mind essence,
the connate of the path is the intrinsically pure three poisons,
and the connate of the result is the state of the three gates of liberation.
Bless me to realize the three kāyas.

The lineage of the path of Ārya Nāgārjuna:

I offer a supplication to Vajradhara, Vajrapāṇi,
Nāgārjuna, Āryadeva,
Kṛṣṇapāda, Candrakīrti,
Brahmin Śrīdhara, and Vīravajra.

I offer a supplication to the great guru Drokmi,
Setön Kunrik, Zhangtön Chöbar,
Palden Sakyapa, and the Lord Brothers,
Dharma Lord Sakya Paṇḍita and Chögyal Phakpa.

I offer a supplication to Könchok Pal,
Dharma Lord Sönam Pal,
Sönam Gyaltsen, Palden Tsultrim Zhap,
the incomparably kind Mahāsiddha Buddhaśrī,
and the glorious gurus. {4}

The bodhicitta of the buddhas of the ten directions
cannot be imputed with the evil taints of concepts
of self, aggregates, perceptions, and so on.
May there be the blessing of the realization of profound
emptiness.

The lineage of *Mahāmudrā without Syllables*:

I offer a supplication to Mahāvajradhara, Lady Tārā,
the great paṇḍita and siddha Vagendrakīrti,
Mahāpaṇḍita Devākaracandra,
and Amoghavajra.

I offer a supplication to the great guru Drokmi,
Setön Kunrik, Zhangtön Chöbar,
Palden Sakyapa, and the Lord Brothers,
Dharma Lord Sakya Paṇḍita and Chögyal Phakpa.

I offer a supplication to Könchok Pal,
Dharma Lord Sönam Pal,
Sönam Gyaltsen, Palden Tsultrim Zhap,
the incomparably kind Mahāsiddha Buddhaśrī,
and the glorious gurus.

At first, having seized the mind free from the two extremes,
tamed the mind with the hook of mindfulness,

and placed the mind in the meaning of profound freedom from proliferation,
bless me with the arising of the gnosis of union.

The lineage of the path of Padmavajra:

I offer a supplication to Vajradhara, Vilāsyavajra,
Anaṅgavajra, Padmavajra, Indrabhūti,
Lakṣmīkara, Kṛṣṇa,
Śrīdhara, and Gayadhara.

I offer a supplication to the great guru Drokmi,
Setön Kunrik, Zhangtön Chöbar,
Palden Sakyapa, and the Lord Brothers,
Dharma Lord Sakya Paṇḍita and Chögyal Phakpa.

I offer a supplication to Könchok Pal,
Dharma Lord Sönam Pal,
Sönam Gyaltsen, Palden Tsultrim Zhap,
the incomparably kind Mahāsiddha Buddhaśrī,
and the glorious gurus.

After all concepts that cling to ordinary appearances of the universe and beings
arise as the appearance of the maṇḍala of the deity {5}
through the yoga of the nine means of the profound creation stage,
may I be blessed such that concepts are purified in the dharmadhātu.

The lineage of the path of Caṇḍālī:

I offer a supplication to Mahāvajradhara,
Lady Yoginī, Vajraghantapāda,
Kūrmapāda, Barzinpa,[3]
Kṛṣṇa, Śrīdhara, and Gayadhara.

I offer a supplication to the great guru Drokmi,
Setön Kunrik, Zhangtön Chöbar,
Palden Sakyapa, and the Lord Brothers,
Dharma Lord Sakya Paṇḍita and Chögyal Phakpa.

I offer a supplication to Könchok Pal,
Dharma Lord Sönam Pal,
Sönam Gyaltsen, Palden Tsultrim Zhap,
the incomparably kind Mahāsiddha Buddhaśrī,
and the glorious gurus.

Bless me to realize liberation from the four extremes,
the ultimate bodhicitta without beginning or end,
by means of the five stages: the stages of the cause, mantra, and gnosis,
and the stages of the secret and nonduality. {6}

The lineage of *Straightening the Crooked*:

I offer a supplication to the victors, Vajradhara and Maheśvara,
Ucita, who obtained the siddhi of immortality,
Kṛṣṇācārya, Śrīdhara,
and Gayadhara.

I offer a supplication to the great guru Drokmi,
Setön Kunrik, Zhangtön Chöbar,
Palden Sakyapa, and the Lord Brothers,
Dharma Lord Sakya Paṇḍita and Chögyal Phakpa.

I offer a supplication to Könchok Pal,
Dharma lord Sönam Pal,
Sönam Gyaltsen, Palden Tsultrim Zhap,
the incomparably kind Mahāsiddha Buddhaśrī,
and the glorious gurus.

Bless me to perceive the profound meaning of emptiness free of
proliferation
and obtain the siddhi of immortality

though the power of firmly placing the vāyus of the rasanā and the lalanā,
which generate the concepts of all dualism, into the avadhūti.

The supplication to the gurus of the short lineage of the path of Indrabhūti:

I offer a supplication to the truly perfect buddha Vajradhara,
Great Indrabhūti, who was predicted by the victor,
his disciple, Lakṣmīkara,
and Guhyaprajñā.

I offer a supplication to the great guru Drokmi,
Setön Kunrik, Zhangtön Chöbar,
Palden Sakyapa, and the Lord Brothers,
Dharma Lord Sakya Paṇḍita and Chögyal Phakpa.

I offer a supplication to Könchok Pal,
Dharma lord Sönam Pal,
Sönam Gyaltsen, Palden Tsultrim Zhap,
the incomparably kind Mahāsiddha Buddhaśrī,
and the glorious gurus.

Bless me to realize the meaning of the *Jñānasiddhi*,
the vajrakāya that does not perish through conditions,
unchanging through the three times,
the great blissful mind essence that pervades all entities.

This verse supplication to the lineage gurus of the eight ancillary path cycles was composed by Bhikṣu Kunga Zangpo.

The supplement that follows Palden Tsultrim:

Buddhaśrī, Ngorchen Dorjechang,
and Palden Dorje.

I offer a supplication to the hidden buddha Kunga Drölchok,
Lhawang Drak, Kunga Nyingpo,

Ratnavajra, Rinchen Gyatso,
Nyingpo Tayezhap, and Kunga Zangpo.

I offer a supplication to Tsewang Norbu,
Ngawang Nampargyal, Kunzang Chöjor,
Lozang Thuthop Je, Nyima Chöphel,
Losel Tenkyong, and the glorious gurus.

Written by Mañjughoṣa.

sarva maṅgalaṃ

2. *Accomplishment of the Connate* Composed by Ḍombi Heruka[1]

Drakpa Gyaltsen

Ḍombi Heruka is credited as the author of several texts in the Tengyur, the most important of which is *Accomplishment of the Connate*. However, that text is not translated in this chapter at all, but rather this chapter presents an instruction for practicing the meaning of that text.

This text has three sections. The first section is not clearly divided into an outline. After some introductory statements detailing vows and differences between how vows are followed in the path of the ascetic who does not rely on a consort and the path of the infant who does rely on a consort, Drakpa Gyaltsen then goes on to detail the connate nature of the cause, the path, and the result. The section on the connate nature of the cause details fifteen dharmas. The connate nature of the path mainly concerns how the path of the ascetic and the infant are practiced. The connate nature of the result begins with signs of the practice and concludes with the seven limbs of three kāyas.

The second section is a detailed discussion of mudras related to the path of the infant. The third section concerns the process of retaining and drawing up the bindu. In *Effortless Accomplishment of the Two Benefits*, Amezhap explains that the practitioner of this instruction is to meditate on themselves as Hevajra according to the six-limbed sādhana.[2]

Ḍombi Heruka is one of the two named disciples of Virūpa, along with Kāṇha. In Drakpa Gyaltsen's *Chronicle of the Indian Gurus*, Virūpa encounters Ḍombi Heruka during the episode when Virūpa reverses the Ganges River. At this time, Ḍombi Heruka is a simple ferryman, taking people across the Ganges River. Ḍombi Heruka and Kaṇhā accompany Virūpa on his most famous adventures, such as stopping the sun and taming the goddess Caṇḍikā[3] and her retinue of cannibal yoginīs. Following the latter episode, Virūpa gave empowerment and complete instructions to Ḍombi. A sudden realizer, he attained realization equal to Virūpa and was sent to East India to tame a king named Dehara. In *Effortless Accomplishment of the Two Benefits*, Amezhap explains that this Ḍombi Heruka is the first of the three siddhas bearing this name.[4]

{8} Homage to Guru Ḍombi Heruka.

Ḍombi wrote *Accomplishing the Connate*[5] based on the following citation:

> Whatever arises connately
> is called "connate."
> Called "connate by nature,"[6]
> all aspects are unified and one.[7]

This is the instruction for practicing its meaning.

There is the connate of the cause, the connate of the method, and the connate of the result; as such, the path is fully completed through the three kinds of connate.

Further, the way this topic is taught is that people wishing to realize the result Vajradhara have two ways to practice the path: the path of the ascetic[8] and the path of the infant.[9] In both paths, the three frugalities are necessary: the frugality of enjoyments, the frugality of the body, and the frugality of the mind.

First, [the frugality of enjoyments] is not permitting one's existing possessions and enjoyments to be squandered by fire, water, enemies, or malicious forces. The frugality of enjoyments is to offer [one's enjoyments] first to the guru and then offer them to the Three Jewels and the ḍākinīs; if there are no material things, offer them mentally.[10]

The frugality of the body is possessing the three vows: the prātimokṣa, bodhisattva, and vidyādhara vows. In each of those, there are both outer vows and {9} inner vows. The outer prātimokṣa vows are the five kinds of vows that an upāsaka or upāsikā protects; the thirteen formally adopted vows of a śrāmaṇera or a śrāmaṇerī; and the two hundred and fifty-three rules of the fully ordained bhikṣu or bhikṣuṇī. The inner [prātimokṣa vow] is retaining the bindu in the body without losing it.

Between the two, the outer and inner bodhisattva vows, the outer are the four defeats and the thirty-six faults. The inner vows are being motivated by compassion for those who are suffering, acting with compassion for the benefit of sentient beings, having a clear and unimpeded mind, and employing the body in every way.

Among the two, the outer and inner vidyādhara vows, the outer vows are protecting the twenty-two samayas: the fourteen root downfalls and the eight secondary downfalls, which are commonly shared from the tantras. The inner vow is abiding in nonconceptual fundamental consciousness.

As such, the three outer vows are the path of the ascetic. The three inner vows are the nonconceptual path of the infant.

The frugality of mind is the two kinds of bodhicitta. The outer bodhicitta is the relative bodhicitta of aspiration and engagement, and the ultimate bodhicitta is free of proliferation. The inner bodhicitta is the relative jasmine bodhicitta and the ultimate bodhicitta of bliss and emptiness. Also, the outer bodhicitta is the path of the ascetic; the inner bodhicitta is the path of the infant.

On the basis of possessing these three vows, {10} there are three methods, upon which arise the result, the three kāyas.

Now then, this is the system of the path instruction of the three connates: the naturally existing connate of the cause; the connate of the method, the method of giving rise to experiences; and the connate of the result, the three gates of liberation and the arising of the three kāyas.

Now, the connate of the cause is explained with fifteen dharmas:[11] for the body, the three nāḍīs are connate; for the voice, exhalation, inhalation, and rest of the breath are connate; and for the mind,[12] the three poisonous afflictions are connate—totaling nine dharmas.

For those connate dharmas, the inner obstacles are the three connate humors of illness. The outer obstacles are the three connate spirits. For the illnesses, there is first, vata; second, blood and pitta combined; and third, kapha. The three spirits are the male class, female class, and nāga class. In this system of the great lord of yogis Ḍombi Heruka, the mind itself is the connate nonarising reality of entities.[13]

In the connate of the method, there are two methods because there are two kinds of people. On entering the path, [the ascetic person] first recalls the guru on one's crown and [then] cultivates precious bodhicitta. The deity yoga is just mentally recalled, and one should engage in the posture of the body according to the technique.[14] The two kinds of voiced inhalations,[15] multiplied by the three limbs,[16] should be requested from the guru. The explanation of the twenty-four dharmas of the intimate instruction of experience is shared with the path of the infant. If it is the path of the infant, then, among the five[17] mudras, avoid[18] the average mudra in the division of best, medium, and average; one should find either the best or medium. With the three preliminary dharmas,[19] after one month[20] the complexion[21] will be accomplished.[22] Sometimes, [the complexion] becomes white.[23] The posture of the body is the same as before.

Next, like Padma and Virūpa, rely on a mudra with the three perceptions. {11} From the first up to the eleventh day, it is impossible that one will not swoon from bliss. Since in both paths[24] there is nonconceptuality for some people, they also revive from such a swoon.

Now, the first experience to arise is the bliss that blazes in the body through the power of the reversal of the downward-voiding and upward-moving vāyus. Warmth and bliss arise together. Bliss arises in the mind. The voice produces laughter, and so on. Occasionally one cries, "Oh no!" As such, one's body, voice, and mind[25] are permeated with the samādhi of so-called "great desire."[26] Since the affliction, desire, is employed as the path, the desire for objects is gradually abandoned. The illness, vata illness, is gradually cleansed. One is free from the female class of spirits. The left nāḍī of the body is brought under control.[27] For speech, inhalation of the vāyu is brought under control. For the mind, also bliss is produced in dreams. The gate[28] of liberation takes the name "without aspiration." As such, those are the eight limbs, the first cause[29] employed as the path.

Second, similarly there are two ways of drawing up the downward-voiding vāyu that cause experience to arise instantly. When bliss arises, the production of consciousness that is clear, light, and endowed with great compassion is samādhi. Since the ultimate degree of clarity is hatred, hatred is employed as the path; the ultimate degree of clarity arises through the condition of an unpleasant object. The illness is both pitta and blood. One is freed from the male class of spirits. The rasanā nāḍī of the body is brought under control. For the voice, exhalation is brought under control. The mind becomes clear and light, and in dreams one levitates cross-legged in the sky, and so on. The gate of liberation[30] takes the name "signless." As such, there are eight through the power of the connate of the cause.

Third, through the power of the two kinds of drawing up the downward-voiding vāyu, simultaneous with the former two, the consciousness that becomes the supreme fundamental state, which is nonconceptual by nature,

{12} is samādhi. Since ignorance of any object is nonconceptual, it is great ignorance. The affliction, confusion, is employed as the path. One is gradually freed from kapha illnesses. One cannot be attacked by the nāga class of spirits. The avadhūti nāḍī of the body is brought under control. For the voice, one obtains control over the resting vāyu. For the mind, there are no equipoise and post-equipoise phases in nonconceptuality, one is neither asleep nor awake, and there is no distinction between sleeping and waking. The gate of liberation[31] takes the name "emptiness." As such, there are eight by the power of the connate of the cause.

Now, for the connate of the result,[32] first is the emergence of the signs; that is, if the three experiences arise in one's continuum, the specific benefit performed for others with the body is that if one sees [someone] suffering an onslaught of illness or spirits, their pain is pacified merely by massaging their body; their suffering is pacified merely by rubbing powder, feces, or urine [on their body].

The signs of the specific benefit performed for others with the voice are that by merely pronouncing "the illness is cured,"[33] the illness is cured, and so on; one can treat epidemics with the supreme accomplishment of words.

The signs of the mind are that dreams first become clear. Next, one can see nonhumans. After that, one recognizes benefit and harm in the experience of meditation.

There are three further [groups of] signs: the signs that arise in this life's body; the signs that arise at the time of death; and the signs that arise in the bardo. The signs of this life are that the body feels light, one's complexion is good, and one has little clinging to food. Any activity is completed merely upon meeting it. The forgotten[34] is suddenly remembered. That is all.

At the time of death,[35] there is no pain of the separation of nāḍīs, no fear of death, no effort to appropriate either a deva or human body, and one is never separate from the experience of samādhi. {13}

The signs of the bardo[36] that [indicate] one feels one has met one's guru in the bardo are that one feels one has seen the face of the Buddha; no matter what kind of body one appropriates, its appearance arises as the excellent deity; one becomes a vidyādhara[37] in the bardo, and so on;[38] and the door of lower realms is blocked in all lifetimes. If those signs arise in this life's body, it is impossible that the signs at the time of death will not occur. If those arise, it is impossible that the signs of the bardo will not occur.

After the signs of this system arise even slightly,[39] one must gradually engage in the secret conduct. At the time of conduct, a vivid cognizance is not asserted. When it seems that concepts are diminishing, in secret rely on feces and urine, also rely on great meat, wear clothes without regard for good or bad, and also associate with companions of both good and bad characters. Primarily, [the time of conduct] is nighttime. During the day one's behavior should comport with one's companions, and one must guard against mundane misdeeds. As such, when one gradually engages in secret conduct, the experiences of the mind stabilize and the three signs,[40] and so on, occur swiftly. Clairvoyance arises. If one is able to benefit others, wear the six ornaments;[41] that is, it is asserted one should engage in the conduct of strict discipline.[42]

In this system, beginning from the first meditation on the path until one attains the result, it is not asserted that one removes obstructing phenomena elsewhere. The obstacles are the three illnesses, the three kinds of spirits, and the three poisons. Those are asserted to self-liberate through sustaining experience.

First, the dharmakāya is the limb of naturelessness, the pacification of all proliferation. That is the path accomplished by [the eight limbs] of the final path. The sambhogakāya has three limbs: the limb of enjoyment together is the blazing of the major and minor marks, the limb of union is having the mother, and the limb of great bliss is the continuum becoming filled with immaculate bliss. It is accomplished by [the eight limbs] of the first path. There are also three limbs for the nirmāṇakāya: The limb of being full of certain compassion is that even though the nonreferential {14} great compassion is nonconceptual, it is a cause of benefiting sentient beings, like a wish-fulfilling jewel. The limb of not being interrupted is the kāya that emanates for as long as there are those to tame, existing without interruption, like the example of a container of water and a moon. This is the limb of accomplishment. There is the limb of not ceasing, the assertion that there is in fact no nirvana for the nirmāṇakāya because the accumulations are all complete, because the māra of death has been conquered, and because attaining power over life is among the ten powers. This is the limb of the aspect of cessation. It is the accomplishment of the middle path. As such, they are the connate of the result. When summarized, there is only division into threes: three causes,[43] three paths,[44] and three results.[45]

samāptamithi

Among the four consorts[46] for union,[47] there is the padminī (red lotus), which is of three types. The superior padminī has a white face,[48] red veins, and an ample body; the veins of her eyes are red; she is typically thin; and, in particular, her waist is thin. Her bird-like legs and arms are red. Her teeth are good. She possesses the qualities of a tathāgata;[49] that is, she belongs to a good family. If one unites with her,[50] the result of the victor is obtained in this life. The middling padminī has white skin, large joints, large bones, a very calm disposition, coarse behavior, a pretty face, a mind[51] difficult to correct, and when she gives birth to children, she gives birth to boys. If one encounters the nāḍī in her, the result is attained within one year without impediment.

The average padminī is called "the white ripener." She has a white complexion. Though her face is fine-looking, her character is ugly; she cannot maintain confidences. Her figure is large. She is tidy. She laughs, gossips, slanders, and criticizes others; she is easily deceived[52] and deceptive in speech. She is not to be relied on.[53] {15}

The superior śaṅkhinī (conch) has yellow skin and red veins. She is competent, with a good disposition, and her word is solid. Her eyes gaze to the side,[54] and their corners are sharp. She can easily understand any topic. She is very intelligent. If one meets with such a woman, one will attain the result in this life. The middling śaṅkhinī appears to be concave when seen from behind and convex when seen from the front. In general, her body is excellent. In particular, her brows are attractive, and her face is a little bright. When she goes to the market, she gazes downward.[55] The height of her face is short. Her chin curves up from her chest. She is very affectionate with her lover. If one joins the nāḍī with that passionate one, [the result will be attained] without impediment within a year and a month.

The inferior śaṅkhinī has yellow skin, her eyes are large, her mind is sharp, and her memory is clear. She cannot stay put and moves frequently; also, her hands cannot remain still even temporarily. Her word is not solid, she cannot focus her mind on explanations, and she also has a bad character. She lives to be seen by men and is always on the lookout for handsome men. She is not to be relied on.[56]

The superior citriṇī (variegated) has blue skin, a long face, thick lips,[57] many wrinkles, good eyes, and a pleasant voice. She is very calm,[58] with gentle conduct, is familiar with and respectful of both human laws and the Dharma,[59] and possesses many auspicious qualities.[60] [From relying] on her, siddhis come quickly, and one will possess necessities.

The inferior citriṇī[61] has dusky skin, with a yellow forehead. She has small, deeply set eyes. She is very agreeable. She is very devoted to men, so do not rely on her.

The superior hastinī (elephant) has a long or wide brow, a short body, and a dusty color. Her conduct is slow, she refrains from touch,[62] and she sits in repose. When that organ becomes larger when uniting with her, {16} since she has many nāḍīs,[63] it is the cause of much good fortune, so rely on her. The middling hastinī has a large torso and is broadminded, her face is bright and high, the shape of her face is wide, and her physique is good. She is incapable of deception. She does not ignore the meaning[64] and is very encompassing. As she is never angry and always good-natured, it is proper to rely on her. The inferior hastinī has physical conduct and speaks many words of praise and blame,[65] saying whatever she likes such as "He rtam."[66] She is a great liar, both easily angered and easily pleased, with many words of praise and blame. She is easily swayed, stingy, and does not rejoice in gifts. She is inappropriate.[67]

Other than the four inferior ones, one should search out the other eight and seek[68] the nāḍī.[69] If one finds the nāḍī, turn one's back on everything,[70] cultivate the vāyu,[71] develop the body with the bindu,[72] and direct oneself toward the meaning of the connate.[73] One will be liberated in this life. The nāḍī[74] is extremely fine. If it is thick, it is bad. It is said to be excellent to ascertain the nāḍī in a very passionate woman. Likewise, with both methods of inhalation, there is using one's own body (the method) and using another's body (wisdom).

samāptamithi

The specific key point[75] the guru mentions that is crucial in the three empowerments at the time of empowerment and when relying on the messenger at the time of the path is (1) the explanation of the method of training,[76] (2) the explanation of the method of holding straight, (3) the explanation of drawing up, and (4) the explanation of the places of spreading.

There are also four parts in the first topic: (1) having eaten beforehand, and so on, explain how to adjust the body,[77] (2) explain holding the vāyu in place,[78] (3) explain the object of visualization,[79] and {17} (4) explain the intimate instruction for practicing the vāyu.[80]

There are also four parts in the second topic: (1) fine like the stamen of a lotus,[81] (2) sharp like the tip of a spear, (3) cutting like the blade of a sword, and (4) smooth like the surface of a mirror.[82]

Third is lowering one's head and elevating others. The first is drawing up soundlessly into the short *A*,[83] then drawing up with sound,[84] and finally drawing up with the mind. "Lowering one's head" definitely causes bliss to spread throughout the whole body.[85]

Fourth is arresting the upper vāyu. First extend the right arm, hold the left nostril, and shake the head.[86] Release and shake. Again hold and shake. That will definitely cause the bindu to spread through all the pores. The body will then become like a ball of cotton. Since the experience arises immediately, this is a very important point.[87]

samāpta[88]

3. Ācārya Padmavajra's *Creation Stage Adorned with the Nine Profound Methods* and *Completion Stage Instruction Resembling the Tip of a Lamp Flame*[1]

This chapter has two main sections. The first is a text composed by Drakpa Gyaltsen called the *Creation Stage Adorned with the Nine Profound Methods*, which summarizes the method of practicing the creation stage sādhana in four limbs, proper to the Padmavajra tradition of Hevajra. Amezhap's *Effortless Accomplishment of the Two Benefits* presents the general structure of Padmavajra's system in this way. First, one understands the view: the inseparability of samsara and nirvana. Second, the path is the method of placing the mind in śamatha along with the stages of the path. Third, one generates confidence by severing all outer proliferation with the nine profound methods. Fourth, the result is the explanation of the seven limbs of the three kāyas.[2]

One of the unique features of this first text, found in the second subsection, is the correlation of the nine stages of śamatha detailed in *Ornament of Mahāyāna Sutras* with the process of meditating on the creation stage. This is still the main approach to reciting the Hevajra sādhana in the Sakya tradition, whether in its six-limbed form or its four-limbed form. This section also details the thirty-two-session approach to systematically meditating on the aspects of the nine-deity maṇḍala of Hevajra, as well as the completion stage. Amezhap explains that the practitioner of this instruction uses the *Saroruha Sādhana*.[3]

The second part of this chapter is a translation of Padmavajra's *Completion Stage Instruction Resembling the Tip of a Lamp Flame*, which is the original text concerning the completion stage text of this Hevajra system and summarized in Drakpa Gyaltsen's text.

Chapter 3 lacks a chronicle of this particular transmission, but it is included here with the understanding that some of these eight ancillary path cycles exclude chronicles because they would have been well-known in Sakya circles during the twelfth century.

According to Kunga Nyingpo's *Chronicle of Ācārya Saroruha*,[4] Saroruhavajra, known interchangeably as Padmavajra, was a prince living in Oḍiviśa (present day Orissa) named Candratilaka (Zla ba'i thig le), presumably a member of the Candra dynasty.[5] Though first in line for the throne and despite the wishes of the king and queen, his relatives, and subjects, Candratilaka had no desire to be the ruler of Oḍiviśa. Oḍiviśa, it should be noted, had long been a Buddhist stronghold. Candratilaka wanted to follow the Mahāyāna in general and the Secret Mantra in particular. In Magadha he discovered that the main country where Mantrayāna was being promulgated was Oḍḍiyāna in the Northwest and so departed for that land. At that time, Oḍḍiyāna was ruled by King Indrabhūti III. Having arrived in Oḍḍiyāna, Indrabhūti appoints Candratilaka as court chaplain and requests that he teach the Dharma. This leads to an encounter with a strange woman who periodically laughs during his teachings. Candratilaka decides to find out who this woman is and eventually asks her to be his teacher. Initially she refuses, but he confronts her over some unusual events he observed at her house. She admits she is in fact a yoginī by the name of Cintā.[6] She mocks Candratilaka's dharma teachings as both tragic and laughable, but nevertheless sends him to Bengal to find a guru named Jalendra, also known as Anaṅgavajra. Jalendra was himself the disciple of the female teacher and emanation of Nairātmyā, Vilāsyavajra.[7] Jalendra initially refuses to give teachings to Candratilaka due to his anger at Cintā for recommending him to the prince but eventually relents, offering Candratilaka his daughter as a support for both the Hevajra empowerment and as a companion for practice. Candratilaka, in the company of his wife and father-in-law, returns to Oḍḍiyāna to resume his position as court chaplain. He offers his wife to Indrabhūti, ostensibly in order to bestow the Hevajra empowerment. The ministers are scandalized because this constitutes a caste violation. The subjects too are displeased. In order to purify the offense, the ministers decide that drastic measures are required—burning Candratilaka and his wife in a pile of brown sandalwood. Both Jalendra and Indrabhūti, very much displeased by the ministers' decision, decide to go to the site of the pyre to recover the bones to be made into small reliquary stupas. When Jalendra and Indrabhūti arrive at the pyre, they discover a small lake, in which Candratilaka and his consort are sitting on a lotus blossom. Candratilaka is given the name Saroruhavajra, Lake-Born Vajra.

It should be noted that five of the main figures in this lineage—Cintā, Jalendra, Saroruhavajra, Indrabhūti III, and Lakṣmī—are all contemporaries and likely active during the ninth century. Indrabhūti and Lakṣmī also appear repeatedly in the lineage lists connected with these eight cycles. Ameshab states that there are three Saroruhas. Kunga Zangpo identifies this person, the disciple of Anaṅgavajra, as the middle Saroruha, but Drakpa Gyaltsen identifies him as the last Saroruha.

Ācārya Padmavajra's *Creation Stage Adorned with the Nine Profound Methods*

Drakpa Gyaltsen

{20} With devotion I prostrate my head to the feet of the greatly compassionate Padmavajra, the great lord of yogins.

The treatise system of this sublime one—the abbreviated features of the approach and accomplishment of the four-limbed creation procedure, which is the antidote to the four kinds of birthplaces in dependence on the Hevajra method of accomplishment and adorned with the nine profound methods—is called "the intimate instruction of the complete path." When that is summarized, however samsara may be, similarly so are the path and result. *Two Sections* states:

> This itself is called "samsara."
> This itself is nirvana.
> Nirvana will not be realized
> through abandoning samsara for another.[8]

The three topics are the naturally abiding cause, the inseparability of samsara and nirvana; the practitioner's practice of the path, which is also practiced as the inseparability of samsara and nirvana; and the totally pure result, the greatly compassionate lord who also asserts the inseparability of samsara and nirvana.

That is the brief explanation. When described in detail, there are four parts: First is the view that realizes the inseparability of samsara and nirvana. The path includes the nine methods of placing the mind with śamatha and the divisions of the path. All outer proliferation is severed through developing certainty in the nine profound methods. The result is explained with the seven limbs of the three kāyas. {21}

I. The View

The view is realizing the cause, path, and result in toto as the inseparability of samsara and nirvana. Within the inseparability of samsara and nirvana of the cause, there is samsara [of the cause]—the cause of the three realms, subject and object, diverse appearances, conceptuality, and the many temporary kinds of suffering—which is nonarising by nature and the same taste, like pouring water into water. Further, [with respect to nirvana of the cause,] the universe, the celestial mansion and its inhabitants, and sentient beings have the nature of the nine deities [of the Hevajra maṇḍala]. For example, though gold may be tarnished, it appears as yellow by nature; likewise, the body and mind, with its concepts, are also understood to be free from proliferation by nature.

The inseparability of the path is the inseparability of both the creation stage and completion stage. The former is the universe appearing as the celestial mansion and the six realms appearing as the deities. Further, that is an assertion that a thing (*chos can*) and its property (*chos nyid*) are the same. Since a celestial mansion cannot be found in the absence of the universe and since deities cannot be found apart from the six classes, those are the inseparability of samsara and nirvana from the perspective of the creation stage. In the gnosis of the completion stage, the impure three realms and the pure maṇḍalacakra gradually dissolve, and one's mind is realized as great bliss. That also is the meaning of the passage:

> In [gnosis] there is no beginning, middle, or end,
> no existence and no nirvana.[9]

The inseparability of samsara and nirvana of the result is that {22} when one has mastered cultivation, one is able to insert the three realms of samsara into the space of a single pore and transform those [three realms] into nirvana, the buddhafield of a tathāgata; that is, the inseparability of samsara and nirvana of the rūpakāya.

The inseparability of samsara and nirvana of the dharmakāya is devoid of accepting and rejecting and devoid of abandoning and obtaining, because everything is realized to be the nature of one's immaculate gnosis, named "the gnosis of transformation." In dependence on the same person, it is said that buddhas and sentient beings merge into one.

As such, the realization of these three occasions [cause, path, and result] as the inseparability of samsara and nirvana can be accepted as the intention of Padmavajra, the lord of yogins. The tantra states:

> Later on reality will be correctly explained:
> there isn't the slightest difference between
> the form of pure gnosis
> and the conceptuality of samsara.[10]

The explanation of the first general topic, the view, is complete.

II. The Stages of Practice

The second topic is the stages of practice, the antidotes of the four birthplaces for the four types of persons. However, when the warmth and moisture birth are divided into two, there are the five limbs in the creation procedure. Since there is meditation on the complete path of the outer shape, one reaches the culmination of the paths of accumulation and application.

The first of the three persons beyond those two [paths] reaches the culmination of the path of seeing in dependence on the path of investigating the nāḍī maṇḍala of the body. The person beyond that reaches the culmination of the path of cultivation by seeing the nāḍīs in the form of vowels and consonants in dependence upon investigating the bhaga maṇḍala. Moreover, the person beyond that who sees a multicolored bindu as the bodhicitta maṇḍala actualizes the ultimate path. That is progressing on the path through the three secret dharma maṇḍalas of the completion stage.

Among the latter are the four persons: those who rely on the creation stage are the beginners, the person who gives rise to small bliss, the person who gives rise to the experience of bliss and emptiness, and the person who gives rise to great experience. Those who possess all afflictions are termed inferior, {23} average, mediocre, and best, respectively termed beginner, one with slight control over gnosis, one with control over gnosis, and one with control over true gnosis. These four reach the culmination of the path of accumulation and application. The specific indications of these will be explained below; if these were explained here, they would be repeated below. Moreover, the position of this ācārya is that the path must be entered gradually. When applied to the creation procedure, the first person meditates on the creation-stage procedure of the deity of the first heat and moisture births. The second person meditates on the second heat and moisture births. The third person meditates on egg birth. The fourth person meditates on the direct realization of the principal as miraculous birth and the retinue as womb birth. The creation of the commitment being is the limb of approach; the entry of the gnosis being is the limb of near-accomplishment; [the limbs of] the accomplishment and the great accomplishment are merging and arising with the critical points of the empowerment. This is the concise explanation.

In the extensive explanation of those, from the perspective of the first warmth and moisture birth, the detailed explanation exists in the treatise and will be explained by the guru. Here, of the pairing just mentioned, after one has obtained the complete four empowerments from the sublime guru, one also obtains the reading transmission of the sādhana. When one practices in four defined sessions, there are two phases: equipoise and arising from equipoise. At the time of equipoise, the field of accumulation is invited before oneself and presented offerings, one performs the confession of misdeeds with the seven branches, and so on. One cultivates the four immeasurables and accumulates merit. Next, one accumulates gnosis by meditating on emptiness, and the two accumulations are gathered.

Following that, one creates the protection cakra, the eight charnel grounds, {24} the celestial mansion, and the seats. Next, nine moons arise from the vowels at the places of the principal and the retinue. Nine suns arise from the consonants. Aside from the sun and moons of the main and intermediate directions, the seed syllables and hand implements in between the sun and moon in the center of the palace merge like water and milk. The complete kāya arises from that; one should imagine it has the nature of the five gnoses. Furthermore, the moon is moisture and the sun is heat, arising from the cause, the vowels and consonants, respectively. This takes the name "the first warmth and moisture birth."

Next, bless the space and the secret; in dependence on entering into union with the three perceptions, the assembly of tathāgatas enters into the mouth, melts at the heart, and descends as two bindus of bodhicitta in the location of the secret place. The bindus issue forth between the sun and moon, transforming into seed syllables and hand implements marked with seed syllables, which all merge into one, blessing the complete kāya as the five gnoses. Since those complete (*sam*) forms of the nine deities enjoy (*bhoga*) great bliss, they are the sambhogakāya. There is no need to meditate on this in detail other than recalling this to mind. This mere recollection should also be understood for the two kāyas below.

Since the father and mother enter into union, the connate gnosis of immaculate bliss arises. Since that is the fire of passionate great bliss, the aggregates, sense bases, and sense elements of the father and mother melt into light; their form becomes a bindu of light. The meaning is that since the father melts, he is gnosis; since the mother melts, she is the dhātu. One should feel that the nondual dhātu and gnosis are the dharmakāya.

Next, imagine the continuum of samādhi as the four goddesses in the intermediate directions. Mentally recollecting, "In order to benefit sentient beings and for the purpose of immaculate great bliss, the principals arise from the dharmakāya bindu of light," [the principal] is invoked in turn with song. The result Vajradhara who arises through the five direct awakenings resembles the created cause Vajradhara. {25} This visualization purifies the universe and inhabitants of the past, which is the first limb, the limb of approach. The principal usually arises here in the abbreviated part of the procedure.

After that, there is the summoning and entry of the gnosis maṇḍala, which is the second limb, the near-accomplishment. Third, both the blessing (of the aggregates, sense bases, and sense elements, the accomplishment), and the conferral of empowerment (with the sealing of the master of the family, the great accomplishment) are combined, because this is a key point of the empowerment. Furthermore, the empowerment deities are invited before oneself and presented with offerings, praises, and supplications. Then, after the empowerment is conferred, the stream of bodhicitta water fills the crown; imagine that one has obtained the vajra master empowerment.

Since one is empowered into the path, [known as] the shape of the creation stage, the culmination of the creation stage is donning the armor, because it is the manifestation of all the adornments connected with the meditation of the purity of the six ornaments. As the stream fills the throat, imagine that one has received the secret empowerment. That empowers one to meditate on the path of self-empowerment (*bdag byin gyis brlabs pa*). Since the culmination of the self-empowerment is caṇḍālī yoga based on the four cakras and since the seal of the four cakras is the support of the vāyu and mind, the self-empowerment is meditated on first. As the stream fills the heart center, imagine that one obtains the gnosis of the wisdom consort empowerment. That empowers one to meditate on the path of relying on a mudra. Since there is an experience of the connate, the six consciousnesses are left naturally on the six sense objects; this is connected with freedom from clinging to the body, voice, and mind. The external sign of that is blessing the six sense bases and the body, speech, and mind. As the stream fills the navel, imagine that one obtains the fourth [empowerment's] supreme great bliss. Thus, [the nine deities of the maṇḍala] are sealed by the master of the family. One should imagine those [masters of the family] as the nirmāṇakāya. Since that empowerment is obtained, the path is not perceiving the appearances of samsara or nirvana, because [the path] is connected with supreme bliss and emptiness. {26} At the conclusion of sealing with the master of the family, one either dissolves the maṇḍala or alternately seals [with the master of the family] without dissolving the maṇḍala and thereafter dissolving the maṇḍala. This sublime one [Padmavajra] includes donning the armor, and so on, with the four characteristics of the third limb. The great accomplishment is obtaining the complete four empowerments.

As such, the beginner should focus and stabilize the mind utilizing the nine methods of placing the mind of śamatha on the basis of the direct realization of the first heat and moisture birth.

Further, to begin, in order to generate realization, it is maintained that one should include creation and completion in the three purities: from the perspective of the creation stage, gathering the wisdom accumulation is the purity of suchness; the complete form of the deities with the fourfold approach and accomplishment is the purity of the individual deities; and the arising of the experiential taste of śamatha is the purity of intrinsic cognizance (*so so rang rig*, Skt. *svasaṃvedana*).[11] Further, it is asserted that there is focusing the mind on the aspect of the deity, focusing the mind on the principal father, focusing the mind on the mother, placing the mind on the nine deities, and placing the mind on the maṇḍala and three realms. For each of those, the guru has explained that there is a stage of engagement, a stage of abiding, and a stage of arising. Among those three, in the stage of abiding there are nine intimate instructions for focusing the mind: placement of the mind, constant or continual placement, definite or repeated placement, near placement, taming, pacification, near pacification, one stream or one-pointedness, and very even placement. To summarize this with a verse:

> There are nine stages of focus:
> placement, continual placement, repeated placement,
> near placement, taming, pacification,
> near pacification, one stream, and very even placement.

Beginning from the rising yoga {27} up to sealing the master of the family, one should meditate with very strict effort. That is [the first placement,] slight placement of the mind. Also, for a beginner, quickness is an important point. When the mind is focused here, clarity is an important point.

Second, in order to meditate with continual placement, dissolve the maṇḍala and abide in the divine pride of the principal; it is also fine at times not to dissolve the maṇḍala. Focus the mind on the central eye. If it is clear, [be satisfied] it is clear; stop and extract the poison of concentration. If it is not clear, [accept] it is not clear; stop and extract the poison of concentration. If one has stopped but the aspect continues to occur vividly, since this is the poison of concentration, redirect one's attention to another entity, such as a vase or a blanket, and then meditate again. If [the visualization] is clear, [be satisfied] it is clear and stop. If [the visualization] is not clear, [accept] it is not clear, stop, and redirect one's attention, recalling [the visualization] through meditation. If a clear visualization does not arise even though one has extracted the poison of concentration through such measures and cultivated them again and again, meditate through recalling [the visualization] verbally. Here, there are also two parts. There is recalling the visualization through one's own recitation, such as reciting, "The veins of the central eye are red," as before, and extracting the poison of meditation and meditating. If that does not make the visualization clear, then another person should begin to recite, "The central eye," and again extract the poison of concentration and meditate. If that does not make the visualization clear, it is said that one should look at the eye and recall it—look at a very beautiful image of the central eye, extract the poison of meditation, and meditate. If at such times the aspect vividly appears as soon as one is no longer meditating, since this is the poison of meditation, redirect one's attention elsewhere.

When clarity [of the visualization] arises through such meditation for the one wishing for clarity, they have arrived at the measure of the purity of the individual deities. If one is able to prevent discursive clarity because one wishes it to be absent, {28} the measure of the purity of suchness is reached. The special experience of śamatha based on that is arriving at the measure of the purity of intrinsic cognizance.

Next, at the time of the session or placement, since the universe and all inhabitants dissolve into the protection cakra that one has meditated on, until finally also the *hūṃ* is meditated on as melting into a bindu of light as the essence of the five families, the completion stage is the purity of the individual deities. Since the meditation on the dark-red aspect, which is like the tip of a butter lamp, is the essence of great bliss, it is the purity of intrinsic cognizance. Since that is meditating without a reference point and since the meditation itself lacks grasping to mere nonreferentiality, it is the purity of suchness. Those are the instructions on continual placement.

Third, definite placement or repeated placement is swiftly returning to mindfulness when the mind becomes distracted externally or becomes internally agitated, by swiftly placing the mind on the object.

Fourth, near placement means that when the mind is fatigued by one visualization, one gives the mind relief by meditating in each session on the uṣṇīṣa, or the crossed vajra at the crown or the fangs of the mouth, and then returning to the previous meditation.

Fifth, taming is understanding the inestimable qualities of samādhi and taming the mind by always recalling the aspect of the deity when the visualization is not clear in all activities.

Sixth, pacification means the mind becomes dissatisfied when there is discursive conceptuality, and one pacifies that by relaxing the mind on the visualization.

Seventh, near pacification means that when unvirtuous thoughts such as covetousness arise, the object [of such thoughts] is pacified in dependence on the visualization.

Eighth, one-pointedness means the mind abides without being externally distracted; there is one-pointed placement on the basis of that.

Ninth, very even placement {29} is the arising of samādhi when the visualization is stable, because practice is not goal-oriented. *Ornament of Mahāyāna Sutras* states:

> Having focused the mind on the object [placement],
> that continuum will not be distracted [continual placement].
> Having swiftly understood there is distraction [repeated
>   placement],
> repeat that [focus] again.
> The intelligent increasingly
> gather the mind within [near placement].
> Because the benefits from that are seen [taming],
> samādhi tames the mind.
> Because the faults of distraction are seen,
> dissatisfaction in [samādhi] is pacified [pacification].

> The occurrence of covetousness, unhappiness,
> and so on are likewise pacified [near pacification].
> Following that, the diligent [one-pointedness]
> naturally attain for themselves
> the [antidotal] activity in the mind.
> Through familiarity with that, there is no [further] activity [very even placement]. [12]

Having stabilized the mind on one part of the body with the instruction of focusing the mind on one part of the body during the creation stage, one then switches to the other parts of the body. (1) In the first session [of the first day], meditate on the central eye; (2) in the second session, recall the three eyes; (3) in the third session, the wrathful wrinkle; and (4) in the fourth session, the nose. If those are not clear, recall the central eye in four sessions or meditate on the central eye for two or three days. In brief, one should meditate on the visualization until it is stable, so that if one wishes for the third eye to be clear, it is clear; if one wishes for [the eye] to vanish, it vanishes.[13] For the following visualizations, meditate in the same way until the visualization becomes very stable.

If one is mentally astute, then in the first session of the second day recall (5) the fangs in the mouth; in the second session, (6) the ears; in the third session, (7) the primary face; and in the fourth session, (8) the primary face and the right white face.

In the first session of the third day, recall (9) the primary face and the right white face; in the second session, (10) the left red face; in the third session, (11) the right two dark faces; and in the fourth session, (12) the left two dark faces and upper face.

In the first session of the fourth day, recall (13) the eight faces; in the second session, (14) the uṣṇīṣa, the ochre hair, and the crossed vajra; in the third session, (15) the head ornaments, such as the bone cakra, the earrings, and so on; and in the fourth session, (16) the whole body along with the throat ornament, and so on. {30}

In the first session of the fifth day, recall (17) the head and the whole body; in the second session, (18) the eight right hands with their implements; in the third session, (19) the eight left hands with their implements, the body ornaments such as the human heads, and the volcano; and in the fourth session, (20) the four feet pressing down on the four māras.

In the first session of the sixth day, recall (21) the principal and Gaurī; in the second session, (22) Caurī; in the third session, (23) Vetalī; and in the fourth session, (24) Ghasmarī.

In the first session of the seventh day, in addition to these five, the principal, and so on, recall (25) Pukkasī; in the second session, (26) Śavarī in the third session, (27) Caṇḍālī; and in the fourth session, (28) Ḍombinī.

In the first session of the eighth day, recall (29) the nine deities and the celestial mansion; in the second session, (30) the charnel grounds; in the third session, (31) the protection cakra; and in the fourth session, (32) the universe and inhabitants.

Just as one gradually trains in the visualizations of the creation stage, focus one's mind on the completion stage, which resembles the tip of a lamp flame. The entire three realms dissolve in stages into the maṇḍala of the universe and inhabitants, meditated on as a bindu of light. When that is clear, it becomes the size of the tip of a lamp flame. When that is clear, it becomes the size of a horsehair. When that is clear, it becomes the size of a horsehair split one hundred times. Finally, rest the mind in emptiness in the same way that warm breath vanishes on a mirror. Having recalled that, focus the mind. If one wishes to do a session or placement, beginning from the recollections up to meditating on emptiness, start from the dissolution of the universe, dissolving it into emptiness. When one wishes to arise, arise from the state of emptiness with the pride of the principal. Recall the purities, sing the song of the vajra, and offer pure aspirations. Following this, abide with the yoga of conduct. Through such cultivation one will see smoke, mirages, fireflies, blazing lamps, and cloudless space during the creation stage, the completion stage, equipoise, {31} and post-equipoise, respectively. It is sad that if one lacks the instruction, one will not see the signs however much one meditates. As such, that meditation in which the five signs are seen repeatedly is the culmination of the path of the beginner.

The arising of the five signs in that way signals that one has transitioned to the stage of the second person, who takes the name "the person who gives rise to slight bliss." Also here, beginning from the invitation of the field of accumulation up to the creation of the celestial mansion, the creation procedure is the same as before, but the creation procedure of the approach, the second "birth from heat and moisture," is abbreviated. The cause Vajradhara, the retinue goddesses, and the result Vajradhara are generated simultaneously in dependence on the moon, sun, vowels, and consonants. The remaining three direct realizations—the entry of the gnosis being, the empowerment, and the sealing of the master of the family—are performed like the previous direct realization. Through the strength of such cultivation, the mind becomes more stable. Through the strength of increasing the expansion and contraction of the vāyu and mind, the body blazes with bliss at the time of gathering merit; the mind is mostly empty at the time of the accumulation of gnosis; and the body and mind are placed in the union of bliss and emptiness at the time of the actual creation and completion stages. From time to time the form of the deity becomes empty and in motion. Dreams that seem clairvoyant arise. Thus, the second person arrives at the level of the path of application.

In the same way, the third person takes the name "the attainer of bliss." When that creation procedure of the approach is abbreviated, the invitation of the accumulation field up to the celestial mansion is the same as before. One instantly imagines the *aṃ* and *hūṃ* on the principal's seat. That is invoked with the recitation of the vowels and consonants, but if one does not recite those, it is acceptable because [the cause Vajradhara] can be created merely from the melting of the syllables. The space and the secret are blessed; the goddesses are also created with the previous method of the issuing forth of the seed syllables. {32} The result Vajradhara is also created from the transformation of a bindu into *aṃ* and *hūṃ*. The three branches of accomplishment, and so on, are the same as before. If one cultivates that, also, the appearance of the deity is primarily the completion stage. Occasionally in the visualization of the aspect of the deity, even though one meditates on Hevajra, one may see it change into many appearances such as Cakrasaṃvara, and so on. One may also see many various deluded appearances such as the cities of the six realms, and so on. The maṇḍalacakra also will become hazy like smoke, and so on. This is the third person arriving at the level of peak on the path of application.

After such experiences arise, the fourth person takes the name "attainer of increased bliss." The way such a person meditates on the gathering of the two accumulations is the same as before. The protection cakra and the celestial mansion are meditated on instantly. The principal is also created instantly. In an instant the space and the secret are blessed and united, and the tathāgatas are invited and enter the father's mouth. [The tathāgatas] melt at the heart, are created as the eight goddesses in the place of organs, and emerge into the main and intermediate directions. As the latter half of the fifth chapter of the root tantra states:

From the union of the churner and churned,
after Gauri emerges in the east,
she stands at the eastern door . . .[14]

The other three limbs are the same as before. This is called "the apparitional birth of the principal and the womb birth of the retinue." Through the power of such cultivation, though one can have a vision of the six realms of samsara in one's experiential appearances, one can also have a vision of the nirmāṇakāya buddhafields of nirvana. At that time there is no division between equipoise and post-equipoise. At that time when there is an effort by the ḍākinīs to cause obstacles and the ḍākinīs fill the sky, they say "give us siddhis," {33} rain down weapons, burn one with fire, and throw one into the ocean. Show the sign and these obstacles will be reversed. If the sign is understood and the ḍākinī shows her own form, since one enters into union with her, one will instantly see the truth. Even if one does not enter into union with her, one will receive empowerment from the nirmāṇakāya and arrive at the level of patience on the path of application.

The person who is beyond that performs the gathering of the two accumulations instantly. As it is said:

One should meditate on the vajra maṇḍala
in the snap of a finger.[15]

The commitment maṇḍala is created instantly. Since one's mind itself has the nature of gnosis, the invocation and entry of the gnosis maṇḍala is discarded. The person discards the seal of the three empowerments, donning the armor, and so on. The person who is beyond patience discards empowerment, sealing the master of the family. It is not that they do not meditate, but rather that they naturally do not visualize the procedure. Of the two paths, the creation stage and the completion stage, they have arrived at the nonmeditation called "dispensing with the creation stage." They are free from the twenty-two samayas, arriving at the level of the highest mundane dharmas of the path of application.

Next, in a single moment the nāḍīs of the maṇḍala of the body manifest[16] and the body arises as the deity, because there is no longer any need to meditate on the external maṇḍala. Since one investigates and meditates again and again on the body maṇḍala, this is the meaning of the explanation given by the gurus of the past: when the body maṇḍala is realized, one obtains the name "siddha." Also, that is called "seeing the truth." The person who transcends the world realizes the meaning of gnosis, arriving at the level of the path of seeing.

After such a realization, they arrive at the head of the path of cultivation. {34} Such a person beyond the path of seeing manifests the bhaga maṇḍala, personally seeing all the nāḍī syllables of the vowels and consonants. They will see the nāḍī syllables of the tathāgatas of the ten directions, the five ḍākinīs, the five families, and so on as undifferentiated from the *bhrūṃ* and *āṃ* in their heart. Due to the stability of samādhi, here they investigate and meditate on the bhaga maṇḍala again and again.

The person who is beyond that manifests the bodhicitta maṇḍala, gathering the ten elements, the five amṛtas, and the five vāyus, which fall where they wish into the nāḍīs and nāḍī syllables. They obtain power over reversal. Their ten elements are realized to be indistinct from the buddhas of the ten directions. Many tathāgatas in a single bindu do not contradict same flavor. That person who investigates and meditates on the bodhicitta maṇḍala again and again applies both the bhaga maṇḍala and the bodhicitta maṇḍala on the level of the path of cultivation.

Since the person who is beyond that arrives at the culmination of conduct because they obtain power over all three maṇḍalas, they rely on a mudra and apply the experience to the mind. Since they impartially enjoy the five castes, brahmins, and so on, they enjoy the four mudras, Locana, and so on. Like the great lord of yogins Virūpa, they are liberated in a single night in dependence on a padminī, arriving at the level of the path of attaining perfection. At the conclusion of that, when the two continuums are liberated simultaneously, the seven limbs of the three kāyas are accomplished. That will be explained below. The second general topic, the explanation of practice, is complete.

III. The Nine Profound Methods

The third general topic is that since all the paths of the four tantra divisions are complete in that direct realization of the path that was explained above and since there is no need to train in them separately, confidence arises in the practitioner. Having generated such confidence, the nine profound methods are called "profound" because of the conviction induced by meditation that realizes everything as complete. {35} Further, this method is many, this method is not incomplete, this method is vast, this method is easy, this method is profound, this method is not difficult, this method is supreme, this method is abundant, and this method is inconceivable. A verse summarizes the meaning:

> This method is many, complete, vast,
> easy, profound, not difficult,
> supreme, abundant, and inconceivable,
> held to be the nine profound methods.

As such, through the means of enumerating those, they are profound because of the nine profound methods. (1) "This has many methods" refers to the path of the four tantra divisions—laughing, gazing, and so on—in a single stream of bodhicitta being complete here.

(2) This method is not incomplete from the perspective of the complete path of the three yānas. From among the four joys at the time of the empowerment, joy replaces the path of śrāvakas, supreme joy replaces the path of pratyekabuddhas, and joy of separation replaces the path of bodhisattvas. (3) This method is vast from the perspective that just as nirvana is transformed into the path, the afflictions are transformed into the path. (4) This method is easy means that the result, great bliss, is accomplished in dependence on not abandoning the five objects of desire, the bliss of the path. This is explained from the point of view of adopting those. Alternatively, since all phenomena of samsara and nirvana are meditated on as a single maṇḍala, it is easy because they are transformed into meditation. (5) This method is profound because beginning from gathering the accumulation of merit, whatever is to be done or has been done is recognized to be one's own mind, the nature of a unique connate gnosis. One is liberated by practicing {36} because the object to be purified and the purifier are not distinct. (6) This method is not difficult because the suffering of hardships and austerities is not employed as the path. One's attitude is relaxed about food because of the yoga of eating, one's attitude is relaxed about the five objects of desire because of the yoga of conduct, and one relies on a mudra through the yoga of passion. Since one abandons suffering based on the bliss of the path, this path takes the name from the perspective of what is abandoned. As such, the sixth takes the name "the profundity of the path."

The three below this point take the name "the profundity of the result." (7) This method is supreme because one meditates on the two stages in a single, definite session (the certainty of session), on one seat (the certainty of place), and the diligent one attains buddhahood in one lifetime (the certainty of time). However, it is explained that even one who lacks diligence will not be delayed more than sixteen lifetimes. (8) This method is abundant because not only is the result, the supreme siddhi, attained on the basis of a single path, it is also explained that the eight intermediate siddhis and all inferior siddhis such as pacifying, and so on, are produced. (9) This method is inconceivable because all supreme and common results are also explained from the perspective of not requiring other causes—substances, and so on—other than being accomplished through the dependent origination of the maṇḍalacakra that inherently exists in one's body, voice, and mind.

Also, when summarized, the meaning of "profound" is twofold: the profundity of the path and the profundity from the perspective of the path. There are four parts in the first topic: the profundity of equipoise, the profundity of post-equipoise conduct, the profundity that permeates both equipoise and post-equipoise, and the profundity connected with profundity. There are three topics from the perspective of the result: {37}profound because there is the cause of swiftly accomplishing the time of the result, profound because all results are accomplished with a single cause, and profound because the result exists naturally perfected in the cause.

In the profundity of the path, the profundity of equipoise is the first two profundities; the profundity of the post-equipoise conduct is both conduct and passion, explained by the fourth and sixth profundities; the profundity that permeates both equipoise and post-equipoise is explained by both the vast method and the fourth, the easy method; and the profundity connected with profundity is the fifth profundity, the profound method itself, which is connected to the view.

The sequence of profundities for those is as follows: First, because the method is profound, it produces the view. Then, when applied to direct realization, "many methods" and "not incomplete" are produced. Next, from the perspective of the profundity that permeates both equipoise and post-equipoise, both "vast" and "easy" are produced. Next, the profundity of practice produces "not difficult." Next, the three profundities from the perspective of the result are produced. As such, the person who has confidence in those nine profound methods will meditate on the two stages of the path with great striving because they have severed all outer proliferation.

IV. The Seven Limbs of the Three Kāyas, The Result

The fourth general topic is the seven limbs of the three kāyas, the result. Among the three limbs of the dharmakāya, the limb of naturelessness is the aspect of the dhātu, the limb of not ceasing is the aspect of gnosis, and the limb of being uninterrupted is the aspect of the nonduality of the dhātu and gnosis. The three limbs of the sambhogakāya are union, consorting with the mother; great bliss, satisfaction with immaculate bliss; and the limb of complete enjoyment, the blazing of the major and minor marks. The nirmāṇakāya has one supreme limb, becoming filled with compassion.

This treatise on the position of the great compassionate lord Padmavajra was written down in the sublime place of glorious Sakya in reply to the many requests of the Śākya bhikṣu Balton Darma Jungne[17] {38} by the Śākya upāsaka Drakpa Gyaltsen, in order to clarify the unclear writings of previous gurus that resemble secret manuals.

samāptamithi

Ācārya Padmavajra's *Completion Stage Instruction Resembling the Tip of a Lamp Flame*[18]

Padmavajra

Having paid homage to Nairātmyā,
the pinnacle[19] of the essence[20] of wisdom,[21]
Anaṅgavajra[22] explained
the instruction on Hevajra,
Resembling the Tip of a Lamp Flame,
in connection with empowerment and instruction.

A practitioner who has obtained the empowerment of Hevajra, possesses samaya, and wishes to accomplish the state of Mahāvajradhara must first seek out a special place, and so on, and balance their health and elements of the body.[23] As such, when the health is very good,[24] settle the body on a comfortable seat[25] and sleep comfortably.[26] Because the accumulation of concentration is varied, it has the nature of the path of accumulation.

Next,[27] rise after the first light of dawn. Having put on clean clothes[28] according to the health and the temperature[29] of the elements of the body, engage in the procedures of waking from sleep and washing. Sit properly on a cushion with clean stuffing, taking a good posture[30] with the body that is even.[31] Similarly, the breath[32] should be very even and the mind should be even.[33] Because everything up to here is to be applied to concentration, it [all] has the nature of the path of application.

Next,[34] imagine that one is Śrī Hevajra with one face and two arms. The right hand holds a vajra and the left hand holds[35] a kapāla. Then, imagine a blue *hūṃ* on top of a sun and moon in one's heart center. {39} Light rays shine out from the blue *hūṃ*, burning up the concepts of all the worlds of the universe and all female living beings.[36] Because those [light rays] return, imagine that one's consort[37] is the nature of the worlds of the universe.

Likewise, imagine that [light rays shine out from the blue *hūṃ*] and burn up [the concepts] of all male living beings. The [light rays] return; imagine that oneself, Śrī Heruka as the nature of all inhabitants of all worlds, purifies others.

Next, imagine there is an *aṃ* on a sun and moon in the heart of the mother. The light from that [*aṃ*] melts the mother into light. Imagine she enters into the heart center of the father. Since one perceives[38] the ultimate suchness that was not seen before, it is the nature of the path of seeing.

The light of *hūṃ* in between the sun and moon in the heart center of the father melts the father into light; imagine the sun[39] is above, the method. The mother[40] is the moon below, wisdom. Imagine the limb of syllables, the eighty inverted consonants surrounding *hūṃ* in between the sun and moon. Likewise, imagine the upright thirty-two vowels in the heart center. The syllable *hūṃ* is imagined to be nondual method and wisdom. The sun and moon are the size of a chickpea. The *hūṃ* is the size of a mustard seed. The vowels and consonants are the size of the tips of hair. This bindu meditation is the nature of the path of cultivation.

Next, light arises from *hūṃ* melting the consonants into light, which dissolve into the vowels. Also, the vowels melt into light, which are then imagined dissolving into the moon. Likewise, imagine that the sun dissolves into the moon, and the moon dissolves into the *u* diacritic. Also, meditating on the gradual vanishing of *hūṃ*[41] is the subtle yoga.

Next, focus the mind on the bindu of amṛta, which is white, shiny, and the size of a tip of hair. {40} Next, imagine that the representation of sound,[42] the nāda, is the size of a tiny particle. Next, focus the mind on the mind alone. This has the nature of the path of attaining perfection, in which entities are abandoned. Following that, meditate on the mind as luminous. Following that, also, the universe and inhabitants are the nature of the father and mother. The father and mother have the nature of the bindu. The bindu has the nature of the subtle. The subtle has the nature of the mind. The mind has the nature of being empty by nature from the start. Meditate that it is free of all extremes, such as beginning, end, and so on. Mahāvajradhara has the nature of the result of the five paths. Based on the levels of individuals, there are differences[43] in enthusiasm for the yoga, namely, focusing the mind[44] for a year, a month, or a day. Next, training on the father and mother is also performed in stages.[45] Alternatively, the two stages are meditated on in a single session. Because some can enter immediately into the [subjects] above, they should focus their minds however they like and should be given the intimate instructions.

The faults are lethargy and agitation. Now, the method of removing lethargy is to uplift the mind by recalling the omniscient gnosis of the Buddha, and then meditate again. Sleepiness is removed by splashing water on one's face and walking around, then meditating again. If one is agitated, develop regret with respect to the objects of samsaric suffering. If that does not pacify agitation, focus on that object,[46] direct the mind itself, and meditate.

There are four sessions. When there is little mental experience, the length of a session should begin with twenty-four minutes, meditating in short sessions. Then meditate for longer intervals. After the mind is slightly stable, then begin with a forty-five minute long session. Likewise, having observed the mind for a little while, one attains experience. The common individual who attains strength of mind can maintain a session of meditation for the length of ninety minutes, three hours, one day, {41} one month, or one year, meditating in short sessions. The signs[47] are that one's health does not decline. Subsequently, chronic illnesses are removed from the body and new ones do not develop. One naturally refrains from negative physical actions, and one engages skillfully in virtues. The signs that arise in the body are trembling, and so on. The best effort in post-session yoga is offering praises and bali prior to the four sessions, and then meditating.

> May all sentient beings obtain
> luminous emptiness
> through whatever virtue is gained
> with *Instruction Resembling the Tip of a Lamp Flame*, composed
> by the one who obtained the empowerment from the lineage of
> gurus
> in connection with the instructions.

The *Instruction Resembling the Tip of a Lamp Flame* composed[48] by Ācārya Padmavajra is complete.

Translated and edited by the Indian abbot Gayadhara and Lama Śākya Yeshe.

sarva maṅgalaṃ

4. *Completing the Whole Path with Caṇḍālī* Composed by Ācārya Kṛṣṇācārya[1]

Drakpa Gyaltsen

Two cycles among the eight ancillary path cycles derive from the famous Indian proponent of Cakrasaṃvara, Kṛṣṇācārya. These are *Completing the Whole Path with Caṇḍālī*, found in chapter 4 and the *Instruction for Straightening the Crooked*, found in chapter 5. The main tradition of Cakrasaṃvara practiced in the Sakya tradition belongs to a system of exegesis traced to Naropa, called "the ultimate secret" (*gsang mtha'*).[2] The ultimate secret tradition of exegesis is exclusive to the Cakrasaṃvara cycles that were introduced to Tibet by Mal Lotsāwa Lodrö Drakpa (c. eleventh century to early twelfth century). Four separate cycles are associated with this tradition: the Cakrasaṃvara systems of the mahāsiddhas Luipa, Ghantapāda, and Kṛṣṇācārya, and the Vajrayoginī system of Mahāsiddha Naropa. The latter system is considered one of the "thirteen golden dharmas of Sakya" and is one of the four primary practices of the Sakya tradition. There are also numerous commentaries and instructions that the Sakya school associates with the ultimate secret tradition of Cakrasaṃvara.[3] Chapter 4, *Completing the Whole Path with Caṇḍālī*, is such an instruction, which distills Kṛṣṇācārya's six treatises, the core of his many works, into its most refined essence. The text is divided into five stages: the stage of tantra, the stage of mantra, the stage of gnosis, the stage of the secret, and the stage of nonduality. Amezhap's *Effortless Accomplishment of the Two Benefits* explains that the practitioner of this instruction is to meditate on the Kṛṣṇācārya system of Cakrasaṃvara.[4]

Drakpa Gyaltsen's text does not provide an account of the life of Kṛṣṇa, as the account of his career had already been composed by Kunga Nyingpo.[5] Amezhap mentions that there are many siddhas named Kṛṣṇa, but of these, this is the one known specifically as Kṛṣṇācārya.

Kunga Nyingpo places Kṛṣṇa in Bengal during the reign of Śrīcandra, 930–975 C.E., the longest reigning monarch of the Candra dynasty.[6] Kunga Nyingpo relates that Kṛṣṇācārya was named Karṇapa, either because he was originally from the southern region of India named Karṇada or because he had long earlobes. Since Kṛṣṇācārya was dark-skinned, he was also called Kṛṣṇa. Kṛṣṇa was a pupil of a guru named Jālandhara and gains slight power based on practicing his guru's instructions, attracting a large entourage of yogins and yoginīs. As is the case with many of the stories of mahāsiddhas, Kṛṣṇa suffered a series of discouraging setbacks after his initial success in practice, including being refused instruction in tantric conduct by his guru due to pridefulness. Kṛṣṇa tells Jālandhara that he is leaving for Devīkoṭa in Bengal. His guru advises against this, observing that Kṛṣṇa will suffer from obstacles created by the ḍākinīs, but Kṛṣṇa disobeys and leads his entourage onward to Bengal.

On the way Kṛṣṇa has four encounters. He first encounters a woman suffering from leprosy. He brags to his entourage that he will cure this woman, yet fails. A beggar in his entourage succeeds in freeing her from the disease. As it turns out, these two were emanations of Heruka and Cakrasaṃvara. After a series of further misadventures—encountering a plowman with an endless flagon of beer (Heruka), a beautiful maiden running a juice stand who humiliates him (Vajravārāhī), and a man in a temple reading a copy of the *Perfection of Wisdom in Eight Thousand Lines*, which Kṛṣṇa cannot read—Kṛṣṇa arrives in Bengal. Here he experiences difficulties consecrating a statue of Lokeśvara at the request of the minister Kuśalanātha, a Buddhist, and manages to get into trouble with the king, who according to this account was a devotee of Bhairava and Kālaratri and thus a non-Buddhist.

At this point in the story, Kṛṣṇa again encounters Heruka in the form of a blue man with Hindu religious markings bearing a skull. The blue man informs Kṛṣṇa that he is the leader of Kṛṣṇa's group, to which Kṛṣṇa haughtily objects. The blue man transforms into Heruka and flies into the sky, leaving Kṛṣṇa begging to become his student. Heruka predicts that Kṛṣṇa will not achieve mahāmudrā siddhi during his life, but he will obtain supreme siddhi in the bardo. This event compels Kṛṣṇa to compose his famous six treatises, mentioned at the outset of *Completing the Whole Path with Caṇḍālī*. He converts Śrīcandra to Buddhism, who then decrees that his subjects are to be Buddhists. This account also records Kṛṣṇa's deathbed request that his body not be burned for seven days.[7] On the fifth day, the king ordered the whole kingdom to gather with the sound of drums.

During the cremation, the body vanishes in the midst of the smoke offering substances such as parasols, banners, and a rain of flowers; the self-arisen sounds of many instruments such as ḍamarus, cymbals, and so on, are heard; and divine scent permeates everywhere.

{44}I pay homage by bowing my head with devotion to the feet of the sublime guru.

On the basis of the intimate instructions of the great Śrī Jālandharapa, the intention of the Mahācārya Kṛṣṇa, the practitioner of strict discipline, is that all of the dharma the Buddha taught is included in Vajrayāna. The three divisions of tantras of Vajrayāna are included in mahāyoga. All the method and wisdom tantras of mahāyoga are included in the nondual tantras of *Hevajra* and *Cakrasaṃvara*. Also, the complete intention of both of those tantras is included in the *Vajraḍāka* and *Saṃpūṭa* explanatory tantras. When the intention of those two is combined, there is the completion stage for which Kṛṣṇa composed six summaries. The basic summary is the *Ornament of Spring*, and the verse summary is the *Secret Principle*. The summary of the direct realization is the *Four Stages*. The summary of the meaning is the *Condensed Essence*, and the summary of yoga is the *Explanation of Vows*. The summary for relying on a mudra is the *Ornament of Mahāmudrā*. Those are included in the *Four Stages*, which is like the heart. The condensed instruction for that is called *Completing the Whole Path with Caṇḍālī*.

I. The Concise Explanation

The view of this ācārya is called "the suchness of bodhicitta without beginning or end and liberated from the four extremes." In order to realize that view, it is held that there is the method of the four or five stages of the path: the stage of tantra, the stage of mantra, the stage of gnosis, {45} and the stage of the secret. In addition to these four is added a fifth, the so-called "stage of nonduality." Now then, though the six summaries explain the stage of the secret as buddhahood, here that must be reconciled with the intimate instructions of the guru. In fact, the five stages stop at the mundane path's supreme mundane dharmas. Then, the [bodhisattva] stages are realized by relying on a mudra, leading to the stage of buddhahood.

Moreover, the five stages are also held to be summarized in triads: the tantra, and so on; the progression, and so on; and the measure of attaining perfection, and so on. Now then, "tantra" refers to the three maṇḍalas supported on the four cakras, and so on, which have existed from the beginning [in the body]. "Progression" refers to progressive visualization. The measure of attaining perfection is clearly seeing the three maṇḍalas that depend on the four cakras as they are.

"Mantra" refers to the *aṃ* in the navel. "Progression" refers to the progression of igniting the fire up to burning the four cakras. "The measure of attaining perfection" refers to trembling, and so on.

"Gnosis" refers to the connate of the connate stabilized in ascending order. "Progression" refers to the amṛta of gnosis of the tathāgata entering through the left calf and experienced from the jewel of the vajra up to the brow. "The measure of attaining perfection" refers to all things arising as bliss, and so on.

"Secret" refers to the prāṇa vāyu. "Progression" refers to removing all the faults of vāyu by meditating after holding the vāyu inside each of the nostrils. "The measure of attaining perfection" refers to the body feeling as light as a cotton ball {46} and that one can avert the obstacles of ḍākinīs through seeing the five signs, and so on.

"Nondual" refers to the fundamental mind of the nonduality of subject and object or appearances and emptiness. "Progression" refers to progressively realizing that all inner and outer phenomena are essentially inseparable. "The measure of attaining perfection" is the attainment of clairvoyance. That is the end of the mundane path.

On the basis of relying on a predicted mudra, one travels through the twelve stages—the pithas, upapithas, and so on—and realizes the stage of buddhahood. This is the conclusion of the concise explanation.

II. The Extensive Explanation

A. The Stage of Tantra

In the extensive meditation of the four stages, first, visualize the stage of tantra at the time of meditation that has been confirmed through hearing and reflection. Sit on a comfortable seat. Having performed the limbs of concentration beforehand, meditate on any maṇḍala for the creation stage such as the thirty-seven-deity maṇḍala, and so on.[8] The half of the deities of the maṇḍalacakra in the principal directions that circle left and the half of the deities in the intermediate direction that circle right enter the right nostril and left nostril in concert with inhalation, and gather into the *hūṃ* of the heart. Finally, the mother Vajravārāhī also gathers into the *aṃ* of the navel, from the light arising from *aṃ*. Visualize the two functional (*las byed*, Skt. *karmakara*) cakras and four upper cakras in stages. Visualize the three nāḍīs and the syllables that block the rasanā and the lalanā. From the *yaṃ* syllable at the rectum, a blue maṇḍala of air arises, marked with pennants. From the *raṃ* in the groin, a triangular fire maṇḍala arises, with one tip facing downward and marked with three flames blazing upward.

The inner circle of the red-colored nirmāṇacakra at the navel has eight petals with the eight series (*a ka ca ṭa ta pa ya śa*) and *aṃ* in the center. The outer circle has fifty-six syllables: thirty-four consonants circling to the right and sixteen vowels circling to the left, to which are added the six short vowels, *a i u e o aṃ*. The black dharmacakra at the heart has eight petals: {47} *bhrūṃ āṃ jriṃ khaṃ* in the four main directions, *hūṃ* in the center, and *ya ra la va* in the intermediate directions. The inner circle of the red [sambhogacakra] at the throat has the four long vowels *ā ī ū ai*, and in the center is *oṃ*. The outer circle has twelve vowels, excluding the four genderless vowels [*ṛ ṝ ḷ ḹ*]. The white mahāsukhacakra at the crown has thirty-two petals, which are free from an array of syllables; in the center is an inverted *haṃ*.

To the right of those [cakras], the red solar rasanā with its mouth facing upward has the nature of fire. Visualize that its entryway is blocked by two upright consonants in pairs between each of the inverted vowels. To the left of those, the [white] lunar lalanā with its mouth facing downward has the nature of water. Visualize that its entryway is blocked by two inverted consonants between each of the upright vowels. Visualize the central nāḍī, which is the size of a horsehair split into hundredths, red, straight, and fine. In concert with exhalation, visualize the four cakras in ascending order based on the rasanā nāḍī. In concert with inhalation, visualize the four cakras from crown to navel. In concert with pausing the breath, visualize only the central nāḍī and *aṃ* at the navel. It is also permissible to visualize [the above] without being in concert with the breath. This [visualization] should be clear and short in length. There is no position concerning the number or length of the session. [The visualization] should become clear in three, five, seven, nine, or eleven days. Some individuals may require up to a month or a year for the visualization to become clear. In brief, since there is no position about a definite amount of time, such as number of days, and so on, one should meditate until the six cakras and the three nāḍīs become extremely clear, like the lines on the palm of one's hand.

This concludes the stage of tantra.

B. The Stage of Mantra

Second, there are two topics in the stage of mantra: (1) the preliminaries and (2) the main subject.

1. Preliminaries

First, at the time of entering the stage of mantra, one's diet should be very nutritious, {48} but only a third of what one ate previously. The key point of the body is that the arms should embrace the knees, like a meditation belt. The thighs should be pressed tightly against the belly. The two feet and the buttocks carry the weight evenly.

Next, in order to ignite the fire maṇḍala of the groin with the vāyu maṇḍala at the rectum, constrict the lower vāyu seven times. Imagine the fire at the groin circling *aṃ* at the navel. Swallow the upper vāyu along with spittle. The upper vāyu dissolves into *aṃ* at the navel. After directing one's consciousness to *aṃ* at the navel, press the upper vāyu down. That is performed forcefully yet briefly. Since one repeatedly meditates on that, five signs arise at the location of the navel: smoke, and so on. Feel that the fire of *aṃ* blazes out of control, one or two finger lengths all the way up to the throat. It spreads to the tongue and the shoulders. One feels thirst and great passion. The caṇḍālī fire becomes strong. It is maintained that until one feels the flame burning out of control, the flame cannot blaze upward and that one should not constrict the lower vāyu. This is the preliminary of the stage of mantra.

2. Main Subject

Next, the second, the actual stage of mantra: When the feeling of the fire blazing out of control occurs, since the rasanā channel on the right causes heat, it is called "the mother of fire." Since the lalanā on the left causes nonconceptuality, it is called "the mother of sleep." Repeatedly open and close the anal sphincter, which is called "the meeting of the tips of the mothers," and then constrict it strongly. The fire of *aṃ* burns the navel cakra and the seed syllables. Then, that fire associated with the right rasanā moves up, burning the [syllables of] the five families of the tathāgatas, the four mothers, and the cakra. Next, the fire burns the throat cakra and its syllables, and similarly, it burns the crown cakra.

After the fire opens the point at the brow, it fills the right nostril or right ear with bliss and fire issues forth, which is meditated on in the space before oneself as the inconceivable tathāgatas of the ten directions. At first train the mind on one tathāgata, then ten, then one hundred, on up to an inconceivable number. {49} The fire enters either the right ear or the right calf of the tathāgatas. The tathāgatas become the same nature as the fire of the rasanā. Since there are some repetitions of fire turning up and turning down, the four cakras of the tathāgatas and the element amṛtas melt together. Like a leech sucking blood, [the amṛta] becomes the same nature as the lalanā of the tathāgatas; this is carried out and leaves through their left ear or nostril. [The amṛta] enters through one's left calf or the left nostril, and as [the lalanā] gradually fills from either the top or the bottom, one gains control over the lalanā, and [the cakras] are restored and filled from the crown down to the navel or from the navel up to the crown. Either way, the crown becomes very full. After the bodhicitta strikes *aṃ* at the navel, the central nāḍī is opened through strong stimulation, and after the [fire] destroys *hūṃ* at the heart and *oṃ* at the throat, it strikes *haṃ* at the crown. Since the bindu of bodhicitta of the melted *haṃ* ignites, the strength of its dripping increases, filling the space between both [cakras] and *aṃ*. Alternately, when meditating on the blazing and dripping through the method of [the bodhicitta] dissolving into *aṃ*, the samādhis of bliss and clarity arise in the body and mind, respectively; there is trembling and shaking, one emits loud noises, and so on. If one wishes to pacify those signs, it is said one should "decapitate the syllables."[9] Inhale [gently] and exhale forcefully three times. If that does not pacify those signs, meditate without visualizing *haṃ*. If that does not pacify those signs, meditate on the area above the heart as hollow.[10] If that does not pacify those signs, visualizing all phenomena as one's mind will pacify them.

This concludes the stage of mantra.

C. The Stage of Gnosis

Third, the stage of gnosis is the progressive meditation on bliss. After the bodhicitta descends from *haṃ* through the path of the central nāḍī and falls into the vajra jewel, that person, in whose continuum the experience of the stage of mantra has arisen, generates experience by means of the sixteen joys, which are stabilized in ascending order. That can arise in oneself in one session on one cushion; it can also arise in days or {50} months.

That stage eliminates the proliferation of the visualization of the stage of mantra. The bodhicitta that descends from the crown falls into the tip of the vajra jewel; one should meditate repeatedly, giving rise to the experiences of bliss, clarity, and nonconceptuality. When those arise, it is the joy of joy. When [bliss] arises there, meditating on the shaft of the vajra is the supreme joy of joy. Further, when that bliss is unbearable, meditate on the base of the vajra, the "separation from joy" of joy. When that bliss is unbearable, focus the mind on the bliss at the navel, the connate joy of joy. These are the four joys included in joy.

When the bliss becomes unbearable, focus the mind on the location one fourth of the way above the navel, the joy of supreme joy. Further, when that bliss becomes unbearable, focus the mind on the bliss in the location two fourths of the way above the navel, the supreme joy of supreme joy. When that bliss becomes unbearable, focus the mind on the bliss in the location three fourths of the way above the navel, the "separation from joy" of supreme joy. When that bliss becomes unbearable, focus the mind on the bliss at the heart center, the connate joy of the supreme joy. When that bliss becomes unbearable, accompanied by a feeling of heart palpitations and tremors, one has reached the culmination of the four joys, which are included in supreme joy.

Further, focus the mind on the bliss at the location one fourth of the way above the heart, the joy of "separation from joy." When that bliss becomes unbearable, focus the mind on the bliss at the location two fourths of the way above the heart, the supreme joy of "separation from joy." When that bliss becomes unbearable, focus the mind on the bliss three fourths of the way above the heart, the "separation from joy" of the "separation from joy." When that bliss becomes unbearable, focus the mind on the throat in the location four fourths of the way above the heart, the connate joy of "separation from joy." Since one focuses on that, when there is a feeling that one's voice is blocked and one cannot speak, this is the culmination of the joys that are included in "separation from joy." {51}

Focus the mind on the bliss one fourth of the way above the throat, the joy of connate joy. When that bliss becomes unbearable, focus the mind on the bliss in the location two fourths of the way above the throat, the supreme joy of the connate joy. When that bliss becomes unbearable, meditate by focusing the mind on the bliss three fourths of the way above the throat at the brow, the "separation from joy" of connate joy. When that bliss becomes unbearable, focus the mind on the bindu of bliss at the crown, the connate joy of connate joy. As such, for all of those, repeatedly meditate on the experience arising in each of those places. However, if the experience does not arise, one must return to that place and repeat the meditation. Through such meditation all things arise as bliss. One will become intoxicated with bliss, becoming unconscious like a drunk. When all that one perceives or sees induces the feeling of being intoxicated with bliss, this is the culmination of the sixteen joys of the state of gnosis. To eliminate proliferation concerning those, meditate on the stage of the secret. This concludes the stage of gnosis.

D. The Stage of the Secret

Fourth is the meditation of the stage of the secret, in which there are two topics: (1) the actual meditation and (2) pacifying the faults of the vāyu.

1. The Meditation

First, in the actual meditation, *secret* refers to the vāyu. *Stage* refers to a progressive meditation. Meditate on the empty space of the two nostrils, which is likened to a hollow egg. Next, balance the life-sustaining vāyu: after the vāyu emerges from the body like incense smoke, meditate that it is sniffed into the base[11] of a single nostril and does not move out. Such meditation stabilizes the life-sustaining vāyu, giving rise to many benefits such as pacifying chronic illnesses, preventing new ones, and so on.

2. Removing Faults of the Vāyu

Second, at that occasion, since all kinds of faults of the vāyu become possible, one should remove those with the procedure of reversing all faults of the vāyu. If one has uncontrollable diarrhea, there is discomfort and pain during movement because the downward-voiding vāyu has been arrested and bliss increases excessively. In order to pacify that, focus on the bliss at the brow. Since one focuses on that, if there is pain in the nasal bone, pain in the crown, {52} or pain in the ears due to roaring sound, the upward moving vāyu has been arrested and bliss increases. In order to pacify that, focus the mind on the bliss at the navel. If there is also a feeling of discomfort and bloating, since the metabolic vāyu is arrested, bliss increases. In order to pacify that, focus the mind on the bliss at the throat. If one feels numbness or paralysis in the lower lip, the vāyu that exists in the tongue is arrested. In order to pacify that, focus the mind on the bliss at the heart center. If one feels queasiness and disturbance in the heart, since the vāyu in the heart is arrested, bliss increases. In order to pacify that, focus the mind on the bliss in the center of the jewel. If one focuses like that, one feels pain and numbness in all joints of the body. If the whole body starts to shake, since the pervading vāyu is arrested, bliss increases in the body. In order to pacify that, meditate on the absence of inherent existence in bliss. If by meditating in that way there is a desire to laugh or one feels compelled to utter exclamations, bliss has increased excessively. Though the bliss is excessive, meditate without perceiving it. If one feels very intoxicated and loses consciousness because of such a meditation, śamatha is predominant. In order to pacify [such effects], meditate on all outer and inner phenomena as illusions. Since one balances [the vāyu] in that way and meditates repeatedly, one's body becomes light as a cotton ball, and one sees the five signs, such as smoke, and so on. When all the ḍākinīs come into one's presence, in order to activate one's experience and exhibit many forms, one will prevent obstacles with signs such as displaying one finger, and so on. If one does not know the signs, one will prevent obstacles through recognizing nonconceptuality. Through such meditation, one is blessed by the ḍākinīs.

This concludes the stage of the secret.

E. The Stage of Nonduality

Fifth, the stage of nonduality refers to the absence of inherent existence of the object and consciousness and meditating after merging the object and consciousness. Since all phenomena are included in one's mind and mental factors, without conceptualizing about external phenomena, one meditates without perceiving all the conceptual sensations of the inner mind. {53} Like pouring water into water, bliss and emptiness are inseparable (*bde stong dbyer med*), clarity and emptiness are inseparable (*gsal stong dbyer med*), and cognizance and emptiness are inseparable (*rig stong dbyer med*). Meditate without perception on nonduality. Through such meditation, one gradually obtains the five clairvoyances and the stage of great bliss. Those are the culmination of the two mundane paths: accumulation and application.

When one reaches the culmination of the stage of nonduality, the predicted mudra will arise. In dependence upon her, the higher perception of the transcendent path arises in dependence on the path of the mudra and conduct. Then, one travels in order on the twelve stages through the pithas, upapithas,[12] and so on, and one realizes buddhahood.

As such, the result of practice is called "the great bliss of the three kāyas," effortlessly accomplishing the benefit of sentient beings without striving, like the sun and its rays. Further, from the seven limbs, the three limbs of the dharmakāya are naturelessness, uninterrupted, and unimpeded. The three limbs of the sambhogakāya are union, great bliss, and complete enjoyments. The limb of the nirmāṇakāya is the one called "totally filled with great compassion."

In order to clarify the somewhat unclear and arcane writings of previous gurus on the instruction of the practitioner of strict discipline Mahācārya Kṛṣṇa, called *Completing the Whole Path with Caṇḍāli*, which is based upon the instruction of the great Śrī Jālandhara, and in response to several requests, this was written at the Sakya retreat place by Drakpa Gyaltsen, a Śākya upāsaka and yogin of the supreme vehicle.

The lineage is Lady Vajrayoginī, Vajraghantapāda, Kūrmapāda, Śrī Jālandhara the Great, Kṛṣṇācārya, Śrīdhara, Gayadhara, and down to the Lord Sakyapa.

samāptamitī

5. *The Instruction for Straightening the Crooked* Composed by Kṛṣṇa Acyuta[1]

Drakpa Gyaltsen

The Instruction for Straightening the Crooked begins by recounting Kṛṣṇācārya's encounter with a yogin named Kṛṣṇa Acyuta, while on the way with his retinue to Bengal. Acyuta taught Kṛṣṇācārya a method called "straightening the crooked" that relies on a forceful method of prāṇāyāma. The instruction here, as indicated by the title, is for straightening out the nāḍīs, vāyus, and bindus. It is of note that Acyuta claims his guru is Śiva and that Śiva's guru is Vajradhara. We have no other details of the life of Acyuta.

Homage to the sublime gurus. {55}

When Mahācārya Kṛṣṇa, the practitioner of strict discipline, left Jālandhara to enter into the conduct, the road on which all yogins before him traveled, later on he came to a great city on the road, where he overheard the conversation of some men who were saying, "Some days ago, a man called Acyuta,[2] who is without aging and death, traveled in the sky."

[Kṛṣṇācārya] asked them, "Where is this man?"

[The men replied,] "He [Acyuta] does not have a certain abode. Sometimes he stays on that cliff over there; sometimes he stays in this small grove over here," and indicated a small grove.

[Kṛṣṇācārya] went to the place where [Acyuta] was meditating and noticed that he was naked, blue in color, with a body like ice. Kṛṣṇācārya prostrated to him without reservation and requested to be accepted as his disciple.

[Acyuta] replied, "I cannot accept you as a disciple. If you do not request instruction, I cannot do as you ask."

[Kṛṣṇācārya] asked, "Who is your teacher?"

[Acyuta] replied, "I am Acyuta, the disciple of Maheśvara, who is the disciple of Vajradhara."

When asked where Maheśvara stays at present, [Acyuta] replied, "He is in union with Uma in the ninth underworld or on the slopes of Meru."

[Kṛṣṇācārya] asked, "When does Maheśvara arise?"

[Acyuta] replied, "He arises simultaneously with the one thousand and two buddhas."

[Kṛṣṇācārya] asked, "Well then, do you assert that this instruction of yours is a Buddhist path?"

[Acyuta] replied, "I do."

Since [Kṛṣṇācārya again] requested [Acyuta] to accept him as a disciple, Acyuta replied, "In that case, this is my instruction," and taught this verse:

> If the vāyu is controlled by the wrathful form,
> one will be free from white hair and wrinkles.
> After being freed from aging and death,
> one will become imperishable, like space. {56}

Now, this is called "straightening the crooked." The crooked nāḍīs are the rasanā and lalanā. The crooked vāyu is exhalation and inhalation. The crooked bindu is the semen and blood. Those are placed in the central nāḍī to straighten them; that is, after the nāḍīs, vāyus, and bindus are controlled, they become the path of buddhahood.

The stages of putting that into practice are to perform massage for several days, and one's behavior should be relaxed. Then, when beginning to meditate, be seated on a comfortable seat. Go for refuge to the Three Jewels, cultivate bodhicitta, feel devotion for the guru who is seated on one's crown, and recall one's commitment deity.

Next, the main subject:

> If the vāyu is controlled by the wrathful form . . .

Position the body well with crossed legs. The two hands should be clenched in vajra fists, resting on the two knees. The two eyes should be rolled back without closing them. The tongue should be on the palate. The teeth should be set and the mouth open. Press the belly toward the spine. Unite the upper and lower vāyus. Gradually slide the two hands forward until the elbows rest on the knees. When one tenses the whole body until one's tendons show, the body trembles slightly. In that way one will control the vāyu. If heat in the heart occurs or a tension headache occurs, release the tension. If those are not pacified by releasing the tension, rise, cry out, and eat food. The above practice should be repeated twenty-one times. After one releases the tension, recognize the mind's clarity and emptiness, releasing the hold and resting. One should engage again with strong effort as before. Since there is no definite length or numbers of sessions, after some time, when the samādhi of clarity and emptiness occur as soon as the body engages in the yantra, one has reached the culmination of the first yantra.

In order to stabilize this, one should perform other yantras. Place the left vajra fist on the heart. Raise the right vajra fist into space and join the vāyus. Tense the body as before and meditate. Then reverse that, raising the left fist and holding the right fist on the heart, training as before. {57} Further, draw a bow both to the right and to the left, and train as before. Further, raise both hands into the sky, tense the body as before, and meditate. Cross the vajra fists at the heart and hold, meditating as before. As such, whichever yantra one holds, when the samādhi of inexpressibility arises in one's continuum, this is the culmination.

If white hair and wrinkles appear, smear saliva on the place where they arise and massage it; that will prevent white hair and wrinkles. Gradually train in the conduct of total freedom (*kun 'dar gyi spyod pa*; Skt. *avadhūtacaryā*) through such actions, disregarding pure and impure with regard to food. Next, one should accomplish the five clairvoyances, traveling in the sky, and immortality. After that, train in the conduct of everything being good (*kun tu zang po'i spyod pa*; Skt. *samantabhadracaryā*). Through that, one progresses gradually through the stages and manifests buddhahood. This naturally pacifies the disturbances of the elements and the body and obstacles of samādhi and mind. The obstacles of the external māras are pacified by the conduct of strict discipline (*brtul zhugs kyi spyod pa*; Skt. *vratacaryā*) through reciting *hūṃ*.

The result is the three kāyas endowed with the seven limbs. There is the limb of naturelessness for the dharmakāya. There are three [limbs] for the sambhogakāya: union, great bliss, and complete enjoyment. There are three [limbs] for the nirmāṇakāya: great compassion, uninterrupted, and unceasing.

This oral instruction of Ācārya Kṛṣṇa, the practitioner of strict discipline, the instruction for straightening the crooked nāḍīs, vāyus, and bindus, was written down at Pal Sakya Monastery. The lineage for this is the same as that for *Completing the Whole Path with Caṇḍālī.*

samāptamithi

6. *Obtained in Front of a Stupa* Composed by Ācārya Nāgārjuna[1]

Drakpa Gyaltsen

Obtained in Front of a Stūpa is a mahāmudrā instruction based on two passages taken from the *Guhyasamāja Tantra*, which according to Drakpa Gyaltsen form the basis for Saraha's *Treasury of Couplets* and Nāgārjuna's *Commentary on Bodhicitta*. Relatively brief, the main focus of the text is identifying the nature of the mind, free from arising, abiding, and ceasing—an inexpressible union of clarity and emptiness. Amezhap's *Effortless Accomplishment of the Two Benefits* does not specify a deity to meditate on with this instruction, which may account for its usage in other Sakya systems when explaining the meditation of mahāmudrā. He outlines the text in five topics: (1) ascertaining the view, (2) accumulating merit, (3), controlling the mind, (4), introduction to reality, and (5) post-realization conduct.

Drakpa Gyaltsen's account of the origin of this instruction begins with Nāgārjuna resisting the amorous advances of the queen of King Dejö Zangpo,[2] much to her anger and subsequent false accusations. Accompanied by Āryadeva, Nāgārjuna flees south to Śrī Parvata, in the region of Andhra Pradesh, where he meets his guru, Saraha, in front of a stupa. Amezhap adds the small detail of Saraha asking them, "Have you not ascertained the mind?"

Saraha is an elusive figure of great importance in Tibetan Buddhism. He is the direct source for the *Laghusaṃvara*[3] and instrumental in transmitting the Guhyasamāja to Nāgārjuna.[4] Amezhap gives one account of Saraha in the *Amazing Storehouse of Jewels*, a history of Guhyasamāja, in which Saraha is described as one of four sons of a brahmin, who ordains with Arhat Rāhula, the Buddha's son, taking the name Rāhulabhadra. He becomes the abbot of Vikramśila. Rāhulabhadra hears that a king from

South India named Visukalpa has retrieved the *Guhyasamāja Tantra* and others from a yoginī in Oḍḍiyāna. Rāhulabhadra requests teachings from Visukalpa, receives them, practices them, and becomes renowned as Saraha.[5] The *Amazing Storehouse of Jewels* further relates that Nāgārjuna was eight years of age when he first meets Saraha/Rāhulabhadra at Nālandā, who grants him novice ordination. Later, Nāgārjuna fully ordains under Saraha/Rāhulabhadra, and receives the empowerment of Guhyasamāja and the explanation of the path.

{60} I devotedly prostrate with my crown to the feet of the sublime guru.

This is titled "Obtained in Front of a Stupa," "Instruction for Ascertaining the Mind," "Meditation on Ultimate Bodhicitta," and "Explanation of Mahāmudrā as Innate."

Saraha composed the *Song of the Treasury of Couplets* based on the bodhicitta of Akṣobhya in chapter 2 of the *Guhyasamāja Tantra*:

> The entities of the three realms
> are meditated on as nonexistent in the ultimate.
> An actual meditation on nonexistence
> is a meditation not to be meditated.
> Therefore, neither the existent nor the nonexistent
> are objects of meditation.[6]

Further, Ācārya Ārya Nāgārjuna composed the *Commentary on Bodhicitta* based on the bodhicitta of Vairocana from chapter 2 of the *Guhyasamāja Tantra*:

> Free from all entities,
> devoid of aggregates, sense elements, sense bases,
> apprehended objects, and apprehending subjects,
> since phenomena uniformly lack identity,
> one's mind did not arise from the beginning,
> having the nature of emptiness.[7]

As such, this is the intimate instruction for both citations. {61}

The lineage is Vajradhara, Vajrapāṇi, Saraha the Great, Ārya Nāgārjuna, Āryadeva, Bhikṣu Kṛṣṇapāda, Candrakīrti, Brahmin Śrīdhara, Vīravajra, Mugulungpa, Se Kharchung, Je Gönpowa, and Jetsun Sakyapa. There are five topics in this teaching for practice: (1) to begin, ascertain the view; (2) next, gather the accumulation of merit; (3) in the middle, control the mind; (4) then, introduce the mind to the reality; and (5) after realization arises, connect it with conduct.

I. Ascertaining the View

Having heard the *Commentary on Bodhicitta*, this is the intimate instruction for practice in order to realize it.

Outer and inner phenomena are not fabricated by a creator such as a vital force, god, and so on, and they are not established from subtle particles, and so on. One's mind is thoroughly adulterated with accumulated traces in samsara without a beginning. That which is accomplished through virtuous and unvirtuous actions is like horses and elephants in a dream. In brief, these are appearances of one's mind.

Now, when that mind is properly investigated, in the beginning it is devoid of a cause of arising, in the end it is devoid of a result that ceases, {62} and in the middle it is devoid of an entity that abides, possessing the nature of luminosity. Though it is empty, its clarity is unceasing. Likewise, that inseparability of clarity and emptiness is called "inexpressible." As such, one should reflect on that for several days until one repeatedly gains confidence.

II. Gathering the Accumulation of Merit

For gathering the accumulation of merit, the place should not be outside or dark. In a spacious and isolated meditation house, face south and offer four maṇḍalas. The four are offered to Vajradhara, the commitment deity, the lineages of the guru, and the root guru.

Then, meditate on the guru at the crown of one's head and make repeated devotions. Go for refuge to the lineage gurus, starting from the Buddha. Offer supplications. Also, offer the maṇḍala and perform supplication as much as one likes, engaging in that for several days.

This is the conclusion of the accumulation of merit.

III. Controlling the Mind

In the middle, control the mind: In an isolated place, adopt a cross-legged posture. One's eyes should be half-closed. Go for refuge and cultivate bodhicitta. Meditate on the guru at the crown and generate devotion. Recall the yidam.

Then, [the *Treasury of Couplets*] states:

> If this entangled mind
> is released, liberation is doubtless.[8]

Release the mind from within, and rest without fabrication in its lucidity, pristine and loose. Do not engage the mind in activities, whether virtuous, unvirtuous, and so on. Since one acts in that way and rests, the mind will be controlled. If it is not controlled but is constantly distracted:

> Allow the ox of the mind to wander.[9]

Having activated the watcher of the mind, allow it to do what it pleases. Since it is allowed [to do what it pleases], it will return on its own. This is the meaning of the passage: {63}

> Just as a crow flies from a ship,
> circles around, and lands once again . . .[10]

By doing so, like a hand that has touched some glue, the measure of controlling the mind is that it is not distracted, it is very languid, forgetful, and as soon one meets any activity, it is perfunctorily performed.

IV. Introduction to Reality

There are three topics in the introduction to reality: (1) identifying clarity, (2) training the mind in freedom from extremes, and (3) generating confidence in inexpressibility.

A. Identifying Clarity

> [Undisturbed concentration]
> is left alone, like water or a lamp's own illumination.[11]

Having first recognized clarity on the basis of unmodified equipoise, because one meditates as before, in the end the mind becomes extremely clear; memory becomes clear; forgetfulness lessens; and when an activity is met, it is diligently performed.

B. Training the Mind in Freedom from Extremes

In the middle, to train the mind in freedom from extremes, the *Commentary on Bodhicitta* states:

> Abiding without reference points, the mind
> has the characteristic of space.
> The meditation of space
> is asserted to be the meditation of emptiness.[12]

To meditate on the meaning of this passage, when investigating one's mind, recall that the mind, like space, lacks beginning or end; that like space, it lacks arising and perishing; and that like space, it lacks a periphery or a center. Rest the mind on that [recollection.] When the mind stirs from resting, one should remember, "Do not follow the past." If concepts about the future arise, remember, "Do not anticipate the future." If concepts about the present arise, meet them directly {64} and remember, "All phenomena are nonarising." The *Nondual Uniformity Tantra* identifies the meaning:

> E MA, the secret of all buddhas
> is that perfect buddhas do not arise.
> Everything arises from nonarising.
> Arising itself does not arise.[13]

C. Generating Confidence in Inexpressibility

Finally, to generate confidence in inexpressibility, merge the experience of the realization of equipoise with all post-equipoise conduct. Determine that inseparable appearance and emptiness, inseparable clarity and emptiness, and inseparable cognizance and emptiness are inexpressible and maintain the experience. The meaning is:

> If there is clinging to something, give it up.
> If there is realization, that is everything.
> No one knows anything more than that.[14]

And:

> Just as an elephant's mind is tractable after training,
> one's mind will relax after coming and going are eliminated.
> Since this is realization, for what purpose would I modify it?[15]

V. Connecting Realization with Conduct

In the fifth general topic, connecting realization with conduct, after slight realization has arisen, train in eating without [discriminating between] pure or impure. Train in companions without [discriminating between] good and bad companions. Train in clothing without [discriminating between] good and bad clothes.

Then, a realization that surpasses the first bodhisattva stage will gradually arise, and one will realize the stage of buddhahood.

This is the removal of obstacles. If there is lethargy, place the mind at the crown. If there is agitation, place [the mind] at the soles of the feet. If obstacles of the elements and body occur, use a rejuvenator (*bcud len*; Skt. *rasāyana*) of the three fruits.[16] If external obstacles of māra occur, gather the body, voice, and mind into the *hūṃ* syllable in the heart and recite *hūṃ*; invigorate the body and mind;[17] and perform the conduct of strict discipline.

The result is the three kāyas endowed with seven limbs: There is the limb of the lack of inherent existence for the dharmakāya. {65} There are the three limbs of union, great bliss, and complete enjoyment for the sambhogakāya. There are the three limbs of great compassion, the uninterrupted wheel of deeds and activities, and unceasingness for the nirmāṇakāya.

"The Explanation of Mahāmudrā as the Fundamental State Obtained in Front of a Stupa" was written by the Śākya upāsaka Drakpa Gyaltsen, in an elevated location two furlongs to the east of the Pal Sakya temple, in order to clarify the unclear writing of previous gurus.

samāptamithi

The lineage: When Ācārya Nāgārjuna was the chaplain of King Dejö Zangpo (*bDe spyod bzang po*), the queen was attracted to the ācārya and slandered him. He departed to Śrī Parvata in the south. By the side of the road there was a stupa constructed by asuras called Śrī Gunavat. The ācārya met the Brahmin Saraha in front of that stupa. From the time this was given to Nāgārjuna up to the Lord Sakyapa Chenpo, this explanation has existed as it appears above.

The direct disciple of Lord Sakyapa Chenpo is Jetsun Drakpa Gyaltsen. From him the teaching passed through Sakya Paṇḍita and intermediary gurus to Könchok Yeshe, from whom it was obtained by the great being, the siddha Palden Gyalwa. He gave it to Nyanton, the Lion of Vinaya. I received it from him. May there be good fortune.

7. *Mahāmudrā without Syllables* Composed by Ācārya Vāgīśvarakīrti[1]

Drakpa Gyaltsen

We have almost no details concerning the life of Vāgīśvarakīrti, other than his caste and reputed siddhis, his position as one of the gatekeepers of Vikramaśīla, and a short note in *Miscellaneous Notes on Individual Sādhanas*[2] concerning an emanation of Mañjuśrī in the form of a child bestowing upon him *The Intimate Instruction on Cheating Death*. His association with White Tārā is well known.[3] He was also one of Drokmi Lotsāwa's direct teachers. In addition to the Hevajra Tantra, he is also associated with the Jñānapāda tradition of the Guhyasamāja Tantra.

Mahāmudrā without Syllables, according to Drakpa Gyaltsen, was a transmission received by Ācārya Vāgīśvarakīrti directly from Lady Tārā. The text begins with a blessing rite of Nairātmyā and then provides a comprehensive, albeit brief, overview of mahāmudrā, one of the two texts in the cycle specifically devoted to mahāmudrā.

Vāgīśvarakīrti's principal contribution to Vajrayāna theory in Tibetan Buddhism is found in the *Seven Limbs*, which provides a full exposition of "the seven limbs of the three kāyas," also known as "the seven limbs of union (*kha sbyor*)." This doctrine is extremely important in the Sakya school, especially with respect to certain principles found in sādhana practice.

The ostensible source of the seven limbs of the three kāyas is the *Compendium of the Gnosis Vajra*:

> Because the three kāyas endowed with seven limbs are realized, one attains the sambhogakāya, union with gnosis, great bliss, the benefit of migrating beings produced because of great compassion, unceasing gnosis, uninterrupted mahāmudrā, and the naturally pure dhātu inseparable with gnosis.[4]

Vāgīśvarakīrti's *Seven Limbs* introduces the seven limbs in the following way:

> The intelligent who are familiar with authoritative reasoning shall praise my assertions
> in this thesis about the seven limbs—
> complete enjoyment, union, great bliss, natureless,
> full of compassion, uninterrupted, and unceasing.[5]

To summarize Vāgīśvarakīrti's explanation of the seven limbs is to do it an injustice. A more comprehensive account of his presentation will require more space than this introduction will allow. However, it would be remiss not to devote a few words to the *Seven Limbs*. The *Seven Limbs* is a polemical text meant to address a controversy over the four empowerments in the Jñānapāda system, a debate once current at Vikramaśīla and now resurrected by contemporary historians of Vajrayāna Buddhism.[6] Vāgīśvarakīrti asserts the fourth empowerment is indeed "the fourth" referred to in the *Ancillary Tantra* of the Guhyasamāja:

> The vase empowerment is first.
> Second is the secret empowerment.
> The gnosis of the wisdom consort is the third.
> That fourth one is also suchness.[7]

Vāgīśvarakīrti states in the introduction to the *Seven Limbs*:

> "In order to realize mahāmudrā" means that the empowerment into the nature of mahāmudrā is to be understood as the fourth.[8]

This point is most closely argued in chapter 3 of the *Seven Limbs*. Vāgīśvarakīrti ruthlessly mocks his opponents for failing to understand that the reference to "the fourth" in the *Ancillary Tantra* is in fact a reference to the fourth empowerment,[9] and that the seven limbs of the three kāyas are solely the result of the fourth empowerment.[10]

{68} I devotedly prostrate with my crown to the feet of the sublime guru. Homage to Lady Ārya Tārā.

On the basis of the mahāyoga *Guhyasamāja Tantra*, the *Hevajra Tantra*, and the words of Ārya Tārā, Ācārya Vāgīśvarakīrti composed the treatises *Seven Limbs, Illuminating the Precious Truth*,[11] and so on. This is the *Mahāmudrā without Syllables*, which is like the essence of those treatises, and the *Light of Amṛta* is the sādhana of Nairātmyā composed by Ḍombi Heruka. Further, *Mahāmudrā without Syllables* was received by Ācārya Vāgīśvarakīrti from Lady Tārā. Ācārya Vāgīśvarakīrti gave this to Ācārya Devākaracandra. Both masters gave it to Ārya Amoghavajra. The latter's disciple was Lama Drokmi. It then was given to Lama Sekhar Chungwa, and then by him to Je Gönpa; the latter gave it to Lama Jetsun Sakyapa.

There are three topics in this instruction: (1) In the beginning, one must be blessed with the blessing of the ḍākinīs, which resembles a vulture's flat tail. (2) In the middle, one meditates the path. (3) In the end, there is the means of obtaining the result, the three kāyas with the seven limbs.

I. The Blessing

The time is any major or minor day of the elementals.[12] The place should be swept. The images should be arranged; in particular, {69} it is performed according to the small manual called the *Heart Maṇḍala of the Ḍākinī*[13] for the fifteen deities of Lady Nairātmyā. If one cannot accomplish that, according to the small manual, use heaps of flowers. Since both of those are strict, their methods are not used. The method is to use fifteen heaps of flowers for the fifteen goddesses of the maṇḍala. If that cannot be accomplished, it is said it is sufficient to meditate on the maṇḍala of the fifteen goddesses in the sky. One should arrange extensive offerings, bali, and so on. If one can accomplish the food offerings, then fifteen; if not, then five. Moreover, arrange whatever offerings one is able. Place the inner offering of alcohol mixed with amṛta before oneself. Arrange two bali offerings. Also place the articles for the feast offering.

Invite the practitioners who have provided some of their wealth to be seated in the rows. They should offer the maṇḍala and flowers, offer a supplication to abide in the deity yoga, and meditate extensively on the direct realization of the fifteen deities of Lady Nairātmyā. They should present offerings and praises and recite [the mantra] as much as possible.

Then, after meditating on the fifteen goddesses, either arranged in front or in the sky, present extensive offerings and praises to them. Send out bali to the host of elementals. Bless the feast and present the first portion to the guru and the ḍākinīs. Enjoy the feast. When content, gather the remainders and send them out. Recite the one-hundred-syllable mantra. {70} Recite benedictions and offer aspirations. Perform the self-protection. Send away the other yogins who will not be present for the rite.

Then, those disciples who wish to request the blessing should wash and be seated in rows. They should begin by offering the maṇḍala, and their donation should be received. After that, they should supplicate the guru:

> Homage and praise to the empty essence,
> truly devoid of all concepts.
> Homage and praise to the embodiment of gnosis,
> the accumulation of omniscient gnosis.[14]

By reciting this three times, they have praised the guru.

Next, they should praise the tantras of method and wisdom, reciting three times:

> Homage and praise to vajra speech,
> which arises from phenomena that lack identity.
> Sever the ignorance of migrating beings
> and show the principle of purity.[15]

Next, the praise of the special method is recited three times:

> Those with the qualities of the perfections,
> the perfect buddhas and bodhisattvas,
> always arise from the protector.
> Homage and praise to the supreme great method.[16]

Then, the supplication is recited three times:

> You who amassed omniscient gnosis,
> the precious chief who explains at length
> the purification of the wheel of existence,
> kindly protect me.[17]

Next, the disciples should generate the confident thought, "My guru is Mahāvajradhara," and arouse strong devotion. The guru also generates understanding through saying, "All phenomena are like dreams. . . ," and so on.

This concludes the preliminary stages of the blessing.

Next, the actual procedure of the blessing is explaining the visualization to the disciple: "Meditate on a tall tree in front of oneself. Next, divide one's body into two bodies. One body is seated at the base of the tree; the other body is naked and {71} climbs that tree. Imagine that one is seated on the top of the tree with knees drawn up to the chest. Look at the base of the tree. At that time a fear of falling will arise naturally."

At that time the disciples should place the feet together and remain in place without the buttocks touching the ground. The body is allowed to move freely. Exhale gradually. That will immediately give rise to the experience. When the experience arises, the reality without syllables is introduced. If the experience does not arise, repeat the previous key points of body and breath. The key point of the mind is to hold onto sun beams and moon beams. Seated on the sun and moon, observe the four continents. Direct the mind down to the top of the tree; then direct it to the base of the tree. Look at one's old body seated at the base of the tree. Investigate, "What are the upper and lower parts of my body? What is my body?" Introduce the meaning that lacks syllables, which is [that the body] isn't anything at all.

At that time there is the activity of the guru: Bless the amṛta, which is placed nearby. While playing the ḍamaru, and so on, the amṛta should be scattered over the entire body [of the disciple]. This is the activity of the body. The activity of speech is reciting the mantra garland. The activity of the mind is that light rays in the form of a red mantra garland pervade the entire body of the disciple; imagine a brilliant red *hūṃ* syllable in the heart center, the support of mind. Also, one should fumigate with gugul,[18] the substance of dependent origination.

After the experience has arisen, it should be accepted with the melodious song of reality, like this:

> There is nothing in your body, hollow
> without flesh, bone, or blood.
> You display your body
> like a rainbow in the sky.

Though your body is without disease or impurities
and never becomes hungry or thirsty,
you display mundane activities
in order to associate with the world.

With nothing to grasp, like the moon in water,
not dwelling among all phenomena,
without pride, unconfused,
homage to you who are without percepts.

You are always in equipoise
in all your pure conduct,
moving, sitting, or sleeping,[19]
homage to you who are without percepts. {72}

Emanating great miraculous displays
through the power of the samādhi of illusions,
while engaged in equipoise on the absence diversity,
homage to you who are without percepts.[20]

Thus, recite this and [have the students] perform prostrations. In between all the verses above, melodiously sing the mantra garland.

Just like a bee does not cling to a flower but travels along collecting pollen, enjoy objects without clinging. This is the introduction to the reality without syllables.

Because of the above, many signs may occur such as trembling of the body, vocal utterances, and nonconceptuality in the mind. That completes the key points. If the mind becomes unconscious, or the body remains like that without being touched, or there is gentle trembling, introduce the mind and rest. If present, enjoy the feast. Offer aspirations and protect the three places with the three syllables in oneself and the disciples.

Recite the following: "All of these experiences are your own mind, the state of a single cognizance. Further, though it does not exist, because it appears, it is illusory. Since it cannot be identified, it is empty. The inseparability of those three [cognizance, appearance, and emptiness] is the so-called 'mahāmudrā without syllables.'" Having explained this, enter into sustaining the experience.

Next, [the disciples] should prostrate to the feet of the guru, present gifts, conclude the activities, perform the protection, and then remain as they like.

This concludes the preliminary blessing.

II. Meditating on the Path

As such, one must explain the intimate instructions to those who have the stream of blessing. There are three topics in that: (1) first, focusing the mind; (2) in the middle, taming the mind; (3) and last, resting the mind in reality.

Each of those three is also divided into three. The three of the first are (1) focusing the mind, (2) keeping it in its resting place, and (3) avoiding the two extremes. The three of the middle are (1) not allowing the mind to escape to the place to where it would move, (2) not allowing the mind to relax where it is placed, and (3) not allowing the mind to either escape or relax. The three of the last are (1) training in the example, (2) training in the meaning, and (3) merging the example and the meaning. These three trios are the concise explanation of the nine fundamental topics.

A. Focusing the Mind

1. Focusing the Mind

To focus the mind on where it moves, be seated on a comfortable seat. {73} Go for refuge with strong devotion to the lineage gurus, beginning from the root guru and Lady Tārā. Cultivate bodhicitta. Meditate on the guru at the crown of one's head. Recall the commitment deity. Wherever one's mind goes, focus it on one place with the rope of mindfulness.

2. Keeping the Mind Where It Is Placed

Having focused the mind, keep it focused without allowing [the mind] to escape elsewhere. Further, if that mind is present before a representation of the Three Jewels, not allowing it to leave from that representation is focusing the mind on the place to which it moved. In addition to that, keeping it there by focusing with the rope of mindfulness is keeping the mind where it is placed.

3. Avoiding the Two Extremes

Not allowing the mind to follow the past or the future is avoiding the two extremes. When one can no longer focus the mind on a representation of the Three Jewels, if a concept moves toward a pillar, a vase, the sound of water, or the scent of an incense stick, also focus the mind on that place where it moves, keep it where it settles, and avoid the two extremes.

These methods will focus the mind. If the mind isn't focused, then to focus the mind, place it at the top of the tree, the top of the sun and moon, and so on, which was done before at the time of the blessing. If those [methods] do not focus the mind, focus the mind on the space in front, the top of the nose, the brow, the navel, and so on, switching repeatedly. Focus the mind with the three key points as before. This will definitely focus the mind.

B. Taming the Mind

1. Taming the Mind

The first part of the second general topic, taming the mind, is not allowing the mind to escape the place to where it moves, which means binding the mind with the rope of mindfulness wherever it moves. Since the mind that is not controlled with mindfulness alone should not be allowed to escape, when it is not controlled with mindfulness, conceptuality falls into the extreme of samsara. If the mind cannot be controlled with mindfulness, since it will escape to a place where it moves, generate the antidote and prevent it from escaping.

2. Keeping the Mind in Its Resting Place

Second, do not allow the mind to relax in its resting place. If the mind remains in its resting place, this becomes śamatha. Since one becomes a śrāvaka, the mind is not tamed. Therefore, as already mentioned, the mind should be withdrawn from the place to which it moved, such as the representation of the Tathāgata, a pillar, a vase, and so on, and placed elsewhere. In the same way, since it is not allowed to rest for a moment, {74} repeatedly changing the object prevents the mind from being overpowered by śamatha, and it [the mind] will be tamed.

3. Not Allowing the Mind to Escape or Relax

Not allowing the mind to escape or relax is not allowing the mind to be overpowered by either discursiveness or śamatha. In brief, if one wishes for śamatha, one has power over śamatha. If one wishes for discursiveness, one has power over discursiveness. Both śamatha and discursiveness must be controlled by the rope of mindfulness. The arising of whichever one wants is the tamed mind.

C. Placing the Mind on Reality

1. Training in the Examples

The first part of the third general topic, placing the mind on reality, has three parts for training in the example: the time of delusion, the time of understanding delusion, and the time of comprehending that delusion has no basis.

First, train in the twelve examples of illusion. Seeing an entire valley filled with water is a mirage. Thinking that this is a lake is the time of delusion. Then, as soon as one arrives down in the valley, one sees that it is a mirage as there is no water. Thinking, "This is not water, it is a mirage," is the time of understanding delusion as delusion. Then, not perceiving the mirage as soon as one arrives in front of it is the time of comprehending delusion as baseless.

Likewise, when in a dream one fights enemies or many relatives and friends arise, it is the time of delusion. In some circumstances, though the appearance of the dream has not ceased, understanding [a dream is a dream] in a dream is the time of understanding delusion. When one wakes up and all appearances have vanished, it is the time of comprehending delusion as baseless. One applies that in the same way to illusions—the moon in the water, fairy castles, rainbows, clouds, lightning, echoes, the city of Candra of Harikela,[21] and so on—and generates a special confidence in the examples of illusion.

2. Training in the Meaning

Next, one needs to apply the meaning. That has two parts: (a) applying it to a recalled appearance, and (b) training in visualization.

a. Recalled Appearances

First, look at any strong affliction. If a strong thought to slay or bind an enemy occurs when hate arises, that is the time of delusion.{75} If one waits a short while after that, the affliction is pacified, which is the time of understanding delusion. Then, having realized there is no truth in that affliction is the time of comprehending delusion as baseless. Therefore, hatred is one's mind. Since one's own mind arises from causes and conditions, it is illusory. If one investigates illusion, it cannot be found and lacks inherent existence; that is the mahāmudrā without syllables. In that case, since "syllable" refers to conceptuality and expression, the absence of conceptuality and expression is the so-called mahāmudrā without syllables. That should be applied to each affliction and meditated.

b. Training in Visualization

Second, training in visualization is (1) giving away the fettering body and mind, (2) giving away the enjoyments that are grasped, and (3) training in the other categories.

i. Giving Away the Fettering Body and Mind

First, invite the guru and commitment deity into the space in front. Offer one's grasping to enemies and friends, and also one's body sundered into pieces. Those are the mind, the mind is illusory, illusions lack inherent existence, and, further, apply one's [mind] to the mahāmudrā without syllables.

ii. Giving Away Enjoyments

Second, likewise, give away all one's enjoyments, and apply the mind to the mahāmudrā without syllables.

iii. Other Categories

Third, training in the other categories: When one arrives in the lower hell realms, one experiences the suffering of being boiled and burned. Also, one is free from that. That is mind, mind is illusion, illusion lacks inherent existence, and, further, apply one's mind to the mahāmudrā without syllables.

Further, see all the buddhas and bodhisattvas in the ten directions; see one hundred thousand buddhas below, Mahāvairocana above, Akṣobhya in the east, Ratnasambhava in the south, Amitābha in the west, Amoghasiddhi in the north, and so on. Imagine, "Amazing, in an instant I have seen inconceivable buddhafields of buddhas." {76} That is also mind, the mind is illusory, illusions lack inherent existence, and, further, apply one's mind to the mahāmudrā without syllables.

3. Merge the Example and Meaning

Third, merge the example and the meaning (1) with effort, (2) without effort, and (3) signs of accomplishment.

a. With Effort

First, merge the twelve examples of illusion, and so on, with the afflictions of hatred, and so on. When describing the examples together, at the time of affliction, say this is an illusion, this is a dream, and so on. Those are also mind, the mind is illusory, illusions lack inherent existence, and mahāmudrā is without syllables. This is mental effort.

b. Without Effort

Second, it is implicitly understood that appearances, sound, and all phenomena of samsara and nirvana simultaneously are the mind; the mind is illusory; illusions lack inherent existence; and mahāmudrā is without syllables. This is the meaning of Saraha's statement:

> The realized do not distinguish between dwelling in a forest or a house.[22]

[And the meaning of the statement in] the *Saṃpuṭa Tantra*:

> Since the mind does not go elsewhere,
> when engaging in all activities,
> such as looking at all forms,
> listening to all sounds,
> eating diverse flavors,

> and talking and laughing,
> that is the continually arising yoga
> of the practitioner who knows reality.[23]

This is one taste, like pouring water into water or oil into oil.

Further, based on this, when the nine key points that were mentioned are included, when extraneous concepts arise due to external conditions, not grasping them from the moment they are encountered is holding the mind in the place to where it moved. Based on that, when the mind is slightly calm, the mind is kept where it was placed. Avoiding grasping to both [discursiveness and śamatha] is abandoning the two extremes. Also, keeping [the mind] in the place where it moved is the time of realization, keeping it where it is placed is the time of understanding, and avoiding the two extremes is the time of comprehension.

Further, as above,[24] if one is never distracted from mahāmudrā, [the mind] will not escape to a place where it would go. Since realization increases exponentially, it will not stay where it is placed. {77} Since there is liberation from grasping, the mind does not slip into either [discursiveness or śamatha]. Therefore, all phenomena are understood, realized, and comprehended in terms of the twelve examples of illusion; the meaning is understood, realized, and comprehended in terms of mind, and so on; and mahāmudrā is understood, realized, and comprehended to be without syllables.

c. Signs of Accomplishment

The signs of accomplishment are with effort and without effort. The signs with effort are equipoise and post-equipoise. The sign without effort is the absence of equipoise and post-equipoise, called "total equipoise." Also, the sign with effort is śamatha. The sign without effort is vipaśayanā. The sign with effort is the antidote to temporary afflictions. The sign without effort is the antidote, freedom from the eight worldly dharmas and the latent afflictions. The sign with effort is that circumstances are sometimes harmful and sometimes not harmful. The sign without effort is that circumstances arise as beneficial. At that moment, freed from sessions, there is no equipoise or post-equipoise. It is the time of appearances arising as one's teacher, the time of things arising as one's guru, the time of afflictions transforming into the path, the time of the five poisons transforming into medicine, the time of concepts arising as gnosis, the time of the elimination of the abyss of the six migrations, the time of destroying the city of the six realms, and the time of appearances transforming into emptiness. The special qualities of realization enter oneself naturally, which are like a fire spreading in a forest or snow falling on a lake or like a full moon. It is a time that resembles meeting a person with whom one was previously acquainted, in which there is no effort of inquiry. Beyond sound and concepts, mahāmudrā is realized as reality without syllables. Given that this is the case, in this system there is no defined time for conduct. When concepts transform into antidotes and {78} companions of realization, from the beginning one commences the secret conduct of not discriminating between good and bad food, neither rejecting or approving conduct, nor discriminating between good and bad companions.

III. The Result

The third general topic, the result, is the three kāyas with the seven limbs. "Natureless" means the pacification of proliferation. "Uninterrupted" means the uniformity of the three times. "Unceasing" means free from the arising and perishing of the compounded. Those three are dharmakāya, the nature. The three limbs of the sambhogakāya are the blazing major and minor marks, union with the mother of an appearance of gnosis, and a continuum moistened with immaculate bliss, which is extraordinarily satiated.

Also, it is maintained there are four kāyas. First, the mind that abides as pure by nature is the svabhāvakāya. Dharmakāya arises from realizing that. The major and minor marks are the vipākakāya.[25] The nirmāṇakāya is the single limb of uninterrupted compassion: nonreferential compassion that acts on behalf of sentient beings. Thus, five limbs are the result of practice, and two are to benefit oneself and others.

This concludes the explanation of the result.

To discuss the meaning a little bit, *mudra* is impressing a seal on all phenomena. *Mahā* means there is nothing higher than that. There are three topics in that. The mahāmudrā of the cause is the dharmatā of the mind. The mahāmudrā of the path has four divisions. The mahāmudrā of the result is the dharmakāya.

The first in the path is the mahāmudrā of the view: hearing and understanding inexpressibility. The mahāmudrā of meditation is training in the meaning and merging the meaning and example. The mahāmudrā of conduct arises spontaneously. The mahāmudrā of experience is the union of bliss and emptiness.

The vajra holder Drakpa Gyaltsen
wrote down the profound hidden meaning
at the insistence of the intelligent piṭakadhara bhikṣu,
Lodrö Tenpa. {79}

For this I beg the compassionate forbearance
of the gurus and the ḍākinīs.
With this virtue may all sentient beings
attain the mahāmudrā of the result.

This so-called *Mahāmudrā without Syllables* granted by Lady Ārya Tārā, the discourse of Ācārya Vāgīśvarakīrti, is complete. I request the forbearance of the assembly of gurus for any faults. May this benefit countless sentient beings. May our obstacles and our retinues' obstacles on the path be pacified.

Sarva maṅgalaṃ

8. Śrī Koṭalipa's *Instruction on the Inconceivable*[1]

The *Instruction on the Inconceivable* is the first and longest cycle among the eight ancillary path cycles and consists of three sections: the root text; the chronicle of the lineage; and the commentarial section, which itself has three subsections including the main commentary and two addenda.

The root text is Koṭalipa's *Stages of the Inconceivable* as translated by Ratnavajra and Drokmi. In the Tengyur an alternate translation exists by Dewe Nyugu (bDe ba'i myu gu) and Gö Khukpa Lhetse.[2] It is quite difficult to discern the discrete stages of the basis or the view, path, and result in the root text. However, it appears that verses 1–68 relate to the basis or the view, verses 69–118 relate to the path, and verse 119 up to the conclusion relate to the result.

The second part consists of a brief chronicle of the lineage. The reader should note that this account of Koṭalipa's life is very different than the account provided by Abhayadattaśrī in the *Hagiography of the Eighty-Four Siddhas.* Here it is clear that Koṭalipa is a native of Oḍḍiyāna and a gardener for Indrabhūti III.

The third part consists of a commentary on the stages of the practice by Drakpa Gyaltsen. Though Kongtrul considers the *Stages of the Inconceivable* to be a general text concerning the completion stage, the Sakya school highlights its association with Nairātmyā. Amezhap's *Effortless Accomplishment of the Two Benefits* explains that the practitioner of this instruction must meditate on themselves as Vajranairātmyā. An interlinear note also mentions that the blessing ritual for Vajranairātmyā in the *Mahāmudrā without Syllables* can be applied to this instruction.

The commentary identifies the root text's subject matter as the five inconceivabilities: characteristics, qualities, power, nature, and essence. These five inconceivabilities are difficult to discern in the root text itself. Drakpa

Gyaltsen presents the path as the method of realizing the five inconceivabilities. Drakpa Gyaltsen's presentation of the seven limbs of the three kāyas weaves the root verses into the seven limbs.

The first of the two addenda identifies "sections" of the five inconceivabilities without specifying actual sections in the root text. Despite the root verses' almost complete dismissal of conceptual yogas, common in Indian mahāmudrā texts, Drakpa Gyaltsen himself clarifies that while in the view there are six negations, in the path there are equally six affirmations, which are the opposite of the six negations. The second of the two addenda is the intimate instruction of the five kinds of antidote.

Intimate Instructions on the Stages of the Inconceivable

Koṭalipa

{82}
In Sanskrit: *Acantyakramopadeśanāma*
In Tibetan: *bSam gyis mi khyab pa'i rim pa'i man ngag ces bya ba*
In English: *Intimate Instructions on the Stages of the Inconceivable*

I prostrate to Śrī Vajrasattva.

Homage to wisdom[3] that arises as the supreme essence,
the nature of inconceivable,[4] nondual[5] space.
I will write of progressing to the stage[6] of perfection[7]
as taught by Bhadrapāda, (1)

the great secret method[8] and wisdom,
the characteristic of inconceivable compassion,
which arises naturally through the domain
of gnosis that is beyond speech. (2)

That [gnosis] is not cultivated through an imagined
visualization
of the form of an entity.
It is the supreme nonduality that self-originates
through the nature of the aspect of bliss. (3)

Vajra holders cannot see bodhicitta
because it is not an entity.

The ultimate is not seen as a duality
because of the distinction between permanence and
impermanence. (4)

This nature of entities
cannot be perceived and is not empty. {83}
Nondual gnosis blazes
through investigating duality. (5)

Everything is an aspect of nonduality;
such dualities do not exist.
The aspect of a uniform single taste
is the supreme inconceivable gnosis. (6)

The supreme nonduality cannot be cultivated
with the conceptuality of a conceptual yoga.
The nonconceptual vajra of bliss
is obtained with the inconceivable. (7)

Both the creation stage
and, similarly, the completion stage are causes of
conceptuality.
Freed from the aspect of duality,
the possessor of traces abandons traces. (8)

Bhadrapāda taught that the stage to which one progresses is
a gnosis free from the aspects of traces,
self-originated, devoid of conceit,
and utterly free of all concepts. (9)

Through the nature of existents and nonexistents,
traces are bonds
severed by the inconceivable
through the nature of nonconceptuality (10)

The jewel mind is tainted
by the mesh of conceptual taints.[9]

By freeing it of impurities, buddhahood itself
is called "nondual gnosis." (11)

The practitioner must always see
everything in a nonconceptual state.
This is the cultivation of samādhi
taught by Bhadrapāda. (12)

That which does not arise by nature
does not cease. {84}
That gnosis is nondual
and truly devoid of all conceptuality. (13)

Buddha Vajradhara, and so on,
explain conceptuality as external.
The meaning of nonconceptuality arises
through possessing the glorious vajra of great bliss. (14)

The whole world truly exists
because of inner and outer conceptuality.
Liberating duality from nonduality
naturally gives rise to gnosis. (15)

Do not meditate on nonentities;
also do not meditate on entities.
The bliss of heroes is without extremes,
abiding in the nonduality of the inconceivable. (16)

Whatever all sentient beings think
dwells as aspects of wisdom's essence.
When the arrow of blossoming compassion
hits the target, there is great bliss. (17)

Since inanimate and animate entities
are not a duality, they exist as aspects.
Those are pure by nature,
like peace, space, and the immaculate. (18)

Nonduality is a merely a name;
even that name does not exist.
Free of demonstrable sense and sensation,
nonduality is great bliss. (19)

Free of all concepts,
without the dualism of duality, supreme peace,
equivalent with space and free of conceptuality—
that is called "nondual." (20)

Cultivate all phenomena
with the yoga of the unconceivable,
taught by Bhadrapāda
in order to progress to the stage of Dharmapāda. (21)

Dividing the nondual into aspects,
the single nature of
the glorious, greatly blissful protector
emanates in different aspects because of migrating beings. (22)

Those deceived by liars
who refer to emptiness as an object
will not realize sublime bliss {85}
because of the bondage of confused concepts. (23)

Pure method and wisdom
are outside the concepts[10] of false imputations.
The great yoga of nondual gnosis
is unique great bliss. (24)

Buddhahood is beyond the domain of the mind
because it is naturally inconceivable,
its nature is everything,
it is self-originated and beyond conception. (25)

All creatures upon the earth
are harmed by the mesh of concepts.

That unique nondual gnosis
is devoid of all conceptuality. (26)

A stream of any size and its bed
are not two parts,
and there is nothing to perceive in the middle.
Nondual gnosis is supreme. (27)

Everything is differentiated in the relative;
duality and nonduality are conceptual.
The great yoga of method and wisdom
is called "the nondual single taste." (28)

Between those with and without desire,
there is nothing to perceive in the middle;
bliss is never truly known.
That is called "nonduality." (29)

Free from a basis of characteristics and characteristics,
devoid of a knower and the known,
the jewel mind is best realized
by abandoning each thing that is without a self. (30)

Because entities lack inherent existence,
also nonentities will not be seen
by realizing eye consciousness.
Nondual gnosis is amazing! (31)

Free from all proliferation,
immaculate like space,
eradicating the mesh of concepts,
nondual inconceivability is supreme. (32)

Bhadrapāda has taught nonduality,
which is like the elixir
that turns heavy wood and stone
into a statue of a deity. (33)

Method, wisdom, and great compassion {86}
are the same, aspects of a single taste.
Gnosis is perfected in it,
the nondual great bliss itself. (34)

Beyond form, sound, and taste,
devoid of smell or tangibles,
the changeless dharmadhātu
is the supreme nondual gnosis. (35)

Free of all concepts,
devoid of subject and object,
the pure nature untainted,
the nondual meaning is the sublime. (36)

Unborn and unceasing,
neither changing nor abiding,
this recognition of supreme nondual gnosis
is mahāmudrā. (37)

Qualities and faults
are aspects described for the mind,
therefore, supreme gnosis is one-pointed.
Gnosis arises naturally from (38)

the nature that lacks conceits
without any meditation at all.
Why? This dharma of inconceivability
is the nondual abode of the buddhas. (39)

Purer than the totally immaculate,
devoid of a meditator and an object of meditation,[11]
all will definitely see the source of glorious bliss
because of the absence of conceptuality. (40)

The manifold forms of the deity,
the form of Vajrasattva, and so on,

all are the reflections of the buddhas.
The assembly of the maṇḍala of yoginīs, (41)

all the wrathful kings,
likewise, the knowledge consort goddesses,
the excellent maṇḍalacakra,
the immaculate aspects of appearance, (42)

likewise, the sutra piṭaka,
further, the stages of the perfections,
mantra, mudra, and mind,
likewise, the accomplishment of the essence mantra, (43)

all explanation of mantra,
the activities of the maṇḍala, the fire offerings,
the recitations, and offering[12] rites—
all arise from nonduality. (44) {87}

The texts of the Śaivas, Sauras,[13]
likewise, the Jains and Vaiṣṇavas,
those who proclaim the authority of the Vedas,
and also those [texts] of others arise by themselves. (45)

This yoga, the abode of the all-knowing,
inconceivable and nonconceptual,
the view called "Samantabhadra,"
is nondual, like a wish-fulfilling gem. (46)

[The siddhis] of traveling underground, the sword, the pill,
the shoes, the vase, the yakṣinī,
the elixir, and the excellent eye medicine
are innately accomplished, not existing elsewhere. (47)

Mantrins should neither meditate on entities
nor meditate on nonentities.
Absence of concepts is freedom—
everything arises by itself. (48)

Also, if buddhahood itself is accomplished,
what need to speak of Śiva, Viṣṇu, and so on?
Its characteristics do not exist,
lacking form, characteristics, and color. (49)

The excellent bearer of the aspect of illusion,
the immaculate nature of entities,
and the aspect of natural luminosity
always rejoice in the source of bliss. (50)

Free from body, speech, and mind,
like a mirror or blazing fire,
the aspect of the bliss of supreme joy
always produces great bliss. (51)

Names and colors are best described
through an explanation that is a combination of words.
Since this is beyond expression,
one cannot easily explain this to others. (52)

However, the desired goal is easy,
using the method of passionate activities.
At the time of the secret offering,
one becomes nondual with the wisdom consort. (53)

Traces are exhausted
from the nature that has a single aspect.
Bhadrapāda taught that
buddhahood itself will definitely be obtained. (54)

Nonduality is not [realized]
because one is empowered with the taints of traces
from the application of various texts
with various different colors. (55){88}

Free from beginning, middle, and end,
devoid of the creation and completion stages,

free from thoughts and thinker,
nondual gnosis is supreme. (56)

Bhadrapāda taught that
buddhahood is called "nonduality."
The sublime siddhas become buddhas
through realizing buddhahood. (57)

Because of explanations that combine words,
buddhahood is designated "nondual."
There is neither buddhahood nor nonduality,
the ultimate is undifferentiated. (58)

When gnosis becomes supreme,
it is far away from the taint of concepts.
The one appointed by heaven is hidden from
all concepts of entities, and so on. (59)

Because of the kindness of Bhadrapāda,
I, the yogi, attained patience
toward that [name] "nonduality"
through the yoga of cultivating experience. (60)

The learned also should exhaust traces
with great diligence,
otherwise, there will be no buddhahood
for incalculable eons. (61)

Traces are exhausted by
the guide, nondual gnosis.
When traces are exhausted,
nonduality is called "buddhahood." (62)

At the time of freedom from traces,
there is no division at all
into medium or ordinary people—
they are called "buddhas." (63)

Bhadrapāda also explained
that through the nature that lacks inherent existence,
wisdom is the support
and method is the generator of entities. (64)

Bhradrapāda taught
that this supreme nonduality
arises from the yoga of one taste
that subsumes them. (65) {89}

Bhadrapāda eloquently stated:
"Without instruction on meditation and reflection,
buddhahood itself is attained
because of the supreme joy of a beautiful woman." (66)

No example can be given
for all phenomena.
The consciousnesses of the eye, and so on,
are devoid of exemplified entities. (67)

The unique state is a support
because it is without beginning or end,
understood to be the excellent, unique state
through the kindness of the guru. (68)

Yoga is explained as the person,
anuyoga is the relative,[14]
the great yoga of nondual gnosis
turns a practitioner into a buddha. (69)

When the sun and moon are seized by Rahu,
there is buddhahood in this life,
arising from the nondual gnosis that melted
from the union of wisdom and the vajra. (70)

The nature of ultimate joy
is devoid of subject and object.

Without doubt, the form of accomplishment
is supreme, nondual compassion. (71)

Any eye can see all form,
superior, mediocre, or inferior.
The sublime eye sees nonduality
through the true nature of the ultimate. (72)

Pleasant or unpleasant sound
can be heard by anyone's ear,
but the supreme, nondual ear
hears the supreme gnosis beyond sound. (73)

Good and bad flavor
can be tasted by anyone's tongue,
but supreme nonduality should be realized
through the six flavors[15] of multiple entities. (74)

Because the scent of musk, and so on,
smelled with the nose is a smell consciousness,
supreme nonduality will be known
by its unique nature. (75)

Because of having been born in different birthplaces
through the nature of contamination,
the complete union of method and gnosis
is the supreme nonduality. (76) {90}

The pervader of all of space,
the independent supreme joy
that arises from the light rays of illuminating gnosis
is the sublime bliss of nondual buddhahood.(77)

Formation, sensation, perception,
matter, and consciousness are
the subsidiary forms of the five gnoses.
The lord of duality is nondual. (78)

The great blissful one is the sixth,
the ruler of the five—
Vairocana, Akṣobhya, Ratnasambhava,
Amitayus, and likewise, Amoghasiddhi. (79)

The connate five elements,
earth, water, likewise, fire and
air, and, also, space itself
are transformed into nondual awakening. (80)

The mirror-like, uniformity, activity,
individually discerning, and dharmadhātu gnoses
are the means of conceptual comprehension.
Be confident in nonduality alone. (81)

With respect to the inclinations of sentient beings,
there are divisions among the texts,
but Śiva, Viṣṇu, Brahma,
and the Omniscient One are one and nondual. (82)

The domain that lacks signs, such as referents, and so on,
and is beyond the mind
is the ultimate, named nonduality.
All verbal proliferations are relative. (83)

There is neither buddhahood nor duality
apart from contingent distinctions of the ultimate.
Connecting realization to space
is also a description of verbal proliferation. (84)

The systematic treatises are to be explained
through different aspects with words,
but nondual buddhahood
cannot be spoken of to others. (85)

The explanation of the sixteen emptinesses,
the investigation of the ten wisdoms,

also the explanation of the buddhas as five,
and the eight relativities are nondual. (86)

See everything as if it
were a reflected appearance in a mirror. {91}
Likewise, the awakening of the Buddha
in this nondual gnosis is inconceivable. (87)

The causes of all births and places
of all living beings,
all three realms,
arise from nondual gnosis. (88)

Here, there can be no doubt that
nondual gnosis is the source of
the oceans, mountains, trees,
roots, branches, vines, and so on. (89)

Mother and father are the same;
these two do not exist.
Everything else arises from the
manifestation of nondual gnosis. (90)

Thus, here the practitioner immediately
attains buddhahood
from the nature of nondual
wisdom conjoined with method. (91)

The supreme pure gnosis,
the text of the lineage of gurus,
from mouth-to-ear,
was taught by Bhadrapāda. (92)

With this, through the kindness of Bhadrapāda,
the completion stage practitioner
will definitely attain buddhahood
through cultivating the inconceivable yoga.(93)

The lineage of Paramāśva, Vīṇapāda,
Indrabhūti, Lakṣmī,
Vilāsavajra, Guṇḍerī,
the greatly compassionate Padmācārya, and (94)

Dharmapāda
[that I] encountered in Bhadrapāda
has the same intention throughout—
supreme nondual gnosis. (95)

Here, all teachings of mantra,
likewise, the system of the perfections,
the sutra piṭaka, and so on,
are only the great bliss of nonduality. (96)

The individual conclusions of
the Jains, Sauras, Śaivas, and so on,
and the dharma of Viṣṇu and Manu
are explained through nonduality. (97)

There is nothing outside nonduality. {92}
Devas, asuras, and ordinary humans,
all are nondual gnosis
perceived as distinct and individual.(98)

Buddha is the guru of all,
merging nonduality and compassion,
endowed with equal measure of means and wisdom,
and classifying emptinesses. (99)

This is Bhadrapāda's text,
the ultimate ocean of gnosis,
resembling milk that when churned
itself gives rise to all other appearances. (100)

Brahma, Viṣṇu, and Śiva,
anyone proclaimed a buddha, and so on,

and the sun, moon, and stars
arise from the ocean of gnosis. (101)

Lakṣmī and Sarasvatī
are the supreme taste of amṛta.
Devas, asuras, and humans,
all arose from amrita. (102)

The virtuous stage of Vajradhara
is also explained to be the thirteenth.
Arising in the form of a triangle,
this is called "the dharmodaya." (103)

In order to obtain buddhahood,
all great bliss arises from the bliss
of the great blazing form of the wisdom consort
through being filled with the sun, moon, and water. (104)

The great lotus has ten million petals,
supreme and common anthers
exist inside it,
perfectly endowed with the vowels and consonants. (105)

Covered with the garb of the sun and moon,
endowed with nine uniform wisdom consorts,
the aspect of dripping and blazing
is the supreme source of the lunar bindu. (106)

The excellent woman who generates joy
bestows the ultimate result in its entirety.
Brimming with pure amṛta,
she is equal with a supreme jewel. (107)

She is the abode of limitless qualities,
the abode of the blissful Śrī Vajradhara,
she creates the happiness of all,
she destroys and creates. (108)

The forms of the deity are manifold, {93}
produced from the ocean of nonduality.
The dharmakāya, sambhogakāya, rūpakāya,
and nirmāṇakāya (109)

turn the wheel of Dharma
for the benefit of all sentient beings
in all the extreme reaches
of all the world systems in the ten directions. (110)

Endowed with the gnosis of ten powers,
the queen of wisdom is the best.
The ḍākinī's lotus is the trail of the animal[16]
progressing to Bhadrapāda's stage. (111)

The animal[17] remains at the gate
of the lotus of the heart, the lotus of the navel,
the lotus of the throat,
and the lotus of the coiled birthplace. (112)

When the movement of feces, urine, and sperm
are encountered at the nine gates,
supreme sight, smell, hearing,
and taste[18] are transformed into knowledge. (113)

The lotus is uniform with the body,[19]
remaining below and above.
She is explained as the wisdom consort,
the mother of all buddhas. (114)

The deity dwelling there in the middle,
the sublime nondual lord,
the omniscient, great, blissful one
will sport in the threefold lotus. (115)

Adorned with fire,
water, earth, and air,

[the purified element] is drawn into the three separate ones
by the knowledge consort's slow movements. (116)

From the union of the tip
with the path of the coiled moon,
the rosary of buddhahood is nondual
in the vajra canal that has a nāḍī. (117)

If thoroughly afflicted because of movement,
after refreshing the coil and the tip,
since one unites the tip of the vajra,
one should imbibe the amṛta. (118)

From that, the body is purified,
one's nature become immaculate,
wisdom is excellent, one is intelligent,
and aging and death are destroyed. (119)

Bhadrapāda taught this yoga
to me without difficulty.
Samādhi is called "amṛta," {94}
truly there is no other superior truth. (120)

By different inhalations through the nose,
the indestructible form of *hāṃ*
via the path of the coiled channel
is carried through the path and is the definitive abode.[20] (121)

That is refreshed at the door,
the pure aspect, luminosity,
called "beginningless nonduality,"
abiding stably in the form of glorious bliss. (122)

After that, expelling the vāyu
and also revealing[21] great power,
[having revealed the definitive path,][22]
the supreme lord is unalterable. (123)

Having attained the thirteenth stage,
defined as the lord of bliss,
the form established without a beginning
turns the wheel of the Dharma. (124)

The stages Bhadrapāda taught
are the brief stages of essential meaning.
Having accepted all that was heard
itself is hearing, reflection, and cultivation. (125)

By Bhadrapāda's kindness,
the one called "Virtuous Koṭalipa"
truly rejoiced
from hearing and cultivation. (126)

Again and again, may I be born
a servant of Bhadrapāda,
other ācāryas and practitioners,
and all sentient beings. (127)

Thus, through these aspirations,
whether or not I become a buddha,
even if I go to hell,
may hell itself be Sukhāvatī. (128)

The limitless yoga of the immaculate stages of the guru,
a mantra treatise for all those with great intelligence,
the section on inconceivable nonduality is the completion stage itself,
This divine form of the essence of treatises on yoga
was written for the purpose of reminding myself who am of little intelligence
because I have a confused mind.

"The Stages of the Inconceivable" composed by the mahāmudrā siddha Śrī Koṭalipa is complete. Translated by the Indian abbot Ratnavajra and the bhikṣu Shakya Yeshe. {95}

maṅgalaṃ

The Chronicle of Ācārya Koṭalipa's Path, the Five Inconceivabilities

Drakpa Gyaltsen

Homage to the sublime guru!

After this was explained by the fully perfect buddha Vajradhāra to the nirmāṇakāya Jñānaḍākinī, she granted empowerment to Ācārya Paramāśva (Supreme Horse) and explained the five stages of the inconceivable. This ācārya was born in the land of Oḍḍiyāna. While Paramāśva was living in a charnel ground, he was repeatedly attacked by the retinue of the precious king of Oḍḍiyāna, Indrabhūti. Paramāśva filled the whole land with horses, which destroyed all the fields of rice. In the end, he gathered the emanations. After taming the king, Paramāśva placed him in the Vajrayāna.

Ācārya Paramāśva gave Mahācārya Vīṇapāda empowerment and instruction. Because Vīṇipāda attained siddhi along with a common flower seller and his conduct was to pass the time playing the tambura, he was called Tamburapāda. At that time, Vīṇapāda tamed the king through causing him to become astonished.

Mahācārya Vīṇapāda gave King Indrabhūti III empowerment and instruction. When the king obtained the precious supreme empowerment, in that one night he instantly attained the supreme siddhi of mahāmudrā from the complete empowerment and instruction. He was able to cause all the citizens of one kingdom to go to the Khecari realm.

King Indrabhūti III gave his queen named Lakṣmī empowerment and instruction. Since she comprehended the ultimate meaning, after realizing the signs of heat with her body, she attained the supreme siddhi of mahāmudrā. {96} Lakṣmī benefited other migrating beings by performing many deeds such as emanating and withdrawing maṇḍalas.

Lakṣmī gave the Ācārya Vilāsavajra empowerment and instructions.

Having obtained the gnosis of heat, he engaged in the victorious conduct of wearing the six ornaments. A native of the east, Vilāsavajra attained supreme siddhi.

Ācārya Vilāsavajra gave Ācārya Guṇḍerī empowerment and instructions. When Ācārya Guṇḍerī was living in a retreat in Oḍḍiyāna, all his meals consisted of a satiating stew made with countless small birds called "guṇḍerī." When he opened his mouth, the birds flew out. With such displays of killing and reviving, he tamed many migrating beings through such actions of destruction and conversion.

Ācārya Guṇḍerī's disciple is identified as the Mahācārya Padmavajra II. Padmavajra had clear images of lotuses on his soles and palms. He was able to place the universe inside of a mustard seed without one becoming larger or the other becoming smaller. He was able to reverse the course of rivers and pass unimpededly through walls and mountains. In particular, he was able to control savage animals with great compassion. He attained supreme siddhi with the principle of the body by relying on a padminī mudra.

Mahācārya Padmavajra gave empowerment and instructions to Mahācārya Śrī Dharmasena (Chos kyi sde). Dharmasena was able to abandon the eight worldly dharmas because correct samādhi arose in his continuum. In all activities he was able to satisfy those to be tamed. He also attained the supreme siddhi of mahāmudrā by relying on the principle of the body.

Mahācārya Śrī Dharmasena gave Śrī Bhadrapāda empowerment and instructions. {97} When he competed in magical power with the lesser Indrabhūti, he defeated the king by emanating ten million heads, and so on. Śrī Bhadrapāda was able to eliminate the king's pride in his form and wealth.

Śrī Bhadrapāda gave Śrī Koṭalipa empowerment and instructions. Koṭalipa was born into the inferior caste of field workers (*so nam pa*), working in the orchards and gardens of the king. He was honest. When he received empowerment and instruction, he attained [both] supreme realization, with no blocks or confusion about the meaning of all the words contained in the tripiṭaka, and the wisdom that eliminated doubts about the four outer sciences, the four inner sciences, and so on. He realized the inseparability of samsara and nirvana in a single teaching from his guru. He set down in writing his understanding based on many sessions of the samādhi of vipaśyana. As such, this is just the story of whatever was said from the perspective of the single lineage of the intention of the nine sublime ones.

ithi

The disciple of Ācārya Koṭalipa was called Bhusanapa because he possessed a carpet of leaves and wore leaves for clothing. His disciple was Karṇapa, called "Karṇapa" because his earlobes were long. Karṇapa's disciple was Vīravajra, who was ordained. Having once accepted a bali offering from the hand of a ḍākinī, Vīravajra journeyed to a city far away; as soon as the winter was cold, he instantly flew to southern Nepal. Vīravajra's disciple was the Tibetan Mangkhar Mugulung.[23] Mugulung's disciple was Kharchung.[24] Kharchung's disciple was Gönpowa.[25] Gönpowa gave the instruction to Lama Sakyapa.[26]

The explanation of the chronicle is complete. {98}

The Clarification of the Instruction on the Inconceivable Composed by Ācārya Koṭalipa

Drakpa Gyaltsen

I prostrate with my head bowed to the feet of the sublime guru.

The lineage of Paramāśva has a total of nine.[27] Then, the system of the unbroken lineage of Koṭalipa, Bhusanapa, Karṇapa, and Bhikṣu Vīravajra establishes (1) the view at the time of the cause, (2) generates and trains in samādhi at the time of the path, and (3) realizes gnosis at the time of the result. It is asserted that everything in the path and result is included in three.

I. The View

Now, to establish the view at the time of the cause,[28] there are twelve definitions that are the basis of the explanation.

The three supports for the instruction of everything in the path and the result are the three times for recognizing those, the three ideas for appraising them, and the three authorities for confirming them.

A. The Support

Now then, the support is the trio of body, voice, and mind. The coarse body is the sense organs and the torso. The subtle body is the three nāḍīs. The coarse voice is the conventions of speaking, laughing, and so on. The subtle voice is {99} the exhalation,[29] inhalation, and pause and the three syllables. From among the support and supported for the mind, the support is the amṛta of the pure bindu of the pure bodhicitta of the nine elements,[30] and the supported manifests as the gnosis known to oneself.

Further, since one being supported on the other[31] is a state of unity, the body and voice are established implicitly by establishing the mind.[32] When the mind is established,[33] there are five inconceivabilities:[34] The inconceivability of characteristics[35] is unmixed and complete. The inconceivability of qualities[36] is like the examples of the wish-fulfilling jewel or the orb of the sun.[37] The inconceivability of power[38] is said to be neither bound[39] nor freed, for example, like a nutmeg flower or sesame oil.[40] Those three[41] inconceivabilities are the method, because they cannot be conceived.{100} The inconceivability of nature[42] is like the example of space. That inconceivability is wisdom, since it cannot be conceived.[43] The inconceivability of essence[44] cannot be disassociated from nor possessed.[45] That inconceivability is the inconceivability of union, because it cannot be asserted as a conception.[46]

B. The Three Times for Recognition

The three times of recognizing the inconceivable: There are inconceivable concepts at the time of sentient beings abiding as the cause.[47] There are inconceivable samādhis at the time of the practitioner cultivating the path.[48] There is inconceivable gnosis at the time of the ultimate result.[49]

Further, at the time of the cause,[50] the trio of body, voice, and mind is subsumed under conceptuality. At the time of the path,[51] the trio is subsumed under samādhi. {101} At the time of the result,[52] the trio is subsumed under gnosis.

C. The Three Evaluations

The three evaluations: If one evaluates the method, the relative truth[53] of all mundane things, it appears and exists in all.[54] If one evaluates wisdom, the ultimate truth, the emptiness of the dharmadhātu, appearances[55] are totally empty and do not exist. If one evaluates[56] the essential nonduality of method and wisdom, while the evaluation itself does not exist,[57] it also is not nonexistent, being union.

D. The Three Authorities

The three authorities for confirming [everything in the cause and the path] are the authority of the authentic compilations of the words[58] of the sugata, the authority of the intimate instructions of the vajra master guru,[59] and the authority of recollection of the practitioner's[60] own experience.

Thus, these are the twelve definitions that are the basis of the instruction. This completes the manner of establishing the view at the time of the cause.

As such, the view that is established is understood[61] at the time of sentient beings abiding as the cause, {102} because after becoming free of the poison[62] of ignorance,[63] one becomes free of the poison of striving of conceptual[64] dualism.

II. The Path

The generation, realization, and training at the time of the path is understood in seven topics: (1) first, focus the mind; (2) in the middle, place the mind on reality; (3) cultivate all conducts; (4) remove the obstructions to concentration, lethargy, and agitation; (5) make progress through the eight kinds of enhancements; (6) apply the signs of the heat of experience to the mind; and (7) in the end, connect with the result through the practice that relies on a mudra.[65]

A. Focus the Mind

Now then,[66] first, to focus the mind, settle the body[67] into its key point, settle the voice[68] into its key point, and settle the mind[69] into its key point. Cultivate bodhicitta.[70] Meditate on the guru above one's crown.[71] Cultivate the pride of the excellent deity[72] and protect the three places. Having fully performed these six limbs of concentration,[73] training in space in the manner of an outer example produces the samādhi that connects nonduality to space. Further,[74] there is the short-distance training {103} and the long-distance training. In each of those, there is both training in the manner of giving punishment and training in the manner of giving a reward.

First is the short-distance training. Focus one's attention on the space four fingerbreadths from the tip of the nose. Meditating with both the body and mind held tensely is training in the manner of giving punishment. Next, meditating with both the body and mind relaxed is training in the manner of giving a reward. Further, train in focusing attention on the space eight fingerbreadths from the tip of the nose. Then, train in focusing the mind on the space sixteen fingerbreadths from the tip of the nose up to a fathom. Whatever experiences[75] of the mind and physical places arise, maintain them in that way. Usually, the [inconceivability of] the nature will arise as emptiness.

Next, for the long-distance training for progress, fully perform the preliminary limbs of concentration.[76] Focus the intrinsically cognizant mind two fathoms in the eastern direction, and so on, and send concepts to the furthest reaches of space. Since one also trains in the manner of giving a reward and punishment, if there is an experience of freedom from extremes,[77] an experience of absence of strength,[78] or an experience of a disabled boat,[79] those should be sustained in that way. {104} Similarly, in order to enhance that, train in all directions,[80] south, and so on. The three experiences above will arise by training in that way.

Based on the experience of freedom from extremes, there is the experience of space,[81] emptiness,[82] pervasiveness,[83] and permanence.[84] Since these four qualities arise, they should likewise be sustained.

This concludes the long-distance training.

B. Place the Mind on Reality

Now then, first, there was focusing the mind; now in the middle, place the mind on reality. Since one trains in the three means after applying the inner meaning to one's mind, there are four bonds in the poison of conceptual effort. First are the three [metaphors of] liberation. There are three manners: applying a name to inconceivable nonarising in the manner of breaking an eggshell,[85] applying the meaning to inconceivable nonarising in the manner of breaking open orpiment ore,[86] and applying samādhi to inconceivable nonarising in the manner of removing a cocoon.[87]

The first[88] of those is applying a name to inconceivable nonarising, because there can be freedom from bondage through a name. The name of the practitioner[89] can be any name at all:

> Nonarising[90] {105} does not arise, like space.
> Arising[91] does not arise, like space.
> Cessation[92] does not arise, like space.[93]

Through such trainings, an experience arises of conceptual grasping to names dissolving into the mind essence without a cessation of clarity. That takes the name, "the three gates of liberation." Likewise, the treatise states:

> Nonduality is merely a name;
> even that name does not exist. [19ab]

. . . .
[I, the yogi,][94] obtained patience for that
which bears the name "nonduality." (60bc)

The *Perfection of Wisdom* states:

Kauśika, matter is a mere designation;
whatever is a mere designation is also dharmatā . . .[95]

Second, in order to be liberated from bondage through the meaning, the meaning is applied to inconceivable nonarising: Investigate any coarse movement of affliction in this intrinsically cognizant mind itself.[96] Having become overpowered by the coarse movement [of an affliction] such as anger, one should investigate the cause[97] in the beginning, the entity that remains in the present, and the result that ceases in the end, and apply this to inconceivable nonarising, which is like space. One should also investigate the location,[98] type,[99] and character,[100] and meditate on nonarising. Through such meditation, the conceptuality of grasping to anger dissolves into the mind itself. {106} As such, the experience of the unceasing clarity of anger arises. The treatise states:

Nondual gnosis blazes
through investigating duality. (5cd)

Third,[101] in order to be free from the bondage of the binding samādhi, samādhi itself is applied to inconceivable nonarising. Internally, the mind is placed in nongrasping; externally, [sense] consciousnesses are muted. First, relax one's body and mind. Then, recall the consciousness by merely looking inward, which causes the arising of the samādhi of bliss and emptiness. If there is external distraction, recall just as before.[102] Second, relax the doors of the sense organs without grasping to any object, and likewise, do not meditate through directing the meditating consciousnesses to an object of meditation. Since one meditates in the manner of not meditating at all, through being free of clinging to an object of meditation, samādhi arises as supreme great bliss. The treatise states:

Free from sense and sensation, (19c)
. . . .
devoid[103] of a knower and the known . . . (30b)

C. Cultivating All Conduct

As a branch for stabilizing those three, there is cultivating all conduct in order to be liberated from the bondage of conditions.[104] First,[105] {107} from the perspective of training on form, placing the eyes on objects set before oneself, whether near or far, such as a flower, and so on, without the sunlight or wind getting into the eyes, is the limb of being supported on those objects.[106] The branch of the body is not moving. The branch of the eyes is not closing them. The branch of the mind[107] is absence of grasping. By training in the possession of all four branches, a samādhi arises without focusing the mind. Next,[108] one trains in looking further and further away[109] and recognizing gnosis from form. In the same way, one should perform the four limbs with sound, and so on, and train. Since one cultivates this instruction of recognizing gnosis from objects, to begin, when the experience of the mind is weak, it is the time when various appearances arise—sometimes one is harmed by conditions, sometimes one is benefited by conditions, and sometimes one is happy.

When one's experience is middling, there is neither benefit nor harm. When the experience of the mind is strong, the concepts of the conditions of objects assist gnosis, like wood added to a bonfire. As soon as one encounters excellent, middling, and inferior conditions of objects,[110] inwardly[111] those transform into the supreme gnosis of the realization of reality. That is the time of beneficial appearances,[112] the time appearances arise as virtuous mentors, {108} the time in which outer and inner are merged,[113] and the time the five poisons[114] are recognized as medicine. The treatise states:

> By realizing eye consciousness,
> nondual gnosis is amazing! (31cd)

And:

> Any eye can see all form,
> superior, mediocre, or inferior.
> The sublime eye sees nonduality
> through the true nature of the ultimate. (72)

D. Removing Obstructions to Concentration

Next, removing lethargy and agitation, the obstacles of concentration, has three topics: lethargy and agitation due to deliberate effort, lethargy and agitation due to conditions, and lethargy and agitation that arises naturally.

1. Lethargy and Agitation due to Deliberate Effort

The lethargy of deliberate effort arises from striving for comfortable beds, and so on, and merit. The agitation of deliberate effort arises from striving for worldly activities such as talking, and so on. To remove that lethargy and agitation, recognize those and having abandoned deliberate efforts for any number of days, that lethargy and agitation will automatically be removed.

2. Lethargy and Agitation due to Conditions

Lethargy due to conditions is lethargy due to eating excessively rich food, drinking too much alcohol, and fatigue. Agitation due to conditions during the day is not isolating from the daily activities of people. Agitation due to conditions at night is not isolating from loud noise. To remove that lethargy and agitation,[115] abandon those conditions for some number of days.

3. Naturally Arising Lethargy and Agitation

Naturally arising lethargy and agitation arise naturally even though the preceding two have been removed. {109} Investigate whether lethargy and agitation occur at the beginning of the session or toward the end of the session. If they arise toward the end of the session,[116] it is the fault of the elements. Thus, reduce the session,[117] and lethargy and agitation will automatically be removed.[118] If lethargy and agitation occur at the beginning of the session, it is an obstacle to concentration. To remove that, in general, there are three approaches: removing lethargy and agitation through conduct, through diet, and through force of mind.

To remove lethargy through conduct, sit on a high seat. If that does not remove lethargy, sit on a high place.[119] The eyes should look at the boundary of the mountains and plains. Invigorate the body and mind. To remove agitation, sit in a low place, slightly drop one's chin toward the chest, or wait until it gets dark.

To remove lethargy with diet, one should not eat prior to concentration. To remove agitation, one should eat before engaging in concentration and drink either a large or small cup of chang.[120] One should take fifty steps and stop.[121] If that does not remove agitation, then double the amount, walk one hundred steps and stop. Further, in general, apply this according to a diagnosis,[122] apply this according to age,[123] and apply this according to season.[124] Such measures will definitely remove lethargy and agitation.

To remove lethargy and agitation through the force of mind, when there is lethargy, train on bodhicitta in the mahāsukhacakra above. Alternately, train on the location of the precious wish-fulfilling gem. {110} First, recall one's mind is in one's heart center, then in the brow, then in the brahma aperture, then four fingerbreadths above the crown,[125] and finally, to the end of space above.[126] As such, take the measure of the mind.[127] However, if one meditates on this for too long, there will be mental discomfort, vata in the heart, and so on. Again, one reverses the process to recall the mind in the heart.

When there is agitation, train on bodhicitta at the place of the *e* dharmodaya below; alternately train on the place of the precious wish-fulfilling gem. That[128] is imagined as a transparent red dharmodaya at the rectum. Look down into that with the mind. As soon as the mind is placed, recall that it exists in the heart. If that does not immediately pacify agitation, it will be removed by holding the narrow path, following, and total understanding. *Holding the narrow path* means that counting agitation immediately dispels it through counting one distraction, a second distraction, and so on. *Following* means being distracted toward an object and then focusing on that object, which swiftly removes agitation. *Total understanding* is said to be dispelling agitation merely by understanding where it is.[129]

If agitation is not pacified by those means, then apply suppression, hang a rope, and clear the narrow path. *Suppression* means putting as heavy a stick as one can support on one's crown and meditating. That will immediately remove agitation. *Hanging rope* means to sweep, make the ground firm, and place a round stick. {11} Above that, tie three ropes to a swing seat. Sit on that with one's feet extending down, which press down on the round stick.[130] Grabbing the rope in front with two hands[131] is the intimate instruction to apply. *Clearing the narrow path* means placing either a stick or a cairn to the right or the left about a cubit in front of oneself. On top of the stick or cairn, place a white stone, then place a black stone on top of the white stone, knock the black stone off with the bamboo cane, and so on. Gaze without closing the eyes. That will immediately remove agitation.

This is the removal of the obstacles to concentration: lethargy and agitation.

E. Progress through the Eight Kinds of Enhancement

Progress through the eight kinds of enhancement includes alternating tightness and laxity, alternating reducing and increasing [the session], alternating meals, relying on the amṛtas of relaxed behavior, the various critical points of mind about alternating, and various objects.

The first four are the application of tightness and reducing the session, and the application of relaxation and increasing the session. First, alternate by sessions.[132] Next, alternate by day;[133] alternate meals;[134] on the second session and day, alternate with alcohol, and so on. Relying on the amṛta of relaxed behavior is easy to understand. The various critical points of mind about alternating enhance progress by the gradual[135] meditation on everything said to be an object of meditation in the sutras, tantras, and so on. {112} "Relying on the amṛta of various objects" means that since one enjoys attractive forms, and so on, one becomes satisfied. Through the power of that, one's realization is enhanced. Those are the eight enhancements.

F. Signs of Heat

Through meditating in such fashion, the signs of the heat of mental experience are produced. To begin, the mind remains [on the object].[136] Confidence in the actual meaning arises. One's slight laziness increases. One has no wish to engage in any activities. One forgets things. As soon as one encounters all activities, one performs them. A special clear memory arises from time to time. One has little desire for food. One can gradually abandon sleep. One can reverse strong, temporary afflictions. One can gradually reverse the conceptual mind for the eight worldly dharmas. Dreams that seem clairvoyant clearly arise. One can expel external and internal parasites at that time. One attains confidence that one will no longer be reborn in lower realms.

G. Conduct Connected with the Result

Finally, since conduct is connected with the result, the conduct of the very unelaborate conduct is the path of the fourth empowerment.[137] At the conclusion of meditating in the manner explained above, ḍākinīs born in nirmāṇakāya buddhafields will make a prediction concerning a young padminī mudra.[138] The position of the ācārya {113} is that when supreme siddhi is realized by relying on[139] an apsara,[140] and so on, both oneself and the mudra should have the perception of the deity upon whom the flower has fallen, such as Vairocana, and so on.[141] One should bless the space of the secret and have the perception of mantra. One should have the perception of dharma, "The supreme siddhi is realized through entering into meditation on method and wisdom."

All the pure essence of the element bodhicitta gathers into the crown from all the nāḍīs of both practitioners when they engage in the union of method and wisdom endowed with those three perceptions. They then experience the four joys[142] descending until they gather in the place of the organs through their respective three nāḍīs.[143] Next, when the solar and lunar bindus are eclipsed by Rahu in the anthers of the supreme place, those pure elements manifest different colors, just like the orb of the sun [descends] into the ocean or when the sun rises. At that time all of samsara and nirvana is seen to be included in that single bindu.[144] That takes the name, "the twelfth stage." {114} That is the final moment of the cause called "contaminated bliss."

Next, to purify the continuums of both the method and wisdom, the method draws up in three different ways: drawing through the right, drawing through the left, and drawing though the middle.[145] In the same way, when drawn up by the wisdom,[146] at the conclusion of that, the purified nine elements move slowly, and because the vāyu is slowly purified, it dissolves[147] into the *haṃ* of the crown after it moves up through the central channel of both [the method and the wisdom]. At that time the experience of the fourth joy arises, stabilized by the mother. At the conclusion of that, since all vāyus and mind dissolve into the central channel, the continuums of both [the method and the wisdom] are liberated simultaneously, and the result—the thirteenth stage, the wisdom of Vajradhara—is realized. This is the meaning of the treatise:

> [The purified element] is drawn into the three separate ones
> by the knowledge consort's[148] slow movements . . . (116cd)

> The supreme path is precisely drawing[149] (121)[150]
> it up the vajra canal that has a nāḍī[151] (117d)
> brimming[152] with pure[153] amṛta.[154] (107c)
> Arising through the three[155] and merging[156] with the three,
> the qualities are perfected[157] and clairvoyance arises.[158]

The explanation of generating samādhi at the time of the path and the method of training is complete.

III. The Result

The system of this ācārya asserts the three kāyas endowed with seven limbs: The first limb in the dharmakāya, naturelessness, is the nonduality of the dhātu and gnosis.{115} The treatise states:

> The ultimate ocean of nonduality . . . (109b)[159]

And:

> The ultimate ocean of gnosis . . . (100b)

The sambhogakāya is summarized in three limbs. There is the limb of great bliss, because it is endowed with special satisfaction with immaculate bliss:

> Defined as the lord of bliss . . . (124b)

And:

> From the great passion of total desire . . .[160]

One's appearances of gnosis[161] together with the mother is the limb of union. Since the major and minor marks blaze, it is the limb of complete enjoyment [of objects of desire].

Further, the nirmāṇakāya is endowed with three limbs. The limb of the cause[162] is being filled with compassion. From the limb of the result,[163] there is the limb of negation because of never ceasing and the limb of establishing[164] because of being uninterrupted.[165] The treatise states:

[T]urn the wheel of Dharma
for the benefit of all sentient beings
in all the utter reaches
of all the world systems in the ten directions. (108)

The explanation of the result from the perspective of gnosis is complete. As such, these very brief words are based on the five kinds of inconceivability and the instruction on the complete path.

samāptamithi

From among the five kinds of inconceivability, in the section on the inconceivable qualities, everything is explained to be differentiated without stirring from the intrinsic nature of dharmatā. A Mahāyāna sutra states: {116}

Though the sun never moves from the sky,
it is blocked by a mountain that everyone sees.
Even though one is certain[166] the sun is carried along
by the chariot of the wind, it is not that way.

Though the nature[167] never moves from the dhātu,
it is blocked by a mountain of conceptuality.
Even though one is certain[168] the nature is carried along
by the wind[169] of concepts, it is not that way.[170]

In the section on view, there are six points of negation: no creation by a cause,[171] no destruction by a condition,[172] no illustration with an example,[173] no accepting and rejecting with an antidote,[174] no purification with a path,[175] and no hope or fear for a result.[176] There are six necessary affirmations[177] when the practitioner practices the path:[178] there is creation through a cause,[179] and so on; moreover, there is suchness,[180] reality,[181] the dharmatā[182] that is accomplished,[183] the gnosis of the connate nature,[184] {117} and the ācārya, the king of the mind;[185] and further, there is the gnosis to be realized, the view of realization,[186] the dharmatā that must be known by each for themselves, proper thinking,[187] and the first stage realized by the practitioner.[188] *śubhaṃ*

[The Intimate Instruction of the Five Kinds of Antidote]

I pay homage bowing my head to the feet of the guru. There are five kinds of antidote: spinning like a wheel, wound like a ball of thread, joining many openings, training without the upper and lower cakras, and training in the very inferior.

I. Spinning like a Wheel

If one feels that the body is swollen, there is pain, and so on, imagine an eight-spoked yellow wheel in the navel, and meditate that the wheel first spins toward the right; if those are not pacified by that, meditate that the wheel spins toward the left. In that way, meditate that since the wheel becomes larger and larger, the body becomes larger and larger. When one feels that the body becomes very large, the wheel is released by the mind and the interior of the body becomes empty, vanishes into space without a trace, and is imagined to be nonexistent. That should immediately solve the problem.

II. Wound like a Ball of Thread

If pain arises because of focusing on a part of the body, such as the heart center, and so on, imagine there is clear tube emerging from that place. Then exhale strongly and imagine the vāyu is blue in color, the size of a split horse-hair, {118} which rolls up outside the body in a shape like a ball of thread. Focus on that for a short while, then release the mind. Next, that becomes larger. In addition, visualize that the vāyu is thicker than before; visualize that it grows from the size of a string to the size of a rope and becomes a ball as before. That should immediately solve the problem.

III. Joining Many Openings

If pain spreads all over the body, many openings appear like the mesh of a strainer. Imagine that the vāyu leaves through those like blue mist. Expel the breath strongly. The problem is solved. It is said there will be little harm to the elements.

IV. Training without the Upper and Lower Cakras

If there is pain and discomfort in the upper body, imagine that above the throat is empty like a bamboo trunk.[189] Imagine that the vāyu leaves in an upward direction as blue mist. Exhale strongly. If there is pain and discomfort in the lower body, imagine the lower body is empty like a bamboo trunk. Then, meditate on the vāyu leaving in a downward direction as blue mist.[190] That will immediately solve the problem.

V. Training in the Very Inferior

If there is much improper jumping, running, and so on, imagine the bottom of one's seat is very low, like a hole. Then, imagine that one's body sinks even lower than that.

The intimate instruction of the five kinds of antidote.

samāptamithi sarva maṅgalaṃ[191]

This word commentary on the essential meaning, summarizing the
meaning,
was written at the request of Phakpe Lha,
who is of good family, supreme in hearing, reflection, and discipline,
by the Sakya upāsaka Drakpa Gyaltsen.
Through this merit may all migrating beings
throughout space attain mahāmudrā.
By the root virtue of writing this text,
after all migrating beings see the essential meaning,
may they quickly attain the stage of Vajradhara
on the stages and paths.

bhavantu
śubham astu sarva jagataṃ

9. *The Path Cycle of the Mudra* Composed by Ācārya Indrabhūti[1]

Drakpa Gyaltsen

Among the eight ancillary path cycles, *The Path Cycle of the Mudra* presents the most detailed and explicit explanation of mudra practice. While it is clear the text is written for practice with a consort, or karma mudra, Amezhap asserts that according to how it is presented in *The Explanation of the Path with Its Result for Disciples*, there are two ways this text has been explained: for practice with an actual mudra and with a gnosis mudra, or a visualized consort. In *The Fortunate Right-Turning White Conch*, chapter 17, Kongtrul comments that even if one is to rely on an actual mudra, training with a gnosis mudra is a necessary preparation.

One of the more interesting features of *The Path Cycle of the Mudra* is the detailed description of how one progresses on the bodhisattva stages to buddhahood through the dissolution of the vāyus that are in "cities"—that is, nāḍī locations that correspond to the thirty-two countries, the renowned pilgrimage sites on the Indian continent.

The text also provides two accounts of the three kāyas: the standard seven limbs of the three kāyas given in the other seven texts belonging to the eight ancillary path cycles and a presentation of the five limbs of three kāyas unique to Indrabhūti II's *Accomplishing Gnosis.*

The text concludes with the account of the lineage, in which three Indrabhūtis are identified, and it is stated that there is both a long and a short lineage for this teaching. In *Effortless Accomplishment of the Two Benefits*, Amezhap states that Indrabhūti II is the author of this instruction.

{120} I devotedly prostrate with my crown to the feet of the sublime guru.

The basic summary:

> Devadatta uses a horse.[2]
> Open the four gates with the nāga.
> Hold desire by pulling the bow.
> The pace of the tortoise causes increase.
> Stop and release the breath.
> The belt is taken to its place with *hi ki*.

When preparing for this path of Indrabhūti, a great lord of yogins, there are four lineages: The verbal lineage is the chronicle of the lineage from Vajradhara down through each guru. The meaning lineage is dependent origination, the account of this arising from that and that arising from this. The symbolic lineage is the lineage of the unerring understanding of the symbols of the vase empowerment, and so on. The blessing lineage is the fourth, and it has five aspects: the blessing of the perfect buddhas, the blessing of the vajra master, the blessing of the commitment deity, the blessing of the ḍākinīs, and the blessing of the view of the essence.

The realization of the three paths arises based on those [four] lineages: There is the path of the creation stage for the one who obtains only the vase empowerment, the path of self-empowerment for the one who obtains the secret empowerment, {121} and the path of the maṇḍalacakra for the one who obtains the gnosis of the wisdom consort empowerment. The person who abides on this last path is endowed with three vows: since the bindu abides in the body, they possess the vow of personal liberation; since great compassion arises for those others who lack realization, they possess the bodhisattva vow; and since bliss blazing in the body is fanned by the vāyu, they possess the secret mantra vow.

Further, in correspondence with the scriptures of the perfect vehicle, the five paths are completed by relying on a mudra. Accomplishing bodhicitta in sixty-four sections, sixteen sections, twelve sections, and so on, as well as the procedure is the path of accumulation. The union of the *bola* and *kakkola*[3] is the path of application.[4] The realization of the mind of the joy of great bliss is the path of seeing. Repeated cultivation of the meaning of the innate (Skt. *nija*; *gnyug ma*) is the path of cultivation. The culmination of the mudra siddhi is the ultimate path.

Now, there are five topics in the explanation of the method of practice: (1) a pure-knowledge consort, (2) equality in body and voice, (3) equality in desire, (4) equality in blessings, and (5) connection with the key points of the intimate instruction.

I. The Pure Knowledge Consort

The [pure knowledge consort] is the meaning of "Devadatta used a horse." That has two topics: (1) the qualities obtained through birth and (2) [the qualities] obtained through training. {122}

A. The Qualities Obtained through Birth

There are three topics in [the pure knowledge consort] obtained through birth. The place-born [pure knowledge consort] is born in a central land and possesses a good character, or she is born in any of the twenty-four regions, or even though she is born in a borderland, she has a special body.

The so-called "mantra-born" or "gnosis-born" [pure knowledge consort] has great power in our own and others' mantras, is fearless in secret conduct, and gives rise to samādhi by nature.

The family-born or connate [pure knowledge consort] is born into a family of secret mantra practitioners, and from among the seven types of yoginīs, she is suited to serve as an attendant and is endowed with any of the five marks of a yoginī. Further, among those [seven], she has a special body due to the power of karma. Her bliss-arousing nāḍīs pervading her entire body are more powerful than those of others. In particular, because the end of her central nāḍī is elongated, it can be exhibited. These are the padminī, hariṇī, śaṇkhinī, and citriṇī.[5]

From the perspective of their age, the twelve-year-old is supreme, the sixteen-year-old is excellent, the twenty-year-old is mediocre, and the twenty-five-year-old is average.

Any of them should have "the fifteen signs of suitability for reliance." There are nine outer signs, three inner signs, and three secret signs. Among the nine outer signs, the signs arising on the body are that she constantly gazes at men, her mouth is dry, and her body hairs are erect. The three signs arising for her voice are erotic conversation, laughter, and meandering speech. The three shared signs are that she has mounted the aspect of the path, begins any activity she encounters, and discriminates among many activities. These are the nine external signs. The three internal signs are that she rejoices in the sublime dharma, has little clinging, and is very compassionate. {123} The three secret signs are that she is devoted to the guru, is not frightened of [secret mantra] and has devotion for secret mantra practice, and is endowed with bodhicitta. Those are the qualities that pure knowledge women obtain through birth.

B. The Qualities Obtained through Training

The qualities obtained through training are possessing the personal liberation vow through going for refuge; generation of the aspirational and engaged bodhicitta and possessing the training of a bodhisattva; receiving the complete four empowerments and possessing the vows of Vajrayāna; and hearing many tantras and instructions and reaching the culmination of hearing and reflection. The *Union with All Buddhas Tantra* states:

> The illusions of women are more extraordinary
> than all pure illusions.[6]

Having found such a person, first purify one's vāyu and maintain the view. Having already gone for refuge and generated bodhicitta, take a cross-legged posture, covering the knees with both hands. Drop the eyes to the tip of the nose. Strongly pull up the lower vāyu, drawing it upward with a slow and long *hūṃ*, and then press down. At that time, if there is pain in the kidney region, rotate the abdomen, straighten up, bind the waist with soft silk, and so on. If there is pain in the head, rotate the head. If there is pain in the upper body, shake the upper body. Since one trains in that way for one week, two weeks, or three weeks, one attains some measure of control over the downward-voiding vāyu.

Further, in order to stabilize that control, boil the egg of a swan or a snowcock with garlic, puncture the side of that egg, and empty the contents. Fill it with goat milk, the six excellent substances,[7] and rock candy. Insert the secret place into that, filling all gaps with dough. Next, draw up [the contents of the egg] step-by-step with slow and long *hūṃ*s, one-third, two-thirds, and all the way. Having drawn it up, {124} follow by drawing up the contents of a brass bowl, and so on. As such, if one wishes to change, [the liquid] should be allowed to descend through the canal of the secret place. If one wishes, one can attain control over lengthening [the secret place].

In the meantime, first, sustain the view. The view, the mind that pervades all entities, is called "the gnosis vajra." Since it cannot be destroyed by compounded conditions, the vajrakāya does not change during the three times. Since [the vajrakāya] is understood to be the nature of all objects of knowledge, it has four characteristics, which are described in *Accomplishment of Gnosis*:

> Pervasiveness, the vajrakāya,
> and changelessness are
> the establishment of perfect gnosis,
> and omniscience is asserted due to that.[8]

When that is practiced, all phenomena are the nature of one's mind itself, clear and unceasing. If investigated, [the mind is] empty; this is called "inseparable clarity and emptiness." That clarity is cognized and experienced by oneself. When investigated, it is called "inseparable cognizance and emptiness." When the body arises as great bliss, all appearances arise as great bliss. When that is investigated, since appearances are empty, this should be understood as the "inseparability of bliss and emptiness." In the beginning, sustain [the view] with hearing and reflection. After that, sustain it naturally by applying the vāyu [yoga]. As such, that training of the vāyu, the demonstration of the horse of Devadatta, can be practiced in the manner of entering into union with a physical mudra, it can be practiced in the manner of gazing and touching, or it can be practiced in the manner of relying on a gnosis mudra. Just as one will quickly arrive at any desired place by mounting a horse, likewise, since [reliance on a mudra] causes one to swiftly arrive at the stage of buddhahood, such is the meaning of the passage, "[Devadatta] used a horse."

Next is the meaning of the passage, "The four gates are opened with the nāga." The person who wishes to practice entering in union with a physical mudra {125} must first search for the tip of her central nāḍī: below the navel, where the rasanā and lalanā split into four tips. Having covered the central nāḍī like the spreading hood of a snake, it is not clear. When those four tips are opened, [the central nāḍī] is clear.

The intimate instruction for that[9] is to make a bolus of felt, shaped like a food offering. The tip should be pointed, and wax should be applied on four finger lengths of its length. The four-finger-length area that is not smeared with wax is held with the hand. Bind the region of both kidneys [of the mudra] with a soft cotton belt and leave it. Above that, place a "saddle," binding the lower edge of the cotton belt above the navel on top of that.

Apply wax to the rectal canal, corresponding with the length of the felt bolus, and insert the bolus. Do not insert it more than four finger lengths. This will cause the lotus to protrude. Mix rock candy and lotus root into goat milk as well as the dirt from the nail of the left ring finger, then apply this repeatedly to all locations. After the four nāḍī tips open, the lower tip of the central nāḍī will be exhibited either two, three, or four finger lengths, based on the difference of whether the nāḍī is good or bad. The passage, "The four gates are opened with the nāga," has five topics. The first of the five topics has already been explained with the training of the vāyu.

II. Equality of Body and Voice

The second topic is the equality of body and voice. Oneself and the knowledge consort must have the stable divine pride of the commitment deity and the ability to accomplish the four kinds of activities based on mantra recitation.

III. Equality of Blessing

The third topic is blessing the vajra and lotus to be joined. The practitioner generates the mother's lotus as a dharmodaya, which arises from an *e* syllable. In the center of that dharmodaya is an eight-petaled lotus, the anthers of which are marked with an *aḥ* syllable. This is stabilized with a mantra. The mother generates the vajra of the father as a five-tined blue vajra marked with a *hūṃ* syllable and meditates on an *oṃ* syllable on the jewel, a *svā* syllable at the jeweled tip, {126} an inverted dark-blue *hūṃ* syllable at the opening, and an upright, dark-red *phaṭ* syllable where the tips meet.

IV. Equality of Desire

The fourth topic, the equality of desire, is employing ordinary desire as the path. That ordinary desire gradually transforms into bodhicitta moistened with great compassion. The thought, "I will attain buddhahood for the benefit of all sentient beings," is the equality of desire.

As such, those are the practices of employing the three kāyas as the path. The equality of body and speech is the nirmāṇakāya, the equality of blessing is the sambhogakāya, and the equality of desire is the dharmakāya.

V. The Key Points of the Intimate Instruction

There are five topics connected with the key points of the intimate instructions: (1) the descent of the bindu of bodhicitta, (2) retention and meditating on bliss, (3) reversing, (4) spreading, and (5) preserving it without loss.

A. Increase the Tissues of the Body

Next, first one must increase the tissues of the body through diet. [One then] expels feces and urine three times, and so on, and then relies on them; rely on mellow, aged alcohol, fresh meat, and goat's milk with rock candy added to it. Also, the preparation of the great maṇḍala will increase the tissues of the body.

B. Descent of the Bindu

Second, in this sequence, the mudra is first regarded as a mental object; [next] without gazing at her, leave her as an object of sound as she speaks erotically; then, finally, she should be gazed upon as an object of sight and meditated on. Mutually exchange the taste of honey and meditate. Kiss, embrace, use the teeth and nails, and meditate. Then, meditating in the manner of uniting with the mudra is called "the descent of the bindu."

C. Retention and Meditating on Bliss

Third is retention and meditating on bliss. That bodhicitta that descends to the jewel is not lost with the three methods of retention. The first method is to open the eyes very widely, place the tongue on the palate, and retain the bindu. If that does not retain the bindu, {127} the second method is retention by pressing down on the upper vāyu and focusing the mind on the bindu. It should be retained, like the simile of a strainer for an ewer,[10] referring to blocking below. If that is difficult to retain, then "Hold desire by pulling the bow," which refers to imagining an upright *phaṭ* drawn upward by an inverted *hūṃ* with twenty-one slow and long *hūṃ*s. It is impossible for the bindu not to be retained by that [method].

Now then, if the power of bliss is weak, one must churn slowly to increase the bliss, referenced by the passage, "The pace of the tortoise causes increase."

If bliss does not spread from the secret place to other parts of the body, to increase it, tighten the lower vāyu slightly, open the eyes, and since one slowly exhales the breath (*dbugs*) for a long while through the nostrils, the samādhi of bliss and emptiness pervades the entire body. This is the meaning of the passage "release the breath."

The sign of retaining the bindu by those methods is that the lower door becomes insensitive, heavy, throbs, spasms, the hairs stand up, one feels the downward-voiding wind, and feces and urine cannot be expelled. When this becomes unbearable and one cries, laughs, exclaims, and so on, it should be reversed. The intention of this ācārya is that after the bodhicitta is sent into the organ, it is stolen from there. So, he asserts practice through the means of the sixteen joys, which stabilizes from below. One can reverse the bodhicitta from the tip of the vajra with the six kinds of movements: clenching and extending with the thumbs and big toes; pressing the abdomen to the spine; rolling the tongue back; rolling up the eyes; after emitting a long *hūṃ*, sounding *hik*; {128} and drawing it upward to the crown with the *hūṃ* of samādhi and *phaṭ*. That refers to the passage, "The belt is [taken to its place] with *hi ki*." Since it is possible there may be excess bodhicitta, one should draw it up two or three times.

D. Spreading

Next, at the time of spreading, if the bindu is not distributed throughout all parts of the body, there will be illnesses, and so on. Fourth, "spreading" refers to spreading the bodhicitta through shaking the head, shaking the upper body, rotating the waist, waving the arms, stamping the feet, crying out, and so on. That is what is referred to by "taken to its place."

As such, one does not avoid the mudra as does a śrāvaka. If one avoids the mudra, the bindu will not increase, and one will resemble a dry cow when milked. That being the case, since it is like milking a cow, the bindu increases and buddhahood arises from the bindu. One should not lose the bodhicitta like an ordinary person. All tantras state that losing it is the source of all faults. Therefore, one should imagine that one has realized the connate gnosis through the descent and reversal of the bodhicitta and abandon desire. By relying on a knowledge consort, the entire body becomes filled with bodhicitta, and the samādhi of bliss and emptiness arises without interruption.

E. Preserving the Bindu without Loss

The fifth general topic is preserving the bindu without loss, with eight subtopics: loss because the body becomes filled with bindu, loss through conditions, loss through illness, loss through spirits, loss through conduct, loss through diet, loss through impaired blessing, and loss through damaged samaya.

1. Loss through Becoming Filled with Bindu

Loss through becoming filled with bindu is loss by virtue of the body becoming entirely filled with bindu. To prevent that, tightly bind the shaft of the vajra with white silk or white cotton, bind the waist with a sash of silk or cotton, strongly shake the two feet, focus the mind on the navel, {129} contract the anal sphincter, and draw the lower wind up with *hi ki*.

2. Loss through Conditions

Loss through conditions is loss upon seeing the knowledge consort. For that, also shake the feet. Imagine that at the tip of the vajra there is a yellow *phaṭ* and a dark-blue *hūṃ*. Draw up with the *hūṃ*, press the upper vāyu down, and also engage in the six movements.

3. Loss through Illness

Loss through illness refers to either loss through a cold condition or loss combined with heat. To prevent that, sleep during the evening and prevent during the day. Soak *Terminalia chebula* in milk, administer a dry powder of the three hot herbs,[11] and rely on a nutritious diet. Apply moxibustion to both the far side and near side of where the elbows reach.[12] Warm a piece of predator hide and also wrap [the vajra] like a case for a vajra and bell.

4. Loss through Spirits

"Loss through spirits" means loss in a dream. To prevent that, burn white mustard seed; mix this with black gugul, the blood of a lotus,[13] and human brains; apply and massage this on the place of the vajra, and so on. Make twenty-one knots in a black cord and recite the mantra of repelling obstructors while tying it on the waist.

5. Loss through Conduct

"Loss through conduct" is loss because of hard work, poor sleep, excessive talking, vigorous walking, and sitting. To prevent that, give up those activities and engage in the six movements. Meditate on *phaṭ* and *hūṃ*. Press down on the lower wind.

6. Loss through Diet

"Loss through diet" is loss through spoiled meat, beans, excess salt, excessively salty water,[14] excessive alcohol, and so on. To prevent that, avoid sleeping after [eating those], drink milk regularly, and eat the garlic preparation called the "daily formula of amṛta."

7. Loss through Impaired Blessings

"Loss through impaired blessings" refers to loss if one neglects bali offerings and feast offerings {130} previously performed. First, descent is difficult; after descent, it is difficult to prevent loss. To prevent that, resume feast offerings and bali offerings.

8. Loss through Damaged Samaya

"Loss through damaged samaya" is the leaking of bindu without the arising of samādhi when any of the fourteen downfalls occur motivated by hatred, and so on. To prevent that, one should receive the full empowerment from the guru. Through the power of that, the bindu will increase immensely, and the liṅga of desire will become firm. At that time, though one thinks one would like to climb on the mudra, one must exercise restraint and not engage in union. After that, bliss will blaze up and nonconceptuality will blaze up. The five signs, smoke, and so on, will gradually arise.

As such, that person in whose body the bindu exists will be blessed by the ḍākinīs. First, one is blessed by four, eight, sixteen, thirty-two inner ḍākinīs, and so on. Then, one is blessed by the outer ḍākinīs. The method of blessing the inner ḍākinīs is that the increased bindu in the body is the pure essence of the five amṛtas. Since those are the five ḍākinīs, they move and increase in the twenty-four places in the body, and so on; nonconceptuality increases; and one is blessed. From such familiarization, one realizes the mudra siddhi, and one attains the result based on the mudra instruction.

When the joys are systematically applied to the stages in order to eliminate proliferation of the path, prior to the sixteen joys being stabilized in ascending order, there is the downward progress of the four joys. To describe that, the joy between the crown and the throat includes four joys; the supreme joy between the throat and the heart includes four joys; {131} the joy of separation between the heart and navel includes four joys; and the connate joy from the navel to the tip of the vajra includes four joys. After gnosis is recognized at the time of the connate, in dependence on training the continuum for a long while, buddhahood is realized at the conclusion of the sixteen joys stabilized in ascending order. When that is cursorily described, since it is stabilized at the navel, joy is realized. The sign of that is the navel cakra becomes white in color, shiny as a mirror, and attractive to all migrating beings. When joy is stabilized at the heart, the shoulders expand, the five clairvoyances arise, and one's strength cannot be overcome, even by one hundred elephants. When joy is stabilized at the throat, if one sticks out one's tongue, it can entirely cover the face, is able to enjoy the amṛta of the three realms, and is the accomplishment of the supreme of words. When joy is stabilized at the crown, one has reached the culmination of the connate joy and realized buddhahood.

If that is described in detail, there are twelve topics: the sixteen joys stabilized in ascending order, the twelve stages, the inner sign of the vāyu rising to the level of twelve finger lengths, the outer sign of knowing the thoughts of others, and so on. Also, in each of the thirty-two lands there are 675 vāyus. Having emptied the cities, based on obtaining empowerment, at the conclusion of the twelfth stage, buddhahood is realized.

When described in [more] detail, when three of the joys stabilized in ascending order manifest—the joy of joy, the supreme joy of joy, and the joy of separation of joy—one manifests the first bhumi based on emptying the four sets of 675 vāyus from the cities—Aryana on top of the head, Jālandhara at the fontanelle, Pulliramalaya at the coronal suture, and Kāmarūpa at the brow—into the central nāḍī. {132} This stabilizes in the remaining half of the secret place of the body. The inner sign is blockage of the vāyu at one finger length. The outer signs of these are not factored in detail apart from a general correspondence. If one wishes a one-to-one correspondence, then in this first stage, the outer sign is said to be knowing the minds of others. Likewise, the connate joy of joy manifests and it is stabilized below the navel. The four sets of 675 vāyus in the cities—Malaya on the tip of the nose, Sindhūra in the two eyes, Nagara at the two ears, and Kaliṅga[15]—are emptied into the central nāḍī. The inner sign is that the vāyu is blocked at two finger lengths. The outer sign is the arising of great compassion and weeping. This is the second stage.

Likewise, between the navel and the heart one realizes the joy of supreme joy, the supreme joy of supreme joy, the joy of separation of supreme joy, and the connate joy of supreme joy. The vāyu and mind dissolve into the inner lands, Mumuni on the chin and Devīkoṭa at the throat. This is the third stage. The dissolution into Kuluta behind the underarm and Arbuda at the two breasts is the fourth stage. The dissolution of the vāyu and mind into Harikela at the heart and Godavari at the navel is the fifth stage. The dissolution of the vāyu and mind into Lampaka at the groin and Kāñci in the middle of the liṅga is the sixth stage. Also, the inner sign is the vāyu being blocked by one finger length at each stage [ending at six finger lengths]. Also, the outer sign is seeing the various forms of migrating beings on the third stage. On the fourth stage, the liṅga is firm. On the fifth stage, since one's continuum is satisfied with great bliss, one cannot differentiate self and other. The outer signs of the sixth stage are enjoying the great bliss of gnosis and seeing the desirable qualities of world. One laughs and dances.

From the heart to the throat, the joy of the joy of separation, the supreme joy of the joy of separation, the joy of separation of the joy of separation, and the connate joy of the joy of separation are again realized. Based on those, the four stages are realized. The way the vāyus and bodhicittas of the eight parts of the body {133} dissolve into the central nāḍī are as follows: the two sets of 675 vāyus of both the White Lady (*dkar mo*) at the tip of the liṅga and Suvarṇadvipa at the anus [dissolve], the seventh stage; similarly, [two sets of 675 vāyus of] Kaṅkana at the thighs and Vindhya at the knees [dissolve], the eighth stage; [two sets of 675 vāyus of] of Pretapuri at the calf and the Ocean (rGya mtsho) at the arch of the foot [dissolve], the ninth stage; and [two sets of 675 vāyus of] Kaumāripa at the big toe and Caritra at the toes [dissolve], the tenth stage. The outer signs are as follows: on the seventh stage, the entire body is observed to be pervaded with great desire; on the eighth stage, various miracles are displayed; on the ninth stage, various sounds are heard; and on the tenth stage, one can arrive in front of the sun without being burned.

On the basis of realizing the joy of connate joy, having gained control over the first quarter [of the area] above the throat, the eleventh stage is realized based on emptying the cities of the four sets of 675 vāyus and bodhicittas—Kashmir at the two shoulders, the border city on the soles of the feet, Nepāla on the occipital region, and Karbuciti at the waist. The inner sign is the dissolution of the vāyu at eleven finger lengths. The outer sign is that one is not covered by faults, like a lotus that grows from the mud. There are three more: The twelfth stage is realized based on the supreme joy of connate joy, the joy of separation of connate joy, and the connate joy of connate joy. For the parts of the body, there is Pūrvavideha at the heart, Uttarakuru in the center of the navel, Aparagodānīya in the eight petals inside the nirmāṇa-cakra, and Jambudvipa at the tip of the secret place. Also, those are said to be Himalaya, Saurastra, Kaliṅga, and Kosala. Based on emptying the city of the four sets of 675 vāyus into the central nāḍī, {134} the twelfth bhumi is realized. The inner sign is the blockage of vāyu at the twelfth finger length. A finger length is a term for each 1,800 [vāyus dissolving into the central channel]. The outer sign is called "the blessing of all the ḍākinīs." In each pore of the body exist innumerable buddhafields. That is the meaning of the passage:

> Those abiding in samaya will see
> the ḍākinīs from afar,
> like a bevy of swans gathered
> on a delightful lotus pond.[16]

As such, the 675 vāyus multiplied by the thirty-two countries is the dissolution of all 21,600 [karma vāyus]. Also, 1,800 multiplied by 12 is the dissolution of 21,600 [karma vāyus]. As such, one reaches the culmination of the twelve stages through the sixteen joys. Since all their powers are combined, after purifying the five concealed nāḍīs, one realizes buddhahood on the thirteenth stage.

Buddha asserted the result in the five limbs: The dharmakāya pervades all entities. Since it cannot be destroyed by anything, it is the vajrakāya. The dharmakāya is immutable. The sambhogakāya is established as the kāya of true gnosis. [The nirmāṇakāya is] the limb of omniscience about that nature and the extent of all objects of knowledge. The *Accomplishment of Gnosis* states:

Pervasiveness, the vajrakāya,
changelessness
is the establishment of perfect gnosis,
and omniscience is asserted due to that.

Previous gurus have stated that the result possesses seven limbs: "The dharmakāya has one limb, naturelessness. The sambhogakāya has three limbs: enjoyment of the Mahāyāna dharma, union with the gnosis mudra, {135} and immaculate great bliss. The nirmāṇakāya has three limbs: nonreferential great compassion, engaging in the benefit of sentient beings without interruption, and never ceasing because of not entering into the nirvana dhātu." This concludes the explanation of the result.

As such, the basis of the intimate instruction is threefold: the four lineages, the five paths, and the one who possesses the three vows. There are five key points of practice included in the sixteen joys and the manner of progressing through the twelve stages by means of the thirty-two inner and outer countries. The result is explained by the Buddha with either five or seven limbs. Thus, the extensive explanation of Ācārya King Indrabhūti's instruction and the detailed explanation of the summarized topics are complete.

Here, from the perspective of lineage, there is the one-to-one lineage that is explained at length and the explanation of the close lineage that was obtained through siddhi.

First, Indrabhūti III's *Amṛta of Reality Intimate Instruction* states:

In the presence of Sukhaśrī,
likewise, Brahma
and the brahminī Siddhavajrā,
then Śrī Vajrabhūtirāja,
then the ācārya after him,[17]
and likewise, the naked ācārya,
Śrī Jñānabhūtirāja,
Ācārya Padmavajra,
and likewise, Ḍombipa,
Anaṅga II, and Śrīdevī,
and likewise, Bee in the Lotus,
the one who entered into the Kila charnel ground,

Princess Lakṣmī,
and I too accomplished the first [stage].[18]

Śrī Sukha is Indrabhūti I, the emanation of Vajrapāṇi. Śrī Vajrabodhirāja is Indrabhūti II. "And also I accomplished the first [stage]" refers to Indrabhūti III. Also, all three are emanations of Vajrapāṇi. {136}

The disciple of Indrabhūti III is the ārya brahmin Ratnavajra. He gave this to the Red Ārya, Prajñāgupta.

When the close lineage is recounted, the Buddha granted this to Indrabhūti I. The latter granted it to Lakṣmī and she granted it to Prajñāgupta. This [account] is found in the *Precious Drop* he composed.[19]

Śrī Prajñāgupta granted this to the great lama Drokmi. He in turn taught it to many disciples, including the Kalyanamitra teacher of the Khön, Könchok Gyaltsen, and many others. The entire instruction was given to the great lama, Sakyapa.

This concludes the explanation of the instruction of Indrabhūti and its chronicle.

PART TWO

Jamgön Kongtrul's Commentary on the Eight Ancillary Path Cycles

Introduction

Chapter 9 through chapter 16 is Jamgön Kongtrul's commentary on the eight ancillary path cycles. His motive for writing this commentary may be found in his autobiography, in a discussion he had with Khyentse Wangpo on the nineteenth day of the first Tibetan month, when Khyentse encouraged Kongtrul to undertake in earnest the composition of a commentary on these eight ancillary path cycles.[1] This discussion also marked the beginning of a ten-year project to assemble *The Treasury of Precious Instructions*, initiated in 1872 and completed with the publication of the final volumes in 1882/83. Kongtrul does not mention when exactly he wrote these texts during this time frame, only that he procrastinated.

Kongtrul considered these eight chapters of a single work, beginning with his commentary on Drakpa Gyaltsen's *Clarification of the Stages of the Inconceivable* (*Fortunate Pure Crystal Mirror*, chapter 15), where the introduction is found. It concludes with the commentary on the *Path Cycle of Mudra* (*Fortunate Right-Turning White Conch*, chapter 16), where the colophon is found. The remaining texts were most likely composed in the order given in Kunga Zangpo's lineage prayer.

For the general structure of Kongtrul's commentaries, he first identifies the source of the teaching and then comments on the instruction. In some cases, he does little more than expand slightly on the original text and rearrange it to provide a more orderly structure, for example, in the commentary on *Straightening the Crooked* (*Essence of Fortunate Curd*, chapter 12). In other cases, especially in *Excellent Tree of Fortunate Bilva* (chapter 13) and *Fortunate Shoot of Dūrva Grass* (chapter 14), the two commentaries most directly concerned with mahāmudrā meditation, Kongtrul expands considerably on the original texts with additional citations. *Excellent Tree of Fortunate Bilva*, the commentary on *In Front of a Stupa* (chapter 6), is the longest of these commentaries and the most detailed. As an instruction on mahāmudrā that descends from the archetypal mahāsiddha, Saraha the Great Brahmin, it certainly earns attention as the most comprehensive commentary in the collection. While *In Front of a Stupa* only gives ten citations, the *Excellent Tree of Fortunate Bilva* adds an additional seventeen. Unlike the other cycles, no particular deity is specified in this cycle. Perhaps the most interesting foray Kongtrul takes in this commentary is found in the section connecting realization with conduct. Here, Kongtrul draws from a Drukpa Kagyu text attributed to Rechungpa, *Root Verses of the Sixfold Cycle of One Taste*, as well as a text by Gönpo Dorje, *Comprehensive Summary of One Taste*, which Kongtrul cites without attribution.

In *Fortunate Shoot of Dūrva Grass*, Kongtrul completely reorganizes Drakpa Gyaltsen's original commentary, moving the cursory breakdown of the mahāmudrā of the view, meditation, conduct, and experience from the end of the text into the discussion of mahāmudrā of the path. In addition, he excises the blessing completely, which reduces the *Mahāmudrā without Syllables* by half and then expands the text with citations and commentary. In *Medicinal Elixir of the Fortunate Bezoar* (chapter 10) and *Fortunate Pure Crystal Mirror* (chapter 15), the main value Kongtrul adds to these commentaries is that he works the copious annotations found in Drakpa Gyaltsen's original commentaries into the main body of the text. The three remaining commentaries, *Fortunate Mustard Seedpod* (chapter 11), *Fortunate Right-Turning White Conch* (chapter 16), and *Fortunate Vermilion Ornament* (chapter 17), are little more than close edits of Drakpa Gyaltsen's originals. Regrettably, in the case of *Fortunate Right-Turning White Conch*, Kongtrul does not provide any further commentary on the progression through the paths and stages described by Drakpa Gyaltsen.

10. Medicinal Elixir of the Fortunate Bezoar

The Manual of Ḍombi Heruka's Accomplishing the Connate[1]

Jamgön Kongtrul

{138} *namo guru vajradharapādāya*

Having bowed to Virūpa, Ḍombipa,
the inseparable five lord founders,
and Khyentse Wangpo who unifies them all into one,
I will set forth the stages of instruction in *Accomplishing the Connate.*

There are two topics in the instruction on *Accomplishing the Connate,* an inner division of the eight ancillary path cycles, composed by the lord of siddhas, Ḍombi Heruka: (1) the lineage from which it springs and (2) the explanation of the main topic, instructions of the lineage.

I. The Lineage

After the fearless lord of yogins, Śrī Dharmapāla, was granted the empowerment into Lady Nairātmyā's maṇḍala of fifteen goddesses and attained the sixth stage, he became renowned as Mahāsiddha Virūpa. He explained the tantras in great detail to Ḍombipa and bestowed upon him the condensed practice of the intimate instruction aural lineage. Ḍombipa himself attained siddhi and explained *Accomplishing the Connate* based on this passage of the [*Hevajra*] root tantra:

> Whatever arises connately
> is called "connate."
> Called "connate by nature,"
> all aspects are unified and one. {139}

After that, in order, there is Naktrö, Garbharipa, Jayaśrī, Durjayacandra, and Bhikṣu Vīravajra. The latter bestowed this instruction to Drokmi. The lineage continues to the Sakya lords,[2] the nephews,[3] and so on, until it finally reaches the omniscient Jamyang Khyentse Wangpo, the single valley through whom flows the great doctrine of all the instructions, through whose kindness I obtained this instruction.

II. The Main Topic: The Instructions

In the main topic of the instructions, there is (1) the general explanation of the way the path is accomplished and (2) the detailed explanation of the main topic, the instructions.

A. The Way the Path Is Accomplished

There are two ways for a person who wishes to realize the result—union, the stage of Mahāvajradhara—to accomplish the path: there is the path of the ascetic with concepts and the path of the infant without concepts. In both paths, three frugalities are necessary: (1) the frugality of enjoyments, (2) the frugality of the body, and (3) the frugality of the mind.

1. Frugality of Enjoyments

If one has possessions to enjoy, having understood they are the fruit of past generosity, it is necessary that those become a partial condition for gathering accumulations. {140} Thus, one should not permit them to be squandered by fire, water, enemies, and spirits. The first portion of them should be offered as a maṇḍala to the guru with a mind without greed or stinginess. The second portion should be offered as a feast to the Three Jewels and the ḍākinīs. The third portion should be offered as Dharma provisions for oneself. If one has no property, do not strive for it. One should understand, without hope and fear, that the bare necessities of food and clothes are sufficient and make mental offerings. This is shared between both paths.

2. Frugality of the Body

Since this body of leisure and endowments is difficult to acquire, it must not be squandered by permitting it to remain in an ordinary state. Hence, it is necessary that one possess the three vows: prātimokṣa vows, bodhisattva vows, and vidyādhara vows. Each of those vows has an outer vow and an inner vow.

The outer prātimokṣa vows are the five kinds of vows that an upāsaka or upāsikā protects, the thirteen formally adopted vows of a śrāmaṇera or a śrāmaṇerī, and the two hundred fifty-three rules of the fully ordained bhikṣu or bhikṣuṇī. Whichever of those vows one has obtained, it should never be allowed to be damaged and should be protected like one's life. The inner [prātimokṣa vow] is retaining the bodhicitta bindu in the body without losing it.

Among the two outer and inner bodhisattva vows, the outer is not permitting the four defeats and thirty-six faults to contaminate one's continuum. The inner vow is being motivated by great compassion for suffering sentient beings; doing what one can to benefit others; and in a state of consciousness that is clear and unceasing, employing one's body in the service of others.

Among the two outer and inner vidyādhara vows, the outer are protecting the twenty-two samayas: the fourteen root downfalls and the eight secondary downfalls, which are commonly shared from the tantras. The inner vow {141} is resting in the state of fundamental nonconceptual consciousness without modification or adulteration.

Those three outer vows are the path of the ascetic. The three inner vows are the path of the infant.

3. Frugality of the Mind

Since one's mind is frugal in not following deluded concepts, it is necessary to never be separate from the two kinds of bodhicitta. From among the outer and inner, the outer relative bodhicitta is generating the aspirational and engaged bodhicittas. Ultimate bodhicitta is remaining in equipoise free from proliferation.

The inner relative bodhicitta is preventing the loss of the jasmine-like bodhicitta. The ultimate bodhicitta is to always abide in the samādhi of bliss and emptiness. Those two are connected with the path of the ascetic and the path of the infant, respectively.

If one properly relies on the three methods on the basis of possessing those three frugalities, the three kāyas will swiftly arise.

B. The Instructions

There are three [connates] in the detailed explanation of the main subject, the instructions: (1) the naturally existing connate of the cause; (2) the connate of the method that gives rise to experience; and (3) the connate of the result, the three gates of liberation and the way the three kāyas arise.

1. The Connate of the Cause

[In the connate of the cause,] there are two connates: (1) the connate nonarising reality and (2) the connate of the cause, one's body.

a. The Connate Nonarising Reality

The first is the reality of the mind that has been connate from the beginning without arising from anything. All phenomena included in samsara and nirvana are included in one's mind. There isn't a single phenomenon that is established apart from the mind. The reality of the mind that has been connate by nature from the start pervades the entire domain of sentient beings. If one investigates that [reality of the mind] by looking within, the essence that is experienced as mere cognizant clarity (*gsal rig*) is clarity, the characteristic of the mind. {142} With respect to its intrinsic nature, that mere clarity does not arise in the beginning, does not abide in the middle, and does not cease in the end. It is not established as an entity of color, shape, and so on. It abides nowhere in the body, inside or out, top or bottom. No matter how much one searches, that clarity cannot be found. No matter how it is analyzed, it cannot be established. That is emptiness, the reality of the mind. As such, that searcher is nothing other than the mind itself and is the clarity aspect. As such, the essence (*ngo bo*) of clarity is empty. The nature (*rang bzhin*) of emptiness is clarity. The inseparability (*dbyer med*) of those two is explained with several names: union, inseparability, inexpressibility, connate reality, and so on. *Accomplishing the Connate* states:

> Why? If one does not meditate with the mind,
> all migrating beings will be meditated on.[4]

Nonmeditation is the meditation
through which all phenomena will be known.
Animate and inanimate entities,
grass, forest, vines, and so on
are [the connate's] own intrinsic nature.
When that supreme one is meditated on with certainty,
there isn't anything apart from those [entities].

As it says, since one abides in equipoise—intrinsic cognizance—in the essence that is not to be meditated in any way, one will be liberated into the dhātu of inseparable emptiness. The foregoing [*Accomplishing the Connate*] continues:

Great bliss is intrinsic cognizance.
That meditation of intrinsic cognizance
will produce siddhi.[5]

b. The Connate of the Cause

Based on not understanding—incorrectly imputing reality as such—once the three poisons and the three doors form gradually, one cycles through the places of samsara; that is called "the connate of the cause." That is explained in this section with fifteen dharmas: the nine dharmas of the three doors and the six obstacle dharmas.

First, the nine features are the three doors: body, voice, and mind. {143} For the body, there are the connate nāḍīs: the central nāḍī, rasanā, and lalanā. For speech, there are the connate exhalation, inhalation, and pause. For the mind, there are the three connate poisons: desire, hatred, and ignorance. The natural shimmer of the three poisons is the connate outer and inner obstacles. The inner obstacles are the three connate humors: the vata illnesses that arise from desire, the pitta illnesses that arise from hatred, and the kapha illnesses that arise from ignorance. The outer obstacles are the female-class spirits that arise from desire, such as *senmo*,[6] and so on; the male-class spirits that arise from hatred, such as *gyalgongs*,[7] and so on; and the nāga-class spirits that arise from ignorance, such as nāgas, pestilential local guardians,[8] and so on. That being the case, it is necessary to practice the path in order to purify the fifteen dharmas, which are connate through the mere formation of the body, after one's mind came under the external power of affliction due to delusion.

2. The Connate of the Method

There are three sections in the connate of the method: (1) the path of the ascetic, (2) the path of the infant, [and (3) the intimate instruction of experience].

a. The Path of the Ascetic

i. The Three Preparatory Dharmas

Among the three preparatory dharmas for the ascetic person with concepts, at the beginning of the entry into the path, there is the meditation on the guru at one's crown. On one's crown, supported by eight lions, there is a jeweled throne, upon which are stacked a multicolored lotus, a sun, and a moon as a seat. Upon this is the root guru in the form of Vajradhara, the lord of all families and maṇḍalas, the embodiment of all the Jewels and places of refuge, the source of all supreme and common siddhis, to whom one offers the special words of supplication. One should also supplicate the lineage. Finally, the guru melts into the nature of light and dissolves into oneself, implanting the blessings of body, speech, and mind, granting the four empowerments, and purifying the four taints. {144} Feeling that one's body, voice, and mind and all one's activities become the nature of the guru's four kāyas, rest in the state of clarity and emptiness without grasping.

The meditation of precious bodhicitta is the strong aspiration, "These parent sentient beings have wandered in samsara under the power of delusion from time without beginning, experiencing inconceivable suffering. How pitiable! For their benefit, I certainly must obtain the stage of Mahāvajradhara, union. The principal cause and condition of that is practicing the profound path of Vajrayāna."

Also, one should verbally repeat many times, "I must obtain the stage of perfect buddhahood in order to benefit all sentient beings. For that purpose, I shall practice the profound path."

The recollection of deity yoga: By reciting *hūṃ*, the place becomes the protection cakra. By reciting *hūṃ*, the interior of that place becomes the celestial mansion. By reciting *hūṃ*, in the middle of that mansion there is a seat composed of a lotus, sun, and the four māras piled upon one another, upon which oneself is visualized as Bhagavān Śrī Hevajra, with one face and two arms, holding a vajra in the right hand and a skullcup in the left hand. He embraces the khaṭvāṅga that represents Nairātmyā, abiding in nondual bliss and emptiness. His three places are marked with the three syllables, white, red, and blue, which are the essence of the three vajras of all buddhas. Recite *oṃ āḥ hūṃ* three times.

ii. The Main Subject

I) The Path of the Ascetic

In the main subject, it is said that the performance of the nine limbs (three by three) in the technique of the physical posture and the two systems of voiced inhalations are learned from the guru personally, as they have not been written down. However, even though the tradition of the intimate instruction is no longer extant, it is very important for the main part of the path of the ascetic and as a preliminary for the path of the infant. Thus, the meaning is complete in the instruction of possessing the method of one's body. This is explained in four parts: {145} the method of purifying, straightening the entry, the method of drawing up, and the place to spread.

A) The Method of Purifying

First, there are four sections in the method of purifying: The method of adjusting the body is placing the right and left feet on the thighs. The explanation of the location to hold the vāyu is to hold it between the navel and the secret place. The object to visualize is the fundamental, shiny, blue vāyu, which is either two or four finger lengths long. The intimate instruction to practice is forcefully joining the upper and lower vāyus, which is said to cause the navel to protrude within three days.

B) The Explanation of Straightening the Entry

Second, since one in fact relies on the path of the karma mudra, it is merely summarized here, but it will be explained below. Since in both paths one must rely at the start on a mental knowledge consort, and since one trains gradually with both methods of voiced inhalations or what has been explained above, when the vāyu is rendered pliable, visualize a passionate woman before oneself. Since one engages in the sport of passion, bliss is induced. One should enter in union using the [three] general perceptions. Generate the descent of the four joys. Since the four nāḍīs do not actually meet, it is necessary to train by imputing that with the mind. That either causes the bindu to descend or bliss to arise, which approximates [the descent of the bindu].

C) Drawing Up

Third, the explanation of the method of drawing up [the bindu]: As soon as the four descending joys are complete, one does not lose even a drop of bindu; that is, lowering one's head and elevating others. First, draw the bindu up soundlessly into the short *a*. Then draw the bindu up with sound. Finally, draw the bindu up with the mind. In each of the three, shake the head. The visualized bindu is pale and shiny, and meditated as returning to the crown. Since one recognizes the four joys stabilized in descending order, bliss arises, spreading throughout the whole body.

D) The Place to Spread

Fourth, the explanation of the place to spread: Inhale {146} and block the vāyu. First, extend the right arm, hold via the left nostril, and shake the head. Release the hand and shake; hold and shake again. Then do the opposite. Visualize the bindu spreading throughout the entire body. That will certainly cause the bindu to spread into every pore of the body. After that, the body will feel like a ball of cotton. Since this causes experience to arise immediately, it is said to be a very important point.

This is the main practice for the path of the ascetic and the preliminary practice for the path of the infant.

b. The Path of the Infant

Second, in the main subject of path of the infant, there are four mothers for union: the padminī, śaṅkhinī, citriṇī, and hastinī. Also, each of these is divided into superior, middling, and inferior, which are examined according to the original text. The ones to be relied upon are the superior and the middling. The inferior one should not be relied upon. Further, the one who is going to rely [upon a mudra] should purify their continuum by accomplishing the complexion with very nutritious food and drink for one month. This will increase the brilliance of one's complexion. One should engage in the visualization, the yantras, and so on, and enter in union with the mental knowledge consort.

In the actual straightening of the entry, there are four nāḍīs that correspond with the four kinds [of mudra]. The nāḍī of the padminī is fine like a thread, sharp like a spear point, keen like the edge of a razor, and smooth like the surface of a mirror. In general, if the nāḍī is very fine, it is best. The tip of the very best nāḍī naturally protrudes through the mere arising of desire. For those that do not protrude, use the method of finding the nāḍī and inserting the tip of the nāḍī into the opening of the vajra. The visualization is to imagine that the avadhūti nāḍī in the navel sways like the head of a snake moved by the wind. One should draw up and spread [the bindu] as before. It is impossible that one will not faint from bliss by engaging in such training for one up to eleven days. Some people will faint from bliss at the start.

c. The Intimate Instruction of Experience

Twenty-four dharmas of the intimate instruction of experience are explained to be shared between both paths. {147}

i. The Eight Dharmas of the First Limb

First, by the power of the downward-voiding vāyu moving and reversing, since bliss and vāyu blaze in the body, there is no definite sequence of arising, as heat and bliss arise together. The mind is pervaded by joy and bliss. One speaks, laughs, and suddenly cries out. (1) That is the samādhi called "pervaded by great bliss." (2) Since the affliction of desire is employed as the path, desire for objects is gradually abandoned. (3) Vata illness is cleansed. (4) One is free from the five classes of female spirits. (5) The left lalanā nāḍī is brought under control. (6) One obtains control over inhalation. (7) Bliss arises for the mind in dreams and in one's experience. (8) The gate of liberation takes the name "without aspiration." Those eight are the first limb in transforming the cause into the path.

ii. The Eight Dharmas of the Second Limb

Second, through the power of drawing up the downward-voiding vāyu, experience will arise immediately. When bliss arises, (1) a consciousness that is clear, light, and endowed with great compassion is samādhi. (2) Since the ultimate degree of clarity produced by unattractive conditions is great hatred, the affliction of hatred is employed as the path. (3) Blood and pitta illnesses are pacified. (4) One is free from the male class of spirits. (5) The right rasanā nāḍī is brought under control. (6) One obtains control over the exhalation of the vāyu. (7) For the mind, clarity and lightness arise, such as levitating in the sky cross-legged, and so on, in dreams and experience. (8) The gate of liberation takes the name "signlessness." Those eight are the second limb that arises from the strength of the connate of the cause.

iii. The Eight Dharmas of the Third Limb

Third, through the power of drawing up the downward-voiding vāyu, simultaneous with the former two, (1) the consciousness abiding as the fundamental state that is nonconceptual by nature is samādhi. (2) Since it is a great ignorance that is ignorant about any object, the affliction of ignorance is employed as the path. (3) Kapha illness is pacified. {148} (4) One cannot be harmed by nāga spirits. (5) The avadhūti nāḍī is brought under control. (6) One obtains control over the resting vāyu. (7) Since nonconceptual mind lacks equipoise and post-equipoise phases, there is no difference between being asleep or awake—one never wakes from sleep.[9] (8) The gate of liberation takes the name "emptiness," and one is free from the duality of subject and object. Those eight are the third limb, and they also arise from the power of the connate of the cause.

When all those are added together, the twenty-four limbs are the connate dharmas of experience.

3. The Connate of the Result

Third, there are three in the connate of the result: (1) first, the way the signs arise; (2) in the middle, the way of engaging in the conduct; and (3) finally, the way the actual result is attained.

a. The Way the Signs Arise

First, once the three experiences arise in one's continuum, three signs will arise in one's body, voice, and mind: The specific sign of benefiting others with the body is that when they perceive there is suffering from the onslaughts of illness and spirits, those [sufferings] will be pacified merely by massaging and rubbing powders, feces, and urine on the bodies [of the patients]. The sign of speech is that when one announces, "The illness is cured!" and so on, merely pronouncing the words of aspiration accomplishes this and that action, because [the voice] transforms into the supreme accomplishment of words. The sign of the mind is that dreams become clearer, after which one sees nonhuman beings, and one then recognizes what is beneficial and harmful to the meditational experience.

Further, three signs arise during (1) this life, (2) at the time of death, and (3) in the bardo.

i. The Signs Arising in This Life

First, in this life, one's complexion is excellent, and one has little clinging to food and clothes. One engages in activities as soon as they are encountered. That which one has forgotten is suddenly recalled.

ii. The Signs Arising at Death

Second, at the time of death, there is no pain from the severing of the vital points [of the body], no fear of death, no aspiration for the body of either a deva or a human, and one is never separate from the experience of one's meditation.

iii. The Signs Arising in the Bardo

Third, in the bardo one feels that one meets the guru; one feels one sees the face of the Buddha; whatever body one has assumed arises in the form of one's excellent commitment deity; and after one becomes a vidyādhara, the door to birth in lower realms is blocked. {149}

b. Engaging in the Conduct

Second, having seen the signs, the way to engage in the conduct is that once the first sign in this system has arisen slightly, one gradually engages in secret conduct. During the day [one's behavior] should comport with one's companions, and one guards against mundane misdeeds. At night, when it is time for the conduct, in no specific order, wear clothes without regard to good or bad and associate with companions also without regard for whether they are good or bad. If one's concepts are few, in secret one should gradually rely on feces, urine, great meat, and so on. This stabilizes experiences in the mind and causes the three signs to swiftly arise and stabilize. Clairvoyance will arise; if it is of benefit to others, it is maintained that one should wear the six ornaments and engage in the conduct of strict discipline.

In this system, beginning with meditating on the first path [of the ascetic] until obtaining the result, the removal of obstacles is not done separately. It is maintained that through sustaining the experience, obstacles, the three illnesses, and the three kinds of spirits will self-liberate.

c. The Actual Result

One obtains the connate of the result in connection with the conduct. That also has three sections: (1) dharmakāya, (2) sambhogakāya, and (3) nirmāṇakāya.

i. Dharmakāya

First, the dharmakāya has a single limb, the pacification of all proliferation. That is accomplished by the third set of experiences on the path.

ii. Sambhogakāya

Second, the sambhogakāya has three limbs: The limb of complete enjoyment is the blazing of the major and minor marks. The limb of union is having a mother of one's own light. The limb of great bliss is the continuum becoming full of immaculate great bliss. That is accomplished by the first set of experiences on the path.

iii. Nirmāṇakāya

Third, the nirmāṇakāya has three limbs: The limb of becoming full of compassion refers to effortlessly benefiting sentient beings while lacking concepts, because of possessing nonreferential great compassion, like a wish-fulfilling gem. The uninterrupted limb refers to the absence of interruption in the nirmāṇakāya through the aspiration to remain [in samsara] for as long as there are those to be tamed, like a pail of water {150} and the form of the full moon. The unceasing limb refers to the fact that, ultimately, the nirmāṇakāya does not pass into nirvana because the accumulations are complete; because the māra of death has been destroyed; and because one has acquired the culmination of the ten powers such as the power of longevity, and so on, pervading everywhere, like the absence of arising and perishing in space. That is accomplished by the second set of experiences on the path. That is the connate of the result, or in other words, the stages of the accomplishing manual of *Accomplishing the Connate*, which include, in brief, the cause, path, and result.

> May the method of instruction on the connate,
> the *intelligent* one's enduring *advice* that nourishes liberation,
> obtain bliss for *limitless* parent migrating beings
> after putting it into practice.[10]

May the chapter on the manual of *Accomplishing the Connate*, composed by Lodrö Taye according to the instructions of the precious lord guru, generate merit.

11. Fortunate Mustard Seedpod

The Manual of the Nine Profound Methods *of Padmavajra*[1]

Jamgön Kongtrul

{152} *namo guru vajradharapādāya*

Having bowed to the supreme siddha Padmavajra,
the inseparable five lord founders,
and Khyentse Wangpo who unifies them all into one,
I shall set forth this manual on the nine profound methods.

From among the eight ancillary path cycles, there are two in the explanation of the stages of the nine profound methods of the great lord of siddhas Padmavajra: (1) the discussion of the source lineage and (2) the explanation of the actual manual of advice that arises from that lineage.

I. The Source Lineage

First, the great ācārya who arrived in secret mantra's place of origin, Śrī Oḍḍiyāna, is known as Saroruha or Padmavajra II. The *Doha Chronicle*, and so on, explain that Anaṅgavajra is one of Padmavajra's names. This tradition asserts that having become the disciple of Anaṅgavajra, Padmavajra composed this treatise. Furthermore, he also composed the ripening empowerment of Hevajra titled the *Island of Barley* (*Nas gling ma*);[2] the creation stage procedure, the *Saroruha Sādhana*; and the completion stage procedure, the *Nine Profound Means*, {153} the *Instruction Resembling the Tip of a Lamp Flame*, other instructions, and so on. Here, the last two [titles] will be explained.

The lineage is traced from Vajradhara to Vilāsyavajra, Anaṅgavajra, Saroruha/Padmavajra, Indrabhūti, Princess Lakṣmī, Kṛṣṇapa, Śrīdhara, and Gayadhara. Drokmi requested this instruction from the latter. It was subsequently transmitted to Setön Kunrik, Zhangtön Chöbar, the five lord founders of Sakya, and then in an unbroken lineage to the lord guru, the omniscient Khyentse Wangpo, through whose kindness I received the transmission.

II. The Actual Instruction

There are two topics in the actual instruction: (1) the concise explanation and (2) the extensive explanation.

A. The Concise Explanation

This treatise on the abbreviated approach and accomplishment of the four-limbed creation procedure—the antidote to the four kinds of birthplaces in dependence on the Hevajra method of accomplishment and adorned with the nine profound methods—is called "the intimate instruction of the complete path." {154} In general, since all meditations on any path of creation and completion appearing individually as this never transcend the essence, the mind essence, and the connate gnosis, inseparable samsara and nirvana are employed as the path. The meaning is stated in the *Hevajra Tantra*:

> This itself called "samsara,"
> this itself is nirvana.
> Nirvana will not be realized
> through abandoning samsara for another.

Thus, this is said to be an intimate instruction based on the meaning of that citation. In the context of the naturally abiding cause, the clear nature of the mind is samsara. The empty nature of the mind is nirvana. Since those two are inseparable as the essence of the mind, when the practitioner practices the path, the basis of purification is samsara, the purifier is nirvana, and the purity of that basis of purification as the essence of the purifier is inseparability employed as the path. The naturally perfected pure result is samsara, transformability is nirvana, and the noncontradiction [between natural perfection and transformability] is realized as inseparability.

B. The Extensive Explanation

Second, in the extensive explanation, to begin, there is (1) the view, realizing that samsara and nirvana are inseparable; (2) the path, the nine methods of placing the mind connected with the path of śamatha; (3) generating certainty with the nine profound methods of severing all external proliferation; and (4) the explanation of the result, the three kāyas endowed with seven limbs.

1. The View

The reason it is necessary to explain the view is that it is mandatory to meditate on the path following the conferral of the ripening empowerment, because it is necessary to sustain the continuity of gnosis and stop the misconception of a personal self. The root tantra states:

> Next, the principle will be correctly explained:
> there isn't the slightest difference between
> pure gnosis endowed with form
> and the conceptuality of samsara.[3]

There are three topics: (1) the inseparability of samsara and nirvana of the cause, (2) the inseparability of samsara and nirvana of the path, (3) and the inseparability of samsara and nirvana of the result.

a. The Inseparability of Samsara and Nirvana of the Cause

First, the inseparability of samsara and nirvana of the cause is described in the root tantra:

> The form of samsara is due to confusion.{155}
> Since samsara is pure in the absence of confusion,
> samsara becomes nirvana.[4]

Since the cause of the three realms is included in relative truth, the various appearances of subject and object; the entity, form, and so on; the outer and inner sense bases, such as the eye; and all the suffering of adventitious conceptuality, such as the three poisonous afflictions, and so on, are samsara.

When an unconfused mind investigates those and realizes them to be nirvana—the ultimate nature that is nonarising by nature—an entity called "samsara" that exists apart from that ultimate nature is not established. Since there is no nirvana established apart from samsara, their same taste, like pouring water into water, is nirvana inseparable from samsara, and is also called "the union of the two truths" in general dharma terminology.

The above should be applied to what follows: The appearances in the universe are the celestial mansion. All inhabiting sentient beings are the nine deities. For example, though gold may have a patina, it appears yellow through its nature. Similarly, even though the body and mind appear with concepts, their essence is understood to be naturally free from proliferation.

b. The Inseparability of Samsara and Nirvana of the Path

Second, in the inseparability of samsara and nirvana of the path, with respect to the creation stage, since the entire outer universe has the nature of a celestial mansion, the former appears as the latter. Since all six classes of migrating beings that inhabit it have the nature of the nine deities, the former appear as the latter. Since the phenomena—the universe and beings, and their nature, the maṇḍala of nine deities—have a support/supported relationship, they are essentially the same. Since the celestial mansion will not be found elsewhere apart from the universe and the deities will not found apart from the beings, samsara and nirvana are termed "inseparable."

With respect to the completion stage, the appearance of the impure three realms and the maṇḍalacakra {156} are respectively included as one taste in dharmatā, the dhātu of emptiness. Since the mind essence is realized to be the great bliss of gnosis, samsara and nirvana are termed "inseparable." This is the meaning of the root tantra passage:

> In this there is no beginning, middle, or end,
> neither existence nor nirvana,
> neither self nor other—
> this is supreme great bliss.[5]

c. The Inseparability of Samsara and Nirvana of the Result

Third, the inseparability of samsara and nirvana of the result means that since one realizes samsara is not established by nature at the time of the culmination of cultivating the path, one can place the entire three realms inside a single pore. Also, those [three realms] arise implicitly as pure buddhafields, nirvana, which is the inseparability of samsara and nirvana of the rūpakāya. Since one realizes all samsara and nirvana to have the nature of the gnosis of the immaculate dhātu, there is nothing to accept or reject and no grasping to renunciation or attainment, termed "the gnosis of transformation." The so-called "merger of buddhahood and sentient-beinghood in one continuum" in dependence on the continuum of a single person is termed "the inseparability of samsara and nirvana of the dharmakāya." As such, the necessity to understand the inseparability of samsara and nirvana in all three contexts—cause, path, and result—is not only the position of this ācārya, but also that of Ārya Nāgārjuna, who states:

> Samsara and nirvana
> are posited by those who do not see the truth.
> Neither samsara nor nirvana
> are posited by those who see the truth.[6]

2. The Path

Second, in the stages of practice, there are two topics: (a) the concise explanation and (b) the extensive explanation.

a. The Concise Explanation

There are four birthplaces that are the basis of purification for the four kinds of persons. Among those four birthplaces, birth from moisture and heat is divided into two, totaling five birthplaces. Since the purifier, the procedure of creation, is meditating on the complete path of outer shape, {157} this results in the culmination of the paths of accumulation and application. There are three persons beyond those [two paths]. The body of the first of these arises as the deity in dependence on the path of investigating the nāḍī maṇḍala of the body and reaches the culmination of the path of seeing. The second of these sees the maṇḍalacakra of the nāḍī syllables in dependence upon the connate bliss of the bhaga maṇḍala and reaches the culmination of the path of cultivation. The third of these sees a multicolored bindu as the bodhicitta maṇḍala and actualizes the ultimate path. This is how the latter three persons progress on the path through the three secret dharma maṇḍalas of the completion stage.

The first of those five are the two persons who practice the creation stage: the beginner and the body maṇḍala practitioner, the person who gives rise to slight bliss. The practitioner of the bhaga maṇḍala is a person who gives rise to the experience of bliss and emptiness. The practitioner of the bodhicitta maṇḍala is a person who gives rise to greater experience. Further, among those four [who practice the creation stage] is the inferior one who is totally bound up with afflictions, the average one who is partially liberated from afflictions, the middling one who is mostly liberated from afflictions, and the best who is liberated from all afflictions.

Among those four persons [who practice the creation stage] are the beginner, the one upon whom gnosis has descended, the one with slight control over gnosis, and the one with control over true gnosis. These four reach the culmination of the paths of accumulation and application.

When applied to the creation procedure, the first person meditates on the direct realization procedure for the first heat and moisture birth, the second person meditates on the direct realization procedure for the second heat and moisture birth, the third meditates on the direct realization procedure for egg birth, and the fourth meditates on the direct realization procedure for apparitional birth for the principal and womb birth for the retinue; that is, the generation of the commitment being is the limb of the approach. Next, the entry of the gnosis being {158} is the limb of near-accomplishment. The key points of the empowerment are the complete limbs of accomplishment and great accomplishment. This is the ācārya's position.

b. The Extensive Explanation

There are two topics in the extensive explanation: (1) the way the four kinds of person progress through the paths of accumulation and application and (2) the way the four persons beyond those [paths] progress on the path toward the culmination of the path of seeing.

i. Progress through the Paths of Accumulation and Application
I) The Beginner

First, among these four persons, the beginner requests the full four empowerments from a lama who holds the lineage. Also, after having obtained the reading transmission of the sādhana, they must practice in four regular sessions. In that practice, there is (1) the yoga of equipoise, (2) the yoga of post-equipoise, [and (3) the measure of signs].

A) The Yoga of Equipoise

In the yoga of equipoise, the beginner must meditate the following in succession according to the direct realization of these recitations: (a) the preliminaries and (b) the main subject: (i) the creation stage, (ii) the nine methods of placing the mind, and (iii) focusing the mind on the completion stage.

1) The Preliminaries

To begin, there are the preliminaries, refuge, generating bodhicitta, and Vajrasattva meditation, which are practiced during the first session. If those are not included in later sessions, it is acceptable.

Next, to gather the accumulation of merit, oneself appears as the Hevajra couple. Light rays shine from *hūṃ* in one's heart, inviting the nine-deity maṇḍala of Guru Śrī Hevajra, whose head is adorned with the form of Akṣobhya and who is surrounded by all the buddhas and bodhisattvas, arising as a rūpakāya from the dharmadhātu. Offer a prostration. The eight goddesses—Gaurī, and so on—emanate from the heart, presenting offerings.

Having already gone for refuge to the Three Jewels, gather the accumulation of merit based on the pure field: confess misdeeds, rejoice in merit, uphold ultimate bodhicitta, go for refuge to the Three Jewels, generate aspirational bodhicitta, generate engaged bodhicitta, and {159} dedicate the root of virtue for the benefit of others. Gather the accumulation of merit on the impure field by meditating decisively, merging one's continuum with the four immeasurables: love, the wish that all sentient beings have happiness; compassion, the wish that they all be free from suffering; joy, the wish that they never be free from happiness; and equanimity, the wish that they be free from attachment to those near and far.

"Gathering the accumulation of gnosis" means arising as an illusory rūpakāya from having realized the dharmakāya. Since one already has the sincere wish to benefit sentient beings, without perceiving any apparent phenomena, rest in equipoise in the inexpressible state of reality. Recall the meaning of the *śunyatā* mantra: having realized that naturally pure emptiness (the object) is nondual with gnosis (the subject), one also thinks that both subject and object are naturally pure.

2) The Main Subject

a) The Creation Stage

In the main subject's creation stage, *paṃ* arises from the state of emptiness, from *paṃ* arises a lotus, and from *raṃ* arises a sun maṇḍala. On top of those is *hūṃ*, from which arises a twelve-tined crossed vajra marked in the center with *hūṃ*. Light radiates from that *hūṃ*. Meditate on the common protection cakra: below is a vajra ground, the horizon is a vajra fence, above is a vajra pavilion, and the area outside is filled with the blazing fire of gnosis. Inside of the protection cakra, meditate on a triangular dharmodaya, inside of which are *laṃ*, *vaṃ*, *raṃ*, and *yaṃ*. From these syllables arise the maṇḍalas of earth, water, fire, and air, with their corresponding general colors and shapes and marked with their respective seed syllables.

The appearance of those maṇḍalas and one's mind merge into one, from which arises the celestial mansion of great liberation, composed of various precious substances, square, with four doors and four-stepped porticos, complete with all features, and beautified with ornaments and decorations. {160} Outside of this are the eight charnel grounds, in which there are the eight trees, eight fires, eight ponds, eight clouds, and eight stupas. Directional guardians, field guardians, nāgas, and yogins reside there. Moreover, inside the celestial mansion, which is surrounded by the terrifying features of the charnel grounds, in the center and in each of the eight cardinal and intermediate directions, from *paṃ* arises a lotus, and from *raṃ* arises a sun maṇḍala. On top of the lotus and sun in the center are the essence of the four māras—Brahma, Upendra, Rudra, and Indra—evenly stacked. On the lotuses and suns in the main and intermediate directions are the eight great worldly ones lying on their backs. On these nine seats are the essence of the thirty-two excellent marks in the form of twice-repeated vowels, like a garland of stars. From the dissolution of these, nine moon maṇḍalas arise, the mirror-like gnosis. Above those are the essence of the eighty minor marks, the thirty-four consonants, and *ya*, *ra*, *la*, *wa*, *ḍa*, and *ḍha* repeated twice, which are as bright as the sun. From the dissolution of these, sun maṇḍalas arise, the gnosis of uniformity. In the center, in between the conjoined sun and moon is *hūṃ*, from which arises a white skull marked with a crossed vajra, which is marked in the center with *hūṃ*. To the left of the skull is *aṃ*, from which arises a dark-blue curved knife marked with *aṃ* on the hilt, the individually discerning gnosis. From the sun, moon, and hand implements in the center merging together into one taste, the kāya is fully completed, the gnosis of the dharmadhātu. One must merely recall each of these gnoses. Further, the moon is moisture and the sun is heat; those two are the cause. Since those arise from the vowels and consonants, this takes the name "the first birth from heat and moisture."

Furthermore, the Bhagavān Cause Vajradhara is blue in color with eight faces. The principal face is blue, the right face is white, the left face is red, and the remaining faces, two on each side, are black. The upper face is soot-colored. Those have three eyes, four bared fangs, and yellow upswept hair. The crown of the head is marked with a crossed vajra. {161} The sixteen hands hold sixteen skulls. In the eight right hands are held an elephant, horse, ass, ox, camel, human, dog, and water buffalo. In the eight left hands are held the deities of the earth, water, fire, air, moon and sun, and Yama and Kubera. His [faces] are adorned with dried skulls. He has a necklace of fresh heads and possesses the six bone ornaments. He stands in the ardhaparyaṅka posture: the two right legs are extended and the toes of his two contracted left legs are directed toward the right thigh. He possesses the nine dramatic moods. The mother, Vajranairātmyā, has one face, three eyes, yellow upswept hair, and two hands holding a curved knife and a skull. Her head is adorned with five dried skulls. She wears a necklace of fifty skulls and is adorned with five bone ornaments. Her left leg is extended and her right leg embraces the father. Both the father and the mother appear standing in the midst of blazing flames of gnosis.

Next, visualize that a red lotus with eight petals and anthers marked with *āḥ* arises from the *āḥ* of the mother's space. A five-tined blue vajra marked with *hūṃ* arises from the *hūṃ* of the father's secret. Bless those by reciting each one's respective mantras. The sound of great bliss as the couple enters into union with the three perceptions invites the tathāgatas, who enter the mouth [of the father]. From the fire of passion, they melt into light in the heart. They descend through the path of the vajra into the space of the mother and transform into eight bindus. Those bindus leave the space of the mother and emanate between the suns and moons in the eight directions, becoming the eight seed syllables: *gaṃ*, *caṃ*, *vaṃ*, *ghaṃ*, *paṃ*, *śaṃ*, *laṃ*, *ḍaṃ*. From all of that merging into one, in the east there is a curved knife; in the south, a ḍamaru; {162} in the west, a tortoise; in the north, a snake; in the northeast, a lion; in the southeast, a bhikṣu; in the southwest, a wheel; and in the northwest, a multicolored vajra. All are marked in the center with their respective seed syllables. Imagine that from those arise the complete kāyas with the nature of the five gnoses.

In the east, black Gaurī holds a curved knife in her right hand and a rohita fish in her left hand. In the south, red Caurī holds a ḍamaru in her right hand and a skull in her left hand. In the west, yellow Vetalī holds a tortoise in her right hand and a skull in her left hand. In the north, green Ghasmarī holds a snake in her right hand and a skull in her left hand. In the northeast, blue Pukkasī holds a lion in her right hand and an ax in her left hand. In the southeast, white Śavarī holds a bhikṣu in her right and a mendicant's staff in her left hand. In the southwest, blue Caṇḍālī holds a wheel in her right hand and a hoe in her left hand. In the northwest, multicolored Ḍombinī holds a vajra in her right hand and makes a threatening gesture with her left hand. All are meditated on with accoutrements similar to those of the principal. As such, one should recall that the complete aspects of the nine deities are sambhogakāya in great bliss.

Once again as the father and mother enter in union, all ṇāḍīs are filled with the pure essence of bodhicitta, which the fire of passion melts into bindus. One experiences the connate gnosis of immaculate great bliss. The fire of the great bliss of passion melts both the father's and mother's aggregates, sense elements, and sense bases into light and is visualized transforming into the form of a bindu of light. The meaning is that the dissolved father is gnosis and the dissolved mother is the bindu, who [together] are imagined as the dharmakāya, the nonduality of the dhātu and gnosis.

Having directed the stream of samādhi toward the goddesses of the intermediate directions, think, "Principal, arise from the dharmakāya's bindu of light in order to benefit sentient beings and for the purpose of immaculate great bliss." In order to recall that:

> Lord with a compassionate mind, arise . . .[7] {163}

The four goddesses who represent the four immeasurables invoke the principal with the vajra song, and the bindu transforms into three parts: below the bindu, a moon arises from the vowels; above the bindu, a sun arises from the consonants; and the bindu in between those is marked with a seed syllable. From those merging, the kāya becomes fully completed with the nature of the five gnoses. Like the cause Vajradhara above, recall the complete faces, hands, and ornaments of the result Vajradhara father and mother. In the center of the conjoined suns and moons within the hearts of the principal and retinue are their seed syllables, radiating light and transforming the universe into the celestial mansion and the inhabiting beings into the nine-deity maṇḍala. The light rays return, dissolving into oneself. This meditation is the limb of the approach. Later, there is familiarization in the five paths. This abbreviated gradual procedure of entry is the root of the creation stage in what follows below.

The summoning and entry of the gnosis maṇḍala: Since light rays shine from the syllable in the heart of the principal, while imagining the nine-deity maṇḍala of the mansion and deities invited into the sky in front, perform the vajra-summoning mudra. Light rays gather into the seed syllable in the heart. Again light rays shine forth. After the maṇḍalas of the commitment beings and gnosis beings become extremely vivid, the light rays return again. From the light rays of the seed syllable in the heart, visualize an infinite number of the eight goddesses, Gaurī, and so on, each carrying their own offering substance, presenting those to the gnosis being, and offering praise. One should use the offering and praise of the words of the tantra. Gaurī arises from one's heart holding a hook, and by touching the gnosis being on the heart, draws it into the protection cakra. Caurī arises from one's heart holding a noose, and by touching the gnosis being on the throat, draws it to the brow of each commitment being and dissolves. Vetalī arises from one's heart holding a chain {164} and causes the commitment being and the gnosis being to merge by touching their feet. Ghasmarī arises from one's heart holding a bell; its sound is imagined to be the essence of the commitment being and the gnosis being. One should perform the mantra and mudra for each one. This is the second limb, the near-accomplishment.

Then, in the heart of the principal and the retinue, in the six places (eye, ear, nose, tongue, forehead, and heart) and the three places [head, throat, and heart] appear lotuses, suns, and corpses. White Mohavajrā arises from *muṃ* in the eyes, blue Dveśavajrā arises from *daṃ* in the ears, yellow

Mātsaryavajrā arises from *paṃ* in the nose, red Rāgavajrā arises from *raṃ* in the mouth, green Īrṣyavajrā arises from *aṃ* at the forehead, black Nairātmyayoginī arises from *naṃ* in the heart, white Kāyavajrā arises from *oṃ* at the crown, red Vakvajrā arises from *aḥ* at the throat, and blue Cittavajrā arises from *hūṃ* in the heart. Recall that all have one face, two hands, three eyes, and upswept yellow hair. They are naked and adorned with five bone ornaments. They have head ornaments made of five dried skulls and necklaces made of fifty dried skulls. They stand on corpses in the ardhaparyaṅka dancing posture with the left leg extended, in the midst of a blazing fire of gnosis. This is the third limb, the accomplishment.

Light rays from the heart invite the five families of the tathāhatas, the four mothers, the eight bodhisattvas, the six goddesses, and the ten wrathful ones. The eight goddesses, Gaurī and the rest, present them with offerings and praise. Because of this supplication, the tathāgatas transform into herukas holding precious vases filled with amṛta and bestow empowerment while reciting verses and mantras. The vidyās sing vajra songs, the bodhisattvas recite benedictory verses, the wrathful ones frighten away obstructors, and the goddesses present offerings.

The stream of bodhicitta fills the area from the crown to above the brow; one receives the vajra master vase empowerment. The taints of the body are purified; {165} one should feel empowered to meditate on the yoga of the creation stage. The ultimate level of the creation stage is connected to donning the armor and meditating on the purities of the ornaments in order to clarify the aspect of mindfulness.

Since the stream of bodhicitta fills the area above the throat, one obtains the secret empowerment, the taints of the voice are purified, and one should feel empowered to meditate on the path, the self-empowerment. The ultimate level of the self-empowerment is the caṇḍālī yoga based on four cakras. Since the seal of the four cakras supports the vāyu and the mind, this is connected to the meditation on the first mental focus.

Since the stream of bodhicitta fills the area above the heart, one obtains the gnosis of the prajñā empowerment, the taints of the mind are purified, and one should feel empowered to meditate on the path of the mudra. Since one experiences the connate joy, as the outer sign of that, one meditates on the blessing of the senses bases; the body, speech, and mind connection with the six sense consciousnesses rests naturally on the six sense objects, free from clinging to body, voice, and mind.

Since the stream of bodhicitta fills the area between the navel and the secret place, one obtains the empowerment of supreme great bliss. The taints and traces of the three doors are purified, and one should feel empowered to meditate on the path of the completion stage. Since that empowerment is obtained, this is connected with meditating on the union of bliss and emptiness without perceiving the dualistic appearances of samsara and nirvana.

Following that empowerment, there is the seal of the master of the family. The excess water overflows, adorning the heads of the principals, father and mother: Gaurī and Pukkasī with Akṣobhya, Caurī and Śavarī with Vairocana, Vetalī and Caṇḍālī with Ratnasambhava, and Ghasmarī and Ḍombinī with Amitābha. One regards those [masters of the family] as nirmāṇakāyas. When practicing this alone, {166} one should seal the empowerment after the entry of the gnosis being. Then, to employ the vase empowerment of the path, recall the purities of the six ornaments and bind the armor: The crown wheel is Akṣobhya. The nature of the earrings is Amitābha. The necklace is Ratnasambhava. The armbands are called Vairocana. The apron is Amoghasiddhi. On each limb is the protector Vajradhara. The *aṃ* of the nirmāṇacakra in the navel is the karma mudra. The *hūṃ* of the dharmacakra in the heart is the dharma mudra. The *oṃ* of the sambhogacakra in the throat is the mahāmudrā. The *haṃ* of the mahāsukhacakra in the crown is the samaya mudra.

In order to employ the secret empowerment as the path, meditate on the caṇḍalī with the four cakras according to the intimate instruction. As the outer sign of the gnosis of the prajñā empowerment, bless the sense bases and the three places as mentioned above. The meaning of the fourth empowerment is recalling the purities, either extensively or concisely:

> His eyes are red due to compassion.
> His limbs are black due to his loving mind.
> The four means of conversion are
> said to be his four feet.
> His eight faces are the eight liberations.
> His hands are the sixteen emptinesses.
> His ornaments are the five buddhas.
> In order to tame the savage, he is wrathful.
> The three realities are his three eyes.
> His flesh is known as Pukkasī.
> Likewise, his blood is Śavarī.
> Caṇḍālī is described as his semen.

> Ḍombinī is his pure marrow and fat.
> His skin is the seven limbs of awakening.
> His bones are the four truths.[8]

Now then, having sealed [the master of the family] as set forth in the above summary, at this time one should rest the mind for as long as possible on the features of the maṇḍala's inhabitants and the celestial mansion. After that, if one cannot recall them, or if one is uncomfortable, visualize lights shining from *hūṃ* in one's heart. {167} After the container and inhabitants of the three realms melt into light, they dissolve into the eight charnel grounds. The eight charnel grounds dissolve into the eight faces. The celestial mansion dissolves into the eight goddesses. The eight goddesses dissolve into the eight faces. Then, engage in the samādhi of placing the mind, as below.

b) The Nine Methods of Placing the Mind

Second, the mantra practice of śamatha based on the nine methods of placing the mind is (1) the focusing of the unfocused mind on the nine methods of placing the mind, on the basis of the beginner's direct realization connected with birth from moisture and heat and (2) stabilizing that focused mind. To begin, there is the purpose of understanding the meaning of the tantra. Also, the three purities include both the creation stage and completion stage. From the perspective of the creation stage, the gathering of the accumulation of gnosis is the purity of suchness. The complete form of the deities in the fourfold approach and accomplishment is the purity of the individual deities. The experience of śamatha is called "the purity of intrinsic cognizance." The form of the deities is the basis for focusing the mind. It is necessary to gradually practice the clear appearance in the principal father, the principal mother, the nine deities, the maṇḍala, and the three realms. For each of those, it is necessary to practice with the three stages: engagement, abiding, and arising. With the stage of engagement, one meditates, as above, on the basis of śamatha, the creation stage. With the stage of abiding, the intimate instructions of focusing the mind are practiced according to the instructions taught by the Buddha in the sutras, which are condensed into four verses in Regent Maitreya's *Ornament of Mahāyāna Sutras*. Ācārya Vasubandhu comments extensively on those verses.

As stated in the root manual: {168}

> There are nine stages of focus:
> (1) placement, (2) continual placement, (3) repeated placement,
> (4) near placement, (5) taming, (6) pacification,
> (7) near pacification, (8) one stream, and (9) very even placement.[9]

i) Placement of the Mind

First is the placement of the mind. When the mind, which is not still because it is attracted and distracted by various outer objects, becomes truly collected, the mind is focused on the object; that is, the mind is slightly placed. Since this is an important point of swift development for a beginner, repeat the creation cycle again and again, or if unable, recall the visualization, slightly place the mind, and meditate without being interrupted by distractions.

ii) Continual Placement

First, focusing on the visualization without being distracted elsewhere is placement through the continuity of that focus. Whether the maṇḍala has been dissolved or not, abide in the pride of the principal deity. To begin, focus the mind on the central eye. If that is clear, when it is clear, stop, and after being slightly distracted, meditate again. If it is not clear, when it is not clear, stop, and after being slightly distracted, meditate again. It is extremely important that the visualizations up to this point are extremely clear. Since stopping the visualization extracts the poison of concentration, this is important at all times. When stopping, if the aspect of the previous meditation vividly arises, because it is the poison of concentration, one should permit distraction to another object, such as a vase, and so on. When the previous meditation is repeated again and again, immediately after that, the visualization will become clear.

If the visualization does not become clear with such efforts, meditate by accompanying the visualization with recitation. That also has two parts: visualizing through one's own recitation means reciting, "The central eye has a white sclera, the pupil of the eye is black, {169} the veins of the eye are red and wrathful," extracting the poison, and meditating. If that measure does not make [the visualization] clear, then the visualization that employs someone else means that someone else recites the aforementioned passage; since the poison has been similarly extracted, meditate. If even that measure does not make the visualization clear, then there is visualization through gazing. Draw a very beautiful central eye and look at it; focus the mind on its features and extract the poison. When one stops, if the aspect of the previous meditation vividly arises, because it is the poison of concentration, one should direct the mind to other things as before. Since one meditates in that manner again and again, when the clear appearances arise vividly for the one who wishes for a clear visualization, one arrives directly at the purities of each deity. If one is able to prevent discursive clarity because one wishes for its absence, one arrives directly at the purity of suchness. Based on that, if one practices śamatha, one arrives at the purity of intrinsic cognizance.

Finally, the stage of arising is the dissolution through the completion stage at the time of the session or placement. [The process of the dissolution]—from the dissolution of the universe and all inhabitants meditated on as external into the protection cakra up to the meditation on the *hūṃ* syllable at the heart melting into a bindu of light possessing the essence of the five families—is the purity of the individual deities of the system of the completion stage.

Since the meditation on the dark-red aspect, resembling the tip of a butter lamp, is the essence of great bliss, it is the purity of intrinsic cognizance. Resting without grasping in a nonreferential state is the purity of suchness.

iii) Repeated Placement

Third, "definite placement" or "repeated placement" is when becoming distracted to something else through forgetfulness, one recognizes that distraction and subsequently applies oneself again to that visualization. One focuses on a visualization, like the eye. When that has been forgotten and the mind is distracted elsewhere, since one immediately refocuses by recalling "I am distracted," the mind is placed on the previous visualization. {170}

iv) Near Placement

Fourth, "near placement" is when the domain of mental discursiveness increases greatly; reduce it again and again, and having narrowed it, place [the mind]. At this time when the mind is fatigued by one's visualization, discursiveness and agitation increase. In each session, alternately focus the mind on the uṣṇiṣa on the crown, the crossed vajra, or the fangs. Since one meditates on the foregoing, there will be relief.

v) Taming

Fifth, having recalled the meaning of the teachings of the Buddha and the treatises on the infinite qualities of samādhi meditation, if the aspect of the deity is clear at the time of any of the four kinds of activity without many types of thought, this is the best. If it is unclear, continually recalling just the aspect of the deity is taming the mind.

vi) Pacification

Sixth, "pacification" refers to reflecting on the faults of distraction when the mind is dissatisfied with discursive conceptuality. That displeased mind is relaxed in a nonreferential state and pacified.

vii) Near Pacification

Seventh, "near pacification" refers to removing the faults of samādhi—such as unhappiness, sleep, fogginess, and so on—when they occur with their specific antidotes or pacifying those faults in dependence on the visualization.

viii) One-Pointedness

Eighth, "one-pointedness" refers to samādhi and its associated factors, which is subsequently meditated on as an effortless stream. When the mind abides on the visualization without external distractions, it is placed one-pointedly on the basis of that.

ix) Very Even Placement

Ninth, "very even placement" refers to naturally entering and gaining control over a samādhi that is effortless and naturally perfected, even though there is no purposeful practice due to gradual familiarization and stabilization of the previous visualizations. {171}

As such, having stabilized the mind on one part of the body in dependence on the nine methods of placing the mind, train by systematically switching to visualizing other parts of the body.

In the first session [of the first day], (1) meditate on the central eye; in the second session, (2) recall the three eyes; in the third session, (3) the wrathful wrinkle; and in the fourth session, (4) the nose. If those are not clear, recall the central eye during the four sessions or [. . .][10] in the following visualizations, meditate in the same way until the visualization is very stable.

If one is mentally astute, then in the first session of the second day recall (5) the fangs in the mouth; in the second session, (6) the ears; in the third session, (7) the primary face; and in the fourth session, (8) the primary face and the right white face.

In the first session on the third day, recall (9) the primary face and the right white face; in the second session, (10) the left red face; in the third session, (11) the right two dark faces; and in the fourth session, (12) the left two dark faces and upper face.

In the first session of the fourth day, recall (13) the eight faces; in the second session, (14) the uṣṇīṣa, the ocher hair, and the crossed vajra; in the third session, (15) the head ornaments such as the bone cakra, the earrings, and so on; and in the fourth session, (16) the whole body along with the throat ornament, and so on.

In the first session of the fifth day, recall (17) the head and the whole body; in the second session, (18) the eight right hands with their implements; in the third session, (19) the eight left hands with their implements, the body ornaments such as the human heads, and the volcano; and in the fourth session, (20) the four feet pressing down on the four māras.

In the first session of the sixth day, recall (21) the principal and Gaurī; in the second session, (22) Caurī; in the third session, (23) Vetalī; and in fourth session, (24) Ghasmarī. {172}

In the first session of the seventh day, in addition to these five, the principal, and so on, recall (25) Pukkasī; in the second session, (26) Śavarī; in the third session, (27) Caṇḍālī; and in the fourth session, (28) Ḍombinī.

In the first session of the eighth day, recall (29) the nine deities and the celestial mansion; in the second session, (30) the charnel grounds; in the third session, (31) the protection cakra; and in the fourth session, (32) the maṇḍala of the universe and inhabitants. Thus, one will obtain the clear appearance of the entire maṇḍala in thirty-two sessions during eight days.

3) The Completion Stage

Third, the completion stage is focusing the mind like the tip of a flame. At the conclusion of each session, the entire universe and inhabitants of the three realms dissolve into the protection cakra, which dissolves into the maṇḍala; the maṇḍala dissolves into the celestial mansion; the retinue dissolves into the principal father and mother; the mother dissolves into the father; the father dissolves into *hūṃ* of the heart; and *hūṃ* melts into a bindu of light; focus the mind on that. Focus the mind on that bindu, which becomes like the tip of a flame. That bindu becomes smaller, like a horsehair. That bindu becomes even smaller, meditated on as the size of a horsehair split one hundred times. Finally, after that vanishes, like breath on a mirror, remain in equipoise on emptiness for as long as one is able.

B) The Yoga of Post-Equipoise

Second, in the yoga of post-equipoise, when arising from that equipoise in the state of pride for oneself as the principal, with one face and two arms, in a state of stable clear appearance, recall the purities through reminding oneself with their recitation. Sing the vajra song, offer the uncommon aspiration, and employ walking, eating, sleeping, and so on on the path in accord with the yoga of conduct.

C) The Measure of Signs

Third is the measure of signs. Seeing the five signs during the meditation of the creation stage, the meditation of the completion stage, or when in equipoise and post-equipoise—experiences of consciousness such as smoke, mirages, flashing lights like fireflies, {173} brilliant light like butter lamps, or like a cloudless sky—generate certainty because those arise from being connected with the key points of the instructions. Without those instructions, one will not see those signs no matter how long one meditates. Having generated diligence, if one sees the five signs and stabilizes them by meditating without interruption, the beginner will reach the culmination of the path of accumulation.

II) The Second Person, the One Who Gives Rise to Slight Bliss

Second, after training on the path of accumulation, [the beginner] transitions into the second kind of person. At this time the practice is the same as before, beginning from the invitation of the field of accumulation up to the creation of the celestial mansion. The abbreviated creation procedure is the instant creation of the cause Vajradhara, the entire retinue, and the result Vajadhara, without depending on the moon, sun, vowels, or consonants. The remaining three direct realizations—the entry of the gnosis being, the empowerment, and the sealing of the master of the family—are the same as before. Through the power of such meditation, the mind becomes increasingly stable. Through the power of increasing the expansion and contraction of the vāyu and mind, bliss blazes in the body at the time of the accumulation of merit. Bliss and emptiness predominantly arise in the mind at the time of the accumulation of gnosis. Bliss and emptiness of the mind and body are unified at the time of the main practice of creation and completion. From time to time the appearance of the deity is empty and in motion. Dreams that seem clairvoyant arise, and one arrives at the level of heat on the path of application through the four empowerments, obtaining a slight bliss and a slight gnosis.

III) The Third Person, the Attainer of Bliss

When advancing beyond that, [the second person] transitions to the third person. {174} The practice at this occasion reduces the components of the creation procedure. The invitation of the accumulation field up to the celestial mansion is the same as before. Instantly imagine *aṃ* and *hūṃ* on the seat of the principals. Those are invoked by reciting the vowels and consonants. It is also permissible not to recite the vowels and consonants and merely create the principal from the melting of the seed syllable. Bless the space and the secret. The goddesses are also created as before from the seed syllables that issue [from the space of the mother]. Also, the result Vajradhara is created from the bindu transforming into *aṃ* and *hūṃ*. The three limbs—accomplishment, and so on—are the same as before. If one proceeds in that manner, also the appearance of the deity is primarily the completion stage. On occasion, the aspect of the deity will be unclear, and one will perceive it transform into many appearances such as Cakrasaṃvara, and so on, even though one is meditating on Hevajra. Also, one will perceive a diversity of deluded appearances, such as the city of the six realms, and so on. The maṇḍalacakra will vanish into mist, like smoke, and so on. Thus, one arrives at the level of peak on the path of application, taking the name, "attainment of bliss" or "power over gnosis."

IV) The Fourth Person

When advancing beyond that, [the third person] transitions to the fourth person. Their meditation is the same as before with respect to the gathering of the two accumulations, but the protection cakra and celestial mansion are instantly created. Inside those, the principals are instantly created. The space and the secret are instantly blessed. Since those are united, the tathāgatas are invited, entering the mouth [of the male principal], melting at the level of his heart, and generated as goddesses in the place of the sexual organs, emerging into the eight directions. The remaining three limbs are the same as before. Here, the direct realization of creating the principals is according to apparitional birth, and the retinue is created according to womb birth. {175} Through the power of such meditation, one can perceive the six realms of samsara in one's experience. One can also perceive the buddhafields of nirvana. At that time there is no distinction between equipoise and post-equipoise, and the body and mind are placed in stable bliss and emptiness. At that time the ḍākinīs make effort to cause obstacles. After the entire sky becomes filled with ḍākinīs saying, "Give us siddhis," they rain down weapons, burn one with fire, and throw one into the ocean. Show the sign and these obstacles will be reversed. If the sign is understood and the ḍākinī shows her own form, since one enters into union with her, one will instantly see the truth. Even if one does not enter into union with her, one will receive empowerment from the nirmāṇakāya and arrive at the level of patience on the path of application.

V) The Persons Who Advance Beyond

The person who advances beyond that instantly gathers the two accumulations. As it is said:

> One should meditate on the vajra maṇḍala
> in the snap of a finger.

The commitment maṇḍala is instantly created. Due to the mind being gnosis in essence, such a person dispenses with the summoning and entry of the gnosis maṇḍala [the limb of near accomplishment]; the person who advances beyond that dispenses with donning the armor, the seal of the third empowerment [the limb of accomplishment]; and the person who advances beyond the latter dispenses with the conferral of empowerment and sealing the master of the family [the limb of great accomplishment]. It is not that they do not meditate, rather they naturally do not visualize the procedure. Among the two paths of the creation stage and the completion stage, they have arrived at nonmeditation, called "dispensing with the creation stage." They become free from the twenty-two samayas and are called "attainers of great bliss" or "great power over gnosis," arriving at the level of the supreme mundane dharmas of the path of application. {176}

ii. Progress on the Path to the Culmination of the Path of Seeing

The second foundation is the way the four kinds of persons progress on the paths of seeing and cultivation. Having arrived at the culmination of the four aspects of the path of application, instantly the nāḍīs, and so on, of the body maṇḍala become evident. Since the nāḍīs themselves are seen as deities, there is no need to meditate on the outer maṇḍala of deities because the body itself arises as the deity. Since one examines and meditates on the body maṇḍala again and again, the meaning of the explanation given by the gurus of the past [is understood]. When the body maṇḍala is realized, one obtains the name "siddha." Also, that is called "seeing the truth." The person who transcends the world realizes the meaning of gnosis, arriving at the level of the path of seeing.

After such a realization, they arrive at the head of the path of cultivation. Such a person beyond the path of seeing manifests the bhaga maṇḍala, personally seeing all the nāḍī syllables of the vowels and consonants. One will see the nāḍī syllables of the tathāgatas of the ten directions, the five ḍākinīs, the five families, and so on as undifferentiated from *bhrūṃ* and *āṃ* in their own heart. Due to the stability of samādhi, they investigate and meditate on the bhaga maṇḍala again and again.

The person who is beyond that manifests the bodhicitta maṇḍala. Since they gather the ten elements, the five amṛtas, and the five vāyus, which fall where they wish into the nāḍīs and nāḍī syllables, they obtain power over reversal. Their ten elements are realized to be indistinct from the buddhas of the ten directions. Many tathāgatas in a single bindu do not contradict same flavor. That person who investigates and meditates on the bodhicitta maṇḍala again and again applies both the bhaga maṇḍala and the bodhicitta maṇḍala on the level of the path of cultivation. {177}

Since the person who is beyond that arrives at the culmination of conduct because they have obtained power over all three maṇḍalas, they rely on a mudra and apply the experience to the mind. Since they impartially enjoy the five castes, brahmins, and so on, they enjoy the four mudras, Locana, and so on. Like the great lord of yogins Virūpa, they are liberated in a single night in dependence on a padminī, arriving at the level of the path of attaining perfection. At the conclusion, when the two continuums are liberated simultaneously, the seven limbs of the three kāyas are accomplished. That will be explained below.

3. Generating Certainty with the Nine Profound Methods

The third general topic is developing certainty with the nine profound methods. Since all paths of the four divisions of tantra are complete in that direct realization of the path, as explained above, and since there is no need to train in them separately, confidence arises in this. Based on this confidence, the nine profound methods are explained for the purpose of authoritatively understanding all meditations.

(1) "This method is many" refers to a single stream of bodhicitta from the perspective of it being complete on this path of the four tantra divisions, laughing, gazing, and so on. (2) This method is not incomplete from the perspective of the complete path of the three yānas. From among the four joys at the time of the empowerment, joy replaces the path of śrāvakas, supreme joy replaces the path of pratyekabuddhas, and joy of separation replaces the path of bodhisattvas. (3) This method is vast from the perspective that just as nirvana is transformed into the path, the afflictions are transformed into the path, which can be understood from the inseparability of samsara and nirvana, as already explained. (4) This method is easy because the result, great bliss, is accomplished in dependence on not abandoning the five objects of desire, the bliss of the path. {178} This is explained from the perspective of what is to be accepted. Alternatively, since all phenomena of samsara and nirvana are meditated on as a single maṇḍala, it is easy because they are transformed into meditation. (5) This method is profound because beginning from gathering the accumulation of merit, whatever is to be done

or has been done is recognized to be one's own mind, the nature of a unique connate gnosis. One is liberated by practicing because the object to be purified and the purifier are not distinct. (6) This method is not difficult because the suffering of hardships and austerities are not employed as the path. One's attitude is relaxed about food because of the yoga of eating; one's attitude is relaxed about the five objects of desire because of the yoga of conduct; and one relies on a mudra through the yoga of passion. Since one abandons suffering based on the bliss of the path, this path takes the name from the perspective of what is abandoned. As such, the sixth takes the name "the profundity of the path." (7) This method is supreme because one meditates on the two stages in a single, definite session (the certainty of session) on one seat (the certainty of place); the diligent one attains buddhahood in a single lifetime (the certainty of time). However, it is explained that even one who lacks diligence will not be delayed more than sixteen lifetimes. (8) This method is prolific not only because the result is accomplished as supreme siddhi on the basis of a single path, but also because it is explained from the perspective of accomplishing all eight intermediate siddhis and the four inferior siddhis, such as pacifying and so on. (9) This method is {179} also inconceivable because all supreme and common results are explained from the perspective of not requiring other causes—substances, and so on—other than being accomplished through the dependent origination of the maṇḍalacakra that inherently exist in one's body, voice, and mind. Also, when summarized, these are included in the profundity of the path and the profundity of the result.

4. The Seven Limbs of the Three Kāyas, the Result

Fourth is the way the result, the three kāyas endowed with seven limbs, is attained. The yogin endowed with the nine profound methods manifests the stage of the seven limbs of the result in dependence upon reaching the culmination of the two stages, the creation stage and the completion stage. With respect to that, the three kāyas are the dharmakāya that is the culmination of one's own benefit, the sambhogakāya that effortlessly produces vast benefits for others, and the nirmāṇakāya that is uninterrupted.

The three limbs of the dharmakāya are essential naturelessness, the limb of the dhātu; the absence of cessation in the nature, the limb of gnosis; and uninterrupted compassion, the aspect of the limb of the inseparability of the dhātu and gnosis. The three limbs of the sambhogakāya are inseparability from the mother of one's own light, the limb of union; a continuum satisfied with immaculate great bliss, the limb of great bliss; and the complete set of special major and minor marks, the limb of complete enjoyment. The nirmāṇakāya is said to have one limb, being filled with nonreferential great compassion. The absence of doubt concerning the accomplishment of those kāyas in this life, the bardo, or within seven or sixteen lifetimes by those of best, middling, and average fortune and diligence is the certainty of Vajrayāna. {180}

Though the completion stage practice for this exists, the instruction of meditating steadfastly, like the flame of a lamp, should be understood elsewhere.

> Having progressed without effort
> upon the inner path of the dance of the miraculous means
> of the instruction of Padmavajra,
> may everyone attain the stage of Lord Vajradhara.[11]

The chapter of the *Instructional Manual of the Nine Profound Methods* from the treatise tradition of Padmavajra was composed by Lodrö Taye according to the command of the precious lord guru. May virtue increase.

12. Essence of Fortunate Curd

The Manual of Straightening the Crooked *by Kṛṣṇa Acyuta*[1]

Jamgön Kongtrul

{182} *namo guru vajradharapādāya*

Having bowed to Kṛṣṇa Acyuta,
the inseparable five lord founders,
and Khyentse Wangpo who unifies them all into one,
I shall compose the stages of the instruction on straightening the crooked.

There are two topics in the explanation of Kṛṣṇa Acyuta's instruction on straightening the crooked: (1) the lineage from which it emerges and (2) the actual explanation of the instructions of the lineage.

I. The Lineage

First, Mahācārya Kṛṣṇa, the practitioner of strict discipline, left Jālandhara to enter into the conduct, the road on which all yogins before him traveled. The ācārya later arrived at the gates of a great city, where he overheard a conversation among some men. One man said, "Some days ago, the one called Acyuta, who traveled in the sky, is without aging and death."

[Kṛṣṇācārya] asked them, "Where does he reside?"

[The men replied,] "He [Acyuta] does not have a certain abode. Sometimes he stays on that cliff over there, and sometimes he stays in that small grove over here," indicating a small grove.

The ācārya went there, noticed a dark-colored naked man with a body like ice meditating there, {183} prostrated to him without reservation, and petitioned, "Please take me as a disciple."

[Acyuta] replied, "I cannot tame you and I cannot [take you as a disciple] without a request for instruction."

[Kṛṣṇācārya] asked, "Who is your teacher?"

[Acyuta] replied, "Maheśvara, who is the disciple of Vajradhara, and his disciple is Acyuta."

[Kṛṣṇācārya] asked, "Where does Maheśvara stay at present?"

[Acyuta] replied, "He is either in union with Uma in the ninth underworld or on the slopes of Meru."

[Kṛṣṇācārya] asked, "When does Maheśvara arise?

[Acyuta] replied, "He arises simultaneously with the 1,002 buddhas."

[Kṛṣṇācārya] asked, "Well then, do you assert that this instruction of yours is a Buddhist path?"

[Acyuta] replied, "I do assert this is a Buddhist path."

Since [Kṛṣṇācārya] requested [Acyuta] to accept him as a disciple, Acyuta replied, "In that case, this is my instruction," and taught this verse:

> If the vāyu is controlled by the wrathful form,
> one will be free from white hair and wrinkles.
> After being freed from aging and death,
> one will become imperishable, like space.

The meaning of this is called "the instruction of straightening the crooked." The crooked nāḍīs are the rasanā and lalanā. {184} The crooked vāyu is exhalation and inhalation. The crooked bindu is semen and blood. Those are placed in the central nāḍī to straighten them. Since the nāḍīs, vāyus, and bindus are controlled, they become the supreme, quick path for progressing to the stage of buddhahood.

The lineage is Vajradhara, Maheśvara, Kṛṣṇa Acyuta, Kṛṣṇācārya, Śrīdhara, Gayadhara, Drokmi Lotsāwa, the five founders, and so on. The omniscient guru Jamyang Khyentse Wangpo, the recipient of the teaching of ripening and liberation, kindly bestowed this.

II. The Practice

Second is the stages of practice of this instruction. To begin, one's behavior should be relaxed for a few days and one should employ massage.

A. The Preliminaries

Then, when engaging in meditation, sit on a comfortable seat, go for refuge to the Three Jewels, and generate bodhicitta as usual. Meditate on the guru on one's crown, generate intense devotion, and recite verses of supplication many times. Instantly recall oneself in the form of the deity of whatever commitment deity one practices. If one conforms to the Sakya tradition, visualize the uncommon object of refuge, the assembly of deities of the Hevajra maṇḍala inseparable with one's guru. Having understood that the guru's mind is the Buddha, their speech is the dharma, and their body is the sangha, one recites five rounds of going for refuge with intense yearning, appealing to the places of refuge until one reaches the seat of awakening. At the end, the objects of refuge melt into light and dissolve into oneself. Imagine that one's three doors transform into the nature of the guru's body, speech, and mind.

One should think, "How unfortunate that all parent sentient beings of the six realms experience only suffering in samsara due to the influence of delusion. In order to free them from suffering, I shall obtain the stage of union, Mahāvajradhara, by practicing the method {185} to attain such a stage, the path of profound Vajrayāna." One should then recite:

> The stage of perfect buddhahood should be obtained for the benefit of all sentient beings. For that purpose, I shall practice this profound path.

On one's crown is a throne of jewels supported by eight lights, upon which is a lotus, sun, and moon seat. Upon that seat is one's root guru in the form of Vajradhara, blue in color, holding a vajra and bell crossed at his heart. He is adorned with silks and jewels and seated with his two feet in vajra posture. Offer any suitable supplications with intense devotion, understanding that he is the union of all jewels of refuge and the source of supreme and mundane siddhis, such as:

> I offer a supplication to the feet of the union of all places of refuge,
> Vajradhara, the kind root guru,
> who is seated on a lotus, sun, and moon seat on my crown.
> Please grant me empowerment and siddhi.

And:

> I offer a supplication to the precious Buddha Guru. Please grant blessings for the special samādhi to arise in my continuum.

Repeatedly offer such supplications with strong devotion. In conclusion, the guru melts into the nature of light and grants blessings by dissolving into oneself. One obtains the four empowerments that purify the four taints. Imagine that one's body, voice, and mind transform into the nature of the guru's four kāyas, and rest in the state of clarity and emptiness without grasping.

To recall the deity, utter *hūṃ*; the place transforms into the protection cakra. Utter *hūṃ* again; the celestial mansion instantly appears inside the protection cakra. Utter *hūṃ* again; in the middle of that celestial mansion, upon a seat of a lotus, sun, and four piled-up māras, oneself is visualized as Bhagavān Hevajra, with one face, two arms, holding a vajra in the right hand and a skullcup in the left hand, embracing a khaṭvāṅga staff in the crook of the elbow, {186} the nature of which is Nairātmyā, present as the essence of nondual bliss and emptiness. His three places are marked with the white, red, and blue syllables, which are the nature of the three vajras of all the buddhas. Recite *oṃ āḥ hūṃ* three times. These are the preliminaries.

B. The Main Subject

Next, for the main subject, there is the meaning of the statement in the root verses:

> If the vāyu is controlled by the wrathful form . . .

Position the body well with crossed legs. The two hands should be clenched in vajra fists, resting on the two knees. The two eyes should be rolled back without being closed. The tongue should be placed on the palate. The teeth should be set and the mouth open. Unite the upper and lower vāyus. Draw up the lower vāyu. Unite the vāyus below the navel. Press the belly toward the spine. Focus on vigorously and gradually sliding the two hands forward until the elbows rest on the knees. Since one tenses the whole body until one's tendons show from the force, all vāyus are controlled. Repeat that twenty-one times. Afterward, release the hold, identify the clarity and emptiness of the mind, and rest. One should engage again with strong effort as before. After twenty-one repetitions, and so on, release, rest, and then increase. Make effort through repeating the number and augmenting the length of the sessions as much as possible.

If strong heat in the heart or headaches arise when intensely training in that yantra, release the hold. If those are not yet pacified, they will be pacified by crying out and eating food. When the samādhi of clarity and emptiness occurs as soon as the body engages in the yantra, one has reached the culmination of the yantra.

The training to modify the yantra in order to stabilize this is as follows: Place the left vajra fist on the heart, raise the right fist into the sky, unite the vāyu as before, and hold and tense the body as before. {187} To reverse that, place the right fist on the heart and raise the left fist into the sky, tensing the vāyu and the body as before. Next, with both the right and left hands, pull a bow and train as before. Then, raise both hands into the sky, tense the vāyu and body as before, and meditate. Next, cross both vajra fists on the heart and hold them, unify the vāyus and hold, tighten the body, and meditate. In between all of those, release the hold and alternate with placement on clarity and emptiness. Whichever of those yantras one holds, the measure of culmination is when an inexpressible samādhi arises in one's continuum. By meditating on these yantras in one's continuum for a long time, one will become free of white hair and wrinkles; wherever those occur, rub one's saliva on that place, which will cause white hair and wrinkles to vanish.

If one reaches the culmination of those yantras, one trains in the conduct of total freedom, enjoying food without regard to its purity or impurity, accomplishing the five clairvoyances, traveling in the sky, and immortality. At that time, since one enhances with the conduct of everything being good, one progresses gradually through the stages and manifests the supreme stage of buddhahood.

At this time the obstacle of disturbances to the elements of the body and mental obstacles to samādhi will automatically be pacified, so there is no need for a separate practice to remove obstructions. The obstacles of external māras will naturally be pacified by reciting *hūṃ* and engaging in the conduct of strict discipline.

The result, the three kāyas endowed with seven limbs, will be obtained. There is the limb of naturelessness for the dharmakāya. There are three [limbs] for the sambhogakāya: union, great bliss, and complete enjoyment. {188} There are three [limbs] for the nirmāṇakāya: great compassion, uninterrupted, and unceasing. Having realized the dharmakāya for one's own benefit and the rūpakāya for the benefit of others, the sambhogakāya and the nirmāṇakāya arise without interruption for as long as samsara exists.

> Having filled a golden teacup of wisdom
> with the amṛta elixir of profound instructions
> that easily dispels the infinite sufferings of birth and aging,
> I have elaborated on it here just a bit.

The manual on straightening the crooked nāḍīs, vāyus, and bindus by Kṛṣṇa Acyuta was composed by Lodrö Taye according to the command of the precious lord guru. May virtue increase.

13. Excellent Tree of Fortunate Bilva

Ārya Nāgārjuna's Manual Obtained in Front of a Stupa[1]

Jamgön Kongtrul

{190} *namo guru vajradharapādāya*

Having bowed to Śrī Nāgārjuna,
the inseparable five lord founders,
and Khyentse Wangpo who unifies them all into one,
I shall set forth the manual on *Ascertaining the Mind*.

Among the eight ancillary path cycles, there are two parts to the instruction called *Obtained in Front of a Stupa*, based on [the encounter between] the great brahmin Saraha, the forefather of the ocean of siddhas of the land of the noble ones (*'phags yul*), and the glorious protector Ārya Nāgārjuna, the second teacher in the doctrine of the victor. Based on the method of meditation, it is also called *Instruction for Ascertaining the Mind*; based on the object of meditation, it is called both *Meditation on Ultimate Bodhicitta* and *Explanation of Mahāmudrā as the Fundamental State*. [The two parts are] (1) the lineage from which it originates, and (2) the explanation of the actual instruction found there.

I. The Lineage

Saraha composed the *Treasury of Couplets* based on the bodhicitta of Akṣobhya in chapter 2 of the *Guhyasamāja Root Tantra*:[2]

> The entities of the three realms
> are meditated on as nonexistent in the ultimate. {191}

An actual meditation on nonexistence
is a meditation not to be meditated.
Thus, neither the existent nor the nonexistent
are objects of meditation.

Ācārya Ārya Nāgārjuna composed the *Commentary on Bodhicitta* based on the bodhicitta of Vairocana from chapter 2 of the *Guhyasamāja Tantra*:

Free from all entities,
devoid of aggregates, sense elements, sense bases,
apprehended objects, and apprehending subjects,
since phenomena uniformly lack identity,
one's mind did not arise from the beginning,
having the nature of emptiness.

This instruction is the condensed essence of those two.

The stages of the lineage of Mahāvajradhara, Vajrapāṇi, Saraha the Great, Ārya Nāgārjuna, Āryadeva, Bhikṣu Kṛṣṇa, Candrakīrti, Brahmin Śrīdhara, Vīravajra, Mugulungpa, Se Kharchung, Je Gönpowa, and the Jetsun Sakya uncles and nephews {192} are a stream of transmission gathered in the great visions of the omniscient lord guru, Jamyang Khyentse, who is my guide.

II. The Actual Instruction

There are seven topics in the explanation of the actual instruction for practice: (1) ascertain the view, (2) gather the accumulation of merit, (3) control the mind in its own place, (4) introduce it to reality, (5) connect with conduct, (6) remove obstructions, and (7) [determine] how the result is attained.

A. Ascertaining the View

There are two topics in ascertaining the view: (1) placing the significance [of the view] in the mind and (2) establishing the topic to be meditated on in the intellect.

1. The Significance of the View

There are three subtopics in the first topic: (1) identifying the entity to be meditated on, (2) the method of meditating on that in equipoise, and (3) the inclusion of the modes of arising in post-equipoise.

a. Identifying the Entity to be Meditated On

The *Commentary on Bodhicitta* states:

> The bodhicitta of the Buddha
> can neither be obscured[3] by the concepts
> of self, aggregates, and so on, nor by percepts,
> but is always asserted to be emptiness.
> The mind moistened with compassion
> is to be meditated on by the diligent.
> Always meditate on the bodhicitta of the
> compassionate Buddha.[4]

The self that is imputed by outsiders is a misconception to be completely discarded. The śrāvakas who impute the aggregates, sense bases, and sense elements, and the Mind Only school that claims all phenomena are only percepts, consciousness is truly existent, and so on may indeed be connected to the path of liberation, but because both are obscured by grasping to extremes, they are not able to abandon the knowledge obscuration. While these positions can be analytically dismantled with the reasonings explained in the treatise systems, {193} doubts can also be eliminated through the points of explanation of the intimate instructions. There is clinging and grasping to the nature of individual phenomena and persons, the two kinds of identity, through the reification of existence based on the connate ignorance, the root of samsara, despite nothing at all being established. Absence of inherent existence is explained as the two absences of identity. Further, the identity of persons is not established at all through grasping to permanence and uniqueness and grasping and clinging to the thoughts of "I" and "mine." The identity of phenomena is externalized clinging to substantial, intrinsic characteristics. Since [grasping] the two identities generates all faults of karma, affliction, and so on, and establishes samsara without a beginning or an end, it is necessary to meditate on the absence of identity in order to abandon samsara. Freedom will be obtained through rejecting the personality view (*'jig tshogs lta ba*, Skt. *satkāyadṛṣṭi*) that grasps self and mine and through exhausting birth through the serial connection of the aggregates caused by appropriating existence.

The principle of absence of identity means that if this so-called self exists, it must arise from self, other, both, or in the three times, but it does not arise from any of those. If the self exists, it must be either the same or different from the aggregates, but neither are established. The phenomena that are the basis of designation of a person—the aggregates, sense bases, and sense elements—cannot be established to arise from self, other, both, or without a cause, and therefore when investigated and analyzed, everything that is apprehended and all apprehensions are not established as truly existent entities. The appearances of a mistaken consciousness's impure traces are not established as truly existent, but should be seen as an illusory display, the forms of a dream, and so on. Though one turns away from clinging to the intrinsic characteristics of the entities of apprehended objects and apprehending subjects by rejecting the two kinds of identity,{194} because grasping emptiness as ultimate and the view of nonexistence are evil views that cannot be cured, it is necessary to abandon them. The *Commentary on Bodhicitta* states:

> Whoever meditates on "nonarising," "empty,"
> "absence of identity," and "emptiness"
> has an inferior nature.
> Those are not to be meditated on.[5]

In reality, since all phenomena of an apprehended object and an apprehending subject appear as mere dependent origination, they are not only empty; if analyzed, since they are not established with an iota of an individual nature, they are neither established as identifiable nor as truly existent, and they cannot be seen as only mind. [The *Commentary on Bodhicitta*] states:

> The Muni explained,
> "All of this is only mind,"
> in order to dispel the fears
> of the immature, but that is not the truth.

In brief, the confirmation of emptiness through the analysis of causes and results, which is the nature of all entities of subject and object (of which the principal [cause] is the connate ignorance of "I" and "mine") through the reasoning of being free from one, and so on, dispels the extreme of existence, while the confirmation of appearances through the reasoning of dependent origination dispels the extreme of nonexistence. The main view is asserting appearance and emptiness in union free from the extremes of existence and nonexistence. When the entity of appearance is confirmed, emptiness is the nonestablishment of the entity or nature of appearances. The apparent mode of appearances is to appear without ceasing; therefore, both [emptiness and appearance] arise inseparably. The *Commentary on Bodhicitta* states:

> Just as the nature of sugar is sweet
> and [the nature of] fire is hot,
> likewise, the nature of all phenomena
> is asserted to be emptiness.[6]

And:

> The relative is asserted to be empty.
> Emptiness is only relative. {195}
> If [the relative] is not [empty,] it won't be produced,
> like products and the impermanent.[7]

All the intimate instructions of India and Tibet first assert that one should understand all phenomena of the apprehending subject and apprehended objects as one's mind. Having confirmed that the mind is empty by nature and not established in any way through grasping it as an entity that exists or does not exist, is or is not, arises or ceases, and so on, in the end, one rests in the view of the dharmatā of all phenomena as the dhātu free from all proliferation.

b. Equipoise

Second, in general, not being distracted from the state of the view is meditation. Further, [meditation] abandons all other perceptions and mental activities apart from mindfulness and attention by merely not losing the state of the view; that is, [meditation] is a naturally settled equipoise through the principle of not meditating at all, as there is no artifice, fabrication, concepts, or analysis. The *Commentary on Bodhicitta* states:

> Abiding without reference points, the mind
> has the characteristic of space.
> The meditation of space is
> asserted to be the meditation of emptiness.

Also, to generate that meditation in one's continuum, it is necessary to possess the support, śamatha, and the supported, vipaśyana. For śamatha, based on the collection of causes of isolation and utilizing the eight factors that abandon the five faults,[8] once the five experiences that arise through the nine methods of śamatha are maintained, when the bliss of the peaceful body and mind arises and continuously sustains those [experiences], it is the characteristic of śamatha included in the stages of concentration. For vipaśyana, initially identify clarity; in the middle, place the mind in freedom from extremes; and finally, develop certainty in inexpressibility and maintain śamatha and vipaśyana in union.

c. Post-equipoise

Third, though all appearances are not established during the space-like equipoise, {196} in post-equipoise when [all appearances] appear clearly according to their mode of appearance, when they appear clearly while being nonexistent—like the entities of the emanated illusions of horses, elephants, and so on—they resemble both the illusionist and his show in terms of how they appear. On the other hand, in terms of how they exist, according to the difference in whether or not clinging arises toward the intrinsic characteristics of horses and elephants, ordinary people cling to appearances, and yogis understand that such appearances are mere dependent origination that are not intrinsically established apart from being mere appearances. Having understood the reality of ultimate bodhicitta, meditation severs the root of existence. The *Commentary on Bodhicitta* states:

> Therefore, the basis of all phenomena
> is peace and equivalent to an illusion.
> Always meditate on emptiness,
> the destroyer of baseless existence.[9]

As such, compassion arises for sentient beings who have not become realized from meditating on emptiness in that way. Since one generated relative bodhicitta and entered into its practice, the nonabiding great awakening is realized and the uninterrupted deeds of buddhahood are produced, which utilize various methods to tame those to be tamed for as long as existence exists. With respect to that, the requirements for first training the mind with the four immeasurables, next, generating aspirational bodhicitta, and gradually practicing engaged bodhicitta are in accordance with the general stages of the doctrine (*bstan rim*). Such requirements are also explained in the *Commentary on Bodhicitta*:

> Generate bodhicitta
> through endeavoring in equipoise.
> There is no other method in the world
> that can accomplish the benefit of oneself and others.
> The Buddha saw no method
> apart from bodhicitta.
> Were the amount of merit obtained
> by merely generating bodhicitta
> to possess form, {197}
> this would fill more than space.
> The amount of merit obtained
> by a person who meditates on bodhicitta
> for an instant
> cannot even be measured by the victor.[10]

The extensive benefits mentioned are the method of training on relative bodhicitta. Here they are abbreviated. If expanded upon, it is necessary to listen in detail to the *Commentary on Bodhicitta*.

2. The Topic to Be Meditated On

Second, for the intimate instructions on the practice of the topic to be meditated on, in an isolated place, relax one's body and mind and reflect in the following way. All phenomena included in the phenomena that arise as appearances of external objects and the inner mind that apprehends them are not created by Brahma, Īśvara, Viṣṇu, and so on, as asserted by tīrthikas. They are also not created by the vital force (*phya*)[11] that determines the destiny of existence[12] famed among Tibetans. [Phenomena] are not composed from particles as asserted by the two divisions of śrāvakas. In order to refute the objections made by the lords of those respective groups, the great brahmin Saraha states in the *Treasury of Couplets*:

> Oh sir, avoid the one who tells lies and misleads.
> If there is clinging, also give that up.[13]

Now then, if one wonders from what do phenomena arise, self and other are grasped out of ignorance and an inability to recognize the intrinsic reality of the mind itself. The concept that grasps to [self and other] is contaminated by traces since beginningless samsara and appears as a diversity of good and bad deluded appearances of accumulated positive and negative karma. For example, even though in a dream there are various positive and negative appearances of humans, animals, houses, and so on, they are only the deluded concepts of the contamination of sleep. After one awakens, the positive and negative appearances are not established as truly existing. [The *Treasury of Couplets*] states: {198}

> [For however long] activity arises from someone's mind,
> for that long it has the nature of the protector.
> Are the water and waves[14] [of the ocean] different?[15]

If one wonders, "Is that mind itself established as truly existent?" when this so-called "mind" is examined (the present clear and knowing consciousness, apart from which there is no other hope), its color, shape, location, foundation, essence, and identity cannot be established at all. The *Commentary on Bodhicitta* states:

> The mind is merely a name
> and nothing other than a name.
> Perception is seen as a name,
> but even names have no inherent existence.
> The victors have been unable to find the mind
> inside, and likewise, not outside
> or in between.
> Thus, the mind has the nature of an illusion.
> The mind does exist as an entity

in divisions of color and shape,
apprehended and apprehender,
male, female, or genderless, and so on.
In brief, the mind has never been
seen and will not be seen by the buddhas.
How can one see
the natureless nature?[16]

As the concise meaning explains, since that entity [the mind] has no cause, at first one cannot find "[the mind] arises from this source, it arises at this time," and so on. In the end when [the mind] ceases, one cannot identify "it goes to this place, this is the result of its cessation." In the middle at the time of abiding, [the mind] does not abide inside the body, above, below, or in the middle. It does not abide in any external object and cannot be shown, cannot be described, and has no form. Dharmatā, which is beyond all identification, is like empty space. Also, the clarity aspect [of the mind], having ceased, does not become empty. {199} The essence of natural luminosity is empty. The empty nature is clear, existing in an inseparable union beyond description, thought, or expression. Saraha states:

It is held that the mind resembles space.
The mind is held to have the nature of space.[17]

Though it is said that [the mind] resembles space, the sign is not established. This is explained from the perspective of the validity of the designation of various conventions, but in reality, space is a noncognizant, inert void, and the mind is cognizant. If the meaning is understood, [the mind] arises as a personally known gnosis. Thus, the meaning of the two are not similar. However, when the mind is investigated with analytical wisdom, the mind is not found. Also, once the investigating concept is pacified, nonconceptual gnosis will arise, and the visual sight of the mind and space will be understood to resemble cessation. Though [the mind and space] are understood as being unseeable, they are described as seeable. The *Collected Verses on the Noble Perfection of Wisdom* states:

Just as "see space" is,
investigate the meaning of "How is space seen?"
Also, the tathāgata explained phenomena should be seen that way.[18]

As such, one should investigate and reflect on that for as many days as it takes for one to attain certainty in that meaning.

B. Gathering Accumulations

The reasoning of these stages of meditation, drawn predominantly from ultimate bodhicitta, not only requires dependence on secret mantra, but also the ācāryas of India and Tibet assert the quick path does not depend solely on empowerment. If the causal accumulation of merit is not gathered, temporary and ultimate bliss will not be obtained, and, in particular, even if the resultant accumulation of gnosis is gathered, {200} without the accumulation of merit, the view of emptiness just as it is will not be realized. The *Collected Verses on the Noble Perfection of Wisdom* states:

> For as long as the root of virtue is incomplete,
> for that long, sublime emptiness will not be attained.[19]

Further, at this time, since the unelaborate activity is primarily explained, also the activity of gathering accumulations is easy. Since the offering of the maṇḍala is presented beforehand, possessing the very great benefit of the full six perfections, and so on, the place should neither have any harmful external distractions nor be filled with dust; inwardly, samādhi should not be unclear. The place should not be a dark, gloomy forest. In a clear and isolated meditation house, sit on a comfortable seat facing south. There should be four maṇḍalas if one can prepare them; if not, one can repeat with the one. First, one should generate sincere bodhicitta, thinking, "I will gather the accumulations in order for the realization of ultimate bodhicitta to arise in my continuum and to place all sentient beings in the state of buddhahood."

Sequentially in the space in front of oneself are the sovereign Vajradhara, the peaceful and wrathful commitment deities, the lineage gurus, and one's root guru, seated as if they were actually present. Arrange a thirty-seven-heap maṇḍala and recite whichever verses one knows, such as *Whatever Offering Substances*,[20] and so on. Visualize separately each of the four accumulation fields above and repeat the offering four times. Also, for the repetition, one should count many repetitions of the verse "The ground is anointed with scent," and so on. After that, with intense devotion imagine again and again that the root guru, the embodiment of all the Jewels, is seated on one's crown. Since going for refuge to the Jewels for the purpose of liberation from the terror and fear of the suffering of samsara {201}is the root of accomplishing the sublime Dharma, the accumulation fields above and the precious Jewel of the Guru who exists throughout space should be used as mental objects. One should recite the words of the fourfold refuge as much as possible. Offer supplications with intense devotion to the general objects of refuge, the root guru in particular, supplications to the lineage, and also the following prayer:

> I supplicate the sovereign Vajradhara
> in the pure buddhafield of the dharmadhātu, Akaniṣṭha,
> the perfect buddha who possesses the seven limbs of union,
> the victor endowed with the four kāyas and five gnoses.[21]

One should merge this with one's continuum. Make effort in maṇḍala offerings, refuge, and supplication in order, without definite sessions and session breaks, until the signs of gathering and blessings arise or for some days, so that the gathering of merit and meditating on the pure continuum will be meaningful.

C. Holding the Mind in Its Own Place

Third, in the middle, holding the mind means adopting a cross-legged posture on a comfortable and soft seat in an isolated place, without allowing distraction in concentration. To begin, one should perform the Mahāyāna refuge in the general way. For the meditation on bodhicitta, [one should think], "Vajra-holding guru, all buddhas and bodhisattvas, please heed me! Just as the bhagavān buddhas and the bodhisattva great beings generated the thought of great awakening, from this time forth until I am on the seat of awakening, I shall generate the thought of great awakening in order to deliver sentient beings who have not been delivered, free those who are not free, provide solace to those without solace, and [assist] those who have not completely transcended suffering to completely transcend suffering." {202}

Having generated aspirational relative bodhicitta through the conduct that employs the door of a secret mantra bodhisattva, similarly, in order to generate ultimate bodhicitta through the strength of meditation, generate bodhicitta by reciting three times, "I shall generate and meditate on the two bodhicittas."

Meditate on the guru at one's crown in their actual form or in the form of Vajradhara and supplicate them with intense devotion. Whatever commitment deity one has, meditate on it vividly and allow the breath to become slower. Then eliminate discursive concepts, and let the eyes be open or closed. Saraha states:

> If one releases this mind that is tied up in worldly distractions,
> liberation is beyond doubt.[22]

Release both the body and mind from within and remain relaxed. Though relaxed, rest comfortably without straining the body and breath or excessively restraining the mind. The key points of the body for concentration are extremely important in every way and must be heeded. With respect to that, the three methods of equipoise are said to be freshness, looseness, and resting in lucidity without fabrication.

Resting in freshness is likened to a brilliant gold nugget. Whatever its nature may be, it is the best of all valuables even though it is unmodified. One rests in one's own nature, an entity free of proliferation from the beginning and devoid of an identity to apprehend, an open clarity that is fresh and free from evaluation.

Resting in looseness is likened to loosening the cord on a bundle. Having totally released the mind so that there is no clinging or grasping, as there is no bondage of affirming or negating, being and nonbeing, good and bad, and so on, it rests loosely by nature. {203}

Resting without modification is likened to a person held in prison who thinks only of escape, but when they remain where they are, they are at ease. When the mind is bound by focal points and opinions, it becomes very perturbed with discursiveness, agitation, and so on. Therefore, the mind should remain at ease, naturally settled in its naturally settled state, without any artifice or modification. What is the need to mention virtuous and nonvirtuous concepts at such times? Since one's understanding was also conceptual beforehand, having abandoned concepts, there is no activity at all in which to engage the mind. As such, though there is no meditation through mental modifications, undistracted mindfulness that does not stray into an ordinary continuum is absolutely necessary. Since one abides in equipoise in that state, the mind is held and the three experiences of abiding gradually arise: slightly stable, somewhat stable, and mostly stable. If through discursiveness and agitation the mind is not controlled, it is said:

> Let the ox of the mind wander.[23]

Without being free of watchful mindfulness, allow concepts to flow. Rest loosely without engaging in doubtful thoughts such as "It is necessary to control the mind. It is necessary for it to be stable," and so on. Since it is allowed to do what it likes, and since it cannot find anywhere to go, it returns to its own place, immediately pacified, and remains. Saraha states:

> Just as a crow flies from a ship,
> circles around, and lands once again.

Since one becomes more and more familiar, the measure of control and stability of the mind is remaining still, like one's hand stuck somewhere with glue, such that it cannot be removed. The outer sign is very languid, forgetful, and as soon as one meets any activity, it is perfunctorily performed. {204} On the other hand, those signs indicate a slightly faulty śamatha, in which subtle lethargy has not been dispelled. When in equipoise, the mind should generate a spacious appearance—open and clear. Free from any desired aim, after the mind develops the force of clarity, an important point is to repeatedly examine it in a firm state of alert clarity, meditating repeatedly.

D. The Introduction to Reality

There are three topics in the introduction to reality: (1) the introduction to clarity, (2) the introduction to resting the mind in freedom from extremes, and (3) generating confidence in inexpressibility.

1. The Introduction to Clarity

Saraha, the great brahmin, states:

> Left alone, like water or a lamp's own illumination,
> I do not accept or reject coming or going.[24]

To practice this, since the clarity and cognizance (*gsal rig*) of the mind is recognized based on the arising of stability of the aforementioned three methods of equipoise, [cognizant clarity] is to be maintained without distraction. Since the true aspect of the mind (the two stable aspects of exposing clarity and cognizance and absence of distraction are grouped as one), the absolute clarity of the mind arises as a genuine, pristine brilliance, like the sun rising in the sky, the crown of vipaśyana shows. The sign of that is clear memory, little forgetfulness, and any activity one encounters is engaged in with great diligence.

2. Resting the Mind in Freedom from Extremes

The *Commentary on Bodhicitta* states:

> Abiding without reference points, the mind
> has the characteristic of space.
> The meditation of space is
> asserted to be the meditation of emptiness.

Having used space to illustrate freedom from extremes, it is to be applied to one's mind and likewise meditated on. Just as for external space there is a conventional designation, "In the beginning it arises here, and in the end it emptied here," likewise, inwardly, when investigated, no basis or foundation for one's mind can be established. {205} Its beginning and end cannot be found. Likewise, just as space does not arise in the beginning nor is destroyed in the end, also one's mind does not arise from anywhere nor is it destroyed by anything. Just as space does not travel to an outer place and return to its own place, likewise, one's mind neither goes to some place nor returns from somewhere. Just as one cannot establish a basis of designation such as "This is the boundary of space, this is its center," because one is unable to identify "This is the boundary of my mind and this is the center," one should recall that it resembles space, which is free of all proliferation, and rest in equipoise. The *Perfection of Wisdom in Eight Thousand Lines* states:

> This meditation of the perfection of wisdom is the meditation of space.[25]

Saraha states:

> The unexamined mind exists like space.
> That space that abides nowhere is free from conventions.[26]

If concepts proliferate on these occasions, since objects of proliferation cannot transcend the three times, also the method of severing such proliferation is taught in the *Sutra of Bhadrakarātrī*:

> Do not follow the past.
> Do not anticipate the future.
> Whatever has passed has ceased.
> The future has not yet arrived.
> Having observed phenomena
> that have arisen at present in this way and that,
> do not be carried away with concepts.
> All those must be comprehended.[27]

If conceptual discursiveness of the mind arises toward objects and entities, actions and agents, good and bad, and so on, immediately control it with mindfulness. {206} Recall, "Do not follow the past," and rest in equipoise in the state that is like nonarising space. Recall the instruction "Do not anticipate the future," and rest in equipoise in the state that is like nonarising space. Whatever experiences of concepts of entities and appearances, good and bad, arise in the present, recognize them immediately, recalling that all phenomena do not arise from the beginning, and rest. The *Union with All Buddhas Tantra* states:

> E MA, the secret of all buddhas
> is that perfect buddhas do not arise.
> Everything arises from nonarising.
> Arising itself does not arise.

3. Generating Confidence in Inexpressibility

To generate confidence in inexpressibility, the realization that arises from equipoise is integrated with post-equipoise conduct. At the time of equipoise, the nature of all phenomena is termed "the space-like emptiness free from all proliferations." At the time of post-equipoise, it is termed "the illusory emptiness," because while the nature or essence is empty, it appears as the aspect of form, and so on. At the time of being a beginner, since the characteristic of equipoise and post-equipoise is absent, at all times there is mainly subsequent knowledge. Once familiarity is stable, when there is a characteristic of equipoise and post-equipoise, where previously one relied on the expectation for effort-based mindfulness, and once mindfulness becomes spontaneous in post-equipoise, one is no longer distracted by subject and object with respect to the arising of apparent objects of the sixfold group. Externally, all appearances, such as form, sound, and so on, are inseparable appearance and emptiness. Internally, all conceptual {207} experiences of the mind are inseparable clarity and emptiness. When the nonconceptual gnosis that arises in between those two arises as inseparable cognizance and emptiness, the reality that can neither be described, imagined, nor expressed is ascertained to be the ultimate dhātu and sustained. It is explained that this is the meaning of Śrī Saraha's statement:

> If there is clinging to something, give it up.
> If there is realization, that is everything.
> No one knows anything more than that.

And:

> Just as an elephant's mind is tractable after training,
> one's mind will relax after coming and going are eliminated.
> Since this is realization, for what purpose would I modify it?

E. Connecting Realization with Conduct

After realization has arisen, connect it with conduct. Regarding the time of conduct, as it is said, "Connect conduct with time." It is necessary to practice each of the conducts mentioned in the *Cycle of Siddhas* and *Essential Texts*,[28] which are applied to the four times, the beginner, and so on: the conduct of Samantabhadra, the concealed secret conduct, the conduct of the strict discipline of knowledge, and the all-conquering conduct.

Regarding the purpose of conduct, when in an isolated place stability in experience and realization arise, one mixes experience and realization with positive and negative conditions to enhance that stability. All employment of the thoughts of the mind while on the path are for the purpose of having the same taste of dharmatā. Though the causes of employment as the path—conceptuality, afflictions, gods and demons, suffering, pain, and death—can be individually employed as the path, all are included within employing conceptuality on the path.[29]

The passage "First, recognize conceptuality"[30] refers to recognizing any sort of positive or negative conditions that arise in any kind of way without engaging in grasping to intrinsic characteristics. {208} The passage "In the middle, mentally abandon self-grasping"[31] refers to anything that arises is not contaminated with negation or affirmation, and thoughts of self-grasping are eliminated. Eat whatever pure or impure food one finds. Associate with good or bad friends without judgment. Wear whatever good or bad clothes one finds without making distinctions. Also, at the start one should engage in those [conducts] little by little and gradually increase.

Finally, one must abstain from any judgmental accepting and rejecting. The passage "Finally, clear the dangerous passage of hope and fear"[32] means that since one acts [without judgment], though concepts of hope and fear arise, such as expectation and disappointment, the hope that a path can be employed and the fear that a path cannot be employed, and so on, those concepts are immediately discarded without grasping them directly because there is no fabrication or modification. As such, having reached the culmination of conduct, a realization that surpasses the first bodhisattva stage will gradually arise, and one will realize the stage of buddhahood.

F. Removal of Obstacles in Meditation

In general, though there are many [methods for removing] obstacles in meditation, deviations, and so on, here this is presented as four: (1) [general] lethargy and agitation; (2) [specific lethargy and agitation]; (3) internally, physical pain; and (4) externally, obstacles of spirits.

1. General Lethargy and Agitation

Though it is said there are many obscurations in samādhi such as agitation, perseveration, racing thoughts, and so on, they are mainly included in lethargy and agitation. There is subtle and coarse lethargy, dullness, fogginess, and sleepiness. There is coarse and subtle agitation, perseveration, doubt, passion, malice, and so on. Though it is said there are many causes of lethargy and agitation, since they arise from the incorrect and improper conduct of the three doors, all explanations in the treatises and oral instructions place importance on proper conduct. Though there are many methods of removing those faults, in general, when there is lethargy, one should lift oneself up by raising one's gaze, {209} tightening the body and mind. The mind and appearances should be vast and vivid spaciousness. For agitation, lower both the gaze and the mind. Do not engage in hope and fear, accepting and rejecting, stillness and movement, or happiness and sadness. Relax the mind in a state of vivid spaciousness. One increases mindfulness that does not allow any distraction from that state. Whether either [lethargy or agitation] arise in the path or not, one should maintain that state by practicing in many short sessions.

2. Specific Lethargy and Agitation

Specifically, if there is lethargy, as it is said [in the root text], "If there is lethargy, place the mind at the crown," directing the mind toward the crown. If that does not remove lethargy, then direct the mind to a light on the crown resembling a brilliant, clear lamp. The mind moves up from the heart as a white bindu connected with a thread, emerging through the aperture of Brahma. Direct the mind into space above the crown.

As it is said [in the root text], "If there is agitation, place [the mind] on the soles of the feet," directing the mind one-pointedly to the soles of the feet. If that does not remove agitation, it will be removed by imagining that the mind moves down from the heart as a black bindu connected with a thread, leaves through the anus, and rests through its weight on the ground.

3. Physical Pain

[The root text] states, "If obstacles of the elements and body occur, use a rejuvenator of the three fruits." Here, since the cause of illness is ignorance, it is generated through motivating karma and afflictions. Since the condition—the incorrect movement of the karma vāyus—disturbs the four elements, the healthy humors (*'du ba*) become unbalanced, and the result is pain and suffering of body and mind. The main method of relative treatment and dependent origination is the antidote to the three pathogenic humors (*nyes pa*), the extended use of the three fruits rejuvenation, which restores good health after the healthy humors become rebalanced.[33] Ultimately, {210} if the practitioner experiences pain, they must recognize that vivid physical and mental pain. It is crucial to meditate on that. Sustain vivid clarity without the mental adulteration of affirming or negating that [vivid physical and mental pain]. On occasion, pull up the root of grasping the self of the one who experiences pain and rest without modification in a state that lacks identification of an entity. Ascertain great uniformity without any hope or fear about being cured or not. Ultimately, the pain, the experiencing mind, and illness are empty, baseless, and without foundation, sustained in a space-like state. Relatively, train the mind with the visualization of sending and taking with great compassion for parent sentient beings who are tormented by suffering and pain, and employ illness on the path.

4. Obstacles of Spirits

[The root text] states, "If there is an external obstacle of spirits, gather body, voice, and mind into *hūṃ* at the heart and recite *hūṃ*, invigorate the body and mind, and perform the conduct of strict discipline." In general, all grasping to the harm of spirits and obstructors is the conceptuality of one's mind. Though spirits and obstructors appear in form, that concept is not recognized for itself, which is nothing other than an experiential appearance of stubborn dualism. It is like apprehending a snake in a rope. Since the rope appears to be a snake, fear arises. Conceptual grasping, which corresponds to the individual actions of the vāyu entering the nāḍī locations of the three poisons in one's karmically ripened body, either causes apparitions to manifest to one in person, or the mind that fears their arising becomes worried with fright, anxiety, and so on. However, one should firmly identify that frightened mind and neither affirm nor negate those concepts that grasp onto demons. Do not think about faults and qualities. Do not engage in any artifice or modification. {211} Since they are recognized as one's mind, sustain that without grasping, clearly, pristinely, and loosely. If such concepts arise in meditation, since they are brought into the path, one becomes very cheerful once the concepts of fear are pacified. Once the harm of obstructing māras has been pacified, they are subjugated.

Though in the beginning those who have yet to master this have difficulty changing their attitudes, and it seems there is little use in virtuous practice, since these [spirits, illnesses, and so on,] are concepts and experiences from the disturbance of the karmic vāyus, if one completely rests those vāyus, gradually [a change of attitude and virtuous practice] becomes effective. During cultivation, merely recognizing concepts arises as virtuous practice.

The specific visualization is having recognized any direct or indirect sign of an obstacle that is under the power of an obstructing māra, meditate on a black *hūṃ* in the heart as the embodiment of one's guru and commitment deity. Gather one's body, voice, and mind into that *hūṃ* and focus one's mind upon it. One should forcefully recite *hūṃ* as many times as one likes, invigorate the body, and engage in the conduct of a madman by jumping, dancing, and so on. This will cause one to be victorious over obstacles.

G. The Result

Since the culmination of practicing the path by such means is connected with conduct, on that basis one obtains the three kāyas endowed with the seven limbs. Further, there is the limb of naturelessness for the dharmakāya. There are the three limbs of union, great bliss, and complete enjoyment for the sambhogakāya. There are the three limbs of one's continuum being filled with great compassion, the uninterrupted wheel of deeds and activities, and unceasingness for the nirmāṇakāya. This is expanded upon slightly in other sources. {212}

> Make effort in this through seeing the effortless accomplishment
> of the supreme stage, which possesses the eight qualities of
> mastery,
> and through the excellent dance of the excellent explanation
> by the great ārya who abides in the lotus buddhafield.

The chapter on the *Manual of the Explanation of Mahāmudrā as the Fundamental State* by Ārya Nāgārjuna was composed by Lodrö Taye according to the command of the precious lord guru.

14. Fortunate Shoot of Dūrva Grass

The Manual of Mahāmudrā without Syllables
Composed by Ācārya Vāgīśvarakīrti[1]

Jamgön Kongtrul

{214} *namo guru vajradharapādāya*

Having bowed to Vāgīśvarakīrti,
the inseparable five lord founders,
and Khyentse Wangpo who unifies them all into one,
I shall set forth the manual on *Mahāmudrā without Syllables.*

There are two topics in *Mahāmudrā without Syllables* from the eight ancillary path cycles, composed by Ācārya Vāgīśvarakīrti: (1) a discussion of the lineage from which it originates and (2) the explanation of the actual instruction arising from that lineage.

I. Lineage

This great paṇḍita, the western gatekeeper of Vikramaśīla, who was taken as an actual disciple of Lady Tārā and in the end attained the gnosis body of Śrī Cakrasaṃvara, is Great Ācārya Vāgīśvarakīrti. It is said that this instruction summarizes the essential points of practice of his many treatises such as the *Seven Limbs*, the *Explanation of Illuminating the Precious Truth*, and so on, as well as the *Light of Amṛta*, the sādhana of Nairātmyā composed by Ḍombi Heruka.

The stages of the lineage are as follows: Lady Ārya Tārā bestowed this instruction upon Vāgīśvarakīrti. Vāgīśvarakīrti gave this to Ācārya Devākaracandra. {215} Both masters gave it to Ārya Amoghavajra. It gradually went to Drokmi Lotsāwa, then Lama Sekhar Chung, Chöje Gönpa, and the Jetsun Sakya uncles and nephews. From them the lineage continued gradually to Jamyang Khyentse Wangpo, the precious lord guru who unified the amṛta of the sublime dharma of sutra and mantra into one river, from whose mouth I heard it.

II. The Actual Instruction

At the beginning of the actual instruction, there is the method of the ḍākinī blessing. However, even though that has not continued to the present day, since the empowerment or blessing of Nairātmyā is useful, that is necessary here.

There are three topics in the actual stages of the instruction: (1) explaining the topic to be understood, (2) explaining the path to be meditated on, and (3) describing the way the result is attained.

A. Explaining the Topic

If it is asked what does *mahāmudrā* mean, *mudrā* refers to sealing all samsara and nirvana with this dharma, just as the decree of a king, and so on, is impressed with his mark. It refers to indicating the reality of samsara and nirvana, just as differences are indicated through emblems such as dharma robes, and so on. {216} It refers to all of samsara and nirvana not going beyond this, just as subjects are unable to transgress the decrees of the king. *Mahā* means there is nothing else higher than this dharma. The *Secret Accomplishment* states:

> Nothing is higher than
> the meditation of mahāmudrā.
> The fourth [empowerment], the cause of the highest,
> is the instrument for direct awakening.[2]

Furthermore, there are teachings on the many meanings of the name in the *Ornament of Mahāmudrā Tantra*, and so on. The *Padmani Commentary* on the *Kālacakra Tantra* explains:

> Since bliss is sealed with nonabiding nirvana or unchanging bliss,
> is superior to the karma mudra and the gnosis mudra, and is free

> from the traces of samsara, it is *mahā*, great. *Mudrā* is the perfection of wisdom that generates all the tathāgatas that have arisen, will arise, and are arising now.[3]

To enumerate its names, Indrabhūti II's *Accomplishing Gnosis* states that ultimate truth, unsurpassed gnosis, Samantabhadra, mahāmudrā, and dharmakāya have the same meaning.

The essence of mahāmudrā is divided into four aspects: it abides nowhere, it is free from characteristics from the beginning, it pervades everything, and it has a space-like nature.

Mahāmudrā has three divisions: cause, path, and result.

1. The Mahāmudrā of the Cause

The mahāmudrā of the cause, or basis, is, in general, the dharmatā of all phenomena, the naturally luminous emptiness free from all proliferation, which pervades all samsara and nirvana. In particular, it is the original reality of the natural state of one's mind that does not apprehend clarity and purity and is free from description, imagination, and expression. The *Garland of Vajras Tantra* states: {217}

> Mudra is the tathāgata's gnosis,
> the stage of nonconceptuality,
> the abode of indivisible Vajrasattva,
> nonconceptual great bliss,
> untainted like space.[4]

2. Mahāmudrā of the Path

The mahāmudrā of the path is as follows: In general, the mahāmudrā of the basis is cultivated with the mahāmudrā of the path, from which arises a genuine realization that is not a realization through abandonment according to the principle that adventitious obscurations are not to be abandoned. The *Garland of Vajras Tantra* states:

> Natureless, free from a basis,
> nondual, without identity, inexpressible,
> the yogin's intrinsic cognizance

> is totally free from the conceptual phenomena
> of aggregates, sense elements, and sense bases.[5]

Specifically, as the *Garland of Vajras Tantra* states:

> Dharma, karma, commitment,
> and mahāmudrā are fully described.[6]

The *Essence of Gnosis Tantra* explains four mudras: dharma mudra, commitment mudra, gnosis mudra, and karma mudra. The tantras and the siddhas explained four mudras, three mudras, and different sequences for those mudras. There are many such inner divisions. In the system of this instruction, view, meditation, conduct, and experience are explained as the fourfold mahāmudrā.

a. Mahāmudrā of the View

The first meditation on the path is the aforementioned mahāmudrā of the view that must be heard from the guru and understood with one's mind. It is the reality of the basis free from indication or expression that has been understood and comprehended on the basis of scripture and reasoning. The *Sutra of Never Wavering from Dharmatā* states:

> All phenomena have never arisen by nature, do not intrinsically abide, are free from all karma and deeds, and are beyond all concepts and conceptual objects.[7]

One should understand that reality is inexpressible from the recurring statements found in all sutras and tantras. {218}

b. Mahāmudrā of Meditation

Generally, the mahāmudrā of meditation is never becoming distracted from equipoise within the state of the view. There are many passages addressing this in the *Commentary on Bodhicitta*, such as the following:

> Abiding without reference points, the mind
> has the characteristic of space.

The meditation of space is
asserted to be the meditation of emptiness.

Specifically, in this intimate instruction it says to merge the example and the meaning. One utilizes the method with the example, contaminated bliss. Having generated immaculate gnosis, the samādhi of the union of bliss and emptiness is employed as the path. Alternately, this is shown with the example of empty space in which no periphery, center, direction, existence, nonexistence, being, or nonbeing can be established in any way. Having applied the example to the meaning that one's mind is empty, free from all extremes of proliferation such as arising, ceasing, abiding, and so on, one practices. There are many similar passages, such as this one in the *Sutra of the Space-like Samādhi*:

Through the blessing of the sublime guru,
one's mind is understood to be like space.
So-called samādhi
is never being distracted from that state.[8]

c. Mahāmudrā of Conduct

The mahāmudrā of conduct is maintaining the conduct of spontaneity. Since a realized practitioner does not engage in any hope for positive things or fear of negative things, there is no grasping or judgment about all the activities that land in one's presence. Whatever appearances arise are directly ascertained. The *Host of Buddhas Sutra* states:

One who wishes to enter the experiential domain of the victors should train in the thought "like space." Having abandoned grasping to analysis, concepts, and perceptions, they enter this domain with a mind that is like space.[9]

The Great Brahmin states:

Just as blazing fire spreads from the forest,
all appearances land before [the mind] in this way.
The root of the mind is recognized to be connate with
emptiness.[10]

Since everything is determined to be emptiness, {219} one should behave spontaneously without any fear toward anything.

d. Mahāmudrā of Experience

Fourth, in general, the mahāmudrā of experience is the different experiences in the mind that arise as a variety without being one-sidedly fixed, having divided the pure and impure parts of the mind once the practice of meditation has hit the key point. When the main reason is summarized, the experience of bliss is being pervaded with the bliss that resembles being unable to feel whether or not there is a body and mind or not knowing whether it is day or night. The experience of clarity is that one's mind is clear as a crystal; there are no other thoughts or cognitions; and one feels that whether one sees an object that is near or far, it is like an appearance of light, even at night. The experience of nonconceptuality is the experience of oneself and everything arising as empty things, like space, without any concepts at all. The essence of all those experiences is free from arising and ceasing and cannot be grasped by nature. If they are understood as nonarising and empty, they can be employed as the path. However, if they are not understood in that way and one engages in realism and attachment to their true existence, one deviates into the three realms. In particular, here, since it is said the experiences of bliss and clarity are in union, the meditator practices the mingled gnosis of the example and meaning, the union mahāmudrā of supreme unchanging bliss and emptiness that possesses the supreme of all aspects. The absence of clinging to bliss and the absence of concepts in clarity beyond everything that is characterized is the meaning of mahāmudrā without syllables.

3. Mahāmudrā of the Result

The result of reaching the culmination of meditating on such a path is realizing the mahāmudrā of the basis and seizing the state of original reality. The reflection of the rūpakāya for the benefit of others arises from the awakening of the dharmakāya and effortlessly produces the benefit of migrating beings for as long as samsara exists.

B. Explanation of the Path to Be Meditated On

In the explanation of the path to be meditated on, {220} there are three fundamental topics.[11] Each of those possess three secondary topics, totaling nine. The three fundamental dharmas are (1) first, focusing the mind; (2) in the middle, taming the mind; (3) and last, placing the mind in reality. The three of the first are (1) focusing the mind, (2) keeping it in its resting place, and (3) avoiding the two extremes. The three of the middle are (1) not allowing the mind to escape to the place where it moves, (2) not allowing the mind to relax where it is placed, and (3) not allowing the mind to either escape or relax. The three of the last are (1) training in the example, (2) applying it to the meaning, and (3) merging the example and the meaning. Since there are three intimate instructions of the key points for each, the brief explanation is that there are nine fundamental topics.

The preliminary practice for all of these is taking a cross-legged position on a comfortable seat in an isolated place. The key point of the body is to be erect. In the space in front of oneself one should imagine Lady Tārā inseparable with the root guru and the lineage gurus, surrounded by an ocean of the objects of refuge, the Three Jewels. With intense devotion one should recite the verses of refuge as much as possible. Taking sentient beings throughout space as the object, generate again and again aspirational and engaged bodhicitta with strong love and compassion. Next, instantly visualize oneself as whichever commitment deity one favors, such as Hevajra, Yoginī, and so on, apparent but lacking inherent existence. Meditate on one's guru, the embodiment of all buddhas, seated on one's crown. Generate heartfelt devotion until tears fall, and one-pointedly supplicate the guru. Supplicate the lineage.

1. Focusing the Mind

a. The Limb of Focusing the Mind

The main subject is the first limb of focusing the mind. Clear the stale air and rest the mind in a nonconceptual state. When conceptuality stirs, it should be immediately controlled with mindfulness. Wherever the mind goes, {221} hold it there one-pointedly.

b. Keeping the Mind in Its Resting Place

The second limb: Since one does not permit that focused mind to become distracted, for as long as one abides with mindfulness and awareness, maintain [that focus] for that long.

c. Avoiding the Two Extremes

The third limb: Without following its path or where the mind arises in the future, in the present the mind stably abides; rest in that state. Since one trains in this repeatedly in short sessions, one will not become weary from the meditation, and conceptual movement will gradually decrease. In addition, place a representation of the Three Jewels, and so on, in front of oneself, focusing the mind on that. If one cannot keep [the mind focused] on that and a concept moves toward a form such as a pillar or a pot, or a sound like the sound of water, or a scent like the scent of incense, recognize the place where it has moved toward and sustain it in that place where it settles. Since one trains in avoiding the two extremes, the sign of focusing the mind is that after the stream of concepts is interrupted, the mind vividly remains wherever it is placed.

If those [methods] do not focus the mind, the procedure for enhancement is to either place or visualize a tall tree in front of oneself and meditate. The key point of the body is to place the feet together, crouching without allowing the buttocks to touch the ground, yet allowing the body to move freely, and exhaling gradually. The visualization is separating one's body into two, placing one's body at the base of the tree. The other body strips naked and then climbs the tree. Imagine that it stays on top of the tall tree, looking down at the base of the tree. Since one looks down at the base of the tree, a clear fear of falling arises. Since one focuses the mind on that, the nonconceptual experience that arises is the mahāmudrā without syllables. If the mind is not controlled by that, the key points of body, breath, and the visualization are just as before. One's body in the treetop seizes the light of the sun and moon. Once seated on the sun and moon beams, visualize that one sees the four continents. Strongly focus the mind on the treetop below. Focus the mind on the base of the tree. Since one focuses the mind on the center of one's body at the base of the tree, {222} the arising of the experience that one's bodies [at the top and bottom of tree] neither exist nor do not exist at all is understood to be the meaning of the reality that is without syllables. Maintain this. Should the mind remain unfocused using that method, or for the purpose of gaining proficiency, switch the object to the center of the space in front, to the tip of one's nose, to one's brow, to one's heart, to one's navel, and so on. Since one focuses the mind with the three key points above, it will definitely become focused.

2. Taming the Mind
a. Not Allowing the Mind to Escape

The first limb is not allowing the mind to escape. If the conceptual mind stirs, immediately control it with mindfulness, do not allow the mind to become distracted toward the object of distraction, and rest directly in the abiding aspect, as before. If [the mind] escapes toward an object, control it with mindfulness by relying on an antidote, prevent it from falling under the power of any distraction. As it is said:

> Conceptuality is great ignorance,
> causing one to fall into the ocean of samsara.[12]

The concepts that are not controlled by the mindfulness of recognition are the root [cause] of falling into samsara. Mere recognition is not enough; it is necessary to liberate those [concepts] into the dhātu of the nature, the absence of inherent existence.

b. Not Allowing the Mind to Relax Where It Is Placed

The second limb is not allowing the mind to relax where it is placed. If the mind is placed somewhere and becomes torpid without a clear, pure aspect, this is faulty śamatha. Since the mind is not tamed, meditate on the physical or imagined representation of the tathāgata and direct the mind toward an object, such as a pillar and so on. After that, switch the mind to another thing and focus. In all instances, [the mind] should be controlled with mindfulness. Similarly, the mind should be allowed to relax for a moment by switching its attention to various objects. Since the mind is never allowed to be dominated by śamatha, the mind is tamed.

c. Not Allowing the Mind to Either Escape or Relax

The mind is controlled with the rope of mindfulness without being dominated by either discursiveness or śamatha alone. If one wishes for śamatha, one has power over śamatha. {223} If one wishes for discursiveness, one has power over discursiveness. Recognize that without allowing the adulteration of distractions either way, [the mind] is liberated without a foundation. The arising of whichever one wants is called "the tamed mind."

3. Placing the Mind on Reality

a. Training in the Examples

The first limb of placing the mind on reality is training in the examples, which has three parts: the time of delusion, the time of understanding delusion, and the time of comprehending that delusion has no basis.

In order to train in those with the twelve examples of illusion, first, when seen from a distance, the entire valley is filled with a mirage. The thought of the valley becoming filled with water as soon as one looks at it is the occurrence of a deluded concept. The arising of the fear "I will die because I will be carried away by the water of this lake" is the time of delusion. When examined closely after approaching the lake, fear is averted through understanding that there is no lake and that it is only the manifestation of a mirage. This is the time of understanding delusion as delusion. As soon as one arrives in that valley, the mirage vanishes without a trace and it can no longer be perceived. This is the time of comprehending that delusion has no basis. Likewise, one should apply these three to all the examples. When the dreamer dreams of fighting an enemy, meeting a friend, and so on, grasping to the true existence of one's form, which is merely an empty figment of the imagination, is the time of delusion. Recognizing a dream through the power of samādhi while the appearance of a dream has not ceased is the time of understanding delusion. Understanding on awakening that the appearance of the dream isn't real at all and lacks true existence is the time of comprehending that delusion has no basis. This [sequence] should be applied to illusions, fairy castles, rainbows, clouds, lightning, echoes, the city of Harikela, and so on. A special confidence will arise, realizing all phenomena have an illusory nature. {224}

b. Training in the Meaning

There are two topics in applying [the three times] to the meaning: (1) applying [the three times] to a recollected appearance and (2) training in a visualization.

i. Recollected Appearance

First, train in any affliction that arises in one's continuum. When intense hatred arises, the unbearable pain of murderous thoughts, such as "That enemy over there must be killed now!" is the time of delusion. After the moment has passed, remaining happy once the anger has been pacified is the time of understanding delusion. The realization that hatred has no true existence, because it is the arising of an adventitious concept of the mind, is the time of comprehending delusion has no basis. When the practitioner investigates, hatred arises from one's mind. The mind is sealed by ignorance, arising through the condition of affliction. Since the nature of those is not established, they have an illusory nature. When the illusion is investigated, since it is not established in any way, it lacks inherent existence. That is the meaning of mahāmudrā without syllables. If it is wondered what that means, a so-called syllable is not established as a thing. It is a verbal expression that arises as a concept of the mind. Because concepts are not established by nature, expressions are not established by nature. As [the root text] states, "the absence of conceptuality and expression," the inexpressible meaning, is the so-called mahāmudrā without syllables.

Saraha states:

> All migrating beings rely on syllables.
> There isn't anyone who is without syllables.
> For as long as there are no syllables,
> for that long one has the best understanding of syllables.
> It is the syllable that is not a syllable.[13]

That indicates that one should apply the same process to desire, ignorance, pride, jealousy, and moreover, all the coarse and subtle concepts of affliction, and meditate.

ii. Training in Visualization

Training in visualization has three topics: (1) giving away the fettering body and mind, (2) giving away grasped enjoyments, and (3) training in the other categories.

I) Giving Away the Body and Mind

After inviting the root guru, the lineage gurus, and the assembly of commitment deities of the four tantra divisions into the space before oneself, {225} imagine they are seated there in person. Imagine that one offers all of them one's grasping to enemies and friends, and that one's body is chopped into many pieces. As such, the object of offering, the material offered, and the one making the offering are all only appearances of the mind. Since the mind is not real, it is an illusion. Since an illusion is not established by nature, one should comprehend it as the mahāmudrā without syllables.

II) Giving Away Grasped Enjoyments

Imagine that one offers without reservation all enjoyments of one's own as well as the valuables belonging to others—clothes, ornaments, private quarters, dwellings, countries, and so on—to the gurus and commitment deities in the sky. Further, the objects of offering, the articles offered, and the one offering are the mind. Since the mind is illusory and illusions lack inherent existence, train the mind in the mahāmudrā without syllables.

III) Other Categories

Visualize arriving in the hell realms below and experiencing the suffering of hot and cold, and so on, such as being boiled and roasted, until the visualization is as clear as being there in person. When panic and fear arise, it is all an appearance of the mind. Since the mind is illusory and illusions lack inherent existence, train the mind in the meaning of mahāmudrā without syllables. In this way, experience the suffering of the other six realms such as the preta realm, and so on. One should integrate the training of the mind on the meaning of everything being mind, illusion, and lacking inherent existence, and train on the places of impure samsara.

Next, place the mind on the visualization in which one encounters all the buddhas and bodhisattvas and their buddhafields moment by moment, such {226} as the one hundred thousand buddhas below, Mahāvairocana above, Akṣobhya in the east, Ratnasambhava in the south, Amitābha in the west, Amoghasiddhi in the north, and so on. Generate enthusiastic joy: "Amazing, in one instant I have seen inconceivable buddhafields." Training the mind on the mahāmudrā without syllables—in which all those are appearances of mind, the mind is an unreal illusion, and illusions lack inherent existence—is training on the pure buddhafields.

c. Explicating the Examples and Meaning

There are three topics in explicating the examples and the meaning: (1) with effort, (2) without effort, and (3) explaining the signs of accomplishment.

i. With Effort

Mingle the twelve examples of illusion, and so on, with the afflictions, such as hatred, and so on. If one is to show them together, when hatred arises, it must immediately be recognized with mindfulness, saying, "This is an illusion. This is a dream." That is mind, mind is illusory, and illusions lack inherent existence, which is the mahāmudrā without syllables. This is the mental effort of mindfulness.

ii. Without Effort

When one has become familiar with the previous training, since after a while effort in visualization is no longer necessary, one realizes all at once that all phenomena included in appearances and sound, samsara and nirvana, are not established anywhere but the mind. Since the mind is not real, is illusory, and illusions lack inherent existence, the mahāmudrā without syllables is realized spontaneously. This is the meaning of Saraha's statement:

> The realized do not dwell in forests or houses.

[And the meaning of the statement in] the *Saṃpūṭa Tantra*:

> Since the mind does not go elsewhere,
> when engaging in all activities,

such as looking at all forms,
listening to all sounds,
eating diverse flavors,
and talking and laughing,
that is the continually arising yoga
of the practitioner who knows reality.

The phenomena of samsara and nirvana {227} are one's mind, the dharmadhātu, the mahāmudrā without syllables, which becomes one taste, like pouring water into water or oil into oil. Further, based on this, when the aforementioned nine key points are included, when extraneous concepts arise due to external conditions, not grasping them from the moment they are encountered is holding the mind in the place where it moves. Based on that, when the mind is slightly calm, this is keeping the mind where it is placed. The avoidance of grasping to both [discursiveness and śamatha] is abandoning the two extremes. Also, holding [the mind] in the place where it moves is the time of realization, keeping it where it is placed is the time of understanding, and avoiding the two extremes is the time of comprehension.

Further, as above, if one is never distracted from mahāmudrā, [the mind] will not escape to a place where it would go. Since realization increases exponentially, it will not rest where it is placed. Since there is liberation from grasping, the mind does not slip into either [discursiveness or śamatha]. Therefore, all phenomena are understood, realized, and comprehended in terms of the twelve examples of illusion; the meaning is understood, realized, and comprehended in terms of mind; and mahāmudrā is understood, realized, and comprehended to be without syllables. It is the time when the aims of this path are accomplished.

iii. Signs of Accomplishment

There are two topics in the signs of accomplishment: (1) signs with effort and (2) signs without effort.

1) Signs with Effort

In the signs with effort, equipoise and post-equipoise are differentiated, there is a time when śamatha is maintained, there is a necessity for antidotes to adventitious afflictions, and sometimes circumstances are harmful and sometimes not.

II) Signs without Effort

In signs without effort, equipoise and post-equipoise are merged, equipoise becomes continuous, the gnosis of vipaśyana arises, one is not oppressed by afflictions, the latent afflictions are subdued, one becomes free from the eight worldly dharmas, and circumstances are beneficial. As such, as soon as there are no sessions or session breaks, and equipoise and post-equipoise merge, it is the time when appearances arise as one's teacher, {228} the time of things arising as one's guru, the time of afflictions transforming into the path, the time of the five poisons transforming into medicine, the time of concepts arising as gnosis, the time of the elimination of the abyss of the six migrations, the time of destroying the city of the six realms, and the time of appearances transforming into emptiness. The special qualities of realization enter oneself naturally, which are like a fire spreading in a forest, snow falling on a lake, or like the full moon. It is a time that resembles meeting a person with whom one was previously acquainted, in which there is no effort of inquiry. Beyond sound and concepts, mahāmudrā is realized as the reality without syllables. In this system there is no defined time for conduct. Once concepts arise as antidotes and transform into companions of realization, one does not accept or reject food, partaking of it whether it is good or poor quality. Since one does not negate or approve conduct, whatever arises is directly cut off. Since companions arise without being good or bad, one associates with whomever one meets. Further, having commenced such secret conduct, bring it to culmination.

C. The Way the Result Is Attained

The three kāyas are held to have seven limbs. The three limbs of the dharmakāya are naturelessness because proliferation is pacified, uninterrupted because the three times become uniform, and unceasing because it is free from the arising and perishing of the compounded. The three limbs of the sambhogakāya are the blazing major and minor marks; union with the mother, self-appearing gnosis; and a continuum moistened with immaculate bliss, which is an extraordinary quality. The single limb of the nirmāṇakāya is uninterrupted compassion, acting on behalf of sentient beings without interruption through nonreferential compassion.

Further, the result is also held to be the four kāyas. First, the mind that abides as pure by nature is the svabhāvakāya. {229} The dharmakāya realized through the power of meditating on that benefits oneself. The sambhogakāya[14] of the major and minor marks, and so on, and the nirmāṇakāya that performs the benefit of sentient beings benefit others. The former two are kāyas of separation and the latter two are vipākakāyas, kāyas of maturation.

> By training the mind on the [mahāmudrā] without syllables,
> all qualities of the syllables are attained.
> This amazing, essential instruction manual
> resembles a deep ocean.

The chapter on the manual of *Mahāmudrā without Syllables* composed by Ācārya Vāgīśvarakīrti was expanded upon by Lodrö Taye in accordance with the command of the precious lord guru [Khyentse Wangpo]. May excellent virtue increase.

15. Fortunate Pure Crystal Mirror

The Instruction Manual of Śrī Koṭalipa's Inconceivable[1]

Jamgön Kongtrul

{232} *namo guru vajradharapādāya*

Having bowed to the nine siddhācāryas
the inseparable five lord founders,
and Khyentse Wangpo who unifies them all into one,
I shall set forth the *Stages of the Inconceivable.*

Now, when these renowned eight ancillary path cycles are precisely divided, six are for the completion stages of Cakrasaṃvara, Hevajra, and Guhyasamāja, and two are connected to the general divisions of tantra. Ḍombi Heruka's *Accomplishing the Connate* and Saroruha's *Nine Profound Methods* are systems commenting on Hevajra, and the latter is the actual completion stage of the Saroruha system. *Completing the Whole Path with Caṇḍālī* and *Straightening the Crooked* are related to Cakrasaṃvara. *Obtained in Front of a Stupa* is related to Akṣobhya Guhyasamāja and *Mahāmudrā without Syllables* is related to the Buddhajñānapāda system [of Guhyasamāja]. The *Inconceivable* and Indrabhūti's path cycles are for the completion stage of unsurpassed tantras in general. Though it appears that the tantras [mentioned above] are connected through their general ripening transmissions to each text, because of the power of the transmission of the special lineage, the empowerment of the intimate instruction system of Hevajra is sufficient to ripen [a student] for all. {233} Also, the eight path cycles are considered to be dependent upon the *Precious Oral Intimate Instructions.*

Now, first, there are two in the explanation of the *Stages of the Inconceivable* by Koṭalipa: (1) explaining the source for confidence, the lineage from which it springs; and (2) explaining the actual instructions of the lineage.

I. The Lineage

First, the perfect Buddha Vajradhara explained the *Stages of the Inconceivable* to the nirmāṇakāya gnosis ḍākinī. She bestowed the empowerment and the instruction of the five stages upon Ācārya Paramāśva in Oḍḍiyāna. Then, in order, it was bestowed to Ācārya Vīṇipada, King Indrabhūti, Lakṣmī, Vilāsavajra, Guṇḍerī, Padmavajra the lesser, Śrī Dharmasena, Bhadrapāda, and finally, Koṭalipa. The lineage runs through this group of ten Oḍḍiyāna mahāsiddhas.

Koṭalipa then composed the stages of the inconceivable called *Accomplishment of Mahāmudrā*. His lineage continued through Bhusanapa, Karṇapa, and Vīravajra. The latter bestowed it to Drokmi Lotsāwa Śākya Yeshe. {234} The lineage then continued to Setön Kunrik, Gönpo Chöbar, and Sachen Kunga Nyingpo without interruption. Then the streams of transmission of instructions flowed together to the omniscient Khyentse Wangpo.

II. The Actual Instructions

There are three topics in the actual instructions: (1) confirming the view at the time of the cause, (2) generating and training in samādhi at the time of the path, and (3) explaining without error the entire path of persons who realize gnosis, attaining buddhahood in a single lifetime at the time of the result.

A. Confirming the View

There are four bases of instruction through confirming the view at the time of the cause: (1) preparing the support for the instruction, (2) the time for recognizing those, (3) the evaluation of them, and (4) the authority of confirmation. Also, when each of those is divided into three, there are twelve topics.

1. Preparing the Support

For preparing the support, among the body, voice, and mind, the coarse body is the supporting sense organs and torso, and the subtle body is the three major internal nāḍīs. The coarse voice is the conventions of talking, laughter, and so on, and the subtle voice is the trio of the exhalation, inhalation, and pause of the vāyu and the tone of the three syllables [*oṃ āḥ hūṃ*]. For the mind, the support is the pure essence of the nine elements that exists as pure bodhicitta amṛta located in the nāḍīs. and the supported is luminosity, the intrinsically cognized gnosis.

The nature of that body and voice is mind. Since the mind is supported and rests upon the body and voice, until the body and mind separate, body, voice, and mind are supported, one upon the other, because they are one entity. Since mind alone is confirmed, both body and speech are implicitly confirmed because there are no phenomena not included in the mind. Though in the confirmation of mind there is no differentiation of the entity into parts, {235} five aspects can be isolated in the inconceivable.

(1) The inconceivability of characteristics is unmixed and complete. Since everything is a cognitive experience (*myong rig*) of the mind, even though there is only one class, there are different ways of understanding: the path of non-Buddhist outsiders and the path of Buddhist insiders. The individual opinions within those paths appear as various analytical philosophical conclusions.

(2) The inconceivability of qualities is like the example of the wish-fulfilling gem. When the same entity encounters the condition of a method, all needs are produced for whomever needs them. It is similar to the example of the sun; the same entity has many different modes of arising through the condition of place. Further, without moving from the intrinsic essence of dharmatā, various paths and philosophical conclusions appear, corresponding with the various types and capacities of those to be tamed, just as the sun that arises in the sky, seen by each person in the country, arises and sets only over the peak of the mountain.

(3) The inconceivability of power is neither bound nor freed. Since the power to generate virtue exists by nature in the mind, it is not bound. It [also] cannot be freed because that will not occur without meeting the proper conditions. For example, when sesame seeds meet the condition of being pressed, oil is produced, but if that condition is not met, oil will not

be produced. Since all causes, paths, and results appear in the mind alone, they are inconceivable because they are beyond theories (the method side).

(4) The inconceivability of nature is ultimately empty of the cause, intrinsic essence, and the result, the inconceivabilities of characteristic, qualities, and power. For example, since one cannot theorize any cause or result for empty space, it is inconceivable (the wisdom side). {236}

(5) The inconceivability of the essence cannot be disassociated from or possessed. Since a second phenomenon cannot exist as a contradiction within a single phenomenon, there is no disassociation. When investigated in detail with reasoning, [that phenomenon] cannot be established with proofs, thus it cannot be possessed. Since it cannot be asserted as an idea, it is inconceivable (union). So-called union does not mean merging existence and nonexistence, meditating on one as two, existing on one side and not existing on the other side, or combining two into one. When sought with an idea of method, everything exists. When sought with an idea of wisdom, nothing exists. Since there is nothing to call "dual," this is called "nondual" or "union"—that is, beyond the range of all thought and expression. Here, it is said that from the perspective of the essence of reality, there are six kinds of nonexistence. Since there is not an iota of an entity established in the mind, there is no generation with a cause. Since the mind is uncompounded, it cannot perish due to compounded conditions. Since the essence is free from all extremes, it cannot be indicated with an example. Since mind cannot be divided into parts, there is nothing to abandon or adopt with an antidote. Since the essence of the mind does not become good by training on a path, there is no training with a path. Since the phenomena of samsara and nirvana are undifferentiated in the space of the mind, there is no hope or fear for a result.

When the practitioner is practicing, the six kinds of existence are employed as the path. There is generation with a cause because experience arises from the third empowerment, and so on. There is perishing due to the condition of lethargy and agitation, and so on. There is indication with an example, such as reflections, space, and so on. There is adopting and abandoning because concepts are abandoned and nonconceptuality arises. There is training with a path since samādhi increases {237} through the methods of enhancement. There is hope and fear since the best obtain the result in this life, the mediocre in the bardo, and the average within seven or sixteen lifetimes. The enumeration of names for this result is "the suchness that never changes through the three times," "the unmodified ultimate reality of things," "the dharmatā that was already accomplished because it naturally exists from the beginning," "the naturally connate gnosis that pervades all samsara and nirvana without being positive or negative," and "Master King of the Mind (sLob dpon Sems kyi rgyal po) because it explicates the result of samsara and nirvana." Further, those are (1) the gnosis that is to be realized; (2) the realized view, that which is to be known personally; and (3) thinking that is in accord with the dharma applied respectively to practitioners of the first stage [of the inconceivable].

2. The Time for Recognizing Those

There are three topics in the time for recognizing those: the times of the cause, the path, and the result.

First, at the time of a sentient being who abides as the cause, there is the web of nāḍīs of the body, the karma vāyus of the voice, and the countless discursive concepts of the mind. Also, due to all three being included in the concepts of the mind, concepts are inconceivable.

Second, at the time of practice, first, the mind is controlled because of the significance of the third empowerment and the instruction to focus the mind on space. The doors at the time of the cause are blessed, like iron coming into contact with the gold-transformation elixir. The body floats, becomes light, and warmth and bliss arise. The voice produces talk, laughter, and spontaneous words. The samādhi of the union of method and wisdom arises in the mind. Also, due to all three being included in samādhi, samādhi is inconceivable. {238}

Third, at the time of reaching the culmination of the path, the three doors ripen into the nature of gnosis, the body appears like a rainbow, and many insubstantial kāyas appear according to the inclinations of those to be tamed. The voice's natural tone of indestructible sound produces limitless dharma-doors, corresponding with the inclinations of migrating beings. Instantly, the mind is capable of knowing as many objects of knowledge as there are and their nature. Because everything is also included in gnosis, gnosis is inconceivable.

3. The Evaluation

There are three topics in the evaluation. If an experiential consciousness evaluates the method—relative truth—the characteristics, qualities, and abilities of objects of knowledge appear in everything. If one evaluates wisdom—the ultimate truth, the emptiness of the dharmadhātu—appearances in the cause, path, and result are totally empty and do not exist. If one evaluates the essential nonduality of method and wisdom, since nothing is found after investigation and examination for an existence or a nonexistence, and since there is neither existence nor nonexistence, union is inconceivable.

4. Authorities

There are three in authority of confirmation: the speech of the sugata, the authentic compilations (*lung*, Skt. *āgama*), and the experience of the practitioner.

The first corresponds with the tripṭaka and the four divisions of tantra spoken by the Buddha. The second corresponds with the lineage beginning from Ācārya Paramāśva up to one's actual vajra master guru and the intimate instruction of the practice to which nothing has been removed or added. The third corresponds with the arising of the experience of method, wisdom, and union through the practitioner's own equipoise. {239} Since that experience is recalled, confidence in dharmatā arises. Those are called "the twelve bases of instruction." Since those are the way the view is confirmed at the time of the cause, it is necessary in the beginning to generate certainty and have comprehension with an evaluation through investigation and examination. Practitioners are obscured by two poisons. Because they do not realize the essence with this [basis of instruction], they must become free from the poison of ignorance that grasps to the intrinsic nature of entities and signs.[2]

B. Generating and Training in Samādhi at the Time of the Path

The second fundamental topic is the necessity of generating and training in samādhi at the time of the path. At the time of the cause, ordinary concepts arise as a stream. The so-called poison of seeking those concepts is an essential obscuration. Here, there are seven topics: (1) focus the mind; (2) place the mind on reality; (3) cultivate all conduct; (4) remove lethargy and agitation, the obstructions to concentration; (5) progress through the eight enhancements; (6) apply the signs of experience of the mind; and (7) connect with the result through the conduct that relies on a mudra.

1. Focusing the Mind

The preliminaries for concentration are remaining alone in an isolated place. If one is elderly, or the season is autumn or spring, or one has a blood or pitta illness, or it is too warm and hot, one should sit in vajra posture with hands in the mudra of equipoise. If one is youthful, the season is winter, one has a cold or kapha illness, or one is [staying] in cold places, one should be seated in the tripod position, with the knees drawn up to the chest, like a cooking tripod. In both postures, the head is slightly tilted, the eyes drop to the tip of the nose, the tongue touches the palate, and the lips and teeth are evenly closed. This is the key point of settling the body. {240} Exhale forcefully three times. This is the key point of settling the voice. Taking one's place in a state of not thinking anything at all, relaxing, and resting for a little while is the key point of settling the mind.

Next, in order to accomplish the path of Mahāyāna, the meditation on bodhicitta is generating bodhicitta with the thought "I will obtain buddhahood for the benefit of all sentient beings. For that purpose, I will meditate on the stages of samādhi."

Meditating on the guru as a branch of perfecting accumulations is as follows: Meditate on one's root guru seated on a lotus and moon above one's crown and generate intense devotion. Recite the lineage supplication by Ngorchen [in chapter 1]. Supplicate again and again from the depths of one's heart, "I supplicate the greatly kind guru father, please cause the extraordinary samādhi to arise in my continuum." Finally, through power of devotion, imagine the guru melts into light and dissolves into one's heart through one's crown. Abandon ordinary concepts. In order to prevent obstacles from arising, recite *hūṃ* and meditate on the form of *hūṃ* inside one's pledged deity, who is inside the protection cakra. Focus the mind. As such, the six limbs of concentration should precede all sessions.

In the main section, the samādhi that connects nonduality to space is the training on external space in the manner of an example. There is the short-distance training and the long-distance training. In each of those trainings, there is both training in the manner of giving punishment and training in the manner of giving a reward.

First is the method of short-distance training. Focus one's attention on the space four finger lengths from the tip of the nose. Meditating with both the body and mind held tensely is training in the manner of inflicting punishment. {241} On the basis of the previous training, meditating with both the body and mind relaxed is the manner of giving a reward. This is the samādhi of the method. Having cultivated that, focus one's attention on the space eight finger lengths from the tip of the nose. Meditating by alternating tension and looseness is the samādhi of wisdom. Having cultivated that, merge one's attention into space from sixteen fingerbreadths up to a fathom and meditate. This is the samādhi of union. The two previous samādhis are faulty and the last one is faultless. In those circumstances, no matter what experience arises when placing the mind—high or low, good or bad—do not engage in any hope, fear, accepting, or rejecting. Sustain that experience naturally. In these circumstances, the typical experience that arises is empty by nature.

Second is the long-distance training for enhancement. When the previous experiences that have arisen become slightly stable, to begin, perform the sixfold preliminaries of concentration in full. Focus one's mind for as long as possible in the eastern direction two fathoms, four fathoms, eight fathoms, sixteen fathoms, and so on, sending one's concepts to the furthest reaches of space. As before, train step-by-step in the manner of punishment and reward, but unlike before, there will be the experience of inexpressible bliss and emptiness free from extremes, an experience of absence of strength through being attached to one seat such that one does not move here and there, and an experience of a disabled boat floating here and there. Those should be sustained without modification. Likewise, by training repeatedly in the manner of punishment and reward—facing south, west, north, [toward] the zenith, and the nadir of space—directly sustain those three experiences.

Based on the experience of freedom arising from those experiences, there is freedom from the extremes of existence, nonexistence, being, nonbeing, and so on, like the example of space. Since nothing is established in any way, there is emptiness. Since it pervades all knowers and objects of knowledge, there is pervasiveness. {242} Since one feels that cannot be destroyed by anything, there is permanence. Thus, there is an experience that arises with these four characteristics: [freedom from extremes, emptiness, pervasiveness, and permanence].

2. Placing the Mind on Reality

There are three topics in the presentation of the path of reality: (1) applying a name to inconceivable nonarising in the manner of breaking an eggshell, (2) applying the meaning to inconceivable nonarising in the manner of breaking free of a spider web,[3] and (3) applying samādhi to inconceivable nonarising in the manner of removing a cocoon.

a. Breaking an Eggshell

When a swan chick has fully developed inside of an egg, if it does not break the shell, it cannot move, but if it breaks the shell, it can move. Likewise, one is bound by deluded concepts because of clinging to a name, but if one recognizes reality as nonarising, after one becomes free of grasping to one's name, one will be liberated. First, there is no person that is born with a name; it is a temporary label, and "This is my name" is a delusion. In the end, when one dies, as a name does not follow one, it naturally ceases, because names do not arise. Even though your name is praised, there is no benefit to your name. Even though the faults of your name are described, your name is not harmed. The text states:

> Nonarising does not arise, like space.
> Arising does not arise, like space.
> Cessation does not arise, like space.[4]

By considering the meaning of this and training, the conceptual grasping to names will dissolve in the dhātu of the nature of the mind, like clouds and mist vanishing into the sky, and the experience of clarity and nonconceptuality will arise. With respect to that, the *Prajñāpāramitā* states:

> Kauśika,[5] matter is a mere designation;
> whatever is a mere designation is also dharmatā.[6]

And, [the *Stages of the Inconceivable*] states:

> Nonduality is merely a name;
> even that name does not exist. (19ab)
> . . . .
> [I, the yogi,] obtained patience for that
> which bears the name "nonduality." (60bc)

Also, that samādhi is named "the three doors of liberation" and when free of the bondage of names, {243} it ultimately touches the inconceivable.

b. Breaking Free of a Spider Web

Sentient beings stuck in a spider web can only be in the place they fell. If they do not break free of the outer web, they cannot move. If they break free, then they can move. Likewise, this mind is bound by various concepts. If one understands those as nonarisen, then one will be liberated. To reflect on the meaning of this, since one coarsely investigates any concepts of affliction in one's mind, when one is under the influence of a coarse movement like anger, investigate its cause of arising first, the entity that remains at present, and the result of cessation in the end. Since no entity at all will be established, apply this to inconceivable nonarising, which is equivalent to space, and investigate. Further, since one investigates in detail from where among one's body, voice, and mind that concept arises, where among those three it remains at present, and what the color, shape, and so on that concept possesses, place the mind on the meaning of seeing that concept does not arise from anywhere, does not remain anywhere, and is not established as any kind of independent entity. By meditating in that way, the conceptual grasping to anger dissolves into the expanse of the mind itself, and the experience of the nonconceptual entity of the clear aspect of anger arises.

> Nondual gnosis blazes
> through investigating duality. (5cd)

That [analysis and meditation] should be combined with the other five poisons, such as desire, and so on, and other concepts, and applied to inconceivable nonarising.

c. Removing a Cocoon

After a silkworm spins its cocoon, it is invisible, but as soon as the cocoon is removed, it is nakedly visible. Likewise, since one meditates in a liberating samādhi, because that samādhi may bind one again, it is necessary to apply that samādhi to inconceivable nonarising. That has two parts: (1) resting without inward mental grasping and (2) loosely resting consciousness on outer objects. {244} First, lightly rest the body and mind. Look inwardly at consciousness. Recall just the entity to be observed and do not conceive anything. Without thinking anything at all, rest in a state of nongrasping. If there is an external distraction, since one again rests as before, the samādhi of bliss and emptiness arises. Second, no matter what kind of apparent objects arise externally, such as form, and so on, loosely rest [one's consciousness] without grasping, free of the effort of the inner sense gates, such as the eyes, and so on. When resting in that way, do not meditate purposefully with a meditating consciousness directed toward one object of meditation. Since one meditates in the manner of nonmeditation—without grasping the characteristics of meditation and without the deluded distraction of nonmeditation—the supreme samādhi of bliss and emptiness arises, free from objects of meditation such as form, and so on, and superior to the previous samādhi. Whichever of the three samādhis arises at this point—method, wisdom, or union—should be directly sustained without rejecting, accepting, modifying, or changing them.

3. Cultivating All Conduct

Cultivating all conduct is that even though attachment and aversion may not arise in equipoise during the prior meditation, it will arise when encountering conditions. In order to be free from the bondage of those conditions, one must train in the limbs of stability.

According to the position of Drokmi Lotsāwa, first, from the perspective of training on form, in a place where the eyes will not be harmed by bright sunlight or cold breezes, place something like a flower, and so on, before you, neither too far nor too close, and look at it with a relaxed gaze. Do not look at anything other than that thing. This is the limb of the unchanging support. Giving up movement is the limb of the unmoving body. Not blinking is the limb of the unmoving eyes. Not purposefully directing the mind anywhere is the limb of the absence of a grasping mind. {245} By training in possession of all four limbs, a samādhi arises without focusing on the object. From the second day to the third day, and so on, gradually place the support further and further away. Finally, recalling the support with the mind a shouting distance away, and so on, and training, is identifying gnosis from form. Having illustrated that, in possession of the four limbs, train on other objects, such as sound, and so on. As such, since one meditates on the instruction of recognizing gnosis in objects for a long while, as the experience of the mind is weak, one is alternately harmed and benefited by objects. When the minor experience arises, objects arise as a mix of alternating harm and benefit. Through cultivating that, the middling experience of the mind is when appearances are neither beneficial nor harmful. Through cultivating that, the strong experience of mind is that as soon as one meets the condition of an object, concepts assist gnosis, just like adding wood to a bonfire.

Further, in the condition of objects, beautiful forms are best, unattractive forms are middling, and ordinary forms are average. Having trained in what is illustrated by that, no matter which condition one encounters—best, middling, or average—the supreme gnosis of realization of reality arises inside. This occasion of supreme samādhi arising immediately upon encountering apparent objects is when one is benefited by appearances, called "the time appearances arise as the virtuous mentor." Since many appear from one entity grasped as "I" and "mine" and many arise as one taste, it is called "the time when both outer and inner are merged." That condition of attachment and aversion to the ordinary is also gnosis arising for the practitioner, called "the time the five poisons are recognized as medicine." At that moment, even though one relies on the five objects of desire, they are not affected by faults. These are also clearly explained in the words of the text. {246}

4. Removing Lethargy and Agitation, the Obstructions to Concentration

In removing lethargy and agitation, the obstructions to concentration, in general, there are three topics in lethargy and agitation: lethargy and agitation due to deliberate effort, lethargy and agitation due to conditions, and lethargy and agitation that arise naturally.

The lethargy due to deliberate effort arises from striving for happiness, such as a comfortable bed, and so on, and merit. The agitation arises from striving in worldly activities, such as talking, debating, and so on. Recognizing the causes of such lethargy and agitation and abandoning those causes for some days will naturally remove them.

The lethargy due to conditions is lethargy due to the condition of eating too much food, drinking too much alcohol, great fatigue, and so on. The agitation due to conditions is the agitation that results from not isolating from the very distracting conditions of the activities[7] of people during the day, loud noise at night, and so on. Whatever conditions there are, since one isolates from those for some number of days, they are automatically removed.

The naturally arising lethargy and agitation is as follows: Even though the aforementioned lethargy and agitation may have been removed, the natural lack of mental clarity and obscuration through lethargy as well as the ceaseless agitated discursiveness of concepts can arise in either a subtle or coarse form. While there may be no fault at the beginning of a session, if it arises at the end of the session, then there is a fault of the elements. One must interrupt one's meditation, rest naturally, and repeat many short sessions, and it will be removed by resting. If there is a fault at the beginning of a session, it is an obstacle of concentration. The three ways to remove it are behavior, diet, and force of mind.

To remove lethargy and agitation with behavior, for mental lethargy, sit on a high seat and lift up the mind. If that does not remove lethargy, since it is a high place, look at the boundary of the mountain and the plain, tightening and invigorating the body, and the mind will remove it. For agitation, sitting on a low seat or in a low place, lowering one's chin so that it touches {247} the Adam's apple, and remaining in the dark will remove it.

To remove lethargy and agitation with diet, when lethargy arises, one should avoid eating prior to cultivating concentration. For agitation, one should administer a cup[8] of chang[9] with food prior to commencing concentration and take a walk of fifty steps. If that does not pacify it, then administer two cups of chang and walk one hundred steps. Further, apply those measures according to diagnosis. If blood or pitta predominate, administer a smaller amount. If kapha and vata predominate, then administer a larger amount. Apply those measures according to age, administering less for the young and more for the old. Apply those measures according to season, administering less in the spring and summer, and more in the fall and winter. Those measures will definitely pacify lethargy and agitation.

To remove lethargy and agitation with the force of the mind, it is said, "When there is lethargy, train in bodhicitta in the mahāsukhacakra above. Alternately, train on the location of the precious wish-fulfilling gem." First, be mindful that one's mind is in one's heart center, then in the brow, then in the brahma aperture, then four fingerbreadths in space above the crown, and so on. Focus the mind higher and higher, and send concepts to the end of space. Once again, it gradually descends back into the heart center. Take the measure of whether or not lethargy has been dispelled. However, if one meditates on this for too long, there will be mental discomfort, vata in the heart, and so on. Thus, since there is a great risk, once the lethargy is removed, then stop. It is said that this will produce visions of the places of the devas, and so on. When there is agitation, train in bodhicitta at the place of the *e* dharmodaya below. Alternately, train on the place of the precious wish-fulfilling gem. First, merely by meditating on an empty space between oneself and one's seat,{248} subtle agitation will be removed. If that does not remove agitation, visualize a transparent red dharmodaya at the rectum. Then, look down into that with the mind, for as long as is suitable. As soon as the mind is placed, directing it toward the heart will remove agitation. If that does not remove agitation, it will be removed by the three concepts about your nature.

Regarding that, "holding the narrow path" means that agitation will be immediately dispelled through counting agitations, such as one distraction, a second distraction, and so on. "Following" refers to being distracted toward any concept and then focusing on that object without wavering. This will swiftly remove agitation. "Total understanding" refers to dispelling agitation merely by recognizing it and understanding that it is one's own mind.

If agitation is not pacified by those means, apply "suppression." Putting as heavy a stick as one can support on one's crown and meditating will remove agitation. "Hanging rope" means sweep the ground, make it firm, and place a round log there. Above that extend two ropes, make a branch for a swing seat, and hang one rope above it. Sit on the seat with one's two feet extended down. The balls of the feet press down on the round log. The mind remains where it is. Grab the rope with both hands, move forward, and also move backward. "Clearing the narrow path" means setting up a round stick or a cairn either to one's left or right and placing a white stone on top of it. On top of that stone place a black stone. Knock those off with a bamboo cane, and so on. Gaze without closing the eyes. Since one rests without grasping, it is said to immediately remove agitation.

5. Progress through the Eight Enhancements

There are eight topics in the enhancement of concentration: {249} the five alternates, relaxed behavior, changing the point, and relying on amṛta.

"Alternate" means first, tightening; second, loosening; third, reducing; and fourth, increasing. In the early morning session, both the body and mind should be tightened. The length should be reduced and shortened. In the late morning session, both the body and mind should be loosened and the sessions extended and increased. In the afternoon session, tighten and reduce, and in the evening session, loosen and increase, alternating each session. In order to slightly enhance that, alternate each day. On the first day, meditate and reduce the length of sessions. On the second day, increase the length of the sessions, and so on. This will enhance one's progress. Fifth, "alternating one's diet" means that in the first session or on the first day, do not eat or drink, and on the second, do eat and drink. Sixth, "generating relaxed behavior" means that one does not block anything that necessarily arises to one's eyes and one enjoys it directly as bliss, the conduct of relying on amṛta. Seventh, "changing the mind to various points" means one makes progress through meditating on the various points of reference that arise in the sutras and tantras in order as taught by the victor. Eighth, "relying on the amṛta of various objects" means that having gone to a vista of brilliant flowers on a plain in the spring, one's continuum is satisfied by indulging the senses in attractive offering objects and pleasing forms. Those enhance realization. In all of those, the sublime point is never wavering from the samādhi of resting the mind in reality.

a. Correcting Errors

At these occasions, {250} though this is not included in the basic outline, there are five topics in the ancillary intimate instruction of correcting errors: (1) spinning like a wheel, (2) coiled like a ball of yarn, (3) the yoga of many passageways, (4) training without the upper and lower wheels, and (5) training in the yoga of heroism.

i. Spinning like a Wheel

If there is a feeling of bloating, pain, and so on in the body, imagine an eight-spoked wheel at the navel. Meditate that the wheel spins clockwise. If that is uncomfortable, meditate that it spins counterclockwise. Since that wheel becomes increasingly larger, meditate on the body also becoming increasingly larger. If one feels it to be very large, release the wheel with the mind. The interior of the body is empty. It vanishes and disappears, and it is imagined to be nonexistent. That immediately frees one from faults.

ii. Coiled like a Ball of Thread

If pain occurs by visualizing a part of the body, such as the heart, and so on, imagine that wherever that pain is, an open passageway arises. Exhale through that and strongly expel the pain. Imagine that the color of the vāyu is blue, the size of a horsehair, coiling into a ball about a cubit outside.

Visualize that for a short while, then release it. Next, visualize that the passageway becomes larger, and also that the vāyu becomes thicker, the size of a thread, then the size of rope, and so on, imagining that these coil, as before. That will immediately free one from faults.

iii. The Yoga of Many Passageways

If there is pain throughout the body, many passageways arise that are like the eyes of a sieve. Exhale forcefully, imagining the vāyu vanishes through all those passageways and disperses. This will immediately release all faults. This is said to be slightly harmful to one's health.

iv. The Absence of the Upper and Lower Wheels

If there is pain and discomfort in the upper body, imagine that above the throat is hollow like a bamboo trunk, imagine again that the upper vāyu vanishes,{251} and forcefully exhale. If there is pain and discomfort in the lower body, imagine the lower body to be like a hollow bamboo trunk, and meditate on the lower vāyu descending and vanishing. If that moves down, strongly hold the lower vāyu. Those will immediately release the fault.

v. The Yoga of Heroism

If there is [a compulsion] to jump, run, and so on, imagine that below the place one is seated is very deep, like a pit. Imagine one's body sinks down. It is said that it is impossible the [compulsion] will not be removed.

6. The Application of the Signs of Experience

Since one has properly meditated according to the stages as they have been explained, to begin, the mind stays where it is wished. Certainty in reality arises. A slight laziness increases, and one has no wish to engage in any activities. One forgets things. As soon as one encounters any activity, one performs it. A special clear memory arises from time to time. One can gradually reverse the distracted, conceptual thoughts about the eight worldly dharmas. Dreams that seem clairvoyant clearly arise. Internal and external parasites leave gradually. At that time, one attains the confidence that one will no longer be reborn in lower realms.

7. Conduct Connected with the Result[10]

Finally, for the conduct connected with the result, since there is no other path for progressing higher than this one, rely on the extremely unelaborate path of the fourth empowerment. When the signs of heat manifest through meditation, it is the assertion of this ācārya that one can associate with apsaras, and so on. If one is relying on the yoga for attaining siddhi, a predicted human woman is held to be the main [type of mudra]. Ḍākinīs born in nirmāṇakāya buddhafields will make a prediction concerning a young padminī mudra. Seek her out, and in the beginning {252} purify her continuum with empowerment and the stages of the preliminaries. One should protect one's three places with the three seed syllables. In an isolated place one should have the perception of the deity. If one is performing the yoga of Akṣobhya, the mudra is generated as Māmaki, or generate the father and mother of whichever family one's flower has fallen on. Blessing the space and the secret is the perception of the mantra. Thinking that for the benefit of all sentient beings, one will attain supreme siddhi based on the union of the method and the wisdom is the perception of dharma.

Since one enters in union with those three perceptions, the entire pure essence of the nine bodhicitta elements gathers at the crown from all the nāḍī locations of both the method and the wisdom. The gathered bindus—the pure element of the method is under the influence of the lunar bindu and the pure element of wisdom is under the influence of the solar bindu—gradually descend through the three nāḍīs individually. As they descend, there is an experience of the four joys.

Finally, when the solar and lunar bindus have been eclipsed by Rahu at the supreme anther, that pure element manifests various colors like the rising sun. At that time all phenomena of samsara and nirvana are perceived inside of a single bindu, just like looking at the lines on one's palm. That is the moment of the cause, called "contaminated bliss," and takes the name "the twelfth stage."

Next, the method draws up in three different ways: first, drawing up through the right nāḍī; then, drawing up through the left nāḍī; and finally, drawing up through the central nāḍī. This purifies the continuum of the nāḍī. Likewise, the wisdom also draws up through the right, left, and central nāḍīs, which purifies the continuum of wisdom. Finally, when the continuums of both are purified, the pure essence of the nine elements is transformed, and since the slowly moving vāyu is very pure, {253} it reverses into the central nāḍī of both and dissolves into the location of *haṃ* in their crowns. At that time, the experience of the fourth joy is stabilized by the mother.

In the end, all the vāyus and minds dissolve into the central nāḍī, the continuums of the method and wisdom are liberated simultaneously, and the result of the thirteenth stage, Vajradhara, is realized. That concludes the stages of the path of generating and training in samādhi at the time of the path.

C. The Result

The three kāyas are asserted in seven limbs. There is only a single limb for the dharmakāya, naturelessness, which is the dhātu and gnosis becoming nondual.

There are three limbs for the sambhogakāya. The limb of bliss is the special satisfaction of the continuum with uncontaminated bliss. Both equipoise and post-equipoise exist in the creation and completion stages at the time of the path, and objects of desire are not abandoned, but employed as the path. The limb of union at the time of the result is that the appearance of objects of desire are not inhibited and become the appearance of gnosis, together with the mother. The limb of complete enjoyment is blazing with the thirty-two major marks and eighty minor marks.

There are three limbs for the nirmāṇakāya: [one limb of] the cause and [two limbs of] the result, negation and affirmation. The limb of the cause is that since the time has arrived to tame all sentient beings, as it is filled with compassion, the nirmāṇakāya is always looking in this way, "Who is next?" For the result, there is the limb of negation because the deeds on behalf of sentient beings to be benefited are unceasing as it is impossible to interrupt them. The limb of affirmation is that since the activity of taming is not interrupted, it is certain deeds to benefit sentient beings will never be interrupted.

That concludes the explanation of the modes of the resultant gnosis. {254} Those topics fully establish and include the cause, path, and result of the stages of the inconceivable.

> May the inconceivable ultimate wisdom
> be swiftly realized through recognizing nonduality.
> May the ocean of gnosis accomplish
> the supreme three kāyas of perfect qualities.

The chapter of "Fortunate Pure Crystal Mirror: The Instruction Manual of Śrī Koṭalipa's *Inconceivable*" was composed by Lodrö Taye according to the command of the lord guru.

May virtue spread.

16. Fortunate Right-Turning White Conch

The Manual of Indrabhūti's Path of the Mudra[1]

Jamgön Kongtrul

{256} *namo guru vajradharapādāya*

Having bowed to the supreme siddha Indrabhūti,
the inseparable five lord founders,
and Khyentse Wangpo, who unifies them all into one,
I shall set forth the manual on the *Path of the Mudra*.

In the manual of the path of the mudra, the oral instruction of Dharma King Indrabhūti, the forebear of all siddhis of the eight ancillary path cycles, there are two topics: (1) the lineage from which it arises and (2) the instructions of that lineage.

I. The Lineage

Though three King Indrabhūtis are known to have arisen in Oḍḍiyāna, in essence they are all emanations of Guhyapati Vajrapāṇi. So-called Mahāsukhaśrī is Indrabhūti I, who attained supreme siddhi along with one thousand queens when the perfect Buddha in person bestowed the empowerment into the maṇḍala of Guhyasamāja. Then, based on his composition of the basic text of this path, the long lineage continues through the line of siddhas and after Indrabhūti III was passed down to the brahmin Ratnavajra and then to the Red Ārya, Prajñākaragupta. {257} The short lineage is Indrabhūti I, Lakṣmīkara, and Prajñāgupta. The latter bestowed this upon Drokmi Lotsāwa, and from him the lineage was transmitted without interruption to the Lord Sakyapa uncles and nephews. Finally, the practice lineage continued to the all-seeing Jamyang Khyentse Wangpo, from whom I directly received the tradition of the great chariot lineage of siddhas as a portion of his kindness.

II. The Instructions

There are four in the actual instruction: (1) preparing the foundation, (2) the extensive explanation of the practice, (3) the way one progresses on the path, and (4) demonstrating the ultimate.

A. Preparing the Foundation

In preparing the foundation, there are (1) the four lineages, (2) the three vows, and (3) the complete five paths.

1. The Four Lineages

The word lineage continues from Vajradhara to the root guru, one after another. The ultimate lineage of the manner of dependent origination is origination based on a first thing, as following that, another thing arises. The symbolic lineage is the unerring knowledge of the meaning of the four empowerments, the vase empowerment, and so on. The fivefold blessing lineage is the blessings of the perfect Buddha, the vajra master, the commitment deity, {258} the ḍākinīs, and the essence. Lineage is complete in these four [lineages].

2. The Three Vows

Realization of the three paths arises in dependence upon lineage. By merely obtaining the vase empowerment, there is the path of the creation stage. By obtaining the secret empowerment, there is the path of self-empowerment. By obtaining the gnosis of the wisdom consort empowerment, there is the path of the maṇḍalacakra. People who dwell on this last path possess three vows: Since their bindu is not damaged in the body, they possess the vow of personal liberation. Since great compassion arises for sentient beings who lack realization, they possess the bodhisattva vow. Since bliss arises through the strength of the increase of vāyu, they possess the vow of secret mantra.

3. The Five Paths

In accordance with the perfection vehicle, the five paths are completed by relying on a mudra. The method and effort of accomplishing bodhicitta in sixty-four sections, sixteen sections, twelve sections, and so on is the path of accumulation. The union of the *bola* and *kakkola* is the path of application. The realization of the mind of the joy of great bliss is the path of seeing. Repeated cultivation of the union of bliss and emptiness is the path of cultivation. The culmination of the mudra siddhi is the ultimate path.

B. The Main Practice

The root treatise states:

> Devadatta uses a horse.[2]
> Open the four gates with the nāga.
> Hold desire by pulling the bow.
> The pace of the tortoise causes increase.
> Stop and release the breath.
> The belt is taken to its place with *hi ki*.

The meaning of that is (1) the practitioner depends only on their own body and (2) the intention of the root treatise is to rely on the mudra, another's body.

1. Relying on One's Own Body

These days it is difficult for people to rely on an actual knowledge consort. Even when relying on another's body, {259} in the beginning it is necessary to obtain stability in a mental knowledge consort, the gnosis mudra. There are two ways for that: (1) the preparation, training in vāyu and maintaining the view; and (2) the main subject, increasing the samādhi of bliss and emptiness.

a. The Preparation

Engage in a proper amount of refuge and generation of bodhicitta. Then sit on a comfortable seat and adopt a cross-legged posture. The two hands should cover the knees. The eyes should fall on the tip of the nose. Strongly pull up the lower vāyu and draw it upward with a slow and long *hūṃ*; then press down. At that time, if there is pain in the kidney region, rotate the abdomen, straighten up, bind the waist with soft silk, and so on. If there is pain in the head, rotate the head. If there is pain in the upper body, shake the upper body. Since one trains in that way for one week, two weeks, or three weeks, one attains some measure of control over the downward-voiding vāyu. In order to investigate and stabilize that control, boil the egg of a swan or a snowcock with garlic, puncture the side of that egg, and empty the contents. Fill it with goat milk, the six excellent substances,[3] and rock candy. Insert the secret into that, filling all gaps with dough. Next, draw up [the contents of the egg] step-by-step with slow and long *hūṃ*s, one-third, two-thirds, and all the way. One will also be able to draw up the contents of a bowl, and so on. If one wishes to change, [the liquid] should be allowed to descend through the canal of the secret place. One can also gain control over lengthening [the secret place]. In the meantime, first sustain the view that possesses the four characteristics, which are described in the *Accomplishment of Gnosis*:

> Pervasiveness, the vajrakāya,
> changeless is
> the establishment of perfect gnosis,
> and omniscience is asserted due to that.

The mind essence, the reality of things, called "the gnosis vajra," pervades everything. Since it cannot be destroyed by compounded conditions, the vajrakāya does not change during the three times. {260} Since [the vajrakāya] is understood to be the nature of all objects of knowledge, when that is practiced, all phenomena are not established to be other than the essence of one's own mind. The characteristic of the mind is unceasing clarity. When its essence is investigated, it is empty. This is called "inseparable clarity and emptiness." That clarity is experienced by oneself. When that is investigated, since it is empty, it is "inseparability of cognizance and emptiness." The body arises as great bliss and all appearances arise as great bliss. When both the body and appearances are investigated, they are empty. Since bliss and emptiness are not different, one should understand that as the nature of "inseparable bliss and emptiness."

In the beginning, sustain [the view] with hearing and reflection. When it has been confirmed, sustain it naturally and apply the vāyu [yoga]. One trains in the vāyu and the view simultaneously.

b. The Main Subject

To accomplish the samādhi of bliss and emptiness, enter in union with the mudra shown with the symbol of Devadatta. First, to rely on a mental knowledge consort, the gnosis mudra, there are five retentions through the key points of the intimate instruction: (1) the descent of the bindu of bodhicitta, (2) retaining it and meditating on bliss, (3) reversing it, (4) spreading it, and (5) protecting [the bodhicitta] from being lost.

i. Descent of the Bindu

Meditate that in front of oneself there is a youthful, beautiful, and dharma-possessing maiden, to whom one is attracted. Meditate on gazing at her and speaking to her erotically. Mutually exchange the taste of honey, kiss, bite, scratch, and embrace one another. When one is dizzy from bliss, because oneself and the knowledge consort stabilize the clear appearance and pride of the pledged father and mother deity, recite the essence mantra. This is the equality of body and voice.

From the *e* of the mother's lotus arises a dharmodaya. Inside that, from *aḥ* generate an eight-petaled lotus with anthers marked with *aḥ*s and stabilize it with the mantra. {261} Meditate on the father's secret arising from *hūṃ* as a blue, five-tined vajra marked with *hūṃ*. From *oṃ* arises the jewel, and from *svā* arises the precious tip. There is an inverted dark-blue *hūṃ* syllable at the opening and an upright dark-red *phaṭ* syllable where the two tips meet. Stabilizing it with the mantra is the equality of blessing.

To employ ordinary desire as the path, bodhicitta motivated by great compassion gradually transforms desire into great bliss. Thinking that one should obtain the state of perfect buddhahood for the benefit of sentient beings is the equality of desire.

Since the three equalities are the nirmāṇakāya, sambhogakāya, and dharmakāya, respectively, the practitioner who employs the three kāyas as the path slowly engages in union and the bindu of bodhicitta descends in stages, beginning from the crown.

ii. Retention and Meditation on Bliss

The bodhicitta that descends into the center of the jewel is prevented from being lost with the three methods of retention. First, stare upward with the two eyes and place the tongue on the palate. Second, if the bodhicitta is not retained by that, press down the upper vāyu and pull up the lower vāyu. Direct attention to the bindu and it will be retained, like the simile of a strainer for an ewer. If that is difficult to retain, then "Hold desire by pulling the bow," which refers to imagining an upright *phaṭ* drawn upward by an inverted *hūṃ* with twenty-one slow and long *hūṃ*s. It is impossible for the bindu not to be retained by that [method].

Now then, if the power of bliss is weak, one must churn slowly to increase the bliss, as referenced by the passage "The pace of the tortoise causes increase." If bliss does not spread from the secret place to other parts of the body, increasing bliss is the meaning in the treatise of "release the breath." Slightly hold the lower vāyu. Open the eyes. {262} Slowly extend the exhalation through the nostrils. The samādhi of bliss and emptiness pervades the entire body.

The sign of retaining the bindu by those methods is that the lower door becomes insensitive, heavy, throbs, spasms, the hairs stand up, one feels the downward-voiding wind, and feces and urine cannot be expelled. When this becomes unbearable and one cries, laughs, exclaims, and so on, the bindu should be reversed.

Though those actual signs arise from relying on a karma mudra, they can also arise with slight retention with the gnosis mudra.

iii. Reversing

The intention of this ācārya is that once the bindu of bodhicitta descends into the space of the mother, it must again be drawn up. Though it is asserted that one practices in the manner of the sixteen joys being stabilized in ascending order, since the gnosis mudra has inferior power, the bindu of bodhicitta is reversed in six aspects from the tip of the vajra, which is the meaning of "The belt is [taken to its place] with *hi ki*": clenching and extending with the thumbs and big toes; pressing the abdomen to the spine; rolling the tongue back; rolling up the eyes; after emitting a long *hūṃ*, sounding *hik*; and drawing it upward to the crown with the *hūṃ* of samādhi and *phaṭ*. Though one engages in such actions, since it is possible there may be excess bodhicitta, one should draw it up two or three times.

iv. Spreading

The meaning of the passage "Taken to its place" is that if bodhicitta spreads into the body and it is not evenly distributed, it is possible illness will occur. Shaking the head, shaking the upper body, rotating the waist, waving the arms, stamping the feet, crying out, and so on will cause the bodhicitta to spread. One does not avoid the mudra as a śrāvaka would. If one avoids the mudra, the bindu will not increase, and one will resemble a dry cow when milked. {263} That being the case, since it is like milking a cow, the bindu increases. Buddhahood arises from the bindu. One should not lose the bodhicitta like an ordinary person. All tantras state that losing it is the source of all faults. Therefore, one should imagine that one has realized the connate gnosis through the descent and reversal of the bodhicitta and abandon desire. By relying on a knowledge consort, the entire body becomes filled with bodhicitta and the samādhi of bliss and emptiness arises without interruption.

v. Preserving the Bindu without Loss

There are eight in preserving the bindu without loss: loss because the body becomes filled with bindu, loss through conditions, loss through illness, loss through spirits, loss through conduct, loss through diet, loss through impaired blessing, and loss through damaged samaya.

I) Loss through Becoming Filled with Bindu

Loss through becoming filled with bindu is loss by virtue of the body becoming entirely filled with bindu. To prevent that, tightly bind the shaft of the vajra with white silk or white cotton, bind the waist with a sash of silk or cotton, strongly shake the two feet, focus the mind on the navel, contract the anal sphincter, and draw the lower wind up with *hi ka*. In general, it is said the bindu will not be lost. The important intimate instruction is to only meditate on the vāyu.

II) Loss through Conditions

Loss through conditions is loss upon seeing the knowledge consort. For that also shake the feet and imagine a yellow *phaṭ* and a dark-blue *hūṃ* at the tip of the vajra. Draw up with *hūṃ*, press the upper vāyu down, and also engage in the six movements.

III) Loss through Illness

Loss through illness refers to loss through a cold condition or loss combined with heat. To prevent that, sleep during the evening and abstain from sleep during the day. Soak *Terminalia chebula* in milk, administer a dry powder of the three hot herbs, and rely on a nutritious diet. Apply moxibustion to both the far side and near side of the point where the elbows reach. Warm a piece of predator hide and also wrap [the vajra,] like a case for a vajra and bell.

IV) Loss through Spirits

Loss through spirits is loss in a dream. To prevent that, burn white mustard seed. Mix the ash with black gugul, the blood of a lotus, and human brains. {264} Apply and massage this on the place of the vajra, and so on. Make twenty-one knots in a black cord, and while reciting the mantra of repelling obstructors, tie it around the waist.

V) Loss through Conduct

Loss through conduct is loss because of hard work, poor sleep, excessive talking, vigorous walking, and sitting. To prevent that, give up those activities and engage in the six movements. Meditate on *phaṭ* and *hūṃ*. Press down on the lower wind.

VI) Loss through Diet

Loss through diet is loss through spoiled meat, beans, excess salt, excessively salty water, excessive alcohol, and so on. To prevent that, avoid sleeping after [consuming those], drink milk regularly, and eat the garlic preparation called the "daily formula of amṛta."

VII) Loss through Impaired Blessing

Loss through impaired blessings refers to loss if one neglects bali offerings and feast offerings previously performed. First, descent is difficult. After descent, it is difficult to prevent loss. To prevent that, resume feast offerings and bali offerings.

VIII) Loss through Damaged Samaya

Loss through damaged samaya is the leaking of bindu without the arising of samādhi when any of the fourteen downfalls occur motivated by hatred and so on. To prevent that, one should receive the full empowerment from the guru. Through the power of that, the bindu will increase immensely, and the liṅga of desire will become firm. At that time, though one thinks one would like to climb on the mudra, one must exercise restraint and not engage in union. After that, bliss will blaze up and nonconceptuality will blaze up. The five signs, smoke, and so on, will gradually arise.

2. Relying on the Karma Mudra, Another's Body

There are five topics in the karma mudra practice with another's body: (1) a pure-knowledge consort, (2) equality in body and speech, (3) equality in desire, (4) equality in blessings, and (5) connection with the key points of the intimate instruction.

a. The Pure-Knowledge Consort

The [pure-knowledge consort] is the meaning of "Devadatta used a horse." In general, karma mudra has two divisions: (1) the qualities obtained through birth and (2) [the qualities] obtained through training.

i. The Qualities Obtained through Birth

There are three topics in [the pure-knowledge consort] obtained through birth: (1) place-born, (2) mantra-born, and (3) family- or connate-born.

I) Place-Born

She is born in any of the twenty-four regions; born in a central land and {265} has a good character; or even though she is born in a borderland, she has a special type of body.

II) Mantra-Born

She has great power in our own and others' mantras, is fearless in secret mantra conduct, and gives rise to samādhi by nature. She is also called "born from gnosis."

III) Family-Born

It is said that the family-born or connate [pure-knowledge consort] is born into a family of secret mantra practitioners or is from among the seven types of yoginīs; she is suited to serve as an attendant; and is endowed with any of the five marks of a yoginī. Further, among those [seven], she has a special body due to the power of karma. Her bliss-arousing nāḍīs, which pervade her entire body, are more powerful than those of others. In particular, since the end of her central nāḍī is elongated, it can be exhibited. These are the padminī, hariṇī, and śaṇkhinī.

From the perspective of their age, the twelve-year-old is supreme, the sixteen-year-old is excellent, the twenty-year-old is mediocre, and the twenty-five-year-old is average. Each of them should have "the fifteen signs of suitability for reliance." There are nine outer signs, three inner signs, and three secret signs. Among the nine outer signs, the three signs arising for the body are she constantly gazes at men, her mouth is dry, and her body hairs are erect. The three signs arising for her voice are erotic conversation, laughter, and meandering speech. The three shared signs are that she has mounted the aspect of the path, she begins any activity she encounters, and gathers many activities. These are the nine external signs. The three internal signs are that she rejoices in the sublime dharma, has little clinging, and is very compassionate. The three secret signs are she is devoted to the guru, she is not frightened of [secret mantra] and has devotion for secret mantra practice, and she is endowed with bodhicitta. Those are the qualities pure-knowledge women obtain through birth.

ii. The Qualities Obtained through Training

The qualities obtained through training are possessing the personal liberation vow through going for refuge; generating the aspirational and engaged bodhicitta and possessing the training of a bodhisattva; receiving the complete four empowerments and possessing the vows of Vajrayāna; and hearing many tantras and instructions and reaching the culmination of hearing and reflection. {266} A tantra states:

> The illusions of women are more extraordinary
> than all pure illusions.[4]
> The division of three gnoses
> is indicated clearly here.[5]

It is said that on the basis of this method, the gnosis of the four illuminations and the four emptinesses can be demonstrated in actuality. Having found such a person, this is the meaning in the treatises of "uses a horse." Just as one will quickly arrive at any desired place by mounting a horse, likewise, since [reliance on a mudra] causes one to swiftly arrive at the stage of buddhahood, the practitioner has previously trained in vāyu and the view.

The meaning of the passage "The four gates are opened with the nāga" is that below the navel of the knowledge consort, the tips of the rasanā and lalanā separate into four, covering the central nāḍī like the spreading hood of a snake. Since the method for opening those four is done according to the intimate instruction, after the four tips separate out, at the lower end of the central nāḍī, the best protrudes four fingerbreadths; the medium, three fingerbreadths; and the inferior, two fingerbreadths. After that, second, as explained in the section on the gnosis mudra, perform the equality of body and voice; third, the equality of blessing; and fourth, the equality of desire. Fifth, in the first of the five retentions through the key point of the intimate instruction, to begin the descent of the bindu, engage in the methods of increasing the bindu with diet, let the bindu descend and retain it, reverse it, spread it, and prevent it from being unequally distributed, as already explained.

C. The Way One Progresses on Path

The means of progression on the path is through the method of stabilizing and transforming the bindu in the body in dependence upon properly training in the path of the mudra. That person in whose body the bindu exists will be blessed by the ḍākinīs. The increased bindu in the body is the pure essence of the five nectars. Since those five are the five ḍākinīs, they move into and increase in the twenty-four inner places; increase nonconceptuality; and one is blessed by the four, eight, sixteen, or thirty-two inner ḍākinīs, and so on. Then, after one is blessed in stages by the outer ḍākinīs, one obtains the mudra siddhi and one obtains buddhahood.

In the section on the pure bindu,{267} there are sixteen joys in descending order. Since the bindu travels from the crown to the throat, there is the joy of joy, the supreme joy of joy, the joy of the joy of separation, and the joy of connate joy. Likewise, there are four joys subsumed under supreme joy, from the throat and the heart. There are four joys subsumed under the joy of separation from the heart to the navel. There are four joys subsumed under connate joy from the navel to the tip of the vajra. Since these are experienced, once gnosis is recognized at the time of the connate joy, one trains the continuum for a long while with the yoga of retaining, reversing, spreading, and distributing the bindu.

The sixteen joys are stabilized in ascending order. From the tip of the vajra to the navel, the four joys subsumed under joy arise. From the navel to the heart, the four joys subsumed under supreme joy arise. From the heart to the throat, the four joys subsumed under the joy of separation arise. From the throat to the crown, the four joys subsumed under the connate joy arise. Those joys, which are stabilized in ascending order, cause the attainment of the stages through the dissolution of six hundred and seventy-five vāyus in each of the thirty-two lands. After the gnosis of the three joys subsumed under connate joy stabilizes in half of the secret place, the first stage is attained. When the gnosis of the connate joy of connate joy is stabilized in the crown, all twenty-one thousand six hundred vāyus dissolve. The cities of the thirty-two places are emptied. Since all their powers are combined, after purifying the five concealed nāḍīs, one realizes buddhahood on the thirteenth stage.

At the occasion of those stages, the inner sign is the blockage of twelve sets of one thousand eight hundred vāyus. The outer sign of the first stage is knowing the minds of others, and so on. Furthermore, because the four joys subsumed by joy are stabilized at the navel, the maṇḍala of the navel is white-colored and hard like a mirror. One is pleasing to all migrating beings. Because the four joys subsumed under supreme joy are stabilized at the heart, the upper arm becomes enlarged, {268} and one obtains the five clairvoyances. One cannot be defeated even by one hundred strong elephants. Since the four joys subsumed under the joy of separation are stabilized at the throat, one can cover one's face with one's tongue, one is able to enjoy the amṛta of the three realms, and one is able to accomplish supreme words. Since the four joys subsumed under connate joy are stabilized at the crown, one sees inconceivable buddhafields in every pore of the body and one arrives at the final stage of buddhahood. If one wishes to understand the way of progressing through the paths and stages as applied to each individual country, it can be understood in detail from Jetsun Drakpa Gyaltsen's discourses.[6]

D. The Ultimate Result

This ācārya stated in the *Accomplishment of Gnosis* that the three kāyas possess five limbs. The dharmakāya has three limbs: it pervades all entities, it is the vajrakāya that cannot be destroyed by anything, and it is immutable in the three times. The sambhogakāya has one limb, the kāya of true gnosis. The nirmāṇakāya is the limb of omniscience about the nature and the extent of all objects of knowledge. The previous lineage masters asserted there were seven limbs. The Dharmakāya has one limb, naturelessness. The sambhogakāya has three limbs: enjoyment of the Mahāyāna dharma, union with the gnosis mudra, and immaculate great bliss. The nirmāṇakāya has three limbs: nonreferential great compassion, engaging in the benefit of sentient beings without interruption, and never ceasing because of not entering the expanse of nirvana (*nirvāṇa dhātu*).

May limitless beings attain the great immutable bliss
of the connate kāya
through the excellent path of the mudra that causes accomplishment,
the supreme, perpetual program of the great-minded.

Because it is meaningful to taste a single drop of {269}
the distilled amṛta of the instructions, which stem without error
from the lineage of the venerable siddhas, the authentic source,
it is valid for those of excellent fortune to nourish liberation.

Each method of instruction is for the diligent
to attain the stage of a sovereign siddha in one lifetime.
It is established by the Vajrayāna scriptures
that even a mere connection with these will allow the attainment of the result in sixteen lifetimes.
Therefore, may those with confidence
in Secret Mantrayāna attain supreme liberation,
relying on this supreme elixir, as difficult to find
as it is for a preta, who does not change its body in one hundred eons, [to find] the ocean shore.

The tradition of instruction in the eight ancillary path cycles was obtained through the kindness of the sovereign of one hundred families, the all-knowing and all-seeing Jamyang Khyentse Wangpo, who explained the manuals of Jetsun Drakpa Gyaltsen and the brief compositions of the *One Hundred and Eight Teaching Manuals of Jonang* [7] in the manner of summarizing extensive explanations. Later, even though he emphatically commanded, "It is necessary to compose an instruction manual" based on the special intention of his pure vision, influenced by the doubt that I was truly incapable of the task, it was neglected for a long while. Following that, for the purpose of fulfilling the wishes of the lord, I, Karma Ngawang Yöntan Gyatso Lodrö Taye Pede, composed this manual in the practice place of the upper retreat of Palpung, Tsadra Rinchen Drak. It was set down nearby in writing by the scribe Losal Sangak Tenzin.

May it be virtuous.

17. Fortunate Vermilion Ornament

Kṛṣṇācārya's Manual of Completing the Whole Path with Caṇḍālī[1]

Jamgön Kongtrul

{272} *namo vajradharapādāya*

Having bowed to Mahāsiddha Kṛṣṇavajra,[2]
the inseparable five lord founders,
and Khyentse Wangpo who unifies them all into one,
I shall set forth the manual on completing the path with caṇḍālī.

Among the eight ancillary path cycles is the manual of completing the path with caṇḍālī composed by Ācārya Kṛṣṇa, the powerful practitioner of strict discipline, who was predicted by the Buddha. There are two topics in its explanation: (1) the lineage from which it originates and (2) the explanation of the actual instruction that arises from that lineage.

I. The Lineage

The position of this great ācārya, who relied upon the intimate instructions of Mahāsiddha Jālandharapa and attained siddhi, is that all dharmas of the Buddha are included in Vajrayāna. The lower tantras of Vajrayāna are included in mahāyoga. Though all say that there are two kinds of tantras in mahāyoga, the method and wisdom tantras, these are included in the *Hevajra Tantra* and the *Cakrasaṃvara Tantra*. Also, all that is compatible in terms of the actual root tantras, explanatory tantras, and so on are included in the *Saṃpūṭatilaka Tantra* {273}and the *Vajraḍāka Tantra*. When the intention of those two is combined, there is the completion stage for which Kṛṣṇa composed six summaries. The basic summary is the *Ornament of*

Spring. The verse summary is the *Secret Principle.* The summary of the direct realization is the *Four Stages.* The summary of the meaning is the *Condensed Essence.* The summary of the yoga is the *Explanation of Vows.* The summary for relying on a mudra is the *Ornament of Mahāmudrā.*[3] Those are included in the *Four Stages*, which is like the heart. The condensed instruction for those six is this, *Completing the Whole Path with Caṇḍālī.*

The lineage is Vajradhara,[4] Vajrayoginī, Vajraghantapāda, Kūrmapāda, Śrī Jālandhara I, Kṛṣṇācārya, Śrīdhara, Gayadhara, and down to the Lord Sakyapa uncles and nephews, and at the end the lineage continues to the greatly kind one who is the river of all tantras, āgamas, and intimate instructions, the all-seeing and knowing Jamyang Khyentse Wangpo, through whose kindness I obtained it. {274}

II. The Instruction

There are three topics in the actual instruction: (1) the concise explanation through the summary, (2) the extensive explanation, and (3) the way the ultimate result is obtained from that.

A. The Concise Explanation

In general, the view of this ācārya is called "the suchness of bodhicitta without beginning or end and liberated from the four extremes." The path of the method of realizing the view is held to have four or five stages. The four stages are the stage of tantra, the stage of mantra, the stage of gnosis, and the stage of secret. When the stage of nonduality is added to those, there are five stages. For each of those five, there is a triad: the tantra, and so on; the progression; and the measure of attaining perfection.

Each of those five stages is also held to be summarized in triads: the tantra, and so on; the progression, and so on; and the measure of attaining perfection, and so on. In the first stage, "tantra" refers to the three maṇḍalas supported on the four cakras, and so on, which have existed from the beginning [in the body]. "Progression" refers to progressive visualization. "The measure of attaining perfection" is clearly seeing the three maṇḍalas just as they are.

In the second stage, "mantra" refers to the *aṃ* syllable in the navel. "Progression" refers to the progression of igniting the fire up to burning the four cakras. "The measure of attaining perfection" refers to the various experiences of trembling, and so on.

In the third stage, "gnosis" refers to the connate of the connate stabilized in ascending order. "Progression" refers to the amṛta of gnosis entering through the left calf and experienced from the jewel of the vajra up to the brow. "The measure of attaining perfection" refers to all things arising as bliss, and so on.

In the fourth stage, "secret" refers to the prāṇa vāyu. "Progression" refers to holding and meditating on the vāyu inside each of the nostrils, which removes all faults of the vāyu. "The measure of attaining perfection" refers to the body feeling as light as a cotton ball, that one can avert the obstacles of ḍākinīs through seeing the five signs, and so on.

In the fifth stage, "nondual" refers to {275} the fundamental mind of the nonduality of subject and object or appearances and emptiness. "Progression" refers to progressively realizing that all inner and outer phenomena are essentially inseparable. "The measure of attaining perfection" is the attainment of clairvoyance. That is the conclusion of the mundane path's supreme dharmas in the path of application.

On the basis of relying on a predicted mudra, one travels through the twelve stages—the pithas, upapithas, and so on—and realizes the stage of buddhahood. This is the conclusion of the concise explanation.

B. The Extensive Explanation

There are five topics in the extensive stages of meditation: (1) the stage of tantra, (2) the stage of mantra, (3) the stage of gnosis, (4) the stage of secret, and (5) the stage of nonduality.

1. The Stage of Tantra

Confirm the root and explanatory tantras of the summary through hearing and reflection beforehand. If unable to do so, it is also fine. There are two topics in the practice of the meditation: (1) the preliminaries and (2) the main subject.

a. The Preliminaries

Having sat comfortably in an isolated place, the preliminary for all dharma practice is the uncommon refuge and the generation of bodhicitta. The principal object of refuge is the guru and Śrī Heruka, inseparable. One should meditate on Heruka Vajrasattva to purify misdeeds and obscurations and recite his one-hundred-syllable mantra. One should offer a maṇḍala in the usual way in order to complete the accumulations. The principal of the field of accumulation is the guru in essence, generated in the form of the pledged deity. The guru yoga to induce blessings is as follows: In the center of one's house, a protection wheel and celestial mansion, on a lion throne, lotus, sun, and Bhairava and Kālaratri is one's guru in the form of Cakrasaṃvara, with four faces and twelve hands, embracing the mother, Vajravārāhī. The retinue is the sixty heroes and ḍākinīs, who each stand in their own places. All the root and lineage gurus, the assembly of pledged deities, buddhas, bodhisattvas, noble śrāvakas, pratyekabuddhas, dharmapālas, and guardians reside inside, outside, above, below, and in all directions of the celestial mansion. {276} Imagine that an inconceivable cloud bank of offerings fills all directions. Having beforehand prostrated, gone for refuge, and presented offerings and praises, offer intense supplications. Visualize that one takes the four empowerments from the light rays from the guru's body. Finally, the retinue dissolves into the root guru. Imagine that the guru dissolves into oneself and dedicate the virtue to awakening. Recite aspirations for the guru's guidance. This is the limb of concentration.

b. The Main Subject

To begin, there is the topic of preventing obstacles and becoming familiar with the samādhi. Since one sets up the dependent origination of the object of purification and the purifier by arranging a large feast, introduce individually the basis of purification, the purifier, the object of purification, and the result of purification in four sessions of the creation stage according to the sādhana of Cakrasaṃvara, train in undistracted meditation, and if one wishes to supplement this, engage in recitation as one wishes. If one purifies a little and meditates, the actual progression of the meditation is to visualize a blue *hūṃ* in the heart and a red *aṃ* in the navel of the principal. Since light shines from *hūṃ*, the half of the deities of the maṇḍalacakra in the principal directions that circle left and the half of the deities in the intermediate directions that circle right enter the right nostril and left nostril in concert with inhalation and exhalation, respectively, and gather in the *hūṃ* of the heart. The mother, Vajravārāhī, also gathers into *aṃ* at the [principal's] navel. Light shines from that *aṃ*, and the interior of the body is empty. Imagine that the two functional cakras, the four cakras of the navel, and so on, the three principle nāḍīs, and the syllables block the rasanā and the lalanā.

The detailed visualization is that from a *yaṃ* syllable at the rectum, a semicircular, blue maṇḍala of air arises, marked with pennants. From *raṃ* in the groin, a triangular fire maṇḍala arises, with one tip facing downward and marked with three flames blazing upward. This is the visualization of the two functional cakras. {277}

The red-colored nirmāṇacakra at the navel has sixty-four nāḍī petals. Its inner circle has eight petals with the eight series (*a ka ca ṭa ta pa ya śa*) and *aṃ* in the center. The outer circle has fifty-six syllables: thirty-four consonants circling to the right and sixteen vowels circling to the left, to which are added the six short vowels, *a i u e o aṃ*. The black dharmacakra at the heart has eight petals: *bhrūṃ āṃ jriṃ khaṃ* in the four main directions, *ya ra la va* in the intermediate directions, and *hūṃ* in the center. The inner circle of the red sambhogacakra at the throat has the four long vowels, *ā ī ū ai*, and in the center is *oṃ*.[5] The outer circle has twelve vowels, excluding the four genderless vowels [*ṛ ṝ ḷ ḹ*]. In the center of the white mahāsukhacakra at the crown, which has thirty-two petals, visualize an inverted white *haṃ*, free from an array of syllables.

Then, in the center of the four cakras, on the right is the red solar rasanā, with its mouth facing upward, which has a nature of fire. Visualize pairs of stacked, upright, red consonants between each of the inverted white vowels, descending from the upper tip to its bottom. To the left is the white lunar lalanā, with its mouth facing downward,[6] which has the nature of water. Visualize pairs of stacked, inverted, red consonants between each of the upright white vowels, ascending from the lower tip to its top. In between those two, the central nāḍī is the size of a horsehair split into hundredths, red, straight, and fine. Those should be clearly visualized in the beginning.

Next, in concert with the exhalation, visualize the cakras in ascending order, from navel to crown, based on the right rasanā. In concert with the exhalation, visualize the cakras in descending order, from crown to navel, based on the left lalanā. {278} When pausing the breath, visualize the central nāḍī and *aṃ* at the navel. Also, the method of visualizing that not in concert with the breath is permissible. Either should be clear and short. As there is no defined number of sessions, the statement that one should meditate for three, five, seven, nine, or eleven days to attain a clear appearance is intended for those of best capacity. Most people will need to meditate for years and months. Whatever the case may be, meditating until the six cakras and three nāḍīs becomes extremely clear, like the lines on one's palms, is an intimate instruction of the stage of tantra alone, the basic yoga of visualization.

2. The Stage of Mantra

There are two topics in the stage of mantra: (1) the preliminaries and (2) the main subject.

a. The Preliminaries

When engaging in this practice, one should reduce one's regular intake of food and drink. Rely on very nutritious food. The key point of the body is that one should sit with the knees drawn up to the chest, with both hands encircling the knees like a meditation belt. The thighs should be pressed tightly against the belly. The two feet and the buttocks carry the weight evenly.

Next, in order to ignite the fire maṇḍala of the groin with the vāyu maṇḍala at the rectum, constrict the lower vāyu seven times. This causes the air maṇḍala at the rectum to stir. Since the blazing fire of the groin strikes *aṃ* at the navel, imagine the fire blazes and relax the lower vāyu. Swallow the upper vāyu and spittle, which dissolve into *aṃ* at the navel. Direct one's consciousness to *aṃ* at the navel. Press down on the vāyu for as long as possible. That is performed forcefully yet briefly. Since one repeatedly meditates on that, one sees five signs, smoke, and so on. Feel that the fire of *aṃ* blazes out of control, from one or two finger lengths all the way up to the throat. It spreads to the tongue and the shoulders. If the signs of thirst and great passion arise, the caṇḍālī fire is growing strong. The flame cannot blaze upward until one feels the flame burning out of control. One should not constrict the lower vāyu.

b. The Main Subject

When the signs of feeling the fire blazing out of control, {279} and so on, occur, there is the "meeting of the tips of the mothers." Since the rasanā channel on the right causes heat, it is called "the mother of fire." Since the lalanā on the left causes nonconceptuality, it is called "the mother of sleep." The tips of both meet in the central channel. Repeatedly open and close the anal sphincter and constrict it strongly. Since one meditates on uniting the vāyus of the vase, the fire blazes from *aṃ*, fills the navel cakra with the light of the fire, and the seed syllables become bright red like red-hot iron. The taints and impurities are burnt away. Imagine that [the fire] is extremely hot to the touch. Next, the flame ascends through the right rasanā like lightning and burns up the seed syllables of the five tathāgata families and the four mothers, as before. Again, the fire moves through the rasanā, burning the seed syllables of the throat cakra, as before. Again, the fire moves through the rasanā. Visualize that it burns the crown cakra in that way.

Although it is explained that after the opening of the point of the brow, there is the [fire and amṛta] entering and leaving the continua of the tathāgatas, practically speaking, after either one's right ear[7] or nostril is filled, the flames fill the expanse of space. One meditates on [the fire] entering and leaving inconceivable tathāgatas in the space before oneself. Further, when that visualization is clear, one should first train the mind on one tathāgata and then according to the stages of familiarization, ten, one hundred, one thousand, and so on, up to an inconceivable number. Those flames enter the right ear or right nostril of the tathāgatas, becoming the same nature as the fire of the rasanā. Since there are some repetitions of fire turning up and turning down inside of their bodies, the four cakras and the pure elements [of the tathāgatas] melt into amṛta and are gathered by the flames. Having become the same nature as the lalanā, [the amṛta] leaves their left nostrils or left ears, {280} traveling inside the lalanā through one's left nostril or ear. Because it fills the crown cakra, it suppresses the heat of the fire and restores the cakras to their previous state. Further, when the amṛta descends through the lalanā, it restores the throat cakra, and the nāḍī syllables become brighter, clearer than before, and radiant. The amṛta descends again and restores the heart cakra. It descends again and restores the navel cakra, and so on, visualized as above. When the flame stirs upward, [the amṛta] enters through the right calf of the tathāgatas and leaves through the left calf, traveling from one's left calf into the lalanā, gradually restoring the cakras from the navel to the crown. One should alternate [the descending and ascending visualizations]. Also, in both cases, since the bodhicitta amṛta of the tathāgatas strikes *aṃ*, strongly activating it, a very fine, clear flame emerges, blazing with light, and blazes longer and longer inside the central nāḍī. It penetrates *hūṃ* at the heart and *oṃ* at the throat, and since it strikes *haṃ* at the crown, *haṃ* melts into bliss. The bodhicitta is white, cool, and shines with white rays of light. It flows down from the crown, like a long thread of white silk, and the strength of joy increases more and more. Next, focus on it dissolving into *aṃ* at the navel or on the gap between the *aṃ* [and the crown]. Finally, one should rest in a nonconceptual state. Meditate on that repeatedly.

In another manual on the *Four Stages*, the cakras that are incinerated by the flame are restored by the continuous flow of the bodhicitta from the *haṃ*. Since the fire blazes in the central nāḍī from *aṃ*, the two syllables are penetrated. The point of the brow is opened and the amṛta that comes and goes from the tathāgatas dissolves into *haṃ* at the crown. The amṛta that simultaneously descends fills the seed syllables of the throat and heart and dissolves into *aṃ* at the navel. This sequence appears in that way. The technique for this is that one repeats the visualization of the four cakras once for each breath {281} and meditates on the blazing and dripping a single time. On the second breath, one mainly focuses the mind on the union of spring and its ornament (*dpyid thig*, Skt. *vasantatilaka*). After that, for one breath, place the mind in nonconceptuality and rest.

Since one cultivates in that way repeatedly, the samādhis of bliss, clarity, and nonconceptuality are generated in one's body and mind. There may be trembling, shaking, uttering loud noises, and so on. It is sufficient to maintain those naturally when some of those [signs] arise. If they are excessive and cannot be pacified, then one should "decapitate the syllables." Inhale and exhale forcefully a few times, and these [signs] should be pacified. If that does not remove them, meditate on the visualization of *haṃ*. If that does not remove them, meditate on the body above the heart as hollow, like a bucket. If that does not pacify them, since one recalls that all phenomena are one's mind and one's mind is empty, they will be pacified.

This is the aspect of the stage of mantra employed as the path, the caṇḍālī yoga of equal portions of nāḍīs, vāyus, and bindus.

3. The Stage of Gnosis

a. The Preliminary

The stage of gnosis is generated by a person who has reached the culmination of experience of the stage of mantra and has generated the experience of the sixteen joys stabilized in descending order. Here in this manual, though the visualization is not clearly explained, it is necessary to identify the four descending joys that occur in other employments of the four stages as the path. Also here, the actual way of performing that due to the influence of such implicit understanding is as follows: At the conclusion of a single occasion of the visualization of the main subject of the stage of mantra, since the stream of the melted *haṃ* descends to the throat, imagine that the gnosis of joy arises when the path of the sambhogacakra fills, and focus the mind upon it. When the stream descends from that, the heart cakra fills, and the gnosis of supreme joy arises. When the stream descends from that, the navel cakra fills, and the gnosis of the joy of separation arises. When the stream descends from that, the cakra of the secret place fills, {282} the inside of the jewel fills with bodhicitta, and one imagines that the gnosis of connate joy arises. If one has trained in the vāyu yoga, in the place of each cakra where one has focused, one holds a vase and after identifying the gnosis, it is necessary to rest in its essence. If the beginner who does not have control over their vāyu emulates the meditation above, after holding an actual vase at the navel, they should just imagine the vāyu gathers in the other places. That is the preliminary.

b. The Main Subject

Focus one's mind on the bindu that is very clear, like a reflection of the moon in the water, which is in the center of those nāḍīs and cakras that are pervaded by bodhicitta, completely full of the bindu of white bodhicitta with a reddish tinge, which descended into the jewel of the vajra.

The meditation on bliss, clarity, and nonconceptuality is the joy of joy. When unbearable bliss arises, draw the bindu into the shaft of the vajra, and focus the mind on it. This is the supreme joy of joy. Next, as the unbearable bliss is gradually drawn up, it is necessary to focus the mind on each place. Thus, when it is drawn to the base of the vajra, it is the separation of the joy of joy. When it is drawn to the navel, it is the connate joy of joy. Thus, of the sixteen moments of joy, four joys are distinguished in the first joy.

Next, drawing [the bindu] to the location one-fourth of the way above the navel and focusing the mind is the joy of supreme joy. Then, drawing it to the location two-fourths of the way above that and focusing the mind is the supreme joy of supreme joy. Then, drawing it to the location three-fourths of the way above that and focusing the mind is the separation of the joy of supreme joy. After that, drawing it up to the heart cakra and focusing the mind is the connate joy of supreme joy. Thus, there are four joys included in supreme joy, the second joy. The sign that the bindu has reached this point is the arising of a feeling of heart palpitations and tremors.

Next, drawing the bindu to the location one-fourth of the way above the heart {283} and focusing the mind is the joy of the separation of joy. Then, drawing it to the location two-fourths of the way above that and focusing the mind is the supreme joy of the separation of joy. Then, drawing it to the location three-fourths of the way above that and focusing the mind is the separation of joy of the separation of joy. After that, drawing it up to the throat cakra and focusing the mind is the connate joy of the separation of joy. Thus, there are four joys included in the separation of joy, the third joy. The sign it has reached this point is that one feels one's voice is blocked and one feels one cannot speak.

Next, drawing the bindu to the location one-fourth of the way above the throat and focusing the mind is the joy of the connate joy. Then, drawing it to the location two-fourths of the way above that and focusing the mind is the supreme joy of the connate joy. Then, drawing it to the location three-fourths of the way above that and focusing the mind is the separation of joy of the connate joy. After that, drawing it up to the center of the crown cakra and focusing the mind on the bindu is the ultimate connate joy of the connate joy. Meditate until all those joys arise in each of their locations. If the experience does not arise in that way, it is necessary to return to the previous location, repeat, and meditate. By meditating in that way, the sign of the bindu reaching that point is all appearances arise as bliss. One becomes unconscious from the bliss as if one were having intercourse or were intoxicated. If one feels intoxicated with bliss merely by perceiving or looking at something, the meditation has reached the culmination of the sixteen joys of the stage of gnosis. Thus, to eliminate proliferation concerning those, one should meditate on the subsequent stages.

4. The Stage of the Secret

There are two topics in the stage of the secret: the actual meditation and removing the faults of vāyu.

a. The Actual Meditation

"Secret" refers to vāyu. "Stage" refers to a progressive meditation. Meditate on the empty space of the two nostrils, which are likened to a hollow egg. {284} Hold a "gentle breath" slightly. Balance the life-sustaining vāyu: After it emerges from the body like incense smoke, meditate that it is sniffed into a single nostril and does not go back. Since one meditates this way for a long while, it is said that the life-sustaining vāyu is stabilized and many qualities arise, such as pacifying chronic illnesses, preventing new ones, and so on.

b. Removing the Faults of the Vāyu

On this occasion, since all kinds of faults of the vāyu become possible, it is necessary to remove those with the procedure of reversing any faults that occur. If one has uncontrollable diarrhea, there is discomfort and pain during movement because the downward-voiding vāyu has been arrested, signifying that the bliss has increased excessively. In order to pacify that, focus on the bliss at the brow. Since one focuses on that, if there is pain in the nasal bone, pain in the crown, or pain in the ears due to roaring sound, the upward-moving vāyu has been arrested and this signifies the bliss is increasing. In order to pacify that, focus the mind on the bliss at the navel. If there is also a feeling of discomfort and bloating, the metabolic vāyu has been arrested and this signifies the bliss is increasing. In order to pacify that, focus the mind on the bliss at the throat. If one feels numbness in the lower lip or one cannot speak, the vāyu that exists in the tongue is arrested and this signifies that the bliss is increasing. In order to pacify that, focus the mind on the bliss at the heart center. If one feels queasiness and disturbance in the heart, the vāyu has been arrested in the heart and this signifies the bliss is increasing. In order to pacify that, focus the mind on the bliss in the center of the jewel. That may cause pain and numbness in all the joints of the body. If the whole body starts to shake, the pervading vāyu has been arrested and this signifies that bliss is increasing in the body. In order to pacify that, meditate on the absence of the inherent existence of that bliss. If by meditating in that way there is a desire to laugh or one feels compelled to utter exclamations, the bliss has increased excessively. Meditate without perceiving the increased bliss. If one feels very intoxicated and loses consciousness because of such a meditation, śamatha is predominant. That will be dispelled by meditating on all outer and inner phenomena {285} as illusions. Those stages of meditation will balance [the life-sustaining vāyu]. Meditation should be repeated. If sustained without interruption, at the culmination, the body will be as light as a cotton ball, and one will see the five signs—smoke, and so on. Gradually, after the ḍākinīs come to activate one's experience, when they display their various forms, one should prevent obstacles by displaying the signs as taught in the tantras. If one does not know the signs, all of those will naturally be removed by resting in a state of nonconceptuality and one will be blessed by the ḍākinīs.

5. The Stage of Nonduality

The stage of nonduality refers to the absence of inherent existence of the object and consciousness and meditating after merging both. Since all phenomena of samsara and nirvana are included in one's mind and mental factors, without conceptualizing about external phenomena, one meditates without perceiving all the conceptual sensations of the inner mind. Further, subject and object are both sensations of bliss, inseparable bliss and emptiness, like pouring water into water. Everything that arises as clarity is inseparable clarity and emptiness. Everything that dissolves into nonconceptuality is inseparable cognizance and emptiness. In brief, meditate without perceiving anything at all in the state of the nonduality of all objects and consciousness. Since one reaches the culmination of such meditation, one gradually obtains the five clairvoyances and the stage of great bliss. Those stages are the culmination of the two mundane paths: accumulation and application.

After one obtains stability in the former stage, that will influence the proper meditation of the later stage. If a beginner meditates on these visualizations fully, in reality, though all [the visualizations described] are only in the stage of tantra, aspects of the three later stages are employed as the path and will be meditated on with devotion. Also, the experience and realization corresponding to each stage will arise.

Because this text is the four stages or {286} the perfection of all paths that depend primarily on caṇḍālī, it is known as "Completing the Path with Caṇḍālī" and "Employing Caṇḍalı as the Path." Because *caṇḍālī* refers to burning the thicket of ignorance and affliction with the fire of gnosis, though a wider sense of the term is that it is a general name for the completion stage, among the different general names, the narrower sense of the term is that it is a description for visualizing the inner fire. The main visualization is this four-cakra visualization. Because it is the condensed, essential topic of the meditation clarified and extensively taught in the *Saṃvarodaya Tantra*, the *Vajraḍāka Tantra*, and the *Sampūṭatilaka Tantra*, its source and purpose are very important.

When one reaches the culmination of the stage of nonduality through practice, there will be a prediction of a mudra by Śrī Heruka, Vajrayoginī, and so on. Search her out and one will obtain the transcendent perception based upon the path of the mudra and profound conduct. After that, since the gnosis of great bliss increases exponentially, the knots of the nāḍīs are gradually released, and one can easily progress without obstacles through the twelve stages, the pithas, upapithas, and so on. Ultimately, one will realize buddhahood.

C. The Result

As such, the result of practice is realizing the stage of the unchanging, supreme great bliss of perfect buddhahood endowed with seven limbs, and having reached the culmination of one's own benefit, effortlessly accomplish the benefit of others without the need for striving, like the sun and its light rays. Further, from among the seven limbs, the three limbs of the dharmakāya are naturelessness, uninterrupted, and unceasing. The first is free from all proliferation, the second arises from the strength of compassion, and the third arises by the power of aspiration. The three limbs of the sambhogakāya are union, great bliss, and complete enjoyments. The first arises from never parting from the apparent aspect of the wisdom consort, one's own radiance. {287} The second arises from one's continuum becoming filled with connate, supreme, and unchanging bliss. The third arises from the extremely pure major and minor marks being perfectly complete. The single limb of the nirmāṇakāya is called "totally filled with great compassion."

> All qualities of the four stages
> are completed by the path of caṇḍālī.
> This supreme elixir of the ocean of secret meaning
> is reasonable for the fortunate ones to practice.

The chapter on the manual of Siddhācārya Kṛṣṇācārya's instruction called *Completing the Whole Path with Caṇḍālī* was composed by Lodrö Taye according to the command of the precious lord guru. May virtue increase.

PART THREE

Ancillary Instructions and Rites

18. The Manual Known as *The Dharma Connection with the Six Gatekeepers* Received by Drokmi Lotsāwa from the Six Paṇḍita Gatekeepers[1]

The Dharma Connection with the Six Gatekeepers is a fascinating cycle, as it is one of the few texts we have in the Sakya tradition that records Drokmi's personal interactions with his gurus at Vikramaśīla. In order, the six paṇḍitas are Ratnākaraśānti, Prajñākaragupta, Jñānaśrīmitra, Ratnavajra, Vāgīśvarakīrti, and Naropa (all late tenth to mid-eleventh centuries). *The Dharma Connection with the Six Gatekeepers* includes four sections: (1) Ratnākaraśānti's *Merging Sutra and Tantra* and instructions, (2) *The Trio for Removing Obstructions by Prajñākaragupta, Jñānaśrī, and Ratnavajra*, (3) Vāgīśvarakīrti's *Clear Mindfulness of the Innate* and instructions, and (4) Naropa's *Mahāmudrā That Removes the Three Sufferings.* There appear to be no Tibetan commentaries on them, other than the summaries by Kunga Drölchok.[2]

Ameshap's *Ocean That Gathers Excellent Explanations* relates that when Drokmi is studying Sanskrit in the Katmandhu Valley, he requests the empowerments of Hevajra, Cakrasaṃvara, Guhyasamāja, Bhairava, and Mahāmaya from the Nepali paṇḍita, Śāntibhadra. Drokmi studies with Śāntibhadra for one year, excelling in his studies and earning the title "translator." Preparing to leave for India, Śāntibhadra encourages Drokmi and his companions to head for Vikramaśīla after they pay respects at Bodhgaya. He tells them there are six gatekeepers (*sgo srung*) at Vikramaśīla:

> Five hundred paṇḍitas who have received royal parasols are at that place. Foremost among them is Guru Śantipa, the one with the twofold omniscience in the age of degeneration. Śantipa is

> the eastern gatekeeper of Vikramaśīla, charged with debating grammar and epistemology. Vāgīśvarakīrti is the southern gatekeeper, charged with debating scriptural dharma. Since these two are equals, they also guide students together. The western gatekeeper is Prajñākaragupta of Oḍḍiyāna, charged with debating non-Buddhist systems. His special expertise is the view, meditation, conduct, and result of equipoise. The northern gatekeeper is Lord Naropa, charged with debating mantra. These two are considered equals. Jñānaśrīmitra of Kashmir and Ratnavajra are the so-called two great pillars in the center. However, they are not considered to have qualities greater than the others, and these five do not have less knowledge than Śantipa. Also, you should request dharma connections with the others.[3]

Amezhap tells us that Drokmi studied under Śantipa for a total of eighteen years, receiving teachings in Vinaya and Prajñāparamitā, including Śantipa's own commentary on the *Perfection of Wisdom in Twenty-Five Thousand Lines*.[4] After these studies, Drokmi received Cakrasaṃvara and other empowerments from Śantipa as well as the special instruction, *Merging Sutra and Tantra*. Drokmi then makes dharma connections with the other five masters listed above and receives instruction from them.

Ratnākaraśānti's *Merging Sutra and Tantra* is exactly what it sounds like, a text on how to practice sutra and tantra in union. It recounts a conversation between Śantipa and Drokmi, and then provides a method of practice for the verse that Ratnākaraśānti utters. Amezhap furthers notes that Ratnākaraśānti explains his view according to the path of the Mind Only school and he practices the creation stage according to the Buddhajñāpāda system. The person who authored the attached meditation instruction as well as the remaining texts is not recorded, but it resembles the style of the eight ancillary path cycles.

The rest of the cycle begins with an interlude and a title list of the five paṇḍitas with whom Drokmi makes dharma connections. While Naropa's and Vāgīśvarakīrti's texts are listed first, they actually come last. First is *The Trio for Removing Obstructions by Prajñākaragupta, Jñānaśrī, and Ratnavajra*.

We know very little about Prajñākaragupta of Oḍḍiyāna, Jñānaśrīmitra of Kashmir, and Ratnavajra other than their works in the Tengyur. These three texts are quite brief and their titles are self-explanatory. The thing of note here is that it appears that the person who put these three texts into writing is Chöje Zhönu Drup, a Sakya master of the thirteenth century.

The next section is devoted to an instruction of Vāgīśvarakīrti, related to *Mahāmudrā without Syllables*, with two parts. The first part of the text is directly attributed to Vāgīśvarakīrti; the second part is a somewhat detailed description of how to meditate in connection with the pledged deity, Hevajra. Notable in the lineage is the presence of Khyungpo Naljor, the founder of the Shangpa Kagyu.

The final section in this cycle is Naropa's *Mahāmudrā That Removes the Three Sufferings.* Naropa himself needs no introduction. Like the Ratnākaraśānti text that begins the cycle, this text also presents a dialogue with Drokmi. No author is given for the final text, but there is a note that the original text was somewhat unclear, and this text represents a reorganization of the original text on behalf of an aristocratic woman named Trinle Kyi.

Merging Sutra and Tantra

Drokmi Lotsāwa

{290} I prostrate with devotion to the feet of the sublime guru.

When Lord Drokmi had completed [his study] of the treatises with Guru Śantipa,[5] as he was departing for Tibet, he offered the latter a little gold and requested practice advice.

[Guru Śantipa] said, "Practice the topics of sutra and tantra."

[Drokmi] asked, "Should I first practice the topics of sutra and then practice the topics of tantra?"

[Guru Śantipa] said, "Practice both inseparably."

[Drokmi] asked, "How should that be practiced?"

[Guru Śantipa said,] "As it says in the *Hevajra Tantra*:

> When the three worlds are transformed,[6]
> all are free from apprehended objects and apprehending subjects.
> However,[7] one must investigate[8]
> the characteristics of entities with all methods.[9]

All topics of the tantras are said to be included in that passage.

The *Collected Verses on the Noble Perfection of Wisdom* states:

> The childish[10] impute existence[11] and nonexistence.[12]
> These two, existence and nonexistence,[13] are phenomena that do not exist.
> A bodhisattva who knows[14] this escapes.[15]

All the topics of sutras are included in that passage."

Having taught the practice of those two nondually, he then said: {291}

> *namo gurupādāya*
> Imputed appearances are the illusory phenomena of one's mind.
> Since one recognizes them to be inherently pure, one is liberated.
> It is important to cultivate with indirect methods.
> The natural progress of the essential meaning,
> evaluating the higher and lower in terms of stages, is a key point.
> Since it is not the domain of the inferior,
> investigate and one should give it to a disciple.

ithi

Now, the practice is to sit on a comfortable seat, with the complete key points of the body for samādhi. The meditation on the desire to go for refuge, generate bodhicitta, and so on is not just a trifle. Sever all that is connected to ordinary thought. Meditate on whichever is one's yidam visualized as the deity. The visualization, the radiation and return of the seed syllable of the heart, and the descent of the blessing should be understood in detail from one's guru.[16] Meditate on the guru upon one's crown, who dissolves, becoming indistinguishable from everything.

Next,{292} since one gazes intensely at appearances and the mind, a deep certainty arises that all phenomena of appearances and mind are like illusions.[17] Do not immediately modify. Also, reification about natural purity from the beginning is instantly eliminated. Nondual samsara and nirvana—vivid in intrinsic clarity and unrestricted in self-liberation—is self-liberated as the dharmakāya. Since that is understood, nonreferential compassion for all sentient beings who do not realize that will arise. That is also termed "inseparability" because it is the state of the dharmadhātu.

There is no fault of reversing the order of method and wisdom. Such a fault is voided by a citation. The *Saṃpūṭa Tantra* states:

> Meditating[18] on emptiness first
> washes the embodied ones.[19]

The *Collected Verses on the Noble Perfection of Wisdom* states:

> Know that these aggregates do not arise and are empty from the beginning.
> Regard the domain of sentient beings who do not reside in equipoise with compassion.
> At those times the buddhadharmas will not be abandoned.[20]

And:

> Wisdom is prior to gift and giver,
> likewise, disciple, patience, diligence, and concentration.
> It upholds virtuous dharmas so they will not be lost.
> This is the single means of demonstrating all dharmas.[21]

[Qualm:] Now then, the *Collected Verses on the Noble Perfection of Wisdom* states:

> For as long as the root of virtue is incomplete,
> for that long sublime emptiness will not be attained.[22]

And the *Hevajra Tantra* states:

> First, bestow poṣadha vows . . .[23]

[Reply:] Those are the easy sequence of arising. Here, it is the necessary sequence of arising. That inseparability is called "emptiness that possesses a core of compassion" or "skill in means that never moves away from wisdom." That is the means of effortlessly progressing on the supreme path. The *Collected Verses on the Noble Perfection of Wisdom* states:

> Though great compassion is generated, a sentient being is not perceived.
> At that time the wise become the object of offering for all migrating beings.[24]

The path is called "the natural progress of the essential meaning." {293} "Evaluating the higher and lower in terms of stages is a key point" refers to such natural progress as evaluating the higher through the view. When evaluating the lower through the means of progress, the virtuous activities of meditation completed by that is the path of accumulation. Clearly ascertaining the general meaning in dependence on any mind of concentration is the path of application. Realizing that [general meaning] is the path of seeing. Through cultivating that, the traces of affliction that have the mode of the knowledge obscuration become very attenuated, which is the path of cultivation. Once each of those subtle taints is pacified in the dharmadhātu, abandonment and realization are totally perfected and activities motivated by the desire to benefit sentient beings are effortless, which is the ultimate path.

A path such as this is not to be given to those inferior ones who have not touched the meaning of reality, but it should be given to a person who is connected with a true, virtuous mentor who understands the nature of samsara, has abandoned grasping to the self of this life, and combines practice into one.

In the end one should dedicate the virtue. One should repeatedly recall the stream of equipoise in post-equipoise.

This intimate instruction of Guru Śantipa is called *The Practice of Merging Sutra and Tantra*, *The Natural Progress of the Essential Meaning*, and *The Intimate Instruction of Blessing the Universe and Beings*.

It is a profound path.

śubha

The Trio for Removing Obstructions by Prajñākaragupta, Jñānaśrī, and Ratnavajra

Drokmi Lotsāwa

namo guru

After Drokmi finished training under Guru Śantipa, the individual intimate instructions and treatises he heard from the other five paṇḍitas were *Dispelling the Three Sufferings* from Nāropa, *Clear Mindfulness of the Innate* from Vāgīśvarakīrti, the *Intimate Instruction of Preventing Obstacles by External Spirits* from Prajñākaragupta, the *Intimate Instruction of Preventing Obstacles of Disturbances of the Body* from Jñānaśrī, and the *Intimate Instruction of Preventing Obstacles in Samādhi and the Mind* from Ratnavajra. The first two of the five should be understood elsewhere. {294} The trio of intimate instructions for preventing obstacles will all be written down together and will be taught separately according to the intention of each ācārya.

Prajñākaragupta's *Intimate Instruction of Preventing Obstacles by External Spirits* states:

> Light shines from the seed syllable[25]
> of the mind's own cognizance, filling the pores of the body.
> Wherever *hūṃ* is recited,
> it is the supreme protection against spirits.

Imagine that light rays shine from *hūṃ* in the navel of the vajra in the heart of whatever deity one is meditating on, filling all pores of the body, and chant *hūṃ* with a strong voice, loud and elongated.

Further, since light rays shine from those as before,[26] one imagines there are vajra walls in all directions, above and below. This is the supreme protection against the three kinds of external spirits.[27] Chanting *hūṃ*, the naked holder of the vajra dances, using undefined steps and hand gestures, and their mind never wavers from the dharmadhātu. This is the supreme protection against the three kinds of external spirits.

Guru Jñānaśrī's intimate instruction is:

> Imagine that in a location of heat and cold,
> on sun and moon seats,
> a vajra and its enclosed bindu spin rapidly,[28]
> removing illness.

The meaning of this is that in the upper body, the location of heat, there is a moon seat. In the lower body, the location of cold, there is a sun seat.[29] On these are a five-tined vajra,[30] and inside of the vase made by the life-pillar nāḍī, within the center of a bindu the size of a chickpea, there is enclosed [either] a *hūṃ*,[31] which is no more than the size of a grain of rice, or the root guru, whichever is appropriate. Expel the breath three times.[32]

After that,[33] having ascertained the visualization clearly, if one meditates on this for a month, undoubtedly one will prevent and remove all illnesses of disturbances. {295}

Guru Ratnavajra's intimate instruction for preventing obstacles to samādhi is:

> One's innately pure mind
> is clarity, appearance, bliss, and all phenomena.
> Greater than the commitment, dharma, and karma [mudras],
> mahāmudrā (*phyag chen*) naturally pervades.
> How can there be any obstacle
> for the practitioner endowed with the fourth mudra?

The characteristic of the original purity of one's mind does not go beyond clarity, the commitment. In general, though the term *phyag* has many presentations, here[34] it refers to natural purity. In general, though the term *rgya*[35] has many presentations, here it refers to pervading[36] everything. In brief, the inseparability of clarity and emptiness is the samaya mudra.

Appearances are the dharmin [characteristics] of the mind. The meaning of mudra is just as before. In brief, the inseparability of appearance and emptiness is the dharma mudra.

Contaminated bliss is karma. The meaning of mudra is just as before. In brief, the inseparability of bliss and emptiness is the karma mudra.

As such, all the phenomena of universe and beings, such as clarity, appearance, bliss, and so on, are great. The meaning of mudra is just as before. In brief, the intrinsic emptiness of all phenomena is mahāmudrā. Obstacles are not possible for the practitioner who knows that.

This intimate instruction of preventing the trio of obstacles was bestowed by Drokmi upon both Se[37] and Rok, by the latter to Nyö,[38] then to Yerpa Gomseng,[39] Siddha Lhabar,[40] Kharak Gompa,[41] Lama Lungphuwa,[42] and Tashi Lungpa.[43] The latter bestowed this upon me.[44]

Since this is the main point of the profound path, conceal it from the unintelligent.

Clear Mindfulness of the Innate

Drokmi Lotsāwa

Homage to Śrī Mahāsukha.

Visualize the supporting maṇḍala. {296} In each nāḍī in the center of the supported six cakras and in each of their petals, the mother is the vāyu and the father is the pure essence. The knowledge generated by those is the son of the inseparable father and mother, bliss. The six sense organs are the father, the six objects are the mother, and the six consciousnesses are great bliss, the son.

The *Hevajra Tantra* states:

> Having abandoned all [ordinary] thoughts,
> by thinking of the form of the deity . . .[45]

The meaning of this is the vase empowerment.

Next, the fire in the secret place ignites *aṃ* at the navel. The gnostic fire endowed with three qualities illuminates the deities, like lifting a lamp in a dark cave. Meditate on uniting the lower vāyu until there is slight stability. This is the meaning of:

> Like the steady flame of the lamp . . .[46]

This is the path of the secret empowerment.

Once *haṃ* at the forehead melts through the force of the crown cakra, meditate on the gradual blazing and dripping until there is slight stability. This is the meaning of:

> Like a falling stream of water . . .[47]

This is the path of the third empowerment.

Also, such meditation is meditating all appearance and emptiness, clarity and emptiness, and bliss and emptiness as intrinsically empty mahāmudrā. This is the meaning of:

> Always remain in equipoise day and night
> with the yoga of reality.[48]

This is the path of the fourth empowerment.

The *Hevajra Tantra* states the profound meaning:

> There is neither meditation nor any meditator.
> There is neither a deity nor any mantra.
> The mantra and deity abide
> from the nature that is without proliferation.[49]

This was composed by Ācārya Vāgīśvarakīrti.

The Intimate Instruction on the Meditation of the Inseparable Two Stages

Homage to the feet of the sublime guru.

The practitioner who wants to meditate on the four empowerments should adopt the full seven features of the Vairocana posture for the body. Relaxing the three doors in self-liberation is the meaning of "Having abandoned all [ordinary] thoughts." Next, go for refuge and generate bodhicitta. Imagine oneself as any deity to which one has devotion. Meditate on the guru on one's crown and {297} arouse intense devotion. The guru dissolves into oneself.

Next, expel the stale vāyu three times and visualize the support and the supported. The soles of the feet are the vajra ground. The crown is the finial of a crossed vajra.[50] The ribs are the vajra fence. The pores are interlaced arrows. The nails are blazing volcanoes. The spread feet are the maṇḍala of air. The groin is the fire maṇḍala. The heart is the earth maṇḍala. The spine is Sumeru. The fathom-length four corners of the unequaled body are the four corners of the maṇḍala. The eyes are the five-colored walls. The teeth are the strands and tassels. The tongue and teeth are the dais of the goddesses. The nose is the ornament of the maṇḍala. The eight feet are the eight pillars. The eight nāḍī petals of the heart are the doors through which the elemental vāyus move in the four directions. In the center of that, meditate on the basic heruka. In the cakra of the secret place, meditate on green Amoghasiddhi embracing the mother, with his right hand holding a sword and left hand holding a sword-handled bell. The mother, Samayatārā, embraces the father while holding a curved knife and skull. There is a retinue of thirty-two goddesses.

In the navel, meditate on yellow Ratnasambhava embracing the mother, with his right hand holding a jewel and his left hand holding a jewel-handled bell. The mother, Ratnatārā, embraces the father while holding a curved knife and skull. There is a retinue of sixty-four goddesses.

In the heart, meditate on blue Akṣobhya embracing the mother, with his right hand holding a vajra and his left hand holding a vajra-handled bell. The mother, Māmaki, embraces the father while holding a curved knife and skull. There is a retinue of eight goddesses.

In the throat, meditate on red Amitābha embracing the mother, with his right hand holding a lotus and his left hand holding a lotus-handled bell. The mother, {298} Pāṇḍaravāsinī, embraces the father while holding a curved knife and skull. There is a retinue of sixteen goddesses.

In the crown, meditate on white Vairocana embracing the mother, with his right hand holding a wheel and his left hand holding a wheel-handled bell. The mother, Buddhalocana,[51] embraces the father while holding a curved knife and skull. There is a retinue of thirty-two goddesses.

At the uṣṇīṣa, peaceful white Vajradhara is seated cross-legged, embracing the mother while holding a vajra and bell and displaying the gesture of teaching dharma. The mother, Vajradhātviśvarī, embraces the father while holding a curved knife and a skull. There is a retinue of four goddesses. The color of each goddess corresponds with the father's color. They stand with left legs extended, hold curved knives in their right hands and skulls in their left hands, and khatvaṃga staffs lean on their elbows.

As such, the gods of the six cakras are the nāḍīs and syllables (the mother) and the pure essences and the vāyu (the father). The generation stage is the son, untouched by the tarnish of conceptuality.

The appearance side is method, the unceasing father; the emptiness side is wisdom, the nonarising mother. The inseparability of those two, or the inseparability of arising and ceasing, is great bliss, the son. Apply the hand implements with those.

In the eyes, there is Kṣitigarbha, who resembles Vairocana. In the ears, there is Vajrapāṇi, who resembles Akṣobhya. In the nose, there is Ākāśagarbha, who resembles Ratnasambhava. On the tongue, there is Lokeśvara, who resembles Amitābha. For the body, there is Nivāraṇaviṣkambhin, who resembles Amoghasiddhi. For the mind, there is Samantabhadra, who resembles Vajradhara. In related order, there is Vajrarūpa[52] up to Dhātviśvarī, who hold curved knives and skulls, and embrace the fathers. None of them need to arise from seed syllables, nor receive empowerment, nor be invited, nor request to depart. They are meditated on by recalling that they form naturally. The gnosis of appearance and emptiness arises primarily from them. This is the path of the vase empowerment.

> Since the sattvas are meditated on in the form of the deity, {299}
> without missing a day, one must examine this thoroughly.
> ....
> In order to best accomplish the benefit of oneself and others,
> there is no other method in samsara.[53]

The explanation of the meaning of this is complete.

Following that, the fire at the rectum ignites *aṃ* at the navel. The form of the caṇḍālī fire is bright, hot to the touch, and very supple. Since fire blazes with these three characteristics, the deities are illuminated like raising a lamp in a dark cave. Allow the fire to get higher in a state of nongrasping. Meditate on stabilizing the lower vāyu slightly by uniting it. The gnosis of clarity and emptiness arises primarily from it. This is the path of the secret empowerment. This completes the explanation of the meaning of "Like the steady flame of the lamp."

Next, the fire of gnosis melts *haṃ* through the power of the crown cakra. There are two types of dripping bodhicitta: like a string of pearls and like a thread of spider silk. Meditate on whichever one likes. The gnosis of bliss and emptiness arises primarily from it. This is the meaning of "Like a falling stream of water." It is the path of the gnosis of the wisdom consort empowerment.

[Next is the explanation of] the meaning of [the following]:

Always remain in equipoise day and night
with the yoga of reality.

For all of those, the father, the secret hand implements of the father, the khaṭvāṅga of the mother, the pure essences, the vāyu, appearance, clarity, cognizance, and bliss are the unceasing method, the rūpakāya. The mother, the secret hand implement of the mother, the nāḍīs, the syllables, and the empty natures are nonarising wisdom, the dharmakāya. Through those, in the generation stage, the fundamental bodhicitta (untarnished by the conceptuality of the eight consciousnesses and [five] afflictions), the skull, and bone ornaments represent not arising and ceasing, the intrinsically empty mahāmudrā, the svabhāvakāya.

In brief, the impure world is the phenomena of samsara. The pure universe is the celestial mansion and all beings are deities. {300} Also, all of that appearance is empty appearance, clarity is empty clarity, cognizance is empty cognizance, and bliss is empty bliss. The meditation is the undistracted mindfulness that recognizes everything in that innate original purity as the nature of intrinsically empty mahāmudrā, but it is not an intellectual meditation. The gnosis of self-liberation arises from that, and it is the path of the fourth empowerment.

This concludes the explanation of "There is neither meditation nor any meditator" and "There is neither deity nor any mantra."

"The Intimate Instruction on the Meditation of the Inseparable Two Stages" (also known as "The Intimate Instruction on Meditating on the Path of the Four Empowerments on One Seat," also known as "The Clear Mindfulness of the Innate") is the essence of Ācārya Vāgīśvarakīrti's instruction to Lord Drokmi. Also, the explanation of all intimate instructions is complete.

The lineage is Lady Tārā to Vāgīśvarakīrti, Lord Drokmi, Khön Könchok Gyalpo,[54] Lama Shangpa,[55] Khön Kunga Nyingpo,[56] Jetsun Drakpa Gyaltsen,[57] the Great Translator,[58] Lama Lungphuwa, Tashi Lungpa, and Khedrup Chöje.[59]

Mahāmudrā That Removes the Three Sufferings

Drokmi Lotsāwa

namo guru

Mahāmudrā That Removes the Three Sufferings is an instruction requested of Lord Nārotapa by Lord Drokmi. [The former said], "When one trains in the treatises of the tantra, the instructions come naturally."

[Drokmi] replied, "I heard the treatises of the tantras from Śantipa."

[Nārotapa responded,] "Excellent. Since you have traveled from far away, employing the three sufferings as the path is very important."

Chanting the True Names of Mañjuśrī Tantra states:

> The suffering of the three kinds of suffering is peace,
> but the three liberations are obtained from the limitless three
> dispellers.
> Liberated from all obscurations,
> abide in uniformity, like space.

There are nine profound points here: {301} (1) In the beginning, the blessings are a very profound point. (2) Prior to every session, going for refuge, generating bodhicitta, and meditating on the deity and the guru are very profound points. (3) Meditating on the innate and ascertaining the meaning of the tantra are very profound points. (4) Controlling the uncontrolled mind and keeping it inside are very profound points. (5) Stabilizing control and holding it externally are very profound points. (6) Remaining in a stable state is a very profound point. (7) Attaining proficiency in the enhancement of remaining is a very profound point. (8) Eliminating a narrow mind and recitation are profound points. (9) Sealing with a nontoxic dedication and sharing with all are profound points.

Having set down Drokmi's speech, if the detailed meaning of these nine points is described, first, there is the supplication for the descent of the blessing, offering a maṇḍala to become a suitable recipient of that, and the meditation and recitation of Vajrasattva in order to purify the recipient of those.

Second, the common preliminaries are going for refuge and bodhicitta. The uncommon preliminaries are meditating on the deity[60] and the guru.

Third, the nature of samsara is the three sufferings. When one sees the innate nature of the mind, the three are dispelled by the dispeller. If one knows the nature of the suffering of suffering, the nirmāṇakāya is obtained. If one knows the nature of the suffering of change, the sambhogakāya is obtained. If one knows the nature of the suffering of formations, the dharmakāya is obtained. Since all of those are known to similarly lack inherent existence, once one is free from the three obscurations, the svabhāvakāya is obtained. This is the meaning of the three lines.

To practice that, all phenomena of the universe and beings, samsara and nirvana, are mind. Clarity is the characteristic of the mind. To train in the potential of emptiness, emptiness is the nature of the mind. To train in the poison of appearance, {302} just as no one made the clouds in clear and empty space, look at one's unmodified, original face. Since it is recognized in that way, though the knower is entirely inside and the appearance is entirely outside, whatever appears is one taste as the vajra gnosis. This is the detailed introduction by the guru.

Fourth, there is an elaborate method and an unelaborate method. First, in the heart, between one's nipples,[61] focus the mind on a bindu the size of a round white mustard seed, which is on top of a moon the size of a split pea. The unelaborate method is that the mind looks at the nature of whatever arises. When cultivated during the day, the experiences of bliss and emptiness and cognizance and emptiness arise. When cultivated at night, the key point is maintaining luminosity.

Fifth, there is an elaborate and unelaborate method. First, focus the mind on any sign inside the pea-sized bindu on the tip of one's nose. The unelaborate method is to look at the nature of whatever appears. Since that is cultivated during the daytime, the experiences of clarity and emptiness and appearance and emptiness arise. When cultivated at night, it is a key point for recognizing dreams.

Sixth, since one knows the intrinsic state of reality, one rests in one's natural state. One rests, maintaining a natural relaxation. Seventh, attain proficiency in abiding vigorously and train in joining the variety to the path.

Eighth, decide that one cannot find anything beyond that final understanding because of the guru's introduction. Decide that after the experience of reflection and meditation, one cannot find that one is deprived of it. Ninth, one should understand that at the conclusion of each session one should seal with a precious dedication to others, which cannot itself diminish.

Though Lord Nārotapa's instruction was divided by the great guru Drokmi into nine points, it was a little unclear and not easy for those of lesser intelligence to understand. Thus, this was written on behalf of Lady Trinle Kyi,[62] a woman from Dringtsam. {303}

If these four points are coordinated with the breath, it is good. The first two points are preliminaries. When meditating on the third point, the full seven-point posture of Vairocana is adopted. Make effort in the path of concentration through the prāṇa and āyama vāyus.[63] Begin by holding the prāṇa inside and meditating on the key point of the application of the activity. Here, a removal of obstructions is not asserted. However, it is said that gaining proficiency in the diversity removes obstructions. The method of gaining proficiency depends on the guru's instruction.

> Since it was recognized that from the beginning the mind does not arise,
> once the original face of the all-basis[64] is seen,
> deathless nonarising is deeply understood,
> and one will certainly attain liberation either in this life, the bardo, or the next life.

This instruction resembles one's heart.

ithi maṅgalaṃ virtue

19. Lineage Supplication of *Parting from the Four Attachments*[1]

Kunga Zangpo and Khyentse Wangpo

{305} I offer a supplication to the three peerless supreme refuges:
the perfect Buddha, the guru of migrating beings;
Mañjughoṣanātha, the powerful heir of the victor;
and Lord Sakya, who was guided by him.

I offer a supplication to the three regents of the victor:
Sönam Tsemo, who mastered the five sciences;
Jetsun Rinpoche, who knows all sutras and tantras;
and the second lord of sages, Sakya Paṇḍita.

I offer a supplication to the three sublime accomplished scholars:
Phakpa Rinpoche, the sovereign of the doctrine;
Könchok Pal, wealthy in the tantras because of hearing, reflecting,
 and meditating;
and Lord Trakphupa, who attained supreme siddhi.

I offer a supplication to the three gurus, supreme guides:
Sönam Gyaltsen, the crown jewel of all beings;
Palden Tsultrim, the lord of the instructions;
and Yeshe Gyaltsen, the omniscient one.

Having offered a supplication to these glorious gurus
and having been clearly seen with their eye of swift-acting compassion,
please bless me to utterly turn away from attachment
to the appearances of this life, which is the basis of ruin.

Please bless me to arouse strong renunciation
for samsara's three realms, which cause constant misery
because of the inexhaustible suffering that is difficult to endure,
and in which there is not even the slightest chance of happiness.

Please bless me to abandon thinking of my own benefit
by meditating thoroughly on the benefit of motherly sentient beings
with the bodhicitta of equalizing and exchanging myself with others,
the single path on which the buddhas and bodhisattvas travel. {306}

Having determined that all phenomena are like dreams and illusions from the beginning
and that appearances are false and empty,
please bless me to arouse in my continuum
the true path of madhyamaka, union that is free from all partiality.

The supplement of the result is [as follows]:

Having turned the mind to the dharma with such meditation,
may all dharma become the path, and having dispelled
every error of the path, bless me so that deluded appearances
arise as the great gnosis of buddhahood.

These verses of supplication to the lineage gurus of the instruction of *Parting from the Four Attachments* were composed by the Śākya bhikṣu Kunga Zangpo at glorious Sakya.

The supplement to the lineage of *Parting from the Four Attachments* composed by Omniscient Ngorchen Kunga Zangpo is inserted after the verse that begins "I offer a supplication to the three gurus, supreme guides."

I offer a supplication to the three who reached the culmination of knowledge and liberation:
Omniscient Evaṃpa,[2] the one predicted by the victor;
Könchok Gyaltsen, his powerful disciple;
and Sönam Senge, the sun of speech.

I offer a supplication to the three illuminators of the doctrine:
Sangye Rinchen, Mañjughoṣa in person;
Namkha Wangchuk, the great being;
and Kunga Lekdrup, the sovereign of scripture and reasoning.

I offer a supplication to the three sublime guides:
Kunga Chödrak, the voice of knowledge;
Kunga Namgyal, the lord of siddhas;
and Tenzin Zangpo, whose wisdom is consummate.

I offer a supplication to the three peerless gurus:
Ngawang Lhundrup, who attained knowledge and siddhis;
Lord Morchen, the all-seeing sun of Dharma;
and Nesarwa, the source of an ocean of instructions.

I offer a supplication to the three supreme guides of all beings:
Kunga Lodrö, the pillar of the doctrine in the age of degeneration; {307}
Lady Chime Tenzin Nyima;
and Jampal Zhönu Dorje Rinchen.

I offer a supplication to the omniscient great abbot, the lord of refuges
who arose in the form of the supreme holder of doctrine, in whom rejoice
all buddhas and bodhisattvas with their loving compassion,
and the world and its gods.[3]

Having offered a supplication to these glorious gurus . . .

This supplement was written at Ladrang Phende Kunkhyap Ling of Palden Lhundrup Teng[4] by the Śākya bhikṣu, the idle Khyentse Wangpo.

śubhaṃ

20. The Mind Training Titled *The Cycle of Parting from the Four Attachments*[1]

Parting *from the Four Attachments,* without question, is the most famous teaching of the Sakya school. It is widely taught by other lineages as representative of the Sakya school's basic point of view. Considered a mind training (*blo sbyong*) text, it is valued for its succinct summary of the stages of the path of Hinayāna and Mahāyāna. For example, it is the first text presented by Kunga Drölchok in the *One Hundred and Eight Teaching Manuals of Jonang.*[2]

Originating in a vision of Mañjuśrī experienced by Sachen Kunga Nyingpo during a six-month retreat on Mañjuśrī, the root text of *Parting from the Four Attachments* is found in Drakpa Gyaltsen's collected works, along with a versified expansion.[3]

The cycle has come down to us in *The Treasury of Precious Instructions* as a collection of six texts. The first text is an account wrtten by Drakpa Gyaltsen of Sachen's pure vision (Sachen being referred to there as the "principal"), and the second text is its verse expansion by Drakpa Gyaltsen. These two form the basis for all later commentaries and are cited repeatedly in Sakya literature. The third text, *Instruction on Parting from the Four Attachments,* belongs to Sakya Paṇḍita and is a brief summary. The fourth text, *Parting from the Four Attachments,* by Nupa Rikzin Drak, is a record of a teaching on parting from the four attachments by Drakpa Gyaltsen. The fifth and longest text, the *Words of the Lord Guru Ānandabhadra,* is a record of a teaching on parting from the four attachments by Ngorchen Kunga Nyingpo, presented in the standard format of the stages of the path (*lam rim*). The final text, *Necklace of Ketaka Gems,* written by Ngawang Lekdrup, weaves together the verses of Drakpa Gyaltsen with the teaching of Kunga Nyingpo and presents it as a four-day teaching program, complete with beginning prayers and concluding prayers for the lama and the assembly.

Parting from the Four Attachments

Sachen Kunga Nyingpo and Drakpa Gyaltsen

{310} When the great Sakyapa Guru[4] reached twelve years of age (1103 C.E.), he practiced the sādhana of Ārya Mañjughoṣa for six months. One day he saw in his direct perception Lord Mañjughoṣa, who was reddish-yellow in color, making the gesture of teaching dharma, seated in the posture of ease on a precious throne in the center of a mass of light, and flanked on the right and left by two bodhisattvas.[5] The principal spoke:

> If attached to this life, one is not a dharma person.
> If attached to the three realms, one has no renunciation.
> If attached to personal benefit, one has no bodhicitta.
> If grasping arises, one has no view.

When the meaning is examined, the entire practice of the path of the perfections is included in the mind training of parting from the four attachments.

samāptamithi

Commentary on *Parting from the Four Attachments*

Drakpa Gyaltsen

May I be blessed
by the kindly guru and
the compassionate pledged deity,
to whom I sincerely go for refuge.

As there is no purpose in behaving contrary to the dharma,
practice in accord with the dharma.
As you requested the instruction on parting from the four
attachments,
please, you must listen to it.[6]

If attached to this life, one is not a dharma person. {311}
If attached to samsara, one has no renunciation.
If attached to personal benefit, one has no bodhicitta.
If grasping arises, one has no view.

First, do not be attached to this life.
The discipline and the trio of hearing, reflection, and meditation
practiced with a focus on this life
is not that of a dharma person—put it aside!

To begin, when discipline is explained,
it is the basis of accomplishing higher realms,
it is the staircase of accomplishing freedom,
and it is the remedy for abandoning samsara.
One cannot do without discipline.

However, the one whose discipline is attached to this life
has the basis of accomplishing the eight worldly dharmas,
has scorn for those whose discipline is inferior,
has jealousy toward those who possess discipline,
has hypocrisy in their own discipline,
and has the seed of accomplishing lower realms.
Put aside pretentious discipline!

The person who engages in hearing and reflection
has the enjoyment of accomplishing knowledge,
has the lamp that dispels ignorance,
has knowledge of the path that guides migrating beings,
and has the seed of the dharmakāya.
They cannot do without hearing and reflection.

The one whose hearing and reflection is for this life
has the enjoyment of accomplishing pride,
has contempt for those of less hearing and reflection,
has jealousy toward those who possess hearing and reflection,
has a corrupt retinue and enjoyments,
and has the seed of accomplishing lower realms.
Put aside the hearing and reflection of the eight worldly
dharmas!

All people who engage in meditation {312}
have the remedy for abandoning affliction,
have the basis for accomplishing the path of freedom,
and have the seed of accomplishing buddhahood.
They cannot do without discipline.

The one who meditates focusing on this life
has distractions even though they stay in retreat,
has conversations of idle gossip,
criticizes those who engage in hearing and reflection,
has jealousy for other meditators,
and is distracted in their own meditation.
Put aside the concentration of the eight worldly dharmas![7]

To accomplish nirvana,
please abandon the attachments of the three realms.
To abandon the attachments of the three realms,
please recall the faults of samsara.

First, the suffering of sufferings
is the suffering of the three evil destinations.
When reflected upon well, one's skin shivers.
If this befalls one, it is impossible to bear.
As the virtue of abandonment is not accomplished,
the field of evil destinations is cultivated,
and those who abide there are pitiable.

When reflecting upon the suffering of change,
those in higher realms go to evil destinies,
Śakra is born as an ordinary human,
the sun and the moon become dark,
and an emperor is born a subject.
Despite confidence through the explanations of scripture,
most people do not understand.
Observe the vicissitudes of humanity that appear to oneself.
Wealthy people become beggars,
loud voices become weak,
many people become one,
and so on, beyond conception.

When reflecting on the suffering of formations,
there is no end to activities.
Though crowds are suffering, solitude is also suffering. {313}
Though jewels and wealth are suffering, hunger is also suffering.
The whole of human life is exhausted in making preparations.
Everyone dies in the process of making preparations.
Even though they die, there is no end to preparations;
they begin making preparations at the start of the next life.

Pitiable are those who are attached to
the mass of samsara's suffering.[8]

If one parts with attachment, misery is transcended.
If misery is transcended, one attains bliss.
This is the experiential song of parting from the four attachments.

There is no benefit in freeing oneself alone.
The sentient beings of the three realms are one's parents.
The one who leaves their parents in a thicket of suffering,
wishing for their own happiness, is pitiable.

May all suffering of the three realms ripen on oneself,
and may all one's merit ripen on sentient beings.
By the blessing of this merit,
may all sentient beings attain buddhahood.[9]

No matter what one may wish, there is no liberation
in a state of grasping to the nature of dharmatā.
When that is explained in detail,
there is no freedom in grasping to existence,
and there is no higher realm in grasping to nonexistence.
Since one cannot grasp both [existence and nonexistence],
put them aside in the state of nonduality.[10]

All phenomena are the domain of mind.
Since a creator cannot be found, such as a vital force, god, or the
four elements,
put them aside in the state of mind itself.[11]

Appearances have an illusory nature
and are produced in dependence.
Since reality cannot be described, {314}
put it aside in the state of inexpressibility.[12]

By merit of this virtue of
explaining parting from the four attachments,
may the seven types of migrating beings
be placed on the stage of buddhahood.

The instruction of parting from the four attachments was composed at Pal Sakya Monastery by the yogin, Drakpa Gyaltsen.

Instruction on *Parting from the Four Attachments*

Sakya Paṇḍita

Homage to the feet of the sublime guru.

In general, having attained human freedoms and endowments, encountered the precious doctrine of the Buddha, and aroused an unfeigned attitude, it is necessary to correctly practice the sublime dharma. For that it is necessary to practice parting from the four attachments. What are they? Do not be attached to this life. Do not be attached to the three realms of samsara. Do not be attached to personal benefit. Do not be attached to things and signs.

When explained, since this life resembles a bubble in the water, the time of death is uncertain. There is no value in attachment. The three realms of samsara resemble poisonous fruit: even though gratifying in the short term, they are harmful in the long run. Whoever is attached to those is deluding themself. If one is attached to personal benefit, this resembles feeding the child of an enemy. Though there seems to be happiness in the short term, one only harms oneself in the long run. Thus, though there is temporary happiness if one is attached to personal benefit, in the long run one goes to an evil destination. If one is attached to things and signs, this resembles grasping water in a mirage. Though it seems to be water at first, it cannot be drunk. Also, samsara is an appearance to a deluded mind. When investigated with wisdom, no essence can be established at all. Therefore, having understood that the mind should not follow the past, the mind should not anticipate the future, and consciousness should engage the present, one should know that all phenomena are free from proliferation.

As such, since there is no attachment to this life, one is not born in evil destinations. Since there is no attachment to the three realms of samsara, one is not born in samsara. Since there is no attachment to personal benefit, one is not born as either a śrāvaka or a pratyekabuddha. {315} Since one is not attached to things and signs, one swiftly attains full buddhahood.

This was composed by Sakya Paṇḍita in accordance with the intention of the great Sakyapa's incontrovertible instruction on parting from the four attachments.

Parting from the Four Attachments[13]

Nupa Rikzin Drak

namo guru

The great Sakyapa Jetsun[14] said:

> Those who wish to strive for the great bliss of nirvana must be free from the four attachments. The four attachments are attachment to this life, attachment to samsara's three realms, attachment to personal benefit, and attachment to things and signs.
>
> There are four antidotes. The antidote to the first attachment is meditating on death and impermanence. The antidote to the second attachment is recalling the faults of samsara. The antidote to the third attachment is recalling bodhicitta. The antidote to the fourth attachment is recalling that all phenomena lack a self, like dreams and illusions.
>
> Four results arise from cultivating such recollections: The dharma becomes the dharma. The dharma becomes the path. The path removes delusion. The result of cultivating such understanding is that the transformation of deluded appearances [arising as] the abundance of gnosis produces buddhahood.
>
> Now, for the first, the antidote to attachment to this life, reflect on the uncertainty of the time of death, reflect on the many conditions of death, and reflect extensively on the fact that nothing is of any benefit at death. After such reflection arises in oneself, there is a sincere wish to engage solely in dharma. At that time dharma becomes the dharma.
>
> Next, the antidote to attachment to the three realms of samsara is recalling the faults of samsara. It may be wondered,

"Though there are such faults in attachment to this life, certainly emperors, Brahma, Śakra, and so on, have supreme happiness?" They also cannot transcend the nature of suffering. {316} Even though their life span and enjoyments last for many eons, in the end they die and perish. Since there is a risk they will be born as hell beings in Avīci hell, one should reflect on the fact that none of them transcend the nature of suffering. When cultivated, the dharma becomes the path.

The thought may arise that since the three worlds never transcend the nature of suffering, the bliss of nirvana is necessary for oneself, and all paths are to be practiced for that purpose. Though such a thought may arise in one's mind, if one strives for personal happiness alone, lacking bodhicitta, one will become an arhat or a pratyekabuddha. Thus, recall bodhicitta, the antidote to attachment to personal benefit. There is no benefit to liberating oneself alone from this nature of the suffering of the three realms. There is not a single one of these sentient beings who has not been one's mother or father. When the thought arises, "If these sentient beings attain the supreme bliss of nirvana, this is easier for them than birth as hell beings for many eons," the path has removed the first delusion, attachment to personal benefit.

Even though one meditates on and cultivates such a thought, since omniscience will not be obtained because of possessing grasping to true existence, it is necessary to recall the absence of identity of all phenomena as the antidote to attachment to things and signs. Furthermore, all phenomena are not established in any way. If grasping to true existence arises, it is the view of permanence. If there is attachment to emptiness, it is the view of annihilation. One should think that all phenomena are like dreams and illusions. If one meditates repeatedly recalling that just as dreams are false, appearances appear to be false, through meditating on merging appearances and one's dreams, the path has removed the second delusion, {317} attachment to things and signs. As such, having reached the culmination of removing all delusion, it is said that delusion arises as gnosis, which means the supreme bliss of the inconceivable qualities of perfect buddhahood are produced, such as the kāyas, gnoses, and so on.

This is the instruction of parting from the four attachments taught by the lord of yogins, Drakpa Gyaltsen.

The Words of the Lord Guru Ānandabhadra[15] The Manual of *Parting from the Four Attachments*

Kunga Lekpai Rinchen[16]

Homage to Guru Mañjughoṣa.

Those who wish to practice listening to the dharma should offer a supplication for generating bodhicitta, such as "Oh, perfect buddhahood should be obtained for the benefit of all sentient beings. For that purpose, I shall hear the sublime dharma and practice for such a goal." After this, ask them to listen.

Here, in the sole path traveled by all sugatas of the three times, the key points of practice of all the profound sutra discourses of the Buddha gathered in one place, the practice of the intimate instruction of parting from the four attachments, are (1) the account of the gurus of the lineage that generates confidence and trust and (2) the actual instruction.

I. The Account of the Gurus of the Lineage

When the great lord Sakyapa, the lord of yogins, was twelve years of age, he relied on and heard the dharma from the great, compassionate Bari Lotsāwa.[17] The Guru [Bari] said, "As the sole heir of your father, you require an education. Since wisdom is a prerequisite for that, you should engage in the practice of Lord Mañjughoṣa," and bestowed the permission and reading transmission for Mañjughoṣa Arapacana. The guru was also the assistant for practice. Since they practiced in the old residence, some slight obstacles arose. {318} [Sachen] did the meditation and recitation of blue Acala and engaged in repelling obstacles through the water protection rite. Having practiced for six months, one day he saw Ārya Mañjuśrī in his direct perception, seated in the posture of ease with the gesture of teaching the dharma and flanked by two bodhisattvas. At that moment Ārya Mañjuśrī spoke [this verse]:

> If attached to this life, one is not a dharma person.
> If attached to the three realms, one has no renunciation.
> If attached to personal benefit, one has no bodhicitta.
> If grasping arises, one has no view.

Since [Sachen] reflected on the meaning of these four lines, experience arose in his mind through the profound intent that included the practice of all sutra discourses of the Buddha found in this verse. Sachen then bestowed these four lines to Lopön Rinpoche,[18] who bestowed them to Jetsun Rinpoche. The latter bestowed them to Sakya Paṇḍita, who bestowed them to Drogön Chögyal Phakpa. He bestowed them to Zhang Könchok Pal, who bestowed them to Gyalwa Drakphupa. The latter bestowed them to the Lord of Dharma, Sönam Gyaltsen Palzangpo, who bestowed them to Lama Palden Tsultrim. He bestowed them to the Lord of Dharma, Yeshe Gyaltsen, who bestowed them to our sublime, glorious guru, Kunga Zangpo.

II. The Actual Instruction

In the topics of the intimate instruction, there are (1) the preliminaries, (2) the main subject, and (3) the conclusion.

A. The Preliminaries

1. Going for Refuge

Going for refuge is Mahāyāna refuge with four features. The way of going for refuge is to go for refuge to the buddha jewel, the peerless individual who possesses inconceivable qualities and has no faults of any kind; to go for refuge to the dharma jewel, the nature and extent of the dharma of scripture and realization that has entered the minds of those in whom bodhicitta is irreversible; and to go for refuge to the sangha jewel, {319}those who properly practice those [two dharmas] with irreversible bodhicitta. Beginning from now until reaching the seat of awakening, one does not go for refuge alone. One goes for refuge wishing that all sentient beings equal with space, beginning with one's parents, obtain the stage of buddhahood for the benefit of all sentient beings. Recalling the meaning of that, one recites:

> From this time forth until reaching the seat of awakening, I and all other motherly sentient beings equal with space go for refuge to the guru, the precious Buddha; go for refuge to the sublime dharma, the nature of scripture and realization; and go for refuge to the noble sangha of bodhisattvas.

At the conclusion of reciting the refuge as much as possible, offer this supplication:

> Through the blessings of the Three Jewels, please bless me so that my mind turns to the dharma, please bless me so that the dharma becomes the path, please bless me so that the path removes delusion, please bless me so that deluded vision arises as gnosis, please bless me so that concepts that contradict the dharma do not arise in my mind even for an instant, and may buddhahood be swiftly obtained.

2. Generating Bodhicitta

While recalling to the mind the meaning of aspirational and engaged bodhicitta—aspirational bodhicitta is "I should attain buddhahood for the benefit of all sentient beings" and engaged bodhicitta is "For that purpose, I will train in the profound stages of the Mahāyāna path"—recite:

> I go for refuge until awakening
> to the Buddha, the dharma, and the supreme assembly.
> Through the merit of generosity, and so on,
> may I obtain buddhahood in order that I may benefit migrating beings.{320}

[Recite:]

> I will obtain buddhahood for the benefit of all sentient beings. For that purpose, I will be diligent in the virtuous activities of body, voice, and mind.[19]

B. The Main Subject

There are four topics in the main subject.

1. Attachment to This Life

The meaning of "If attached to this life, one is not a dharma person"[20] is that it is necessary that one not be attached to this life. If one is attached, just as when one is attached to water in a mirage, a mirage is unable to relieve thirst, likewise, though one engages in discipline, hearing, reflection, and meditation, since it serves the purpose of accomplishing abundance in this life, it does not become authentic dharma. Thus, as Śrī Vasubandhu states in the *Treasury of Abhidharma*:

> Abiding in discipline endowed with hearing and reflection
> always applies to oneself in meditation.

Likewise, on the basis of pure discipline, first engage in hearing. After that, reflect on the meaning. Since it is necessary to meditate on the meaning, having eliminated doubts, (1) reflect on the difficulty of acquiring freedoms and endowments in order to generate the attitude of wishing to practice the dharma until it arises and (2) reflect on death and impermanence for the purpose of supreme diligence in the practice of dharma.

a. The Difficulty of Acquiring Freedom and Endowments

Ācārya Śāntideva states in the *Introduction to the Conduct of Awakening*:

> This freedom and endowment, which is very difficult to acquire,
> will accomplish an individual's meaningful goals.
> If this benefit is not accomplished here,
> where will it be met later?[21]

Since this human body of freedom and endowment, the foundation of accomplishing the sublime dharma, is difficult to acquire, meditate repeatedly thinking, "A pure dharma is necessary when these have been acquired."

When these are slightly expanded, there is (1) the difficulty to acquire them through cause, (2) the difficulty to acquire them through number, (3) the difficulty to acquire them through example, and (4) the difficulty to acquire them through nature.

i. Cause

The cause for the attainment of the pure human body of leisure and endowment is the accomplishment of virtuous actions such as discipline, and so on, {321} and the requirement to abandon unvirtuous actions. Since the sentient beings of the three realms accomplish little virtue and engage in many unvirtuous behaviors, meditate on the difficulty of acquiring freedom and endowment through the cause.

ii. Number

When looking at the realms of sentient beings, there are as many hell beings as there are atoms of the earth. There are as many pretas as there are snowflakes in a blizzard. There are as many animals as there are lees of fresh chang. In comparison, those who have attained the pure human body are quite few. Thus, meditate on the difficulty of acquiring freedom and endowment through number.

iii. Example

Introduction to the Conduct of Awakening states:

> For that reason, the Bhagavān has said
> it is extremely difficult to attain a human birth,
> like a sea turtle placing its neck through the hole
> of a wooden yoke drifting on the ocean.[22]

Though there are inconceivable kinds of sentient beings, being born a human is just a mere possibility. It resembles the possibility that a sea turtle in the ocean who rises to the surface every one hundred years will be able to place its neck through the hole of a golden yoke drifting on the waves of the ocean. Thus, meditate on the difficulty of acquiring freedom and endowment through example.

iv. Nature

Since it is extremely rare to be born free of the eight lacks of freedom, such as being born a mute, a barbarian, and so on, and to have the complete ten endowments, meditate on the difficulty of acquiring freedom and endowment through nature.[23]

b. Death and Impermanence

To reflect on death and impermanence, Ācārya Aśvaghoṣa explained:

> In this way, death stands before
> all lives.[24]

Death is the certain end of all lives. {322} Thus, meditate on the necessity to practice Dharma immediately. If that is explained a little further, one should (1) reflect on the certainty of death, (2) reflect on the uncertainty of the time of death, and (3) reflect that only dharma is of benefit at the time of death.

i. The Certainty of Death

In general, all compounded things have the nature of impermanence, and in the end they must perish. The *Sutra of the Extensive Play* states:

> The three realms are impermanent.
> The birth and death of migrating beings are equivalent to
> watching a show.
> A sentient being's life is like a flash of lightning in the sky,
> passing by as swiftly as a mountain waterfall.[25]

In particular, Ācārya Aśvaghoṣa states:

> If the vajra body—
> the body of the Buddha
> adorned with the major and minor marks—is impermanent,
> what need is there to mention this water-bubble body?[26]

One must reflect, thinking, "Though the perfect Buddha demonstrated nirvana and attained the stage of deathlessness, it is certain that ordinary people must die."

Ācārya Aśvaghoṣa states:

> Though great seers with the five clairvoyances
> can travel without impediment[27] into the sky,
> they will never arrive anywhere
> that is not the domain of death.[28]

Thus, meditate on the thought "No matter where one is born in the three realms, since there is no place unharmed by death, death is certain."

Death is certain because the conditions of death are many and the conditions for living are few. As Ācārya Nāgārjuna states in the *Necklace of Gems*:

> The conditions of death are many,
> the conditions of life are few.
> Those are the conditions of death.
> Therefore, always practice the dharma.[29]

Thus, meditate on the thought "Even though there are places asserted as conditions for living, and also food and enjoyments, since even these can become conditions for death, death is certain."

ii. The Uncertainty of the Time of Death

Since some die in the wombs of their mothers and others die as soon as they are born, one can see for oneself that it is uncertain when an elder, a youth, or an adult will die. Reflect on the way the time of death is uncertain and meditate.

iii. Only Dharma Is of Benefit at the Time of Death

When the time of death has arrived, since it will not be averted by anything—a dominant voice, power, a large retinue, enjoyments, heroics, and so on—death is certain. When one dies, only dharma is of benefit. In that respect, since one practices the dharma for as long one lives, one will have no regrets at the time of death. Since one is also confident in being born in a good destination, the mind is at ease. Thus, it is necessary to practice the sublime dharma. Meditate on the thought "I must practice the dharma immediately because the time of death is uncertain."

2. Attachment to the Three Realms

The statement, "If attached to the three realms, one has no renunciation," means that if one is attached to the three realms, even the practice of dharma will not become the path of awakening. Thus, one must not be attached to samsara. The faults of samsara are explained for that reason, and therefore once all of samsara is perceived to be the nature of suffering and the attitude of wishing to abandon it and striving for liberation arise, the faults of samsara are explained in order to generate that realization. Also, since birth in samsara arises from careless, unvirtuous behavior because one does not know which causes and results of karma to accept and reject, one reflects on the causes and results of karma in order to know which causes and results of karma to accept and reject. {323}

a. The Faults of Samsara

The *Possession of the Root of Virtue Sutra* states:

> The desire realm has faults;
> likewise, the form realm has faults,
> and the formless realm has faults.
> Nirvana alone is seen to be faultless.[30]

No matter where one is born in the three realms, it possesses faults. {324} The *Sutra of the Close Application of Mindfulness of the Sublime Dharma* states:

> Hell beings experience the fires of hell.
> Pretas experience hunger and thirst.
> Animals experience being eaten by one another.
> Humans experience short lives.
> Devas experience absence of shame.
> There isn't so much as a pinpoint
> of happiness in samsara.[31]

Thus, meditate on the thought "Wherever one is born in those three realms has the nature of suffering." Even if there are enjoyments, since they are only enjoyments of suffering, the pure dharma of traveling the path of awakening must be practiced in order to become free from that suffering. When that is elaborated a little, reflect on the three sufferings: (1) the suffering of suffering, (2) the suffering of change, and (3) the suffering of formations.

i. The Suffering of Suffering

There are three topics: (1) reflecting on the suffering of hell beings, (2) reflecting on the suffering of pretas, and (3) reflecting on the suffering of animals.

I) The Suffering of Hell

There are three topics: (1) reflecting on the suffering of the cold hells, (2) reflecting on the suffering of the hot hells, and (3) reflecting on the suffering of the temporary, peripheral hells.

A) The Suffering of the Cold Hells

The first of the eight cold hells is called Arbuda ("blister"). One is born either between great snow mountains where there is neither sun nor adequate shelter, or inside of ice. Since the body is struck by a very cold wind, the entire body erupts in blisters. The life span there is explained in the *Treasury of Abhidharma*:

> The life span of Arbuda is
> exhausted once every one hundred years when a sesame seed
> is removed from a bushel of sesame. {325}
> The life span of the others is multiplied by twenty.[32]

Through the condition of being even colder than the last, Nirārbuda ("cracked blister") is so called because blisters crack open, seeping lymph, pus, blood, and so on. Huhuva is so called because it is even colder than the last. There is immense suffering, and one clearly wails with the sound *hu hu*. Hahava is so called because there is suffering from cold that is even greater than the last. Since one cannot even cry out, one softly moans *ha ha*. Aṭaṭa ("chattering teeth")[33] is so called because the cold is even greater than before. One cannot utter a sound, whether loud or soft, the entire body becomes totally frozen, and the teeth clench. Utpala ("blue poppy") is so called because one is struck by strong winds that are much colder than before. The surface of the skin becomes blue and splits into eight pieces. Padma ("lotus") is so called because the blue skin decays and peels off when struck by the wind. The body becomes red and splits into many pieces. Mahāpadma ("great lotus") is so called because it is so cold that one becomes completely frozen. The entire body, inside and out, becomes like stone and splits into sixteen or more pieces. Because the outside of the body has split open, the small intestines, the colon, the sigmoid colon,[34] and so on splinter. One should reflect on these sufferings again and again.

B) The Suffering of the Hot Hells

The first of the hot hells is Saṃjiva ("live again"). The sense organ of the body is born on a ground of burning iron. Since there is great self-grasping to the very tender body, everything that one picks up with the hands becomes a weapon. All beings who see one another think of each other as enemies. They stab and cut each other's bodies into pieces with these weapons. A sound comes from the sky, saying, "Live again." {326} Since the body is struck by a cold wind, it becomes tender, as before.

Kālasūtra ("black line") is so called because the hell guardians place eight, sixteen, or more black lines on one's body, cut it with saws, split it with axes, and so on. There is an unimaginable experience of suffering. Saṃghata ("crushing") is so called because this tender body is pressed between mountains, which are like the heads of goats and sheep, and there is extreme suffering. Raurava ("wailing") is so called because hell guardians chase one on a ground of burning iron, and one flees to a white house. Thinking that one can escape to this place, one arrives inside. The door of the house closes automatically, and it becomes a house of burning iron. Impenetrable, there is no chance of freedom, fire blazes on its own, there is immense suffering, and there are sounds of wailing. Mahāraurava ("great wailing") is so called because other than the characteristics being the same as before, the house has two stories. Tapana ("inferno") is so called because the hell guardians impale one on a stake of burning iron from the anus to the crown, and one suffers. Pratapana ("great inferno") is so called because one is impaled on a trident from the anus to the crown, the right and left points pierce the right and left shoulders, and one suffers. Avīci ("unbearable") is so called because the ground of burning iron is burning with fire, and one cannot differentiate this fire from one's body. One infers from the burning and the sound of wailing that there is another sentient being here. The *Treasury of Abhidharma* states:

> A single day of the lower devas
> of the desire realm
> equals fifty human years.
> Their own life span is five hundred years.
> For the upper devas, double both.
> . . . .
> In the six hells, Saṃjiva, and so on, in this order,
> a single day equals the life span of the desire realm devas.
> Therefore, they resemble the desire realm devas.
> Life in Pratapana is half a minor eon; in Avīci,
> one minor eon.[35] {327}

Fifty human years is a single day for the four great kings. Thirty of those days is a month. Twelve of those months are one year. Thus, five hundred of their years equals the life span of the four great kings. Also, the life span of the Saṃjiva hell is five hundred of its years calculated on the basis of that day. Likewise, one hundred human years is a single day for the Trayastriṃśa devas, and their life span is one thousand of their years. Making that into a single day, the life span of Kālasūtra is one thousand of its own years. Taking two hundred human years as a single day, the Yama devas live for two thousand of their years. Taking that as a single day, the life span of Saṃghata is two thousand of its own years. Taking four hundred human years as a single day, the Tuṣita devas live for four thousand of their years. Taking that as a single day, the life span of Raurava is four thousand of its own years. Taking eight hundred human years as a single day, the Nirmāṇarataya devas live for eight thousand of their years. Taking that as a single day, the life span of Mahāraurava is eight thousand of its own years. Taking one thousand six hundred human years as a single day, the Paranirmitavaśavartino devas live for sixteen thousand of their years. Taking that as a single day, the life span of Tapana is sixteen thousand of its own years. The life span in Pratapana is half a minor eon; in Avīci, one minor eon.

C) The Suffering of the Temporary, Peripheral Hells

There are four topics.

1) Kukūla

Kukūla ("pit of embers") exists on the periphery of the hot hells. There, the inside of a pit is filled with embers. One enters that pit, and all one's limbs burn. When one lifts the right foot, the left foot burns. When one lifts the left foot, the right foot burns. One's small intestines, colon, and so on burn, and the openings of all sense organs emit smoke.

2) Kuṇapa

In Kuṇapa's ("putrid swamp") muck are all kinds of impure things, such as excrement, and so on. One falls onto one's face or back. {328} Imagining that all of one's sense gates are filled with impurities, one suffers. Inside of the muck are insects with iron beaks, and so on, who pierce and cut all of one's limbs and hands to the bone, and one suffers immensely.

3) Kṣuramārga

If one passes beyond Kuṇapa, one arrives on top of the very sharp Kṣuramārga ("plain of razors"). The flesh of one's feet is cut to the bone, and one suffers. Within this is Asipattravana ("forest of swords"). All tree limbs are weapons such as swords, and so on. Because one seeks sanctuary from the threat of the power of karma, one stays near the forest. When the forest is stirred by the wind, all weapons cut one's limbs to pieces, and one suffers immensely.

Ayaḥśalmalīvana ("thorn grass mountain") is a high mountain that one thinks one should go toward and climb. Eight-inch and sixteen-inch downward-facing iron thorns pierce the whole body, and one suffers. After reaching the peak, crows and owls pluck out one's eyes, pull out one's brains, and so on, and one suffers. After thinking that one has arrived at the peak, as one descends, the iron thorns face upward and pierce one's body. When one is at the base of the mountain, wolves, dogs, foxes, and so on eat one's limbs. Since they tug the body between them, it separates into pieces, and one suffers. Moreover, one is stretched by nails on the ground of burning iron. Through being stretched by iron tongue nails, one suffers from being plowed, and so on. This is also a part of the temporary peripheral hells.

4) Vaitaraṇī

Vaitaraṇī ("river") is a river of ashes beyond Kṣuramārga, which carries one's body away, burning it inside and out. The river is guarded all around by hell guardians, and one suffers. {329} Reflect on those sufferings. Reflect and meditate repeatedly on the thought that it is necessary to practice dharma to be free from those sufferings.

II) The Suffering of Pretas

In reflecting on the suffering of pretas, there are three topics: (1) external obscuration, (2) internal obscuration, and (3) the obscuration of food and drink, also called "the obscuration of the obscured."

A) External Obscuration

Through the power of nonvirtues such as greed, and so on, there is birth in the preta kingdom. Even though exhausted by hunger and thirst, a preta can see nothing to eat or drink. Thinking that in the distance there are mountains of cooked rice, and so on, and a great kingdom of water, the preta travels there. Since it is a very tiring and arduous journey, the preta suffers in body and mind. When arriving there, what appeared as a mountain of cooked rice are white rocks or heaps of white earth, and what previously appeared as a kingdom of water turns out to be either a mirage, blue earth, or blue slate. Since there is nothing to eat or drink, the preta suffers immensely.

B) Inner Obscuration

In addition to the previous suffering, a preta consumes a small portion of food and drink, but since its mouth is as narrow as the eye of a needle, the food does not fit, the mouth is torn open and bleeds, and it suffers. Then, since the food will not fit in the preta's throat, which is as narrow as a horse-hair, even though it eats, the texture of the food becomes rough and tears its throat, and it suffers from heat. Next, even though the food reaches the preta's stomach, which is comparable to a mountain in size, it feels full. Since the drink does not have the power to remove the food, it suffers again.

C) The Obscuration of Food and Drink

A preta travels everywhere in search of food and drink, chased by other preta leaders. Beaten and terrified, it suffers. The one who finds a little food and drink fears it will be stolen by the others. Since the preta consumes that small portion, as before, there is the suffering of being unable to fit the food in the mouth, and so on. {330} When that food reaches the stomach, the food and drink blazes with fire through the power of karma, burning all the intestines, colon, and so on. The preta is burned from the inside. Some pretas suffer because the flames come out of their sense organs. Such immense suffering is an intense suffering that must be experienced until the karma is exhausted. Thus, meditate on the thought "Since at present I have been born a human being, it is necessary to practice dharma for traveling the path of awakening."

III) The Suffering of Animals

In reflecting on the suffering of animals, there are (1) those that live in the depths and (2) those scattered about.

A) Animals in Depths

The creatures in the ocean—crocodiles and so on, whose numbers resemble the amount of lees in hard alcohol—are packed together and suffer from confinement. Since they are driven in all directions by the waves of the ocean, they have no definite abode. They are never at ease as there is no certainty they will meet as friends or that they will associate with anyone. The larger animals eat the smaller animals. The bodies of the larger animals, such as crocodiles, have the suffering of being pierced by spears, and so on. Also, the animals that live in the dark gulfs between the continents are devoid of light and cannot see one another. Because they live piled on top of one another, confined, weighted down, very confined, and pressed together, their bodies are cut to pieces. When it is time to find food and drink, there is none, and they suffer.

B) Animals on the Surface

Domestic animals carry loads that are too heavy, are tied to plows, milked, fettered with iron chains, beaten with whips and sticks, and used for various jobs. In the end, because they are slaughtered for their meat and sold to others, who kill them for their excretions, pearls, wool, bones, and hides, they suffer.

Wild animals have no certain abodes. Since they are hunted for their meat, they are pierced with arrows and chased by dogs into ravines, {331} canyons, and so on. Even if they escape being stabbed with weapons, in the end they experience the suffering of being slain, and so on. Reflect on the general suffering of animals, their inability to think and speak clearly, and their specific sufferings. Thus, meditate on the thought of the necessity of practicing a pure dharma.

ii. The Suffering of Change

In reflecting on the suffering of change, for example, reflecting on the example of a deva due to the power of past karma, a deva's palace, clothes, food, and so on arise merely through being imagined. Also, the bliss of female devas is limitless. However, when the devas are struck by the five omens of death and the five omens of immediate death, their mental suffering is even greater than the suffering of the hells. Once they die, even though they were a king like Śakra, they are born as servants among humans, and so on. The devaputras, like the sun and moon, the light of whose houses can illuminate the four continents, are born in the darkness between continents. Since they cannot even see their hand extended and withdrawn, they suffer. Even one who becomes an emperor in the end becomes a servant to the servants of the retinue.

The example of humans is that a powerful voice becomes weak; a wealthy person becomes impoverished; even though there are many people, ultimately the family line comes to an end; one fears whether or not one will encounter an enemy; one fears whether or not one will be parted from friends; one cannot find what one desires; one's expectations do not bear fruit; and so on—these sufferings are beyond conception.

The example of the asuras is that they fight and strike each other with weapons and sever limbs, having very angry natures. Since they are jealous of the prestige of the devas, they have inconceivable mental suffering.

iii. The Suffering of Formations

The pervasive suffering of formations is that since the activities of humans are inconceivable, they never end. {332} Actions are wasted. Since one thinks, "I need this and I need that," a human lifetime is exhausted in counting, and work never ends. When it is time to die, one suffers immensely because one's wishes remain unfulfilled. The wealthy suffer when their wealth is robbed by thieves, taken by the powerful, and so on. Paupers suffer immense fatigue due to searching.

In brief, meditate on the thought "No matter where I am born in the six realms, it never transcends the nature of suffering. Since I am suffering right now, I must practice the pure dharma."

b. Reflecting on the Causes and Results of Karma

As explained already, birth in samsara, which has the nature of suffering, is produced by the cause, unvirtuous behavior. To avoid such a birth, it is necessary to avoid the cause. When that is summarized, meditate thinking, "I must avoid the cause, all nonvirtue, and also accomplish even the smallest virtue as much as possible."

When that is elaborated a little more, there are three topics: (1) reflecting on unvirtuous karma, (2) reflecting on virtuous karma, (3) and reflecting on neutral karma.

i. Reflecting on Unvirtuous Karma

There are three topics: (1) reflecting on the nature of unvirtuous karma, (2) reflecting on the result of unvirtuous karma, and (3) advice for avoiding that result.

I) Reflecting on the Nature of Unvirtuous Karma

There are ten types of negative karma. Three are physical nonvirtues: Taking life is deliberately killing anything, from an insect to a human or a human fetus, with an intention motivated by any of the three poisons. Taking what has not been given is appropriating the belongings of others as one's own, even so much as a husk of rice. Apart from people whom one esteems and are close, sexual misconduct is wishing to have relations with the partners of others; those who uphold the banner of the dharma, like novices; those who are keeping the one-day vows; those who are under the guardianship of their parents; or having relations during the day, even with one's own partner, and so on.[36] {333}

Four are verbal nonvirtues: Lying is speaking words and meanings understood by others in order to confuse others by changing their perception. Calumny is speaking to others in order to divide them from their other friends. These are motivated by desire. Harsh words is speech harmful to others with a loud voice, whether purposeful or not. It is motivated by hatred. Idle speech is profuse, meaningless chatter about this and that and speaking without any direction, which interrupts one's own or others' virtuous practice.

Three are mental nonvirtues: Covetousness is motivated by desire. It is the thought that one is entitled to enjoy the enjoyments and wealth of others out of the desire to obtain other people's abundance for oneself. Malice is motivated by hatred. It is the thought that if harm is inflicted on another person, how fitting it is that they suffer immensely. Wrong view is motivated by ignorance. It is the thought that the teachings of a pure guru are untrue, such as the existence and nonexistence of the cause and result of karma, the four truths, the Three Jewels, and so on, and in addition, that happiness is the result of virtue and suffering is the result of nonvirtue.

II) The Result of Nonvirtuous Karma

There are two results: (1) temporary results and (2) ultimate results.

A) The Temporary Results

The temporary results are a short life; impoverished enjoyments; one's spouse, and so on, behave like enemies; one is criticized by others; conflicts with one's friends occur; one hears unpleasant speech; one's speech is held as false, lacking a source; {334} one's expectations are fruitless; one meets with great terrors; one's view becomes distorted, and so on.

B) The Ultimate Results

The ultimate results are that, since one engages in minor nonvirtues, one is propelled to an animal birth; since one engages in middling nonvirtues, one is propelled to a preta birth; and since one engages in major nonvirtues, one is propelled to a hell birth.

C) Advice for Avoiding the Result of Unvirtuous Karma

As such, since one engaged in those nonvirtues motivated by the three poisons, the result does not transcend the three evil destinies. Thus, one should commit to abstain from them even at the cost of one's life and avoid them with body and speech.

ii. Reflecting on Virtuous Karma

There are three topics: (1) reflecting on the nature of virtuous karma, (2) reflecting on the result of virtuous karma, and (3) advice for accomplishing virtuous karma.

I) The Nature of Virtuous Karma

The nature of virtuous karma is to abandon the aforementioned ten nonvirtues and motivated by an absence of desire, hatred, and ignorance, accomplish the ten virtues as much as possible.

II) The Result of Virtuous Karma

There are two results: (1) temporary results and (2) ultimate results.

A) Temporary Results

The temporary result is longevity; great enjoyments; one is in harmony with one's spouse, and so on; one obtains fame in all quarters; one is in harmony with friends; one's sense organs are clear; one's word is powerful; one's aspirations are fruitful; one is fearless; one has a correct view, and so on.

B) Ultimate Results

By engaging in a small amount, a middling amount, or a great amount of the ten virtues, one will attain the awakening of either a śrāvaka, a pratyekabuddha, or unsurpassed awakening.

III) Advice for Accomplishing Virtuous Karma

As such, the result from engaging in the ten virtues is attaining any of the three kinds of awakening. Since even obtaining the stage of a śrāvaka frees one from fear of samsara and evil destinies, {335} one should accomplish virtuous karma as much as possible.

iii. Reflecting on Neutral Karma

There are three topics: (1) reflecting on the nature of neutral karma, (2) reflecting on the result of neutral karma, and (3) advice for transforming neutral karma.

I) The Nature of Neutral Karma

The nature of neutral karma is eating food, engaging in handiwork, and so on, impartially, without virtuous or unvirtuous motivations.

II) The Result of Neutral Karma

Since the result of neutral karma does not deliver either happiness or suffering, one enthusiastically practices crafts impartially.

III) Advice for Transforming Neutral Karma

The advice for transforming nonvirtuous karma into virtuous karma is to transform it with motivation. For example, when eating food, think that one is nourishing the creatures in one's body. After building up one's body, use it for hearing, reflection, and so on. Also, when coming or going, imagine one goes to meet the guru for the sublime dharma, and visualizing statues of buddhas and bodhisattvas to one's right side, imagine one circumambulates them respectfully, showing the right side of the body, and go in that way.

3. Attachment to Personal Benefit

The statement "If attached to personal benefit, one has no bodhicitta" means that having seen the suffering of all of samsara, as explained above, since one engages in any of the minor, middling, or major virtues in order to be free from that suffering, one may attain the stage of a śrāvaka or a pratyekabuddha. However, they are not able to fulfill their own benefit or greatly benefit others. Since it is a hinderance to obtaining perfect buddhahood, one must not strive for one's benefit alone, but rather one should obtain perfect buddhahood for the benefit of all sentient beings. Buddhahood will not arise from incomplete or erroneous causes and conditions. For example, when warmth and moisture do not come together, like winter, even if one plants a seed of rice, it will not grow. {336} Even if one plants the seed wishing for rice, a harvest of rice will not be produced. Just as when rice seed (the cause) and manure, moisture, and warmth (the conditions) come together, a harvest of rice will grow for the one who desires it, so too does full awakening. As stated in the *Direct Awakening of Mahāvairocana*,[37] the cause arises from great compassion. The root arises from bodhicitta, and the culmination is reached due to skillful means. In order to practice the meaning of that, there are four topics: (1) cultivating love, (2) cultivating compassion, (3) cultivating bodhicitta, and (4) training in those practices.

a. Cultivating Love

There are four in cultivating love: (1) meditating on friends, (2) meditating on neutral people, (3) meditating on enemies, and (4) meditating on all sentient beings.

i. Meditating on Friends

There are three in meditating on friends: (1) recognizing one's mother, (2) recalling her kindness, and (3) cultivating love.

I) Recognizing One's Mother

For example, considering one's present mother, one's present mother is not only one's mother in the present but she has also been one's mother for many lifetimes. Ācārya Nāgārjuna's *Letter to a Friend* states:

> Were they the number of pills the size of juniper seeds,
> the earth could not hold the line of one's mothers.[38]

A sutra states:

The amount of mother's milk a single sentient being has drunk
cannot be contained in the four oceans.
The number of horses and cows fathers have given to one sentient being
surpasses the realm of Brahma.[39]

II) Recalling Her Kindness

The kindness of each of our mothers is immeasurable. When you were conceived in her womb, for a period of nine or ten months, her body was heavy and fatigued. When you were born, she endured suffering equal to the separation of her mind and body. After you were born, you could neither understand nor use language, like a grub turned over by a plow. She protected you with a loving mind and looked upon you with loving eyes. {337} She gave you delicious food from her tongue and wiped away your feces with her hand. She fed you with her hands. She prepared whatever food and clothes she could. She removed you from all harm. After you grew larger, she risked her life to give you wealth. She trained you in all kinds of subjects, such as writing, reading, and so on. In brief, reflect upon whatever kindness she offered, benefiting and protecting you from all harm.

III) Cultivating Love

The nature of love is described by Ācārya Buddhaśrījñāna:[40]

Accomplishing the benefit of migrating beings
is called "great love."[41]

Since a loving mind is the wish that all sentient beings possess happiness and the causes of happiness, in connection with generating bodhicitta, think, "May my kind mother have happiness and the causes of happiness." In connection with desire, think, "How wonderful it would be if she had happiness and the cause of happiness." In connection with aspiration, think, "She must have happiness and the causes of happiness!" Meditate on this without distraction and recite those passages. As such, recognize one's mother in this life as one's mother, and having recalled her kindness, meditate on love. Change the meditation to those who are neutral, enemies, and all sentient beings.

b. Cultivating Compassion

As such, if one trains well in the meditation on love, compassion will arise through its power. As it is said:

> Love is the water of compassion,
> which truly grows from suffering.[42]

Therefore, one should meditate on compassion. The nature of compassion is described by Ācārya Buddhaśrījñāna:[43]

> So-called compassion
> totally protects all who suffer.[44]

When one sees the object, suffering, and there is a mind that wishes to be free of that, (1) meditate on friends, (2) meditate on those who are between being friends and enemies, (3) meditate on enemies, and (4) meditate on all sentient beings. {338}

First, the three topics are like recognizing one's mother, recalling her kindness, and meditating on love, as above. The meditation on compassion is to meditate on one's mother whether she is living or deceased. Clearly visualize her before oneself. In connection with generating bodhicitta, think, "How sad it is that my kind mother is suffering and devoid of happiness. It is necessary to free her from suffering and the cause of suffering. When my mother's situation is observed, she has only suffering and the causes of suffering. How sad that she experiences that. I must free her from such suffering." Next, change to neutral beings, then to enemies, and finally to all sentient beings, and meditate on the unfabricated compassion that arises.

c. Cultivating Bodhicitta

As such, compassion arises and through its power, bodhicitta arises. As it is said:

> The root of that is asserted to be compassion,
> the thought to always benefit sentient beings.[45]

Therefore, the conclusion of that is meditating on the relative bodhicitta of exchanging oneself and others:

> May the suffering of all sentient beings ripen upon me.
> May my virtue ripen upon them.[46]

Recite the words "May all the suffering and unhappiness of the sentient beings who are equal with space, ripen upon me. May all my merit, happiness, and advantages be obtained by all sentient beings," and meditate on this with a sincere mind.

d. Training in Those Practices

Training in those practices is the conduct of a bodhisattva—abandoning harming others and accomplishing their benefit as much as possible. In particular, this is the practice of the six perfections for ripening oneself and ripening others through the four means of gathering, and so on, {339} as found in the *Ākāśagarbha Sutra*, Śāntideva's *Compendium of Training*, the *Introduction to the Conduct of Awakening*, and Nāgārjuna's *Necklace of Gems*.

4. If Grasping Arises, There Is No View

The meaning of "If grasping arises, there is no view" is that even though relative bodhicitta may have arisen satisfactorily, if it is combined with grasping to true existence, one falls into the extremes of permanence and annihilation, and there will be no liberation. Therefore, to remedy grasping to things and signs, the meditations of both śamatha and vipaśyana are required. As it is said:

> Having understood that the faults of affliction are destroyed
> by vipaśyana endowed with śamatha,
> first, to find śamatha, one must have
> neither attachment to the world nor delight.[47]

Here, there are three topics: (1) cultivating śamatha, (2) cultivating vipaśyana, and (3) cultivating śamatha and vipaśyana in tandem.

a. Cultivating Śamatha

In an isolated and pleasing place that is guarded by a dharma king and without harm, free of the thorns of concentration, such as people passing by, noise,[48] and so on, sit on a comfortable seat. At the beginning of all sessions, go for refuge and generate bodhicitta. The feet are in vajra posture, the hands are in the gesture of equipoise, the tongue rests on the palate, the spine is straight, and the eyes should neither be too open nor too closed. Maitreyanātha states:

> On the basis of true stability,
> place the mind on the mind.
> In order to fully distinguish phenomena,
> there is śamatha and vipaśyana.[49]

Śamatha is one-pointed placement of the mind on an external or internal object, such as a black pebble, and so on. Neten Chang Zang[50] said, {340} "The *Samādhirāja Sutra* explains there are two approaches: meditation that focuses on a statue of the Buddha and, prior to that, meditation that focuses on a pebble." Though there is no difference in the method of the one-pointed placement of the mind, since one is focusing on a statue of the Buddha, it becomes close mindfulness of the Buddha and the merit is greater. Therefore, meditate that in front of oneself on a jewel throne, lotus, and moon is Buddha Śākyamuni, with a color like pure gold, the right hand touching the earth, the left hand making the gesture of equipoise, wearing saffron dharma robes, and seated in vajrāsana. Meditate focusing on that statue and especially on the ūrṇā at his brow. Otherwise, one can meditate on Amitābha, who is red in color, with both hands in meditative equipoise. It is said it is sufficient to meditate on the visualization with the seat, and so on, as before.

As such, meditating on śamatha prior to vipaśyana is the meaning of "First, to acquire śamatha, one must be . . . ." When śamatha is cultivated well, the mind can dwell for months and years on any kind of object. However, śamatha alone is insufficient. Vipaśyana meditation is necessary as a remedy for pulling out afflictions from the root. Further, the mind that investigates the reality of inner and outer phenomena with discerning wisdom discerns that freedom from the extremes of existence, nonexistence, permanence, annihilation, and so on is vipaśyana.

b. Cultivating Vipaśyana

Cultivating vipaśyana has three topics: (1) establishing that apparent objects are mentally fabricated, (2) establishing that the mind is illusory, and (3) establishing that illusions lack inherent existence. {341}

i. Establishing that Apparent Objects Are Mentally Fabricated

Are the diverse appearances of objects that appear as a diversity—horses, elephants, men, women, walls, vases, blankets, and so on—without causes? Are they created by a vital force, god, and so on? Are they created by the four elements and particles? They are not emanations of the Buddha, but they arise because traces of such appearances of objects have been planted in one's mind from beginningless time. The creator of all of those is the mind. Meditate on the thought that there is no creator other than the mind.

ii. Establish the Mind as Illusory

The *Samādhirāja Sutra* states:

> The forms conjured by an illusionist
> do not exist as they appear.
> All phenomena should be understood in that way.[51]

Also, as explained before, those diverse objects are like dreams and illusions, just as when a dreamer experiences happiness and suffering in a dream, upon waking they recognize it was all false. Therefore, meditate until certainty repeatedly arises that these appearances in the mere relative are like reflections inside a mirror.

iii. Establish that Illusions Lack Inherent Existence

As such, meditate on the thought that though the appearance of those illusory objects that appear as a diversity appear in the mere relative unceasingly, when examined there is not so much as a hundredth of a hair that can be established in the ultimate.

c. Cultivating Śamatha and Vipaśyana in Tandem

Having confirmed step-by-step that the appearance of objects is fabricated by the mind, and so on, and having understood and ascertained that the appearance of objects is emptiness free from all extremes of proliferation, the mind understands the inseparability of that and the reality of objects, becoming one taste, like water poured into water or ghee poured into ghee. {342} Focus the mind on that and meditate one-pointedly. Since one meditates on that continuously, one gains familiarity. An impartial compassion guided by emptiness arises for all sentient beings who do not understand that, deluded grasping to things is averted and "deluded appearances arise as gnosis." One obtains the stage of buddhahood that has the nature of the three kāyas.

C. The Conclusion

Sealing with the dedication is the conclusion of all sessions. In this way, the cause of dedication is the root of virtue of one's profound samādhi meditation. Dedicating all roots of virtue gathered by oneself and others is included in one place. All that is dedicated—even the stage of perfect buddhahood—is made into a mental object and dedicated to all sentient beings equal with space for the purpose [of attaining perfect buddhahood].

Having made a petition through recognizing that appearances are like dreams and illusions, dedicate with whatever dedications from sutra and the treatises one knows, such as:

> By this virtue may all migrating beings
> gather the accumulation of merit and gnosis
> and obtain the two sublime [kāyas]
> that arise from merit and gnosis.[52]

Thus, having been encouraged by the great mantradhara vajradhara, Lama Kunga Lekpa, the master of the precious qualities of scripture and realization, having heard this twice from the lord of dharma, the all-knowing Kunga Zangpo, and having taken his two feet upon my crown, this was written down as notes by Bhikṣu Kunga Lekrin. Having presented this to the dharma lord guru, it was corrected and edited.[53]

Virtue. *maṅgalaṃ* {343}

The Necklace of Ketaka Gems

The Explanatory Method for the Manual of Parting from the Four Attachments *Mind Training Composed by the Bodhisattva Kunga Lekrin*

Ngawang Lekdrup[54]

namo guruve

Having perfected the sixteenfold emptiness that originates from the ocean of perfect aspirations,
the activity of the light of compassion that pacifies, cools, and illuminates is beautified by the image of a deer,
cannot be represented by a piece of camphor, and enjoys knowing the fortunate blue water lily as a friend—
I bow with my hands to that supreme moon of teachers, Guru Mañjughoṣa.
The personal embodiment of gnosis of all victors, holding a sword,
exhibited the major and minor marks with great love,
condensed the great tradition of introducing the children of the victors in four topics,
and graced the ear with the positive sound of instructions.
This prerequisite outline for giving explanations
according to the undisputed treatise, which causes that system to arise,
is promulgated so those newly placed on the throne of giving explanations
may obtain the wish-granting cow of oral explanations.

The guide whose continuum has been purified by bodhicitta—the virtuous mentor in possession of the characteristics of what is to be explained—will systematically lead the fortunate disciples to the jeweled island of liberation through the path of *Parting from the Four Attachments*. Out of many texts, such as the manual of Jetsun Rinpoche in the manner of an experiential song, the notes composed by Lord Sakya Paṇḍita[55] and Nupa Rikzin Drak, the manual composed by the omniscient dharma king Sönam Senge,[56] the manual composed by Mahāpaṇḍita Namkha Palzang,[57] and so on, these days the standard manual is the one composed by the bodhisattva Kunga Lekpa Rinchen, the patrilineal nephew of Vajradhara [Kunga Zangpo], who sets down the utterances of the lord guru [Kunga Zangpo]. In this system, to begin, in a pleasing temple, and so on, arrange offerings, and so on, before an image of the Bhagavān Muni and his retinue. The master should face the images and with folded hands begin with the seven-limbed prayer, "In the worlds of the directions, as many as there are . . . ." Generate aspirational and engaged bodhicitta with the verses found in the *Introduction to the Conduct of Awakening*, reciting "Until reaching the seat of awakening . . . ," and refresh one's bodhisattva vow. Having gone for refuge, whatever subject matter is extracted for the disciples should be meditated on for one session. Seal with the dedication, "By this merit, may all living beings . . . ."[58] This is the procedure for the following days.

When the master recites the mantra to eliminate māras[59] for the disciples seven times, the disciples prostrate and then sit in the row. Then, encouraged by the master, they recite the *Heart of the Perfection of Wisdom Sutra* once, beginning with the verse "Unutterable, unthinkable, inexpressible . . . ," and at the conclusion, recite the single verse:

> Please completely pacify
> all outer and inner
> harmful obstacles
> to accomplishing full awakening.[60]

Recite, "By this merit . . . ."

When slowly reciting "Glorious root guru" and the appended arrangement of the lineage prayer beginning from "I offer a supplication to the three peerless supreme refuges," the assistant for offerings distributes flowers to the beginning of the row and gathers them from the end of the row. The assistant makes three prostrations, stands, and with a bow announces:

> The maṇḍala is offered as a gift for requesting the profound teaching of the sublime Dharma in the presence of the glorious, sublime guru, the embodiment of all buddhas of the three times.

Then, the thirty-seven-heap maṇḍala is offered. If it is wished, add "Whatever offering substances . . ."[61] and "From now until the seat of awakening . . . ."[62] Next,{345} motivated by the great compassion to liberate all sentient beings from I, the master, should speak in a loud and clear voice:

> Now then, recall the generation of supreme bodhicitta with the thought, "The stage of perfect buddhahood should be attained in order to benefit all sentient beings equal with space. For that purpose, I will listen to the profound dharma and practice the meaning." Also, the conduct of listening to Dharma is taught in the *Garland of Incarnations*:
>
> > While sitting on a low cushion,
> > maintaining glorious restraint,
> > gazing with joyful eyes,
> > imbibing the amṛta of words,
> > and generating devotion, with one-pointed respect[63]
> > and a tranquil, unsullied mind,
> > generate reverence and listen to the dharma,
> > just as a patient listens to a physician's instructions.[64]
>
> One must avoid lying down, leaning, turning to one's side, or having one's back to the master, and so on. Whether sitting or kneeling, one must possess the conduct of devotion. One should not speak. The mind must be attentive.
>
> The *Inconceivable Secret Sutra* states:
>
> > Human birth is difficult to find
> > when the path of the Buddha arises in the world.
> > Alas, one who is faithful and listens to the dharma
> > is very rare in this world.[65]
>
> Having assembled those conditions so the dharma can be heard, it is necessary to listen with joy and enthusiasm. In particular, the sutras state, "Listen carefully and keep this in mind!"[66] Those

who do the opposite will not focus their mind on the words of the dharma, which is the fault of an inverted container. Even if they focus their minds on the words, they do not maintain their attention, like a container with a broken bottom. Even if they maintain mindfulness and attention, {346} *Pedagogical Strategies* states:

> Pride, lack of faith,
> disinterest,
> outer distraction, inner absorption,
> and weariness are the faults of listening.[67]

Such people may be proud, thinking, "I am better in many ways than this one giving explanations because of my knowledge, qualities, and so on." They may lack faith, thinking, "The one giving explanations has this fault." They may be disinterested, thinking, "I know this dharma that is being explained." They are distracted, examining outer things such as form, and so on, or distracted by games and jests. They may be occupied with thoughts of the three poisons or engaged in samādhi or equipoise. Or, they may be tired of hearing the dharma, thinking, "If they would take a break from explaining the dharma, it would be good." Whichever of these six taints one has is the fault of the sullied container. It is necessary to abandon the three faults of the container. Further, it is necessary that the master and the disciples rely on the six perceptions and practice the six perfections. The six perceptions are thinking that the master is a physician, the ones listening to dharma are patients, the dharma is the excellent medicine, the afflictions are a severe illness, the diligent practice is the treatment for the illness, and this dharma of the sugata should remain for a long while because of the sublime people and this method due to there being no deception in the Tathāgata. Possession of the six perfections is definitely necessary: The teacher granting the words and the disciples presenting offerings for the purpose of receiving the teachings are generosity. Abandoning unfavorable circumstances for explanation and listening is discipline. Not having aversion to arduous conduct of body and voice is patience. Enthusiasm for explaining and listening is diligence.

One-pointed focus on the dharma is concentration. Discerning the words and meanings is wisdom. {347} Please listen, keeping those things in mind.

> **Here, in the sole path traveled by all sugatas of the three times[68] . . . Yeshe Gyaltsen Palzangpo.**

Yeshe Gyaltsen gave this to the all-knowing Kunga Zangpo, the jewel in the crown of Tibetan scholars and the second Munīndra of the degenerate times. The latter gave this to the sublime regent, Kunga Wangchuk. He then gave this to the tutor, Chökyi Gyalpo. The latter gave this to omniscient Könchok Lhundrup. He then gave this to Könchok Gyatso, the eye of great scholars. The latter gave this to Jetsun Ngawang Choklek Dorje. He gave this to his nephew, Kyenrap Tenzin Zangpo. The latter gave this to his nephew, Jampa Ngawang Lhundrup. He gave this to Omniscient Morchen, Ngawang Kunga Lhundrup. The latter gave this to Jamgön Nesarwa. He gave this to Pal Sakyapa Ngawang Kunga Lodrö Sangye Tenpe Gyaltsen Palzangpo. The latter gave this to Jetsunma Chime Tenpe Nyima. She gave this to Jamyang Khöntön Ngawang Dorje Rinchen. The latter gave this to my root guru [insert name here]. Pleased with us, that one gave this to us with great kindness.

One should know how to alter this in accordance with the name of each from whom this dharma was received.

II. The Actual Instruction

In the topics of the intimate instruction, there are (1) the preliminaries and (2) the main subject . . . diligent in the virtuous activities of body, voice, and mind . . .

. . . is recited three times.

B. The Main Subject

There are four topics in the main subject.

1. Attachment to This Life

The meaning of "If attached to this life, one is not a dharma person"

. . . is stated by Jetsun Drakpa Gyaltsen:

First, do not be attached to this life
. . . . .
put aside the concentration of the eight worldly dharmas! {348}

[I]t is necessary that one not be attached to this life . . . . Thus, meditate on the difficulty of acquiring freedom and endowment through example.

iv. Nature

Because it is extremely rare to be born with all eight freedoms and ten endowments, they are difficult to acquire. The eight freedoms [are listed]:

These eight who lack freedom are hell beings,
pretas, animals, long-lived devas,
barbarians, those with wrong view,
those who live when a buddha is absent, and mutes.[69]

As such, it is necessary to be free from the eight places that lack freedom. In that regard, hell beings are pierced by intense suffering. Pretas have the nature of mental pain. Animals are completely confused and their minds are mostly without shame and modesty. The long-lived deities have the negative conditions of wrong view and live in a place where strong pride arises. Barbarians behave mistakenly with respect to what to accept and reject—marrying their mothers, and so on—and find it difficult to meet sublime people. Those with wrong view do not consider virtue to be the cause of higher realms and liberation and assert the Three Jewels, the result of karma, and so on, to be false. The people born in the world when the Buddha is absent have no interest in the sublime cause of accomplishment. Mutes have a fault with their tongues. Since those eight are confused about what to accept and reject and they are outside the conventions of dharma, they have no freedom to practice the dharma. Therefore, it is very rare to obtain the basis of freedom because most migrating beings of the six realms live where there is no freedom.

In terms of the ten endowments, there are five personal endowments and five external endowments. The five personal endowments are:

> Born human, born in a central country,
> with complete faculties, with faith in the foundation [vinaya],
> and without negative actions.[70]

The rarity of birth as a human being has already been explained above. {349} Birth in a central country is also rare. Ārya Asaṅga said that a central country is a place where any of the fourfold assembly dwell, and where they do not live is a border land. The area where the fourfold assembly do not live is as wide as space, and the area where they live appears as narrow as the axle of a chariot.

The rarity of complete faculties is addressed in the *Compendium of Training*:

> Though it is difficult to acquire complete faculties,
> it is also difficult to hear the Buddha's dharma.[71]

It is rare to have faith in the foundation because obtaining sincere faith in the well-spoken sublime dharma and vinaya appears only one time in a hundred. It is also rare to be without negative actions, because it seems that many people themselves engage in the deeds of immediate retribution, encourage others to engage in them, and cultivate joy when others perform them.

The five external endowments are:

> The Buddha arrived, he taught the dharma,
> the doctrine is present, there are followers of that doctrine,
> and there is sincere appreciation due to others.

The arrival of a buddha in the world is very rare. The eons in which a buddha arrives are called "light eons,"[72] and those in which a buddha has not arrived are called "dark eons." Since in this present eon one thousand buddhas will arrive, it is called Fortunate Eon. Then, following sixty dark eons, there is one light eon called Array of Qualities. Next, after ten thousand dark eons, there is a light eon called Great Fame. Next, after three hundred dark eons, there is a light eon called Like a Star. As such, no more than four light eons arise in ten thousand, three hundred sixty dark eons. Further, in a light eon, because it is said that the life span of living beings increases even when a buddha has not yet arrived, {350} [the eon] of the non-arrival of a buddha has elapsed.

Thus, the teaching of dharma is rare because those to be tamed are not suitable recipients for dharma, and so it is explained that the buddhas will not teach the dharma. Our teacher, having manifested the way of buddhahood, stated in the *Sutra of the Extensive Play*:

> I have obtained an ambrosial dharma that is
> profound, peaceful, free of proliferation, luminous, and
> uncompounded.
> I shall dwell silently in the forest,
> because even if I explained it, others would not understand.[73]

The Buddha dwelled [in the forest] with little concern. Brahma, the lord of the Sahā universe, presented him with a one-thousand-spoked golden wheel and supplicated the Buddha to turn the wheel of dharma, explaining that the need had arisen.

It is rare that the doctrine of the buddhas is present, because after the five past buddhas of this Fortunate Eon complete their teachings, there will be no doctrine until later buddhas arise.

It is rare that there are followers of the doctrine who can introduce the doctrine of the buddhas to oneself and others, because most people in the world practice non-Buddhist teachings and turn their backs on the doctrine of the buddhas. There are also many with the conceit of introducing the doctrine of the buddhas to people. They may have thought about the systematic[74] words of those who have commented on the intention of the sutras and tantras, yet having merely heard them and not effectively understood their meaning, these fools introduce others to train on whatever little they can remember. Finally, there are also vacuous people who have engaged in much hearing, explanation, and meditation and have conceit about their knowledge of the piṭakas, who seem like frightened rabbits running away at the sound of thunder.

Sincere appreciation due to others is rare because there are many who reward those of wrong livelihood, who live by taking what they can get, renunciants who do not enjoy worldly activities and householding but who recite texts as a basis for alms food, and it is rare that alms are provided to those engaged in meditation. {351} Therefore, having all these factors on the basis of a single human body is as rare as a star appearing during the day. Thus, one should also meditate based upon the difficulty of acquiring freedom and endowment in terms of nature.

b. Death and Impermanence

To reflect on death and impermanence . . .

Meditate on the thought, "I must practice the dharma immediately because the time of death is uncertain."

Once again, when repeating this in order to generate certainty in the mind, this evening, in your rooms, each of you should adopt the posture of concentration on a comfortable seat and rest until your uneven breathing naturally settles. When thought arises suddenly, do not allow yourself to be under its power, and having completely interrupted it, engage in the stage of contemplation. Repeat everything as above between "There are (1) the preliminaries, (2) the main subject . . ." and "Meditate on the thought, 'I must practice the dharma immediately because the time of death is uncertain.'"

Then again, repeat everything once more to generate certainty.

C. The Conclusion

When one wishes to rise from that session, [say]:

> **Sealing with the dedication . . . . In this way, the cause of dedication . . . dedicate with whatever dedications from sutra and the treatises one knows . . . .**

In between sessions, pass the time by engaging in activities consistent with the dharma in a state inseparable from the essence of the practice of the main subject. Now, please engage in the stages of contemplation.

[Recite the single verse] from the *Garland of Incarnations*:

By this merit, having attained the stage
of the omniscient one and subdued the enemy, faults,
may I rescue living beings from the ocean of existence,
tossed about by the waves of birth, aging, and death.[75]

The master recites the single verse by Ārya Asaṅga:

May any of the inconceivable merit I have gained
from this explanation of the precious, sublime dharma of the
Mahāyāna
transform all migrating beings into stainless vessels of
the precious, sublime dharma of the Mahāyāna.[76]

The disciples recite the altered version:

May any of the inconceivable merit I have gained
from hearing the precious, sublime dharma of the Mahāyāna
transform all migrating beings into stainless vessels of
the precious, sublime dharma of the Mahāyāna.

Together recite the verse composed by Chögyal Phakpa:

By my power may I utterly destroy
the power of Māra, the textual systems of non-Buddhists,
all serpents of darkness who fabricate facsimiles of dharma,
and all others who cause harm to migrating beings![77]

In addition, the verse from the *Aspiration of the Conduct of Samantabhadra*:

When circling through all of existence,
may inexhaustible merit and gnosis be attained.
May there be methods, wisdom, samādhi, and liberation—
an inexhaustible treasury of qualities![78] {352}

Day two is the same as the first day. Speak in a loud and clear voice:

The stage of perfect buddhahood should be attained in order to benefit all sentient beings equal with space. . . . "I must

practice the dharma immediately because the time of death is uncertain."

Since that causes one to abandon attachment to this life, one will not fall into lower realms. Following the stages of the instruction to cause the mind to turn toward the dharma, now offer the new stages of contemplation:

2. Attachment to the Three Realms

The statement "If attached to the three realms, one has no renunciation" means,

. . . as stated by Jetsun Rinpoche:

To accomplish nirvana
. . . . .
the mass of samsara's suffering.

If one is attached to samsara's three realms, "even the practice of dharma will not become the path of awakening . . . imagine one circumambulates them respectfully, showing the right side of the body, and go in that way."

Once again, when repeating this in order to generate certainty in the mind, this evening, in your rooms, each of you should adopt the posture of concentration on a comfortable seat and rest until your uneven breath naturally settles. When thought arises suddenly, do not allow oneself to be under its power, and having completely interrupted it, engage in the stages of contemplation. Complete the first portion of the preliminaries and main subject from the trio of the preliminaries, main subject, and conclusion, repeating once, "If one is attached to samsara's three realms, even the practice of dharma will not become the path of awakening . . . ," and so on. Third, the conclusion is the same as the first day.

Day Three:

The stage of perfect buddhahood should be attained in order to benefit all sentient beings equal with space. . . . (1) the

account of the gurus of the lineage that generates confidence and trust and (2) the actual instruction.

In that case, history and the instruction for contemplating the preliminaries and main subject have been well presented.

Because of the second topic, "If one is attached to samsara's three realms . . . imagine one circumambulates them respectfully, showing the right side of the body, and go in that way," {353} one will not wander in samsara, since one has abandoned attachment to the three realms. Having completed the stages of instruction that cause the dharma to turn into the path, now to offer the new stages of contemplation:

3. Attachment to Personal Benefit

The statement "If attached to personal benefit, one has no bodhicitta" means . . .

As Jetsun Rinpoche already explained:

If one parts with attachment, misery is transcended.
. . . . .
may all sentient beings attain buddhahood.

Having seen the suffering of all of samsara, . . . and Nāgārjuna's *Necklace of Gems*.

Once again, when repeating this in order to generate certainty in the mind, this evening, in your rooms, each of you should adopt the posture of concentration on a comfortable seat and rest until your uneven breath naturally settles. When thought arises suddenly, do not allow oneself to be under its power, and having completely interrupted it, engage in the stages of contemplation. From the trio of the preliminaries, main subject, and conclusion, after going for refuge and generating bodhicitta, repeat the third of the four topics in the main topic as above:

The statement "If attached to personal benefit, one has no bodhicitta" means . . . and Nāgārjuna's *Necklace of Gems*.

Third, the conclusion—sealing with a dedication, and so on—are the same as found at the end of the main text.

Day Four:

> **The stage of perfect buddhahood should be attained in order to benefit all sentient beings equal with space. . . . (1) the account of the gurus of the lineage that generates confidence and trust and (2) the actual instruction.**

In that case, history and the main subject have already been completed as above:

> **The statement "If attached to personal benefit, one has no bodhicitta" means . . . and Nāgārjuna's *Necklace of Gems*.**

Therefore, since one has abandoned attachment to personal benefit, one does not deviate into the state of a śrāvaka or a pratyekabuddha, and the stages of instruction of the path that remove delusion are complete. Now, to offer the new stages of contemplation: {354}

4. If Grasping Arises, There Is No View

> **The meaning of "If grasping arises, there is no view," is . . .**

. . . as Jetsun Rinpoche says:

> **No matter what one may wish, there is no liberation**
> . . . .
> **put it aside in the state of inexpressibility.**

> **. . . even though relative bodhicitta may have arisen satisfactorily . . . One obtains the stage of buddhahood that has the nature of the three kāyas.**

Once again, when repeating this in order to generate certainty in the mind, this evening, in your rooms, each of you should adopt the posture of concentration on a comfortable seat and rest until your uneven breathing naturally settles. When thought arises suddenly, do not allow yourself to be under its power, and having completely interrupted it, engage in the stages of contemplation. From the trio of the preliminaries, main subject, and conclusion, after going for refuge and generating bodhicitta, repeat the fourth of the four topics in the main topic as above:

> **"If grasping arises, there is no view," . . . One obtains the stage of buddhahood that has the nature of the three kāyas. . . . Seal with the dedication . . . .**

. . . when one wishes to rise from that session.

> **In this way, the cause of dedication . . . dedicate with whatever dedications from sutra and the treatises one knows . . .**

Therefore, since one abandons attachment to things and characteristics, it is the quick method of attaining full buddhahood. The stages of instruction that cause deluded appearances to arise as gnosis are complete. In brief, the essence of all Mahāyāna sutras, the entire path of the perfections, is totally complete. Since Mañjughoṣanātha's profound instruction on *Parting from the Four Attachments* was received according to the speech of our guru, our virtuous mentor {355} is now finished. Based on experience through initial intense effort, a special experience in the mental continuum will definitely be born. Fortunate persons who follow the profound instruction, and so on, please act on behalf of the great benefit of the doctrine and sentient beings. In gratitude for receiving the entire instruction, present either a long or a short maṇḍala offering. Since each of you listened properly to the explanation of the Mahāyāna dharma, and it is necessary to dedicate merit without perceiving the three spheres, offer pure aspirations so that the inestimable heap of merit will not go to waste.

In between sessions, having removed your hat, dedicate offerings to the perfect sangha, and so on, offer extensive general dedications, and release the assembly.

A dedicatory verse:

> How wonderful! The essence described by the ocean of discourses,
> tasted well by the munis of the past,

is given to all in the family of the sugatas—
what else can there be aside from the two truths and bodhicitta?

Therefore, the oral instruction of Mañjughoṣa that has the power
to increase wishes,
the method of explanation that does not mix sutra and tantra, is
placed on the tip of a banner,
the victory banner that pleases all scholars, raised
free of fearing the dark snake partisans.

By the pure virtue that arises in this way (*idam*),
having purified the realm of migrating beings like the sun's
procession north (*udag*),
the Muni's dharma proclaimed to the four continents of the world
(*evaṃ*)
should be practiced without effort, like eating porridge (*odanam*).

This explanatory method of parting from the four attachments, called the *Ketaka*, which removes the impurities of fabricated systems, {356} was written by the wandering vagrant, Ngawang Lekdrup—who has taken on his head the dusty feet of many tutors who practice dharma correctly and who give explanations of dharma, chiefly the Evaṃ Tartse Khenchens, father and sons, the dharma kings of the great treasure of limitless compassion—at Evaṃ Chöden, having carefully investigated the *Entryway to Dharma* by Lopön Rinpoche Sönam Tsemo, the history of the dharma composed by Ngorchen Jampeyang Könchok Lhundrup, and so on.

May good fortune and the flame of glory ornament the world.[79]

21. Increasing the Two Accumulations

A Systematic Arrangement of the Offering Rite to the Gurus of the Path with Its Result[1]

Kunga Chöphel

This is an offering ritual to the lineage of the gurus of the Path with Its Result. It is adapted primarily from five texts: Kunga Gyaltsen's *Common Supplication to the Guru* and *Uncommon Supplication to the Sublime Guru*, and Lodrö Gyaltsen's *Homage and Offering to the Lineage of the Path with Its Result*, *Ocean of Hearing*, and *Offering the Maṇḍala and Supplication to the Guru*. The text *Increasing the Two Accumulations* is not included in the published editions of the Path with Its Result literature, and virtually nothing is known of its author except that he was a seventeenth-century figure.

{358} *oṃ svasti*
Homage to Śrī Hevajra, nondual with the guru.

Here, from among the preparations, main subject, and conclusion, those who wish to practice the common guru yoga should engage in the preparations. In an isolated and pleasing abode, one should sweep and arrange any statue inside of which has been placed the nails, locks of hair, and so on of the previous gurus, or a painting, or a molded image one can acquire. In front of that image, on a shelf covered with cloth, scatter flowers. Above that, place a tripod, upon which is placed a practice maṇḍala, smeared with scent, with five heaps. This is surrounded by the two water offerings[2] and the five welcoming offerings.[3] If one can prepare it, one should ornament the stepped shelves with a garland of offerings, canopied victory banners, and so on.

Before oneself, prepare an offering maṇḍala, which is no smaller than six inches in diameter, with scented water and clean rice.

> *oṃ vajra yakṣa hūṃ*
> *oṃ vajrajvala anala hana daha paca matha bhañjaraṇa hūṃ phaṭ*
> *oṃ svabhāva śuddho sarvadharmāḥ svabhāva śuddho 'haṃ*
>
> From the state of emptiness arises *oṃ*, from which arises vast and wide containers made of precious substances, {359} inside of which *oṃ* melts, filling those with water offerings, flowers, incense, lamps, scent, and food formed of divine substances. Other inconceivable offerings, such as music, streamers, and so on, fill all of space.
>
> *oṃ vajra arghaṃ āḥ hūṃ . . . oṃ vajra śabda āḥ hūṃ, oṃ vajra dharmāraṇi . . .* , and so on.
>
> Beginning from this moment until seated on the seat of awakening, I and all sentient beings, equal with space, go for refuge to the venerable, glorious, and sublime root and lineage gurus, the embodiments of the body, speech, mind, qualities, and activities of all tathāgatas of the ten directions and three times, the sources of the eighty-four thousand sections of the dharma and the sovereigns of the noble sangha. {360} We go for refuge to the perfect Buddha Bhagavāns. We go for refuge to the sublime dharma. We go for refuge to the noble sangha. [Recite three times.]
>
> I prostrate and go for refuge to the guru and the precious Three Jewels. May you please bless my continuum.
>
> I will practice the profound path in order to attain the stage of perfect buddhahood for the benefit of all sentient beings. [Recite three times.]
>
> *oṃ svabhāva śuddho sarvadharmāḥ svabhāva śuddho 'haṃ*
>
> From the state of emptiness arises a *bhrūṃ*, from which arises a celestial mansion made of various precious substances, adorned

with four doors and four pediments, and decorated with all ornaments, complete in all ways. In the center of this is a jeweled throne supported by eight great lions, upon which multicolored lotus and sun and moon maṇḍalas are stacked one atop the other. Upon that is one's sublime root guru, the embodiment of all victors of the three times, their heirs, and disciples, in the form of Vajradhara, the sovereign of all families. His color is as blue as blue sapphire, limpid, and shining with light. He has one face and two hands, which hold a vajra and a bell crossed at his heart. His face smiles wrathfully. His mood is graceful and passionate. His long hair is bound into a black topknot on his crown and the remainder hangs in locks. He is adorned with jewels and bone ornaments, and he wears clothes of multicolored silk. Many light rays shine from his form {361} as he sits in vajrāsana with a regal posture.

Surrounding him are the lineage gurus in the form of Vajradhara, seated facing inward. In the East is the assembly of pledged deities. In the South are many perfect buddhas in sambhogakāya and nirmāṇakāya forms. In the West is the sublime dharma of the Mahāyāna in the form of volumes wrapped in brocade, and so on. In the North is the noble sangha, in the form of many householders, renunciants, and yoginīs. Surrounding them are innumerable dharmapālas, wealth deities, and so on, like a billowing cloud bank.

Light rays shine from all their hearts and invite the root and lineages gurus, pledged deities, the Three Jewels, the dharmapālas, and the wealth deities from their natural abodes, *oṃ vajra samājaḥ*.

I pay homage with devotion to the Dharma king of the three realms, who is endowed with inalienable wisdom and compassion, the embodiment of all tathāgatas, the source of all sublime dharma, the father of all bodhisattvas, the guru of all śrāvakas and buddhas, the refuge of the whole world and its devas. Great paṇḍita of Sakya, the lord of the dharma, please guide me at all times with your great love.[4]

I bow to the lotus feet of the guru,
whose body is like a jewel, endowed with the vajras,

by whose kindness great bliss
arises in an instant.[5]

You ripen all disciples
through adopting the forms of the victors, their heirs,
renunciants, upāsakas, householders, and so on,
and all migrating beings.

Just as the intense heat of the rays of the sun
cannot be produced without a magnifying glass,
likewise, the blessings of the Buddha
will not be produced without a guru.

Therefore, all buddhas are pleased
by pleasing you.
I go for refuge to you, the guru,
who combines the Three Jewels into one.

I bow to that glorious guru,
the embodiment of all buddhas, {362}
the precious treasury of dharmas,
and the form that includes all sanghas.

In order to ripen disciples,
you display the five tathāgatas as
the five aggregates.
Buddhalocana, and so on, are the four elements.
Protector, your sense organs are
Kṣitigarbha, Vajrapāṇi,
Ākāśagarbha, Avalokiteśvara,
Mañjuśrī, Nivāraṇaviṣkambhin,
Maitreya, and Samantabhadra.
The ten wrathful ones, Yamāntaka, and so on,
are parts of your glorious body.
You display form, and so on, as vajra goddesses.

Having transformed afflictions into gnosis,
great being, your wisdom

emanates all perfect buddhas
through your activities that spread everywhere.

Vajradhara, lord of all buddhas,
you have abandoned all traces of obscurations
and perfected all qualities
through the yoga that unifies all into one.

Your activities are marvelous.
Whoever relies unwaveringly on you
will immediately be blessed
and will instantly attain perfect buddhahood.

Furthermore, they will accomplish all abundance.
Therefore, supreme vajra master,
bowing to you with all things,
be my refuge in every way.

I shall please you
with outer, inner, secret, and ultimate offerings—my body,
enjoyments, all personal connections, and even my life.
For as long as we all
have not obtained the stage of liberation,
we shall present you
with a cloud of supreme offerings
that exceeds that of the liberation of Samantabhadra.

May those activities that please you
be accomplished.
May you avoid all those who are displeasing.
May all rely upon you.

If it would please the protector,
I will even abandon attaining
unsurpassed awakening
for the purpose of accomplishing your activities.

In every birth after birth,
I will accomplish your activities. {363}
By this virtue may we all
accomplish deeds that please you.[6]

Your physical conduct is pure,
endowed with conduct pleasing to the Buddha.
Your activities of speech are abundant,
covering the whole maṇḍala of knowledge.

The thoughts of your mind are very profound,
knowing the nature of all phenomena.
You are endowed with an ocean of qualities,
pleasing to all who are wise.

You, lord of dharma, possess
the activity of ripening all sentient beings.
Welcoming you causes prestige.
Relying upon you causes supreme wisdom.

One becomes fearless by relying upon you.
The source of happiness is serving you.
To the glorious lord of dharma who is like that,
to the supreme guru, I offer a supplication.

All buddhas have stated,
"Having given up other offerings,
present offerings to the guru."
Therefore, may the guru be pleased
by all things.
In this life and other lives
until buddhahood is attained,
may I dwell before the feet of the guru,
never to be parted!
May an offering be made with all offerings,
may the sublime dharma always be heard,
and may their commands be accomplished![7]

I pay homage to all gurus,
the embodiments of all buddhas,
the precious treasury of all siddhis,
those freed from all faults.

I pay homage to Vajradhara,
who perfected merit and gnosis,
the nature of emptiness and compassion,
the glory of samsara and nirvana.

I pay homage to Nairātmyā,
the dharmadhātu, the perfection of wisdom,
the illusory form of great bliss,
the mother who gives birth to all sugatas.

I pay homage to Virūpa,
who trained in all knowledge,
diligently attained the supreme stage, {364}
and benefited others with deeds out of love.

I pay homage to Kāṇha,
who benefited others with his strict discipline,
after his mind was liberated
by following the profound instruction.

I pay homage to Ḍamarupa,
who dwelled in the strict discipline of a siddha
and was liberated from mundane conduct
by seeing the meaning of the sublime truth.

I pay homage to Avadhūtipa,
who behaved without duality in the manner of a child,
after attaining siddhi
through total diligence in the profound path.

I pay homage to Gayadhara,
skilled in all knowledge,

who attained mastery of samādhi
and tamed Tibet.

I pay homage to Śākya Yeshe,[8]
the compassionate one fluent in two languages,
who fulfilled the hopes of disciples
through holding the precious treasury of the sublime dharma.

I pay homage to Jetsun Kunrik,
who held all the tantras and sutras,
having relied on his guru with faith
and possessed great magical power.

I pay homage to Chöbar.
In order for you to benefit others,
you mastered samādhi, clairvoyance,
and miraculous abilities through diligence in practice.

I pay homage to Kunga Nyingpo,
the Sakyapa, the lord of yogis,
who constantly benefited others
with great compassion.

Because you comprehended all dharmas
from Mañjuśrī in person,
you were unconfused about all knowledge
and became the guru of great scholars.

I pay homage to Sönam Tsemo.
Because you accomplished activities of immeasurable merit
and increased your gnostic wisdom,
you became the supreme friend of migrating beings.

I pay homage to Drakpa Gyaltsen,
the lord of all vajra holders, {365}
who saw the truth of all phenomena
and crossed the ocean of secret mantra.

I pay homage to Palchen Öpo.[9]
You are a treasury of many intimate instructions,
possessing a stable mind
and constantly intending to benefit others.

I pay homage to Palden Döndrup.[10]
Because you accomplished many eons
of gathering merit and gnosis,
you perfected all tenets.

I pay homage to your body
that generates great faith at its mere sight
and is adorned with the collection of
unmistaken, faultless discipline.

I pay homage to your supreme speech,
pure speech free of meaningless sound,
which satisfies the ears of limitless disciples
with distinct elocution.

I pay homage to your liberated mind,
in equipoise free of concepts,
entering evenly to the minds of migrating beings,
a treasury of samādhi and dhāraṇī.

I pay homage to you who attained mastery
over explanation, debate, and composition
because you comprehended the entire
maṇḍala of knowledge.

I pay homage to your great love
that never neglects the benefit of others
because you are free of all references
and endowed with great compassion.

I pay homage to your great power
that conquers the power of Māra

with the great force of wisdom, love, and diligence,
and transforms afflictions into the path of awakening.

I pay homage to the lord of activities,
who engages in benefiting others
with various emanations
for as long as samsara exists.

I pay homage to the powerful king
who produces all needs and wants, pleases all
from the precious victory banner,
and grants the result of excellent, abundant wealth.[11] {366}

I pay homage to you, the incomparable one,
the embodiment of the gnosis of all buddhas
gathered into one, who shows the body of an ordinary person
in order to benefit others.

The Three Jewels are you.
You are the Three Jewels.
Therefore, I pay homage with devotion
to you in every way.

Supreme teacher, homage to you.
Supreme refuge, homage to you.
Supreme guide, homage to you.
Supreme guru, homage to you.

I pay homage to all those
who have been touched by your body,
have heard and upheld your speech,
and have been brought to your mind.

I pay homage to Sönam Gyaltsen,[12]
the bodhisattva mahāsattva,
one of great analytical intelligence,
the holder of secret mantra who possesses supreme strict discipline.[13]

I pay homage to the excellent activities of
the one who possesses marvelous great wisdom,
like the gem placed on top of a victory banner,
and who bestows all desires on migrating beings.[14]

I pay homage to Dharma Lord Zhangtön,[15]
who held the Three Jewels as the guru,
gloriously stabilizing the culmination of experience
and realization with the samādhi of the two stages.

I pay homage to Trakphukpa,[16]
diligent in one-pointed practice,
wealthy with the glory of the two purposes,
born from the two accumulations of merit and gnosis.

I pay homage to you, sole teacher,[17]
who discerned the truth of the knowable
through wisdom that realizes reality
and is never distracted by other deviations.

I pay homage to you,
supreme glorious root guru,[18]
endowed with discipline, hearing, reflection, and cultivation,
who kindly shows the unmistaken path with love.

I pay homage to the lord of dharma endowed with the five gnoses,
the one who protects all migrating beings
with the excellent wealth of the two accumulations, {367}
having seized the tip of the victory banner of the two stages.[19]

I bow to the mahāsiddha, Buddhaśrī,
the lord of dharma, by whom
the supreme gnosis of the peak of the path of application
was attained by cultivating profound samādhi.

I pay homage to the one who pleased migrating beings
with a festival of amṛta of all-knowing speech

and whose excellent activities
became the glory of disciples.[20]

I bow to the feet of the glorious guru,
endowed with the altruistic mind that pleases the Jewels,
who possesses the excellent, glorious, beneficial qualities
to overcome the opposition.[21]

I bow to the feet of Guru Mañjuśrī,
whose glorious fame shakes the three regions,
who penetrates all there is to know
and comprehends an ocean of discourses.[22]

I bow to the sublime guide of disciples,
the lord of wisdom,
who sees the truth of all tantras,
whose festival of ripening and liberation spreads in the ten
directions.[23]

I pay homage to the snake-hooded siddha scholar,
endowed with the glory of an ocean of limitless tantras,
illuminating the doctrine of Vajrayāna
with the light rays of his crest-jewel intimate instructions.[24]

I bow to the protector of the Muni's doctrine in Tibet,
who increased the power of the body of vast merit
and frightened all the wild animals of false teachings
with the lion's roar of the discourse of the sugata.[25]

I offer a supplication to the lord of dharma, the supreme guide,
who possesses an abundant treasury of all amazing qualities
through relying on the guru as the Three Jewels in person,
and possesses the activity of increasing the great secret doctrine.[26]

I pay homage to the glorious guru,
who perfectly holds the doctrine of the Buddha,
whose conduct accords with the precious, sublime doctrine,
the magnificent one in the middle of an ocean of sangha.[27] {368}

I bow to that lion of precise speech,
who properly pleased the gurus
and the assembly of superlative deities with supreme faith
and held the treasury of many tantras and intimate instructions.[28]

I offer a supplication to the brilliant scholar, the virtuous mentor,
the one cared for by the protective tutor, the Three Jewels in person,
wealthy in discipline, hearing, reflection, and cultivation,
whose effortless activities spread in one hundred directions.[29]

I bow to the lion of speech of the profound and vast three vehicles,
the dharma lord, the supreme guide with three collections,
all buddhas throughout the three times in person,
whose activities liberate the three realms throughout space.[30]

I bow to the embodiment of root and lineage gurus, the source of all siddhis,
the precious Jewels, the source of all virtues,
the venerated lord of dharma, the source of all sutras and tantras,
and the glorious guru, the source of all blessings.[31]

I bow to the one whose activity of excellent scholarship
possesses the glorious qualities of the queen's abundant intelligence
through the light rays of brilliant wisdom that shine
in the vast space of infinite objects of knowledge.[32]

I bow to the dharma lord, the supreme refuge of migrating beings,
the one who upholds the victory banner of good fortune and fame
for the doctrine, pleasing to all with loving compassion,
and protects the fortunate with excellent wealth.[33]

I bow to the excellent wealthy, fortunate bee,
the scholar who upholds the banner of fortune and fame,
who possesses the anthers of effortless merit
of the thousand-petaled blossom of excellent wisdom of eloquent explanations pleasing to all.[34]

I offer a supplication to the peerless guru,
the one who guides all migrating beings to the stage of the four kāyas,
the embodiment of the victors who effortlessly accomplishes the two benefits,
the heart son of the glorious root and lineage gurus.[35] {369}

I supplicate the peerless dharma lord
who clarified the Buddha's doctrine
with space-like, vast wisdom
in order to free limitless migrating beings from existence.[36]

I offer a supplication to the supreme guide of migrating beings,
the one who performed the deeds of the Muni, the source of all virtues,
whose wisdom clarifies, just as they are,
the vast range of objects of knowledge in its entirety.[37]

I offer a supplication to the tutor, the precious supreme jewel of space,
whose scholarship sheds the warm light rays of the path of ripening and liberation
in the vast sky of infinite disciples.
Please bless my continuum.[38]

I bow to the sovereign of the ocean of maṇḍalas,
Vajradhara who holds the saffron robes of altruism,
the lord of dharma who effortlessly accomplishes merit and gnosis,
which are the foundation of benefit and qualities in abundance.[39]

I bow to the one endowed with precious bodhicitta,
the guru who adorns the crowns of infinite sugatas,
who holds that great banner of doctrine of the Three Jewels,
having been held close by the glorious root and lineage gurus.[40]

I bow to the one whose excellent activities protected migrating beings,
who shone with one hundred thousand brilliant lights of love and compassion,

whose body shone with abundant glory
in the maṇḍala of space of virtuous actions.[41]

I offer a supplication to the supreme guru,
the victorious king of precious, effortless altruisim,
who offered a supplication to the tip of the victory banner of deep faith
and bestowed the wealth of the two benefits on faithful migrating beings.[42]

I bow to the one endowed with one thousand lights of virtue,
the servant of the oceanic doctrine of the Muni's abundant power,
who removed the darkness of ignorance with the light of wisdom,
possessing the extensive maṇḍala of great loving compassion.[43] {370}

I offer a supplication to the feet of the one whose activity is excellent,
the embodiment of the vajra of glorious bodhicitta,
the precious source of well-being and happiness, the holder of the essence
of three vows, the heart of the doctrine of the Buddha.[44]

I offer a supplication to the feet of the most supreme guru,
who caused the lotus patch of many disciples to increase,
who vastly increased the maṇḍala of very clear wisdom and love
in the vast space of infinite objects of knowledge.[45]

I offer a supplication to the lord regent of Palden Kunga Zangpo,
beautified with the precious ornaments of marvelous discipline,
the heart son of an ocean of loving guides.
Please bless my continuum.[46]

I offer a supplication to the feet of the omniscient guru,
whose body is formed of the merit of the two positive accumulations,
whose voice proclaims the qualities of the pure discourses,
and who is endowed with a loving mind that shows the path of liberation.[47]

May the feet of the one who grants the excellence of the two
benefits be firm,
the treasury of all power of wisdom and love,
whose stream of marvelous merit and wisdom
increases positive activities in the ten directions.[48]

I offer a supplication to the protector who pleases all fortunate
ones,
who increases positive activities in the ten directions,
endowed with the wisdom maṇḍala of effortless omniscience and
love
in the sky of increasing virtue and good fortune.[49]

I offer a supplication to the peerless powerful sun
of scholars, who shines rays of light of effortless activities
and increases the maṇḍala of effortless bodhicitta
in the vast space of pure discipline.[50]

I always pay homage with devotion
to all perfect buddhas
who engage in benefiting beings
in all worlds of the ten directions.[51]

I pay homage to the sublime dharma,
the path of supreme renunciation, {371}
pure and unadulterated,
virtuous in the beginning, middle, and end.

I pay homage to the sangha, the supreme assembly
of buddha heirs, pratyekabuddhas, and arhats,
the object to whom devas and humans make offerings,
the supreme field of merit.

I pay homage to all virtuous mentors,
who abide in discipline, are endowed with hearing and reflection,
dwell in samādhi and equipoise,
and uphold the doctrine of the sugata.

I pay homage with supreme faith,
in all ways, bowing with bodies
equal in number to the atoms in a field,
presenting all suitable offerings.

I present offerings to the assembly of gurus and the Three Jewels,
with water for washing and drinking, flowers, incense,
lamps, perfume, food,
umbrellas, banners, and the sound of music.

With my mind, I present
every kind of offering article
in infinite worlds,
which have no owner.

I present a cloud bank of offerings
arising from my faithful mind,
an ocean of many qualities, with their offspring
equal with space.

I offer supreme amṛta,
which becomes the basis for all siddhis,
the supreme samaya of all victors,
beyond inferior objects.

Unsurpassed bodhicitta,
freed from all concepts
after all taints of obscuration are dispelled,
be pleased with great bliss![52]

Drinking water below, drinking water above,
drinking water that emits an array of lights,
and drinking water of various kinds strewn everywhere
are presented to the great beings, the glorious gurus.

oṃ guru buddha bodhisatva
saparivāra arghaṃ pratīccha svāhā {372}

Flowers below, flowers above,
flowers that emit an array of light,
and flowers of various kinds strewn everywhere
are presented to the great beings, the glorious gurus.

oṃ guru buddha bodhisatva saparivāra puṣpe pratīccha svāhā

Incense below, incense above,
incense that emits an array of light,
and incense of various kinds strewn everywhere
are presented to the great beings, the glorious gurus.

oṃ guru buddha bodhisatva saparivāra dhūpe pratīccha svāhā

Lamps below, lamps above,
lamps that emit an array of light,
and lamps of various kinds strewn everywhere
are presented to the great beings, the glorious gurus.

oṃ guru buddha bodhisatva saparivāra aloke pratīccha svāhā

Perfume below, perfume above,
perfume that emits an array of light,
and perfume of various kinds strewn everywhere
are presented to the great beings, the glorious gurus.

oṃ guru buddha bodhisatva saparivāra ghande pratīccha svāhā

Food below, food above,
food that emits an array of light,
and food of various kinds strewn everywhere
are presented to the great beings, the glorious gurus.

oṃ guru buddha bodhisatva saparivāra naividya pratīccha svāhā

Music below, music above,
music that emits an array of light,

and music of various kinds strewn everywhere
are presented to the great beings, the glorious gurus.

oṃ guru buddha bodhisatva saparivāra śabda pratīccha svāhā
oṃ vajra ghande ranita praranita saṃpraranita sarvabuddha kṣetra pracalite prajñāpāramitā nāda saṃbhaveta vajradharma hridaya santvaṣaṇi hūṃ hūṃ hūṃ ho ho ho akhaṃ svāhā
oṃ sarvavita pūrapūra sura sura āvartaya āvartaya hoḥ {373}

Since this great precious wheel
is offered to all sugatas,
may the wheel of existence be stopped
and the wheel of dharma turn.

oṃ guru buddha bodhisatva saparivāra cakraratna pūjite āḥ hūṃ

Since this precious jewel
is offered to victors and their heirs,
may poverty and penury end
and wealth be abundant.

oṃ guru buddha bodhisatva saparivāra maṇiratna pūjite āḥ hūṃ

With the offering of this queen,
may the darkness of ignorance end
and may method and wisdom be connected
once the meaning of the dhātu of wisdom is realized.

oṃ guru buddha bodhisatva saparivāra striratna pūjite āḥ hūṃ

With the offering of this minister,
may the limitless doctrine be upheld,
replete with the outer, inner, and secret vehicles,
accompanied with all qualities.

oṃ guru buddha bodhisatva saparivāra mahatratna pūjite āḥ hūṃ

With the offering of this precious elephant,
having cleared away all evil devas
and mounted the unsurpassed vehicle,
may I travel to the city of the omniscient.

oṃ guru buddha bodhisatva saparivāra hastiratna pūjite āḥ hūṃ

With the offering of the precious supreme horse,
may we be freed from the hobbles of existence,
obtain the strength of the supreme magic power,
and may I travel to the buddhafields.

oṃ guru buddha bodhisatva saparivāra aśvaratna pūjite āḥ hūṃ

With the offering of a precious general,
having overcome the enemy afflictions
and destroyed the opponents,
may I obtain supreme fearlessness.

oṃ guru buddha bodhisatva saparivāra viraratna pūjite āḥ hūṃ
{374}

With a devoted mind, I offer the supreme guru
every supreme form in all times and directions,
endowed with excellent shape and color and a garland of attractive ornaments.
Please accept this and grant supreme, unsurpassed siddhi.

oṃ guru buddha bodhisatva saparivāra rūpa kāmaguna pūjite āḥ hūṃ

With a devoted mind, I offer the supreme guru
every supreme word and pleasant sound,
qualities that are produced intentionally and naturally in all times and directions.
Please accept this and grant supreme, unsurpassed siddhi.

oṃ guru buddha bodhisatva saparivāra śabda kāmaguna pūjite āḥ hūṃ

With a devoted mind, I offer the supreme guru
every pleasing scent in all directions and times,
such as snakeheart sandalwood, lignum aloes, and so on.
Please accept this and grant supreme, unsurpassed siddhi.

oṃ guru buddha bodhisatva saparivāra gandhe kāmaguna pūjite āḥ hūṃ

With a devoted mind, I offer the supreme guru
every supreme taste in all times and directions,
tasty and nutritious, building up the body and mind.
Please accept this and grant supreme, unsurpassed siddhi.

oṃ guru buddha bodhisatva saparivāra rasa kāmaguna pūjite āḥ hūṃ

With a devoted mind, I offer the supreme guru
every special texture in all times and directions,
smooth, soft, and snug.
Please accept this and grant supreme, unsurpassed siddhi.

oṃ guru buddha bodhisatva saparivāra sparśe kāmaguna pūjite āḥ hūṃ

oṃ vajra bhūmi āḥ hūṃ The foundation is totally pure, a mighty golden ground.

oṃ vajra rekhe āh hūṃ Circled by an outer range of iron mountains, in the center is *hūṃ*, Sumeru, the king of mountains. In the east is Pūrvavideha. In the south is Jambudvipa. {375} In the west is Godānīya. In the north is Kurava. There are Deha and Videha, Camara and Avarācamara, Śāṭha and Uttaramantrin, and Kuru and Kaurava. There are mountains of gems, wish-fulfilling trees, wish-fulfilling cattle, and uncultivated harvests.

There are precious wheels, precious jewels, precious queens, precious ministers, precious elephants, precious horses, precious generals, treasure vases; offering goddesses of beauty, garlands, music, dance, incense, flowers, lamps, and perfume; the sun and moon, parasols, and banners of total victory—all this abundant wealth of devas and humans, with nothing missing, is offered to the glorious root and lineage gurus, the assembled deities of the maṇḍalas of pledged deities, the buddhas, the sublime bodhisattvas, the assembly of guardian dharmapālas, and yakṣa wealth deities. Please accept this with compassion for the benefit of sentient beings. Having accepted this, please bless my continuum to complete the two accumulations, merit and gnosis. Please bless me to purify the two obscurations and their traces. Please bless me so that the special samādhi of the two stages arises in my continuum. Please bless me to obtain the stage of the two kāyas.

I supplicate the precious guru, the embodiment of all refuges,
the greatly kind lord of dharma.
See me with unparalleled, kind compassion
and bless me in this life, the next, and the bardo. {376}

I supplicate the precious guru, the embodiment of all guides,
the greatly kind lord of dharma.
See me with unparalleled, kind compassion
and bless me in this life, the next, and the bardo.

I supplicate the precious guru, the embodiment of all pledged deities,
the greatly kind lord of dharma.
See me with unparalleled, kind compassion
and bless me in this life, the next, and the bardo.

I supplicate the precious guru, the embodiment of all buddhas,
the greatly kind lord of dharma.
See me with unparalleled, kind compassion
and bless me in this life, the next, and the bardo.

I supplicate the precious guru, the embodiment of all sublime dharmas,
the greatly kind lord of dharma.
See me with unparalleled, kind compassion
and bless me in this life, the next, and the bardo.

I supplicate the precious guru, the embodiment of all sanghas,
the greatly kind lord of dharma.
See me with unparalleled, kind compassion
and bless me in this life, the next, and the bardo.

I supplicate the precious guru, the embodiment of all bodhisattvas,
the greatly kind lord of dharma.
See me with unparalleled, kind compassion
and bless me in this life, the next, and the bardo.

I supplicate the precious guru, the embodiment of all śrāvakas and pratyekabuddhas,
the greatly kind lord of dharma.
See me with unparalleled, kind compassion
and bless me in this life, the next, and the bardo.

I supplicate the precious guru, the embodiment of all dharmapālas,
the greatly kind lord of dharma.
See me with unparalleled, kind compassion
and bless me in this life, the next, and the bardo.

I supplicate the precious guru, the embodiment of all wealth deities,
the greatly kind lord of dharma. {377}
See me with unparalleled, kind compassion
and bless me in this life, the next, and the bardo.

After that, offer the seven-heap maṇḍala one hundred times and alternate with the thirty-seven-heap maṇḍala and supplication as much as possible.[53]

These offering substances, a cloud of various offerings equal in number to the atoms of the ocean,
with light rays shining in the ten directions adorned with ornaments, on the tips of the light rays
gemstone lotuses, equal in number to the atoms of the ocean, give off light from their centers, spreading everywhere,
equal in size to one billion worlds, producing wealth of all that is desirable among the amazing objects of desire of devas and humans,
a cloud of offerings emanated by a mind virtuous in every way, just like the emanations of Samantabhadra,
spreading everywhere in all directions of space, just like the dharmadhātu, abiding until the realm of sentient beings comes to end—
may the king of dharma,[54] the victor, the victor's heirs, pratyekabuddhas, and those victorious over the enemy[55]
be pleased with all these offerings presented in a maṇḍala that entirely encircles them![56]

From now until the seat of awakening,
may my body, enjoyments,
and virtues of the three times
be offered to you with devotion
in order to benefit sentient beings.
You, sublime source of virtue,
endowed with eyes that see all,
please think of me with love.
Please accept these offerings of mine,
and having accepted them, please bless me.[57]

oṃ guru buddha bodhisatva saparivāra ratna maṇḍala pūja megha samudra spharaṇa samaya hūṃ

I regret all the natural misdeeds I have done
from time without beginning {378}
with body, voice and mind,
because of being under the power of karma and afflictions,
and the assembly of faults

of transgressing the three vows,
and confess them in the presence of those worthy of offering,
with the intention to refrain from them henceforth.

I rejoice in all the merit
of the amazing activities of the guru,
the victor, the victor's heirs, the pratyekabuddhas,
the arhats, and commoners.

I request the gurus and the buddhas
to turn the profound and vast
wheel of dharma
in order to ripen and liberate all migrating beings.

With folded palms I supplicate you
to remain forever without entering nirvana
for as long as sentient beings exist
and perform the benefit of migrating beings.

I go for refuge with constant faith
in the supreme guru, the Buddha,
the dharma, and the sangha
until seated on the seat of awakening.

I shall generate bodhicitta
and engage in the conduct of awakening
in order to obtain perfect awakening
for the benefit of all sentient beings.

Assembly of loving gurus,
endowed with the clear eye of gnosis,
and all victors and their heirs,
please heed me for a moment.

Please protect me,
a weakling of inferior intelligence,
and all sentient beings
blinded by ignorance,

heaved by the tempest of karma,
submerged in the ocean of existence,
overpowered by the crocodile of afflictions,
and tormented with unbearable suffering.

Despite our best efforts,
it is difficult to find an opportunity for freedom.
Please extend the hand of your compassion {379}
and free us from the ocean of existence.

With rays of gnosis,
please remove the thick darkness of ignorance,
the basis of all accumulations,
the cause of all improper thinking.

With the sword of wisdom,
please cut through the thickets of self-grasping,
the ground that produces the faults and downfalls of existence,
the generator of all concepts.

With your great power, O Protector,
please transform into great gnosis
all delusion, hatred, and desire,
pride and jealousy.

Since my mind has been under the power of afflictions,
in existence from time without beginning,
please cleanse any accumulated taints of traces
with the water of gnosis.

Please turn back the winds of karma
that hurled me into the ocean of suffering,
rendering me powerless
through the power of my own evil deeds.

Please pacify the sufferings
of suffering, change, and formations,

such as birth, aging, illness, and death, and so on,
emanated by karma and affliction.

Please turn back the activities of Māra,
who totally deceives sentient beings
away from the methods, refuge, purity,
and deliverance of the Mahāyāna.

Please turn my mind away
from meaningless activities
such as the pursuits, acquisitions,
and veneration of the worldly.

Please destroy the wheel of samsara
that turns on its firm axle (the all-basis consciousness),
with its spokes (the twelve limbs of dependent origination),
and its rim (suffering).

Please stop in every way
the inferior motivation of the śrāvakayāna,
striving for solitary peace
because benefiting others overwhelms us. {380}

May my body, voice,
and, likewise, my mind
be of great benefit in every way
to all sentient beings.

Please pacify
all outer and inner
harmful obstacles
to the accomplishment of perfect awakening.

At all times please establish
conducive conditions effortlessly,
such as virtuous mentors, supreme companions, the sublime
dharma,

excellent abodes, requisites, and so on.

Please accomplish longevity, health, wealth,
the permanent aspirations of migrating beings,
and whatever goals they desire,
in accordance with the dharma.

When my life force is abandoned,
may I be led to the Khecari realm
by the supreme guru, Heruka,
and innumerable powerful ḍākinīs.

Just as all of you who are endowed with the ten powers
attained the supreme stage,
as stated in many descriptions,
I too will attain it.

Since I and others are completely exhausted
by the suffering of existence,
please have patience for any faults that appear,
exposed while we are ignorant.

Having gathered all this merit
and the merit of others into one,
may perfect buddhahood be swiftly attained
in order to benefit all sentient beings.

In all my lifetimes, may I have
a good family, form, and wealth,
wisdom, abundant power,
health, and longevity.

May I please the buddhas who have arisen,
always practice the sublime dharma,
and make every kind of offering
to the oceanic assembly of the noble sangha.

May I always hear the discourses pleasing to all
and see the victory banner of your body.
May I always be sustained {381}
by your excellent glory.[58]

May the paths of awakening be completed
through the power of faith, love, and diligence.
May buddhafields be purified
and sentient beings ripened.

Like the great wish-fulfilling gem,
may I fulfill all that is desired in the minds
of all sentient beings
and satisfy all migrating beings.

In dependence on me, may all migrating beings
enter the profound path
and attain the great awakening,
abiding neither in existence nor peace!

Since wisdom purifies the two obscurations,
may I have the great wisdom
endowed with profound wisdom
and vast wisdom![59]

Endowed with the banner of discipline,
upholding the excellent banner of dharma,
having created a support for the banner of the doctrine,
may the banner of freedom be raised!

Having perfected the glorious two accumulations,
the basis of the arising of the protector, the glory of migrating beings,
may the glory and wealth of the three kāyas be effortlessly accomplished.
May I become the glory of existence and peace!

May I have the excellent strict conduct of
accomplishing the excellent fortune of all migrating beings,
the excellent activities
produced from excellent aspirations!

After I follow the
the victor and the victor's heirs,
may his merit and the merit of others
be dedicated.

Furthermore, in this life
may all negative conditions be pacified,
may there be long life, health, and abundance,
and may there always be happiness!

By the blessings of the truth of the
compassionate, unsurpassed guru,
the victors, the victor's heirs, and arhats, {382}
may there be accomplishment according to what was dedicated.

Offer this supplication:

I prostrate with devotion and go for refuge to the stainless lotus feet of the sublime guru, the embodiment of all bodies, speech, minds, qualities, and activities of the tathāgatas of the ten directions and three times, the lord of dharma, the king of dharma, the master of dharma, the abundance of all the wealth of the sublime dharma, the sublime glory of samsara and nirvana.

Please bless me and all sentient beings with body, speech, mind, qualities, and all activities.

Please bless me so that all obstacles of humans, nonhumans, harmful elementals, injuries, calamities, misfortune, and outer and inner obstacles arising from my past karma and temporary conditions be totally pacified.

Please bless me that my life, prestige, wealth, and mastery are abundant.

Please bless me so that no concepts arise that turn me toward samsaric existence—all distractions of the eight worldly dharmas, signs, and so on—or any concepts that turn me toward nirvana, such as being overwhelmed at benefiting others, aspiring for my own peace, and so on.

Please bless me to have a pliable mind, vigilance, right mindfulness, and attention.

Please bless me to have a pure collection of disciplines, samayas, and vows, and to not be sullied with taints of misdeeds, obscurations, downfalls, and faults.

Please bless me to have abundant faith, compassion, and wisdom, and having unified the two bodhicittas, may the sublime appearance of the dharma that includes scripture and realization {383} and a special pure realization[60] arise in my continuum.

When it is my time to die, bless me to be free of attachment to this life and to this world, to have joy and supreme mental clarity without the arising of even the slightest pain and suffering in my body and mind, to truly see the guru, the assembly of deities, and the assembly of heroes and yoginīs, to be greeted by their inconceivable emanations after sublime samādhi arises in my continuum, to be free of all fear of the bardo, and after leaving behind the whole domain of Māra and Yama, to be born on the supreme stage of the vidyādharas, the khecaris, and so on.

Please bless me to be free of mundane and transcendent deterioration in all lives and worlds, to obtain the abundant wealth of existence and peace, to truly uphold the oceanic collection of discourses of the tathāgatas of all times and directions, and having pleased the sublime guru with everything and made progress on the paths and stages with ease, to swiftly obtain the stage of Mahāvajradhara, endowed with the four kāyas and five gnoses.[61]

From the periphery, the objects of offering melt into rays of light and dissolve into the root guru. The root guru dissolves into one's crown and is seated in one's heart in the center of an eight-petaled lotus, {384} on top of a moon maṇḍala, which is the white aspect obtained from the father, and a sun maṇḍala, which is the red aspect obtained from the mother. At all times one should reflect on the blessings and the protector as one's refuge and companion. Remain for a little while in equipoise with faith and one-pointedness in reflection. When one rises from the sessions, recite:

Glorious root guru
seated on a lotus in my heart,
care for me with compassion
and please grant me the siddhis of body, speech, and mind.

The offering water of an ocean of hearing collected from everywhere,
the flowers of qualities, a cloud of incense of discipline,
a lamp of wisdom, a perfumed lake of faith,
the sublime ambrosia of samādhi,
the sweet music of melodious praise,
the celestial mansion of my body beautified
with an umbrella of love, a victory banner of discernment,
and a string of pennants of courage
are offered to the lord of dharma,
who is seated firmly in the center of the lotus at my heart.
Supplicating him with true devotion,
may it please the guru of migrating beings![62]

In birth after birth, may I be inseparable from the guru,
enjoy the wealth of dharma,
and having perfected the paths and stages,
may I attain the stage of Vajradhara.

In every birth after birth,
may I have a good family, intelligence, absence of pride,
compassion, devotion to the guru,
and dwell in the samaya of the glorious guru.

May I and all who become my disciples
be diligent in karma and its result, skilled in the meaning of the discourses,
have pure discipline and diligence in hearing, {385}
and spread the doctrine of the Muni in the ten directions.

Like the powerful king on the top of a victory banner,
may the crown ornament of superlative deities

grant supreme siddhi to the practitioner,
and may there be the good fortune of the peerless guru!

These subjects can be seen in the writings of Lord Sakya Paṇḍita, and so on, as well as in the writings composed by previous masters, such as the *Beautiful Ornament of the Three Tantras*, and so on.

Through the merit of composing this, may the siddhis
of myself and all others please the root guru,
may the two accumulations, both temporary and permanent,
increase,
and may we follow the conclusion in this lifetime.

Increasing the Two Accumulations: A Systematic Arrangement of the Offering Rite to the Gurus of the Path with Its Result was arranged by Bhikṣu Kunga Chöphel according to the tradition of Lord Evaṃpa[63] and written down by Tashi Wangchuk.

For the creation on the occasion when there are no heaps as the basis for creation, condense the visualization as follows:

In the space in front of oneself is a jeweled throne supported by eight great lions, upon which multicolored lotus and sun and moon maṇḍalas are stacked one atop the other. On that is one's sublime root guru, the embodiment of all victors of the three times, their heirs and disciples, in the form of the perfect, complete buddha, Vajradhara. His color is blue. He has one face and two hands, which hold a vajra and a bell crossed at his heart. He is adorned with jewels and bone ornaments such as a jeweled crown, and so on, and he wears clothes of multicolored silk. His body is adorned with all the major and minor marks. His voice is endowed with sixty melodious tones. {386} His mind knows the nature and extent of all there is to know. He is smiling, seated, and pleased with you. Surrounding him is an encircling assembly of lineage gurus, the assembled maṇḍalas of pledged deities, buddhas, sublime bodhisattvas, and the host of guardian dharmapālas. Light rays shine from their hearts, inviting the assembly

> of the root and lineage gurus, buddhas, sublime bodhisattvas, and guardian dharmapālas, *oṃ vajra samājaḥ*. I pay homage with devotion to the dharma king of the three realms, who is endowed with inalienable wisdom and compassion.

. . . and so on. May it be virtuous.

22. Procedure for Preparing Barley Liquor from the *Śrī Samvarodaya Tantra*[1]

Kunga Lodrö

This text consists of a close read and explication of a procedure for preparing alcohol, drawn from the *Samvarodaya Tantra* and its commentary by Ratnarakṣita. It is somewhat unclear who this Kunga Lodrö might be. Kongtrul gives no lineage at all for this text. Given the devotion expressed in the colophon, this may be Chöje Sepa Kunga Lodrö,[2] one of Ngorchen's direct disciples. Another supportive piece of evidence is provided by Amezhap, who notes that Sepa Kunga Lodrö received the entire body of Cakrasaṃvara empowerments, commentaries, and instructions from Ngorchen Kunga Zangpo.[3]

{388} The mind is purified by drinking the amṛta of the one-taste yoga.
The body is purified by going to places such as the pithas, and so on.
I always pay homage, bowing my head to the protector of the
maṇḍalacakra
in the supreme central place and the supreme guru.

I shall compose the procedure for preparing liquor
as taught in the *Śrī Samvarodaya*
in order to make offerings to the outer and inner ḍākinīs
and accomplish the gnosis of great bliss.

Here, having entered the door of the precious tantras of unsurpassed great yoga, the foundation of practicing the path is samaya. Further, there is both the method for those who do not have samaya to receive samaya by receiving empowerment and maintaining the collection of samayas guarded so that those received will not be impaired. The conferral of empowerment is also connected with the gaṇacakra. On that occasion liquor is required. Second, to maintain the collection of samayas, the Lord Sakyapas include the samaya of eating in the basis of samaya.[4] Between the daily practice [of the samaya of eating] and specific times, the latter is asserted to be the gaṇacakra. Similarly, the assertion of the greatest of great vajradharas of India and Tibet is that liquor is necessary for maintaining the collection of samayas. {389} Not only that, when the body is exhausted by completion stage [practice], liquor is also shown to be a supreme *rasāyana*[5] for developing the tissues.

In terms of liquor, excess liquor, when used out of desire, causes shameless intoxication devoid of pure conduct, is the enjoyment of maudlin fools, and harms the tissues of the body and virtue. Therefore, it should be avoided like dog vomit by those who properly practice mantra. The detailed explanation can be understood in *Letter to Benefit Disciples*[6] composed by Ngorchen Kunga Zangpo. {390}

Now, the meaning of so-called prepared liquor[7] is explained in five topics according to the commentary on the *Samvarodaya* root tantra: (1) the validity of using liquor, (2) the procedure for making valid liquor, (3) the manner of drinking the liquor that has been made, (4) the faults of drinking liquor in absence of the procedure, and (5) the benefits of properly relying on liquor.

I. The Validity of Using Liquor

Though there are countless teachings in other tantras, for now, there is this citation from the eighth chapter of the *Samvarodaya Tantra*, the section on offering to the deities of the gaṇacakra:

> Offer whatever one can find,
> mead, cane spirits, or wine.[8]

Next, from the section on singing and dancing:

> With the convivial festivities of liquor . . .[9]

In chapter 10, in the section on making offerings to the kinswomen:[10]

> Here be diligent. One should make offerings of liquor and meat
> to the vajra goddesses.[11]

And:

> Food and liquor to drink . . .[12]

Chapter 24, on rasāyana, states:

> One should make offerings to the deities
> with equal portions of liquor and bali.[13]

Chapter 32, on bali offerings, states:

> Rapid accomplishment of activities is not possible
> without liquor and bali.[14]

The latter part of the chapter states that for the accomplishment of samaya in gathering the remainder bali:

> Having taken a mouthful of liquor,
> make the blazing mudra . . .[15]

Chapter 25, on stabilizing with liquor, states:

> From where will gnosis arise without liquor?
> What will transform consciousness?
> Despite its benefit to consciousness and gnosis,
> all migrating beings are confused concerning liquor.[16] {391}

And:

> There is no offering other than liquor,
> just like a burnt offering without oil
> or the dharma without a guru
> or liberation without the dharma.
> A samaya other than liquor
> does not arise anywhere.[17]

And:

> In the places, fields, chandohas,
> meeting places, and charnel grounds,
> the object of offering and the offerer are connected with
> the supreme offering of amṛta,
> auspiciousness, bliss, and joy
> taught in other tantras,
> and also in the offerings of the ancestral gods, humans,
> marriages, and brahmins,
> at the commencement of the battles of warriors,
> for the benefit of the good fortune of merchants,
> to accomplish the success of commoners,
> when making offerings to renunciants,
> when there has been lengthy explanation,
> when doing a burnt offering consecration,
> when practicing circumambulation of the places,
> when making offerings to the invited yoginīs,
> and when accomplishing mantras.
> One should understand those many circumstances
> and not attribute fault there.
> To hear the remaining explanation,
> Guhyapati, listen![18]

Thus, it is said that there are infinite needs for manufactured liquor.

II. The Procedure for Making Valid Liquor

Here there are three topics: (1) the concise explanation of the divisions of liquor; (2) the extensive explanation of the procedure for making the six kinds of liquor, such as liquor made from amalaki,[19] and so on; and (3) the principal procedures of manufacturing liquor in terms of place and time.

A. The Concise Explanation

The concise explanation of the divisions of liquor are described in twelve lines:[20]

Arising from substances[21] and, likewise, roots
are liquors made from fruits and flour.[22]
From trees and, likewise, cane,
the things that grow on the surface of the earth
are explained as the five kinds of mead.[23]
Eight kinds of flour are described,
and there are seven kinds of fruit.
Those should be understood in that order.
They grow as sharp, bitter, hot,
sweet, and smooth.
Liquor is described in [various] names
corresponding with what grows in various lands.[24] {392}

B. The Extensive Explanation

The extensive explanation is the following passage:

> Take two zho[25] of the medicine, śigru,[26]
> ....
> Emulate the [liquor of the] country.[27]

There is amalaki liquor, dhātaki flower[28] liquor,[29] patraka liquor,[30] cane liquor,[31] śigru liquor,[32] and śobhañjana liquor.[33] Further, the covering for fermenting with heat, the substances, and so on, the container, generating the mash[34] as nāgas, fumigating with gugul and making offerings, and generating the deity are applied in the procedure that occurs below.

C. The Principal Procedure

[The *Samvarodāya Tantra* states:]

> Having understood procedures for [manufacturing] various
> liquors,
> emulate the [liquor of the] country.[35]

The commentary states, "'Emulate the country' should be understood as 'emulate the liquor of the country.'"[36] In this country of Tibet, the liquor cooked from barley, wheat, and so on, ferments in two or three days. The procedure for that is as follows: Having received the empowerment for entering the door of this tantra, if the mantra practitioner who possesses samaya is a householder, they should have obtained the empowerment of the wisdom consort, or else they are a renunciant. They make the liquor through praising a woman who has obtained empowerment, or if one is unavailable, it is done alone.

The method for that is as follows: The brewer should have continuously practiced the direct realization of Cakrasaṃvara if male, and Vajravārāhī if female. {393} In between sessions one should maintain the pride of the deity.

First, one needs a clean vessel for cooking the liquor. The grain, such as barley, wheat, and so on, should be cleaned and fumigated with gugul. Make offerings with flowers. After that, place the vessel with water on the stove, recite the mantra of the deity, and ignite the fire. After stopping the cooking, it is time to spread the mash. Spread it on clean felt, and so on. Herbs free of insects are added in the proper amount as a fermenting agent to cause fermentation.[37] Clean a clay fermentation vessel, fumigate it with gugul, and offer flowers.

The preliminaries for the liquor are to prepare a clean and large pile of roadside grass or cloth, and so on, and imagine that facing oneself are the nāga kings, Ananta, Vāsuki, and Varuṇa, with human upper bodies, coiled snake tails for lower bodies, and with hoods above their heads, embracing wives who resemble themselves on the left.

Recite *oṃ aḥ vajra varuṇaya hūṃ svāha, oṃ aḥ vajra anantaya hūṃ svāha, oṃ aḥ vajra vāsuki hūṃ svāha*, and make a proper offering of white flowers. Next, show one's right hand in the manner of a hood, extend one's right hand, and recite, *oṃ varuṇa ananta vāsuki oṃ bhakṣa agaccha mahānāga adhīpati sarva bhur bhuva phaim hūṃ svāhā*. Having offered the milk bali, present offerings as before, and imagine that the nature of the three nāgas in the milk is poured into the vessel. Place the lees in that vessel, and instantly generate the thirteen-deity maṇḍala of Bhagavān Cakrasaṃvara inside the vessel. This maṇḍala with its retinue {394} dissolves and transforms into an orange *maṃ*. From *maṃ* arises the goddess of liquor, who has one face, eighteen arms, and is perfectly beautiful. She shines with light rays like the light of the sun, gathering the universe and its inhabitants, which she holds as a variety of excellent elixirs. In her right hands are a sword, arrow, hook, skull, vajra, victory banner, a string of pearls, bell, and the mudra of supreme generosity. In her left hands are a shield, bow, noose, khaṭvāṅga, water jug, vase, spear, hoe, vīṇa, and counting mala. She is adorned with jewel ornaments. She has three eyes. Meditate on her body that subjugates the three realms. One should imagine that the place overflows with her form, liquid, and gnostic amṛta, possessing the nature of great bliss. For as long as there is no foam, it should be kept warm with cloth and venerated. Then, strain the water, which is free of insects, through the fermented mash; diligently maintain the pride of the excellent deity; and recite the mantra while stirring the strained water. This is the procedure. The liquor prepared according to that procedure will taste delicious, bitter, sweet, and so on. Also, the tantra states:

> Varuṇa, Vāsuki, and Nanda
> are meditated on the seat there.
> Begin with flowers, fumigate with gugul,
> and offer the bali.[38]

And:

> All comes from Mount Mandāra,[39]
> transforming into the river that flows through the middle.
> The so-called Ocean of Milk
> falls like butter and honey.
> The goddess who imbibes the moon
> exists in the form of Vajravairocanā.[40]
> In the center of the body, Vairocanā
> melts with Heruka. {395}
> That supreme network of ḍākinīs
> in union with all the heroes,
> all become one taste.
> The amṛta has a fearsome female form,
> which plunders, acts, and enjoys.
> Therefore, it is the essential amṛta.[41]

Further:

> The goddess of liquor arising from that
> has the form of a passionate maiden,
> her color like the rising sun,

shining like liquid lacquer,
and her body adorned with all jewels,
with light like the color of a red lotus.
The form that arises from the red *maṃ*,
beautiful with eighteen hands, is
the goddess who holds various essences
and subjugates the three realms.
Her right hands hold a sword, arrow, hook,
skull, vajra, victory banner,
likewise, a string of pearls and a bell,
and the ninth has the mudra of supreme generosity.
Her left hands hold a shield, bow,
noose, khaṭvāṅga,
water jug, vase, spear,
hoe, vīṇa, and a counting mala.
She is in the full bloom of youth.
The beautiful goddess has three eyes.[42]

And:

When the procedure is complete,
the supreme liquor will arise.
When thinking of the manufactured liquor,
it should be used daily.
This preparation is supremely beautiful.
The manufactured liquor is delightful.[43]

And:

They grow as sharp, bitter, hot,
sweet, and smooth.[44]

And:

The nature of merit
is acquired by some from pleasing the guru.[45]

The meaning of these miscellaneous citations is discussed in the *Padminī* commentary:

> Therefore, to preserve samaya and please the guru, the explanation of liquor is {396} "The nature . . . ," and so on. "Some" refers to the yogis whose merit preserves samaya. "From pleasing the guru" the mundane and transcendent benefits are obtained. Further, never be separate from the samaya substance.
>
> Thus, there is no doubt that [liquor] is the main samaya substance. This is the principal procedure. Having set out the herbal ingredients according to country, season, and potency, wise mantrins engage in the preliminary torma offering. In front of oneself as the excellent deity, there is the nature of the three nāga lords, Ananta, Vāsuki, and Varuṇa. On the seat [made] of bunches of grass,[46] and so on, fumigate with a vessel of gugul smoke and make offerings. Inside that vessel mix the pulverized śobhañjana, and so on, with water. Imagine that inside the vessel Śrī Cakrasaṃvara embraced by Śrī Vajravārāhī melt into great bliss. From this arises *maṃ*, which is the liquor goddess meditated in the form having the nature already described. She exists in the form of the liquid amṛta of gnosis, which has the nature of great bliss. Always be very devoted and happy.[47]

III. The Manner of Drinking the Liquor

After blessing the amṛta, one can enjoy it. If that is connected with gaṇapuja, one should bless the amṛta according to each circumstance, take some up with the karma vajra, and taste it. The way it is tasted {397} can be understood from the gaṇacakra rite composed by Ngorchen Kunga Zangpo.[48] The way the liquor is blessed and tasted in the commentary of this tantra is not solely during the gaṇapuja, but there is also a special requirement of the samaya-bearing mantrin to use liquor at all times. The tantra shows to which object the offering is made:

> To explain the activity in particular,
> Guhyapati, listen!
> Always make the offerings

to the guru, heroes, and yoginīs,
and practice presenting offerings.[49]

The passage "with the mantra *oṃ āḥ hūṃ*" explains reciting *oṃ āḥ hūṃ* and making offerings. With what is the offering made? It is made with the blessed liquor. How is the liquor blessed? Apply this stanza:

Always bless
with the mantra *oṃ āḥ hūṃ*.
One should understand purification
with the mantra *ha hoḥ hrīḥ*.
With the syllable *ha*, the color is enchanting.
With the syllable *hoḥ*, the smell is abundant.
With the syllable *hriḥ*, the force is overwhelming.
Thus, one should consume the nectar.[50]

As such, what are the faults of drinking liquor without the blessing?

If those who crave liquor
drink without the three deities, and so on,
there is no doubt it will become poison
and the siddhis of mantra will not arise.[51]

Even if one blesses it, one should drink liquor without becoming intoxicated. If one becomes too intoxicated:

Whoever becomes intoxicated
will experience many obstacles.[52]

The commentary states:

> Now, to explain the continuous practice, "To explain the activity in particular . . . ," and so on, means the drink of the practitioner. {398} "To the guru, heroes, and yoginīs" means the guru, the heroes, and the yoginīs. It is taught in this way: A wheel on the right hand, which has the nature of Vairocana, arises from *hoḥ*. Meditate on the form of the blessing with the *hoḥ* syllable. Above that there is an eight-petaled red lotus that arises from *ha*. Med-

itate on the form of the blessing that has the nature of Amitābha with the syllable *ha*, and cover this with the left hand. Observe the *hrīḥ* syllable, which has the nature of Akṣobhya, existing on a sun on top of the substance. Recite the mantra *ha hoḥ hrīḥ* three, five, or seven times. Since the mantra *oṃ āḥ hūṃ* is above the substance, on the right, left, and in front, recite only that. This procedure for pleasing will please the guru, the heroes, and the yoginīs. Also, one can then use it oneself.

Next, the faults of not using that procedure is taught by, "drink without the three deities, and so on . . ." The three deities are *oṃ āḥ hūṃ*, the nature of Vairocana, Amitābha, and Akṣobhya.[53]

Having performed a lotus roll with both hands, in the right hand one takes the skull vessel of liquor, or lacking that, one imagines that any vessel is a skull. One covers the top with the left hand, and the manner of blessing is understood from the text. Drink as the root tantra states:

> If experienced like the drink of peace,
> one will always obtain siddhis.[54]

Maintaining the pride of the deity, engage in the yoga of eating and drinking.

Having utilized that procedure, should one share this with all?

> Do not share with those who injure the guru, {399}
> slander the guru, or injure sentient beings.
> For them, that amṛta is poison.
>
> The result of siddhis will not be accomplished.
> The past buddhas have said
> mantrins should avoid these people.[55]

Thus, those with samaya should not be deceptive and should not share [with such people,] because it is said:

> As stated in the procedure, do not deceive
> the gathering[56] of yogins and yoginīs.
> Do not examine common things
> to see if they are good or bad.

For that reason, the so-called gathering
obtains siddhis and permissions.[57]

Just as the five amṛtas of one's own body have the nature of the five families, externally, the liquor prepared according to procedure and blessed has the nature of the five families.

The hearth is the dharmodaya.
The mash is known as the pure amṛta.
What is the liquor? Vajrayoginī.
Who is the pride? Heruka.
Who is the color? Padmanarteśvara.
Who is the fragrance? Ratnasambhava.
Who is the taste? Amoghasiddhi.
Who is the force of the vāyu? Oneself.[58]

This is just a brief explanation. The extensive procedures and divisions should be understood from other tantras:

These divisions of liquor
should be understood elsewhere in the tantras.[59]

IV. The Faults of Drinking Liquor in Absence of the Procedure

[The following passage states:]

Intoxicated by liquor, the mantrin
will have sensual longings and crave intercourse,
likewise, dance and sing, {400}
quarrel and be deludedly cheerful,
will criticize others and break [their vows]—
they will roast in the Raurava hell.
Once all yoginīs become angry,
they will terrify one with illness and misery.
Tormented with terror,
the sinner is led to hell.[60]

V. The Benefits of Properly Relying on Liquor

[The following passage states:]

> Liquor bestows the results of wisdom, intelligence, strength,
> happiness, and good fortune.
> One will attain the unsurpassed result
> with all eight qualities of mastery.[61]

First, gather the material of the liquor, which is pure and not obtained through misdeeds. According to the procedure, it should be cooked and fermented. Then, it should be blessed according to the procedure by a samaya-bearing mantrin. If it is enjoyed with the thought of offering to a deity, it is certain that one will manifest the form of Śrī Heruka, possessing the eight qualities of mastery.

> I have set this text down in accordance with the statement of my guru:
> "The liquor used by practitioners who have entered the doorway
> of the unsurpassed secret yoga
> should be made according to the procedure taught in the tantra."

> By this merit, may all migrating beings {401}
> always enjoy the food of the two stages,
> the supreme amṛta churned by the intimate instructions of the guru
> from the oceans of tantras.

This [Procedure for Preparing Liquor] was composed at Pal Evaṃ Chöden Yöntan Rinpoche Dume Jungne by Vidyādhara Kunga Lodrö, a small child born of the teachings of Lord Kunga Zangpo, Mahāvajradhara, the embodiment of all buddhas of the three times, at the repeated urging of the vajraholder Sangye Pal,[62] the virtuous mentor from Tsawa Rong.

sarva maṅgalaṃ

23. Blazing Brilliance and Strength

The Sādhana and Permission of the Eight Deities of Śrī Vajramahākāla Pañjaranātha[1]

Jamgön Kongtrul

The final text is a permission ritual for the uncommon eight-deity Mahākāla composed by Jamgön Kongtrul.

{404} Mind emanation of Śrī Heruka,
king of the guardians of the doctrine,
and your swift messengers, protect me.
May there be no obstacles to my dharma plans.

The three topics in the bali rite and permission of the eight deities of the glorious protector from the *Vajrapañjara Tantra*, his siblings, and their activity emanations, set out concisely, are the preparations, main subject, and concluding stage.

I. The Preparations

The disciple must have obtained empowerment into unsurpassed yoga. The specific time is the twenty-ninth day. Having gathered the requisites, set up an image of the protector. Place the triangular, jewel-shaped bali on a tripod. A little lower and in front of that, place an eight-sided offering bali. Arrange whatever offerings one can. There is also a tradition of placing the bali in the center of a three-cornered dharmodaya maṇḍala. If it is an occasion where only the bali rite is being performed, on a high shelf in front of oneself, place the two balis for one's yidam and protector, which are made from nine excellent food stuffs and adorned with flesh and blood. In front of those, on a slightly lower shelf, arrange an eight-sided offering with bali offerings of flesh and blood. Also, gather the required preliminary offerings, and so on.

II. Main Subject

A. The Sādhana

Bless the preliminary bali, the place, and the articles. {405} The preliminary self-generation is the class of herukas led by Hevajra, or the generation, recitation, dissolution, and arising, such as any of the wrathful kings like Vajrapāṇī. Perform the rite of the bali offering however it is done for the yidam, otherwise, perform the concise blessing common to the unsurpassed tantras.

> Purify with *svabhāva*, and so on. From the state of emptiness, in the sky before oneself, on top of defeated enemies and obstructors, in the center of a great charnel ground, a lotus arises from *paṃ* and a sun arises from *raṃ*. On top of the sun is a dark-blue *hūṃ*. Light shines from that, destroying enemies, obstructors, and savage beings. The light returns to *hūṃ*, which transforms completely into a huge, blazing Vajramahākāla, whose color is the darkness of time. He has one face and two hands. The right hand holds a curved knife above his heart and the left hand holds a skullcup filled with blood below his heart. He holds an emanation gaṇḍi on the middle of both forearms. He has three eyes, bares his teeth, and his yellow hair sweeps upward. {406} He is adorned with a diadem of five skulls, a necklace of fifty heads dripping blood, the six bone ornaments, and snakes. He wears a tiger skin skirt and a crown of multicolored silks with ribbons. He stands on a corpse in the posture of a crouching dwarf. To his right are black birds, to his left are black dogs, behind him are wolves, in front of him there are black men, and above him in the sky is the emanated messenger, a garuḍa. He has Akṣobhya on his crown and stands in the middle of a blazing fire of gnosis. He is surrounded by a retinue of innumerable assemblies of primary and secondary emanations.
>
> To his left, blue Ekajāti arises from the syllable *trak*. She has

one face and two hands, which hold a vase filled with amṛta to her heart. She wears an upper garment of white silk and a tiger skin skirt. Her hair is wound into a single braid, which hangs to the left. She has a wrathful countenance. An ocean of blood arises from *trak* in her vast belly, in which is *bhyoḥ*, from which arises Śrīdevī Kāmadhātviśvari, riding an ass. In the first right hand she holds a sword and in the second right hand she holds a skull filled with blood. In the first left hand she holds a javelin and in the second left hand she holds a trident. She has a tiara of five dried human skulls, a necklace of fifty fresh heads, and is adorned with six bone ornaments. She wears an upper garment of elephant hide, a lower garment of cowhide, and a skirt of felt tied with a belt of a powerful nāga. She has three eyes and bares her fangs with a human corpse in rigor mortis in her mouth. {407} She is adorned with a poisonous snake as her right earring and a lion as her left earring. There are spots of blood, smears of grease, and piles of great ash arranged on her body. She is extremely emaciated. The sun and moon rise from her navel. She roars *hūṃ* and *bhyoḥ* in the midst of one hundred thousand mātṛkas[2] and flesh-eating ḍākinīs.

In from of them, *ya* emanates from the heart of the protector, and *ma* emanates from the heart of the goddess. Kālayakṣa arises from *ya*. His right hand holds a curved knife, and the sun rises from his upraised, open left palm. He wears a cloak of human skin. To his left, from *ma* arises Kāliyakṣi. Her right hand holds a golden razor, and the moon rises from her upraised, open left palm. She wears a garb of black silk and has a coral braid. From the heart of the father emanate two *tri* and from the heart of the mother emanates a *bhyo*, which transform into the Putra brothers and sister. Black Putra arises from *tri*, with one face and two hands. His right hand holds a razor-sharp sword and his left hand holds a skull filled with brains and warm blood, from which he drinks. He wears a bark sash and garb of black silk. Black Bhata arises from *tri*. He wears a sash of silk and a tiger skin. In his right is a samaya staff, and in his left hand he holds a human heart, from which he drinks. Rākṣasī Ekajāti arises from *bhyoḥ*. She holds a golden curved knife in her right hand and an intestine in her left hand. Blood drips from her eyes. Fire blazes from her mouth.

Also, all five are black in color, wear the accoutrements of male and female Mönpas, and are adorned with human heads. They are very wrathful, fearsome, and aggressive, {408} standing in the manner of destroying savage beings. They are majestic in the middle of a firestorm.

Furthermore, surrounding them to their right is a column of one hundred men adorned with battle gear, to their left is a column in the form of bhikṣus, one hundred black bhandhes wielding phurbas follow behind, and one hundred black women lead the way. Furthermore, inconceivable messengers such as black birds, black dogs, wolves, and so on, with the remains of samaya breakers, surround them.

Both siblings—Mahākāla and Mahākālī—are marked with *oṃ* at their foreheads, *āḥ* at their throats, and *hūṃ* at their hearts. Light rays shine from the *hūṃ*s, inviting Mahākāla from the heart of Vairocana in Akaniṣṭha and Mahākālī from her natural abode.

While holding the vajra and bell, recite:

Protector, arise from the seat of all tathāgatas.
Now is the age of the five degenerations.
Come and remain in this evil place
and guard the doctrine of Śākyamuni.
In order to benefit us,
please come to this place.[3]

oṃ śṛi mahākālaya mahākālidevī e hye hi
jaḥ hūṃ vaṃ hoḥ
oṃ padmakamalāya stāṃ

Light rays shine from one's heart, inviting the Karmanāthas and their retinue from their residence at Vajrāsana in India and, in particular, from the seats of the previous gurus, *om vajra samāḥ.*

Karmanātha, residing at the seats of the deceased gurus,
now is the age of the five degenerations.
Come and remain in this evil place
and guard the doctrine of Śākyamuni.

In order to benefit us,
please come to this place.

[The two invocation mantras:]

ali ali ma ja ja śaṃ śaṃ li śi de a śva ded mo smugs putri a li ma jaḥ jaḥ nag mo sha la rub ja ja, oṃ ro ru ro ru ru tri ca pa la a śug me ma hūṃ ma bhyoḥ jaḥ jaḥ

At the conclusion of the two mantras, which invoke the males and the females, invite with:

om vajra samājaḥ ehye hi
oṃ śṛi mahākālaya mahākālidevī e hye hi {409}
jaḥ hūṃ vaṃ hoḥ
oṃ padmakamalāya stāṃ

The outer offerings:

oṃ śrī mahākālaaya mahākālidevī grihṇidaṃ arghaṃ svāhā padyaṃ svāhā, oṃ vajra puṣpe . . . śabda aḥ hūṃ

Cup the palms face up for the samaya mudra of the protector. Interlace the fingers for the samaya mudra of the goddess.

oṃ śrī mahākālā mahākālidevīye samayasmara, samayamātrikama, samayarakṣantu

To *ali ali* append *samayasmara* in order to place the karmanāthas in samaya. The entrustment of activities:

Śrī Vajramahākāla, siblings, and your retinue of servants and loyal subordinates, accept this vast *bali* offering. Do not transgress the commands and samayas of the glorious root and lineage gurus. Protect your samaya. Guard the doctrine. Extol the Three Jewels. In particular, with methods of pacification, please eradicate all evil intentions, plans, and conflicts of the host of misleading obstructing enemies who harm and injure the doctrine of

> the Buddha, the holders of the doctrine, and us yogins and our retinue, creating obstacles to our accomplishment of the path. If they cannot be tamed with methods of pacification, please eradicate them with whatever means are appropriate—frighten and oppress them, divide them, threaten and subdue them. In brief, pacify all obstacles to accomplishing the dharma; support the accomplishment of our intentions and plans we wish for that accord with the dharma; and propagate and increase the doctrine, the doctrine holders, and all worldly people.

With vajra-folded palms, open and facing up, recite the following three times for the siblings:

> *oṃ mahākāla mahākāli devī e hye hi namaḥ* {410} *sarvatathāgate bhyo viśva mukhe bhyaḥ sarva thakaṃ udgate spharaṇa imaṃ gaganakhaṃ grihṇadaṃ baliṃtaye svāha*

At the end of the mantras of the siblings and the two invoking mantras append *akaro*, and so on, which are recited three times. Make offerings to the karmanāthas. Make offerings as above and present the bali:

> *oṃ śrī mahākālāya śasanaupahariṇi eṣa apaścimakālo ayaṃ idaṃ ratnatraya apakariṇi yadi pratijñasmara sitada idaṃ duṣṭaṃ kha khā khāhi khāhi mara māra ghriṇa ghriṇa bhandha bhandha hana hana daha daha paca paca dina dinamekana hūṃ phaṭ oṃ roru roru vitiṣṭha badhotsī kāmala rakṣasī hūṃ bhyoḥ hūṃ*

Append *oṃ āḥ hūṃ* to the two invocation mantras and present the inner offerings to the karmanāthas.

The praise:

> *hūṃ*
> I praise you, fierce one,
> the destructive bodhisattva
> with the savage form of a rakṣasa
> who terrorized the city of Tripura.

I praise you, one with a garland of heads,
who is black, squat in form, very brilliant,
with a curved knife in the right hand that destroys savages
and a vessel full of the blood of savages in the left hand.

I praise the one who holds samaya,
whose raging steps shake the ground,
whose terrifying laughter topples Sumeru,
and who rips out the hearts of samaya breakers.[4]

Śrīnātha Mahākālaya,
the great deva, brilliantly blazing, black one of great power,
the ferocious son of Mahādeva,
the great lord of the host, Mahākālaya,
the Black Fortunate One, the enemy of the city of Tripura,
the guardian of the whole doctrine is Mahākāla.
The axial pillar of the wheel of dharma is Mahākāla.
The war god of samaya holders is Mahākāla.
Come here and accept this ornamental bali! {411}
Accept this bali of red flesh and blood!
Accept this food of Jambudvipa!
Accept this bali of the first portion of medicine and blood!
This is solemnly presented as thanks for entrusted activities in the past.
Please solemnly accept this so that you recall your entrusted activities in the present.
Please protect my retinue, repel our negative conditions,
and pacify the multitude, all hateful enemies, harmful obstructors,
māras, and obstacles.
Quickly accomplish activities to increase the doctrine.[5]

And:

bhyoḥ
I bow to Kāmadhātviśvari,
she whose powerful body, voice, and mind
subjugated the desire realm entirely
and brought the desire realm under her power.

Śrīdevi, your body is
overwhelming like the massif of Sumeru,
brilliant like blue sapphire,
and effulgent like the rays of the sun.
Your blazing yellow hair sweeps upward,
your bloodshot eyes are as swift as lightning,
you bare your fangs with a human corpse in your mouth,
and your hands are occupied with a skull filled with blood
and terrifying weapons.
You are adorned with human heads, jewels strung on bone,
nāgas, a lion, iron chains,
and marks of blood and grease.
You wear a coat of fresh hide and felt.
You ride at night, mounted on an ass with a blaze.
You are extremely emaciated and hideous.
I pay homage to she whose form is terrifying.

I bow to you, the one whose melodious, roaring voice
subjugates the three realms
with the sound of a thousand peals of thunder
and shakes the three worlds.

I bow to you, whose mind naturally dwells in peace,
but enters existence through the power of compassion
and conquers the host of māras
through wrath, fear, and aggression. {412}

Invincible Śrīdevī, mistress of the three realms,
come here and accept this . . . .

Add the praise and entrustment of activities.
Now, the karmanāthas:

The terrifying forms of the Yakṣa father and mother,
with accoutrements of fearsome aggression,
destroy the māras and obstructing enemies.
I praise the great father and mother guardians of the doctrine.

Black Mönbu Putra, you
wear a bark sash on your body
and hold a mendicant's staff of *gośīrṣa* wood in your hand.
I praise you, Black Putra.

Mönbu Bhata, you have a striped, tiger-fur coat,
wear a silk sash on your body,
and hold a sharp samaya stick in your hand.
I praise you, Mönbu Bhata.

Mönmo Golden Razor,
Mahākālī with a flaming mouth,
you hold a golden razor in your hand.
I praise you, Kālī.

A hundred great black women
depart and lead the way.
The column on the right
is the one hundred men adorned with battle gear.
The column on the left
is the one hundred śrāvaka arhat bhikṣus.
The terrifying ones who follow behind
are the one hundred black mantrins wielding kīlas.
I praise the entire retinue.
I also offer praise during the three times.

Should one wish, also perform the extensive praises. If one wishes to perform the very concise praise, the following is sufficient:

Putra, you complete all glorious activities.
Your color is black, with billowing flames.
You are majestic with a fearsome stance, holding a staff of *gośīrṣa* wood.
I praise you, great messenger, tamer of the savage.

Come here and accept this presented offering....

Append the verses of the entrustment of activities. This suffices for the bali rite.

For the permission, {413} in order to bless the continuums of the disciples, one should recite the following mantras as much as one can. Those are the protector's three mantras—the near essence mantra, *oṃ mahākāla hūṃ phat*; the essence mantra, *oṃ mahākālāya hūṃ hūṃ phaṭ svāhā*; and the *śasana* root mantra—and the goddess's essence mantra, *oṃ ro ru.* The invocation mantras of the karmanāthas can be recited as much as one likes.

Next, having offered the general bali offering to the ḍākas and ḍākinīs,[6] for the permission, the qualified disciple should wash, begin with prostrations, and be seated in the row. The offering assistant should distribute flowers, collect half of them, and offer the maṇḍala; half of the flowers should be left in the hands of the disciples. The master begins:

> To begin, sincerely think you are requesting this permission for Vajramahākāla brother and sister in order to obtain the stage of Vajradhara, the lord of the four kāyas, in order to benefit sentient beings and in order to remove obstacles on the path for accomplishing that. Further, this Mahākāla originates in chapter 15 of the *Vajrapañjara Tantra* and the extensive tantra of the *Four Vajra Seats.* The lineage descends from siddhas such as Brahmin Vararuci, and it is ornamented by the intimate instructions of the gurus, such as the Palden Sakya uncles and nephews, and so on, who composed the practices and the samayas. There are many extensive and concise empowerments and permissions for Śrī Mahākāla Pañjaranātha, in terms of rituals and commitments. Among the permissions, there is the common permission and the uncommon permission that entrusts one with the hand implements. This is the latter permission.
>
> First, because there are preliminaries, there are three topics in accomplishing those: (1) the preliminaries pleasing to the five internal and external ḍākas and ḍākinīs, (2) the main permission endowed with blessings, and (3) the concluding stages for the master.

I. Pleasing the Ḍākas and Ḍākinīs

Pleasing the ḍākas and ḍākinīs is accomplishing the maṇḍala and presenting offerings.

II. The Permission

In the permission, there are (1) preliminaries, {414} (2) the main section, and (3) conclusion.

A. Preliminaries

There are five sections in the preliminaries: (1) offering the maṇḍala and supplication, (2) generating bodhicitta with the preliminary daily confession, (3) taking the vows of the five families, (4) requesting for the specific topic, and (5) emanating the basis of the body for the blessing.

1. Offering the Maṇḍala and Supplication

To begin, please offer the maṇḍala.

The students offer a maṇḍala.

Next, please repeat this supplication after me three times:

I bow to the lotus feet of the guru,
whose body is like a jewel, endowed with the vajras,
by whose kindness great bliss
arises in an instant.

Embodying the nature of all buddhas,
I supplicate the supreme guru,
who possesses the body of all-knowing gnosis
and conquers the wheel of existence.

From now on, treasury of precious explanations,
supreme one, please grant me your kindness.
I shall never abandon your lotus feet

> and go for refuge elsewhere.
> By the great power of the hero of migrating beings,
> supreme guru, please appear to me.

2. The Preliminary Daily Confession

Please repeat after me three times the preliminary daily confession to generate bodhicitta:

> I go for refuge to the Three Jewels . . .[7]

3. Taking the Vows of the Five Families

To take the vows of the five families, please repeat the following after me three times:

> All buddhas and bodhisattvas . . .[8]

4. Request for the Specific Topic

To request the specific topic, please repeat the following after me three times:

> Embodiment of the vajra body, speech and mind of all buddhas of the three times, precious, sublime guru, please bless me with the body, speech, and mind of Vajramahākāla and grant me the permission. {415}

5. Emanating the Basis of the Body for the Blessing

One should meditate on this visualization one-pointedly. Imagine that the master is Bhagavān Hevajra, with eight faces, sixteen arms, and four legs, who is in union with the mother Vajranairātmyā. In the sky in front, there is the nine-deity maṇḍala of Bhagavān Hevajra, the lineage gurus, and inconceivable numbers of buddhas and bodhisattvas. In front of them is the bali and the image. Surrounding these are the eight charnel grounds, in the center of which, on top of a lotus, sun, and a corpse, is

Vajramahākāla Pañjaranātha. On his left is Ekajāti. Inside of her vast belly is Śrīdevī Kāmadhātviśvari. In front of them are Kālayakṣa and Kālayakṣī, in front of whom are the three Mönbu Putra siblings and their retinue of columns of attendant messengers. Moreover, living in the charnel grounds are hundreds of thousands of primary emanations and millions of secondary emanations of directional guardians, field guardians, ḍākas and ḍākinīs, piśācis, the eight classes of gods and demons, the male and female arrogant ones, and also the assembly of ḍākas and ḍākinīs of three places, who are the abundance of the brilliant body. With their speech, they proclaim the sound of *hūṃ* and *bhyo* like thunder. Their minds are diligent in guarding the doctrine in a state of bliss and clarity. Please imagine that all of this is actually present in front of you.

Next, light rays emerge from the heart of the guru, who is visualized as Heruka, and touch the heart of the front-created dharmapāla, invoking his mind. From his heart a blue *hūṃ* separates, leaves through his nostrils, {416} circles your bodies three times, and enters your mouths. The blue *hūṃ* remains on a sun seat imagined in your hearts. Light rays shine from it, burning away all karma, afflictions, and the great karmically ripened body with the fire of gnosis. The foot of *hūṃ* dissolves into the body. The body dissolves into the head. The head dissolves into the bindu. The bindu dissolves into the nāda, which now vanishes like breath on a mirror, imagined to be emptiness free from all proliferation.

From the state of emptiness, on top of defeated enemies and obstructors, in the center of a great charnel ground . . . you transform completely into Vajramahākāla . . . in the middle of a firestorm. Visualize this.

B. The Main Section

Following the preliminaries, there are three sections in the main section: (1) the permission of body, (2) the permission of speech, and (3) the permission of mind.

1. The Permission of the Body

Among the first, repeat after me the supplication for the permission of the body three times:

> Please bestow upon me right now
> the vajra body of all buddhas.

With special devotion, imagine that infinite rays of light shine from *hūṃ* visualized in the heart of the guru as Heruka. They strike the heart of the dharmapāla in front, invoking his mental continuum. Infinite gnosis protectors arise from *hūṃ* in his heart, and again light rays shine from his heart, inviting inconceivable numbers in the form of the dharmapāla from the heart of Vairocana Sāgara.[9] Some are the size of Sumeru and some are as small as sesame seeds, emanating in the rays of light, arriving with the sound of *hūṃ* and *phaṭ*. They dissolve into your foreheads and {417} in the upper, middle, and lower parts of your bodies. Once again light rays shine and invite inconceivable numbers of Śrīdevīs, who dissolve. Again, light rays shine and infinite numbers of Kālayakṣa, Kālayakṣi, and the three Mönbu Putra siblings are invited from their residence at Vajrāsana and, in particular, from the seats of the previous gurus, who [then] dissolve. Furthermore, [the light rays] invite inconceivable numbers of buddhas, bodhisattvas, and yoginīs, who transform into the forms of the protector siblings and their attendants, falling like a great shower, and are imagined dissolving into one's body.

Having recited this, fumigate with gugul and the incense of the protector, and recite each mantra three times: the Hevajra mantra, beginning with the *aṣṭa* mantra up to the essence mantra, the *śasana* mantra, the *roru* mantra, and the two invocation mantras [of the karmanāthas]. Play music and strongly invoke the blessings.

With that, the permission of the body is accomplished.

2. The Permission of Speech

Among the first, repeat after me three times the supplication for the permission of speech:

> Please bestow upon me right now
> the vajra speech of all buddhas.

Imagine that among the mantras in the heart of the guru, who is visualized as Heruka, are the near-essence, essence, and root mantras. In the heart of the front-created Mahākāla is a sun, on which is a five-tined blue vajra marked with *hūṃ* in its center. Imagine that surrounding it is the near essence mantra, *oṃ mahākāla hūṃ phaṭ*; outside that is the essence mantra, *oṃ śrī mahākālāya hūṃ hūṃ phaṭ*; outside that is the root mantra, *oṃ śrī mahākālāya śasan . . . dinamekana hūṃ phaṭ*; and outside of that is the Śrīdevī's mantra, *oṃ roru roru vitiṣṭha badhotsī kāmala rakṣasī hūṃ bhyoḥ hūṃ*. {418}

Visualizing yourselves as the dharmapāla, in your hearts, which resemble an eight-petaled lotus blossom, a lotus arises from *paṃ* and a sun arises from *raṃ*. On this sun is *hūṃ*, which dissolves and becomes a five-tined blue vajra. At the navel is a sun marked with *hūṃ*. After that, because of one's devotion, light rays shine from the heart of the guru. Since the light rays strike the heart of the front-generated Mahākāla, the mantra garland, blazing with light rays and its sound, emerges from his heart and leaves through his mouth, one mantra after another. The mantras are arranged around *hūṃ* in your hearts, and some of them dissolve into *hūṃ*. Light rays shine from the guru and the front-created deity, and also from the heart of Vairocana Sāgara, inviting inconceivable root and essence mantras, which are blazing, to resound with the sound of thunder and enter your mouth. Further, inconceivable vowels and consonants of the speech of the buddhas and bodhisattvas in the form of syllables are invited and dissolve into *hūṃ* and the mantra garland in your hearts.

Fumigate the disciples and recite the mantras three times, beginning from the deity mantra. Strongly invoke the blessings with the visualization.

> Now, you should pick up your malas or a flower and repeat after me to receive the reading transmission. Since the mind of the protector is invoked by the light rays from the heart of the master, each of the mantras leaves from his mouth making their sound, in the way one lights one candle with another. The mantras enter your mouth, and the near essence, essence, root, and Śrīdevīs mantras are arranged successively around *hūṃ* in your hearts. Again, the light rays from the heart of the front-generated protector {419} invoke the karmanāthas, and the mantra garlands emerge from their hearts, which are meditated on as surrounding the mantras of the siblings. While repeating this three times, imagine the first repetition is in the manner of the commitment being, the second is in the form of the gnosis being, and the third stabilizes the gnosis being in the commitment being. Thus, repeat these mantras after me.

Begin by having the disciples repeat in order the protector's mantras three times, the goddesses' mantras three times, and then the karmanāthas' mantras. The invocation of the males is:

> *ali ali ma ja ja śaṃ śaṃ li śi de a śva ded mo smugs putri a li ma jaḥ jaḥ nag mo sha la rub ja ja*

The invocation of the females is:

> *oṃ ro ru ro ru ru tri ca pa la a śug me ma hūṃ ma bhyoḥ jaḥ jaḥ*

It is said it is sufficient to repeat the two invocation mantras; the slaying and curse mantras need not be repeated.[10]

Next, after receiving the reading transmission:

> Please scatter flowers on the master and repeat this supplication three times:
>
> > Protector, grant this to me.{420}
> > Protector, please bless me.

The master then places his vajra on the heads of the disciples and repeats three times:

The protector shall grant this.
The protector blesses this one.

With that, the blessing of speech has been accomplished.

3. The Permission of Mind

In order to request the permission of mind, repeat after me three times the supplication for the permission of mind:

Please bestow upon me right now
the vajra mind of all buddhas.

With devotion, one should imagine that light rays shine from the heart of the guru and strike the front-generated Mahākāla siblings. From their hearts arise inconceivable numbers of hand implements of the principal and retinue—the curved knife, skull full of blood, sword, javelin, trident, staff of gośīrṣa wood, samaya staff, golden razor, and so on, the sounds of the mantra, and light rays—which dissolve into the vajra and seed syllable in your hearts. Infinite gnosis hand implements arise from the hearts of the buddhas and bodhisattvas of the ten directions, melt into light, and dissolve into your hearts.

Fumigate the disciples; invoke the gnosis implements by reciting the mantras, beginning with the root mantra; and play music.

That accomplishes the permission of mind.

Next, after the eight-petaled lotuses of your hearts close, imagine the tops are sealed with five-tined half-vajras. After this has been stabilized in you, imagine they always accompany you.

Place the vajra on the disciple's heads. Recite twice:

tiṣṭha vajra

C. Conclusion

There are four sections in the concluding procedures: (1) commanding activities, (2) giving the reading permission for the sādhana, (3) advising never to be separate and to maintain secrecy, and (4) offering a maṇḍala and accepting samaya with a promise. {421}

1. Commanding Activities

For the purpose of commanding the activities, set one's intention in the following way:

Insert a glorious flame in the bali offering and place it on the heads of the disciples.

Imagine that this bali offering is like a cloud bank of Mahākāla siblings, their servants, attendants, and emissaries. Above the protectors, the root guru is surrounded by the assembly of lineage gurus, along with inconceivable numbers of buddhas, bodhisattvas, ḍākas, and ḍākinīs of the three places.

Fumigate, and at the end of the essence mantra, the long dhāraṇī, the goddesses mantra, and the two invocation mantras of the Putras, add:

samaya samaya rakṣantu

Śrī Mahākāla siblings, servants, attendants, you must guard your samaya and never transgress the samayas of the sovereign Vajradhara, Brahmin Vararuci, Norbu Lingpa,[11] Śraddhavarma, Lotsāwa Rinchen Zangpo,[12] Mal Lotsāwa Lodrö Drak,[13] the five Sakya founders, Dampa Kunga Drakpa,[14] and the glorious root and lineage gurus. Protect the doctrine. Until these vidyādharas obtain buddhahood, protect them from all negative conditions and obstacles! Remove all opposition to them! Accomplish all positive conditions! In general, subjugate, guard against, and be a refuge from all enemies, obstructors, and obstacles to the doctrine of the Buddha in general and these vidyādharas in particular! {422} You must accomplish any commands of these vidyādharas that accord with the dharma!

Next, generate faith for the special objects and imagine that the gurus, buddhas, bodhisattvas, ḍākas, and ḍākinīs melt into light and dissolve into Mahākāla. Light rays shine from him and strike Śrīdevī, the attendants, and their retinue, who melt into light and dissolve back into Mahākāla. He also melts into light, which enters in your crown apertures. Since he becomes nondual with you, imagine that you have abundant power.

Play music.

2. The Reading Permission

To give the reading permission for the sādhana, this dharmapāla has four types of sādhanas: sādhanas in the form of the lord of the host, sādhanas like an attendant, sādhanas like Yama, and sādhanas like a yakṣa. Among the sādhanas like an attendant, there is the solitary male sādhana, the solitary female sādhana, and the combined male and female sādhana. In all those sādhanas, there are intimate instructions for the approach, the accomplishment, and the application of activities, which you have been empowered to practice on the proper occasion.

3. Advising Never to Be Separate and Maintain Secrecy

Having become protected by the power of the permission and the reading transmission, the characteristic is that the guardians will never be separate from you, like the body and its shadow. You must protect pure samaya. You should endeavor in the torma offerings and feasts. You must not so much as show the name of the glorious protector and his retinue to those who lack samaya and those who cannot become recipients of secret mantra.

4. Offering a Maṇḍala and Accepting Samaya with a Promise {423}

Please offer a maṇḍala.

After the maṇḍala is offered, then:

Please repeat after me three times:

Whatever the principal commands,
I will do all that.

Please repeat after me three times:

Henceforth, I offer
myself to you as a servant.
Accept me as a disciple
and please employ me in any way.

The permission has now been accomplished.

Recite aspirations and benedictions:

With this merit . . .

III. The Concluding Stages for the Master

Refresh the offerings and bless them in the general manner. Present the outer offerings:

oṃ śrī mahākālaaya mahākālidevī grihṇidaṃ arghaṃ . . .

Append *oṃ āḥ hūṃ* to the essence mantra and present the inner offering. Praise with one verse:

I praise you, fierce one . . .

And:

I bow to Kāmadhātviśvari . . .

And:

> Putra, you complete all glorious activities . . .

Offer a supplication:

> Please pacify the obstacles of myself and my disciples, grant us siddhis, and accomplish all that we wish.

Recite the one-hundred-syllable mantra and request forbearance:

> Whatever I have not prepared, whatever was defective,
> whatever I have done with a confused mind
> or asked to be done,
> I request the forbearance of the protector for all.
>
> *oṃ*
> You who perform all benefits for all sentient beings,
> please grant the corresponding siddhi.
> Even though you have departed for buddhafields,
> please return once again.

At the end of that, recite either *om vajramahākāla saparivāra yati gaccha* or *om vajra muḥ*.

> The gnosis being departs and the commitment being dissolves nondually into me.

Recite whatever aspirations and benedictions one likes.

Here, this uncommon permission with the fastening of the hand implements can be understood from the text by Dampa Kunga Drak:

> May the stable flagpole
> of the great secret doctrine be upheld
> and the activities that are
> victorious over the dark side strongly blaze!

The special guardians of the Path with Its Result Oral Instruction (from *The*

Treasury of Precious Instructions that epitomizes the eight major traditions of practice lineages in Tibet) were extracted from the works of Jetsun Rinpoche and the sādhana and permission of Chögyal Phakpa, and arranged by Karma Yöntan Gyatso, also known as Lodrö Taye, for ease of recitation, at the retreat place of the residence of Deshek Dupa in Dzongshö, Derge. May excellent virtue increase.

Abbreviations

BDRC	Buddhist Digital Resource Center (formerly Tibetan Buddhist Resource Center), www.bdrc.org.
Dg.K.	Derge Kangyur (sDe dge bka' 'gyur): Derge edition of the Tibetan canonical collection of sutras and tantras.
Dg.T.	Derge Tengyur (sDe dge bstan 'gyur): Derge edition of the Tibetan canonical collection of commentarial treatises.
DNZ	Jamgön Kongtrul Lodrö Taye. *The Treasury of Precious Instructions. gDams ngag rin po che'i mdzod.* 18 vols. Delhi: Shechen Publications, 1999.
G	*The Collection of All Tantras. rGyud sde kun btus.* 30 vols. Delhi: N. Lungtok and N. Gyaltsan, 1971–1972. BDRC W21295.
Gö	Koṭalipa. *Stages of the Inconceivable. Acintyakramopadeśanama. bSam gyis mi khyab pa'i rim pa'i man ngag.* Dg.T. rgyud, *wi* (Toh. 2228).
HT	*Hevajra Tantra. Kye'i rdo rje zhes bya ba rgyud kyi rgyal po.* Dg.K. rgyud, *nga* (Toh. 417).
L	*The Explanation of the Path with Its Result for Disciples. Lam 'bras slob bshad.* 21 vols. Dehra Dun: Sakya Centre, 1983–1985. BDRC W23649.
Nar.T	Narthang Tengyur (sNar thang bstan 'gyur): Narthang edition of the Tibetan canonical collection of commentarial treatises.
P	*Yellow Volume. Pod gser ma.* In *Lam 'bras Slob bshad.* Dehra Dun: Sakya Centre, 1983–1985. BDRC W23649.
SKB	*Sa skya bka' 'bum.* 15 vols. Dehra Dun: Sakya Centre, 1992–1993. BDRC W22271.
ST	*Saṃpūṭa Tantra. Saṃpūṭanāmamahātantra. Yang dag par sbyor ba zhes bya ba'i rgyud chen po.* Dg.K. rgyud, *ga* (Toh. 381).
Toh.	*A Complete Catalogue of the Tibetan Buddhist Canons*, edited by Hakuju Ui et al. Sendai, Japan: Tohoku University, 1934.
VT	*Vajrapañjara Tantra. Āryaḍākinīvajrapañjaramahātantrarājakalpanāma. 'Phags pa mkha' 'gro ma rdo rje gur zhes bya ba'i rgyud kyi rgyal po chen po'i brtag pa.* Dg.K. rgyud, *nga* (Toh. 419).
ch., chs.	chapter, chapters

f., ff.	folio, folios
p., pp.	page, pages
v., vv.	verse, verses
vol., vols.	volume, volumes

Notes

Series Introduction

1. Jamyang Khyentse Wangpo ('Jam dbyangs mkhyen brtse dbang po, 1820–1892), Chokgyur Dechen Lingpa (mChog 'gyur bDe chen gling pa, 1829–1870), Mipham Gyatso (Mi pham rgya mtsho 1846–1912), and many more masters were involved in this movement, including Kongtrul's guru Situ Pema Nyinche (Si tu Pad ma nyin byed, 1774–1853). See Smith, *Among Tibetan Texts*, 247–50; Jamgön Kongtrul, *Treasury of Knowledge, Book 8, Part 4: Esoteric Instructions*, 25–48; Ringu Tulku, *The Ri-me Philosophy of Jamgön Kongtrul the Great*; etc.
2. The specific text by Shes rab 'od zer that expounds the eight chariots is *Meditation's Ambrosia of Immortality* (*sGom pa 'chi med kyi bdud rtsi*). A study of this has been done by Marc-Henri Deroche: "'Phreng po gter ston Shes rab 'od zer (1518–1584) on the Eight Lineages of Attainment." According to Deroche, "This text may be considered as an (if not the) original source of the '*ris med* paradigm' of the eight lineages of attainment" (17). It is interesting to note that the eight lineages are arranged in a different sequence in that text—Nyingma, Kadampa, Shangpa Kagyu, Lamdre, Marpa Kagyu, Zhije, Jordruk, Dorje Sumgyi Nyendrup—which may have been more chronological than Kongtrul's preferred order.
3. One finds this idea developed in the volume on esoteric instructions in *The Treasury of Knowledge*, where Kongtrul describes in incredibly condensed detail the basic principles and sources of these eight lineages. It is expounded in the catalog of *The Treasury of Precious Instructions* (*DNZ*, vol. 18), published in English as *The Catalog of The Treasury of Precious Instructions*, trans. Richard Barron (Chökyi Nyima). Also see Stearns, *Luminous Lives*, 3–8.
4. Barron, *Catalog*, 21.
5. *The Treasury of Precious Instructions. gDams ngag rin po che'i mdzod* (*DNZ*), 12 vols. (Delhi: N. Lungtok and N. Gyaltsan, 1971–1972). Known as the Kundeling printing.
6. *The Treasury of Precious Instructions. gDams ngag rin po che'i mdzod* (*DNZ*), 18 vols. (Delhi: Shechen Publications, 1998). Known as the Shechen printing.

Translator's Introduction

1. In general, the translations and transmissions of Drokmi Lotsāwa form the core of the four translators whose translations and transmissions serve as the basis for the Sakya school's Vajrayāna teachings—Lochen Rinchen Zangpo (958–1055), Drokmi Lotsāwa Śākya Yeshe (992–1072), Mal Lotsāwa Lodrö Drakpa (late eleventh to early twelfth century), and Bari Lotsāwa Rinchen Drakpa (1040–1112).
2. Jamgön Kongtrul, *Jonang*, ch. 9, guidebooks 44–51.
3. See Catherine Dalton, "Enacting Perfection," 104n111. The reason for the absence of much discussion of the seven limbs of the three kāyas also may be that authors in the Buddhajñānapāda tradition, of which Vāgīśvarakīrti is but one, more commonly referred to these seven limbs as the seven yogas. However, it is clear the Sakya tradition regards Vāgīśvarakīrti authoritative, always referring to this doctrine as the "seven limbs of the three kāyas" or "the seven limbs of union."
4. Jamgön Kongtrul, *Jonang*, ch. 9, guidebooks 52–57.
5. Thubten Jinpa, *Mind Training*, chs. 38–43.

1. Supplication to the Lineage

1. *Lam skor phyi ma brgyad kyi brgyud pa'i gsol 'debs ngor chen kun dga' bzang po mdzad pa kha skong mañjughoṣas mdzad pa. DNZ* 6, pp. 1–6.
2. *rDo rje nags khrod.*
3. *'Bar ba 'dzin pa.*

2. *Accomplishment of the Connate*

1. *Ḍombi he ru ka mdzad pa'i lhan gcig skyes ces bya ba. DNZ*, pp. 8–17. *P*, pp. 387–400.
2. As several of these names were taken by more than one Indian siddha, Amezhap identifies to whom among them these verses refer. Amezhap also provides the same verses as Kunga Zangpo (*Effortless Accomplishment of the Two Benefits*, p. 434, line 5).
3. Caṇḍika is one of the names of the goddess Durga.
4. Amezhap, *Effortless Accomplishment of the Two Benefits*, p. 649, line 4.
5. Ḍombi Heruka, *Accomplishing the Connate*, Dg.T. rgyud, *wi* (Toh. 2223).
6. NOTE: In reality, the connate is the fundamental mind essence. TN: Reading *P*, *don*; for *DNZ*, *rten*.
7. *HT*, Dg.K. f. 13a, lines 2–3. Jetsun Drakpa Gyaltsen writes in *Possessing Purity* (*SKB* 6, f. 269b, lines 1–4), "Now then, if it is asked what entity is connate, that is called 'connate by nature.' That being the case, there are two types of connate: example and meaning. If it is asked what is the meaning [of connate], 'by nature'

means that it has been so from the start but is not produced dependently. If it is asked why that is the case, 'All aspects are a single vow.' This means that when all phenomena are summarized, they are free from all proliferation."

8. NOTE: Conceptual.
9. NOTE: Nonconceptual.
10. NOTE: This is the same in both paths.
11. NOTE: The view that understanding is sufficient.
12. NOTE: Multiplied by clarity, emptiness, and union.
13. NOTE: Confirmation of connate wisdom.
14. NOTE: The body is seated cross-legged. The hands are in the gesture of equipoise. The spine is vertical. The head is slightly tilted forward with the eyes falling on the tip of the nose. The breath is even. The mind is slightly relaxed and at rest.
15. NOTE: Gentle and strong.
16. NOTE: Straighten [one's head] in the middle. Next, bend the head to the right twice; then bend one's head to the left twice. Then bend right, bend left, and then bend in the middle. Drop it forward and train in that for a long time. Then one should do it forcefully. Both [gentle and strong] vocal inhalations will result in a [deeply reddened] complexion.
17. Omitted in *DNZ*.
18. Omitted in *DNZ*.
19. Guru, bodhicitta, and pledged deity.
20. NOTE: Of the uninterrupted gentle and strong vocal inhalations.
21. NOTE: By practicing the vocal inhalation uninterruptedly.
22. NOTE: The complexion of the face becomes deeply reddened. NOTE: When the patron called Drala reached fifty years, he went before the great guru. Since he engaged in cultivating this instruction, his samādhi rapidly arose. He was able to reside in equipoise in each samādhi for fifteen days. At that time, when his face was observed, it reddened little by little.
23. NOTE: Appearing so little by little.
24. NOTE: Of the ascetic and the infant.
25. NOTE: Which does not arise in a definite order.
26. NOTE: The sequence of stability.
27. NOTE: Since Ācārya Virūpa asserts that it is the nāḍī to the right of the avadhūti, this is a slight contradiction. Here, it appears as he [Ḍombi Heruka] stated it. The other teachings, such as the gate of liberation, the illness, and so on, slightly correspond.
28. NOTE: Free from the concept of an apprehending subject.
29. NOTE: The first of the five sets.
30. NOTE: Liberated from an apprehending subject.
31. NOTE: Free from both an apprehended object and an apprehending subject.
32. NOTE: Since the samādhi of the trio of bliss, clarity, and nonconceptuality arise, the three nāḍīs and the three vāyus are brought under control, the three

illnesses and the three classes of spirits are brought under control, and dream experiences and the gates of liberation are realized.

33. NOTE: Through a mere aspiration.
34. NOTE: This will be explained below.
35. NOTE: If experience arises in one's continuum, even if one is a lazy person, one will attain the result of a vidyādhara.
36. NOTE: If one does not accomplish the time of death.
37. NOTE: And one follows the conclusion.
38. NOTE: Also, in this system it is asserted that even in the bardo the average practitioner will attain the result after following the conclusion.
39. NOTE: [After the signs of this system arise just a little,] it is possible to realize the state of Vajradhara with nothing other than the path of the ascetic. Alternately, based on a mudra that one has cultivated from an initial prediction, [one must gradually engage in the secret conduct].
40. NOTE: Of the body, and so on.
41. NOTE: If one accomplishes the two activities of destruction and conversion, one is considered a practitioner. Having abandoned family, clan, and high status [engage in the conduct of strict discipline].
42. *brtul zhugs kyi spyod pa*, Skt. *vratacaryā*. A *vrata* (*brtul zhugs*) is a type of strict vow or observance that a Vajrayāna practitioner adopts for the purpose of testing the stability of their experience.
43. NOTE: Three sets of five.
44. NOTE: Three sets of eight.
45. NOTE: This is given the name the *Rootless Path with Its Result*. This is said to be very profound. In the context of the extensive path, all paths are included in the path of the fourth empowerment, all views are included in the view of the fourth empowerment, all conclusions are included in the conclusion of the fourth empowerment, and all times of death practice are included in the time of death practice of the fourth empowerment.
46. NOTE: There are twelve kinds of mudra, among which eight are to be relied upon and four are to be avoided.
47. NOTE: From the perspective of the nonconceptual child.
48. NOTE: Which are a cause for the arising of bliss.
49. NOTE: The concept of destroying the lord of death.
50. NOTE: She is the support of the path of the swift messenger that generates great bliss.
51. NOTE: Compared with [a mudra who is] scared of the practitioner.
52. NOTE: By a man.
53. NOTE: Because she causes obstacles to siddhis.
54. NOTE: At men.
55. NOTE: As she is not able to look at others.
56. NOTE: Since obstacles will arise.

57. NOTE: "Slightly soft" following *P*, *cung zhig sha sob* for *DNZ*, *cung zhig sbom pa*, "slightly thick."
58. NOTE: Of good character.
59. NOTE: Of good character.
60. NOTE: She will increase the longevity and wealth of the practitioner.
61. NOTE: Here, the medium citriṇī was omitted. Lama Drokmi stated that she was forgotten.
62. NOTE: She does not embrace men.
63. NOTE: Though these are not the central nāḍī, she has many nāḍīs that cause bliss.
64. NOTE: She is learned in errors, and so on.
65. NOTE: Aimless.
66. NOTE: Babble.
67. NOTE: Because she will cause obstacles for the practitioner.
68. NOTE: Like Virūpa.
69. "Seeking the nāḍī" refers to the practice of finding the lower end of the female's central channel in the vagina and inserting its tip into the end of the male's central channel in the penis.
70. NOTE: With the three frugalities.
71. NOTE: With the vocalized inhalations.
72. NOTE: Through food.
73. NOTE: It is impossible that the three signs will not arise.
74. NOTE: In all the citriṇīs.
75. NOTE: In the system of Ḍombi Heruka.
76. NOTE: Vāyu.
77. NOTE: Place the left leg over the right thigh between the navel and the groin, like the ear of an ox. TN: This is like the cow-faced posture or gomukhāsana in postural yoga.
78. NOTE: With the mind.
79. NOTE: The swirling blue vāyu is imagined to be four and two finger lengths.
80. NOTE: The forceful method of uniting the upper and lower vāyus, which will cause the navel to protrude in three days.
81. NOTE: When uniting with any of the four consorts.
82. NOTE: In this way, the avadhūti nāḍī possesses the four characteristics of the head of a snake swaying in the wind.
83. NOTE: And shaking the head.
84. NOTE: To mix with that.
85. Elevating others is not addressed.
86. NOTE: Inhale strongly.
87. NOTE: Out of the two paths of Ācārya Ḍombipa, first accomplish the complexion by means of the first vocalized inhalation of the path of the nonconceptual infant. Next, when relying on a mudra, it is necessary to train in the

vāyu beforehand. Also, there is (1) training the vāyu, (2) straightening the entry of the bindu, (3) the method of drawing up, and (4) the method of spreading. First, explain the posture of the body, the place of holding the vāyu, the visualization, and the method. In the first, there is straightening. Second, after a yellow swelling arises below the navel, look downward. After a large swelling of feces and urine arises, in that gap of two fingerbreadths, visualize a blue vāyu and meditate while uniting the vāyu. After three days, meditate on the size of the gap between those two.

88. *DNZ* gives *sarva maṅgalaṃ*.

3. Ācārya Padmavajra's Creation and Completion Stages

1. *sLob dpon pad ma ba dzra gyis mdzad pa'i bskyed rim zab pa'i tshul dgu brgyan pa dang rdzogs rim mar me'i rtse mo lta bu'i gdams ngag rje btsun grags pa mdzad pa bcas tshan sbrel la ldeb. DNZ*, pp. 19–41. *P*, pp. 419–45.
2. Collected Works, vol. 22, p. 441, lines 2–3.
3. Ibid., p. 441, line 6.
4. The reader cannot help but note the similarities between this account and the slightly later account of Padmasambhava and Mandarava in the *Zangs gling ma* biography attributed to Yeshe Tsogyal. See Yeshe Tsogyal, *Life of the Lotus Born*, 45–46.
5. Historically speaking, the Candra Dynasty has always been regarded as a strong supporter of Buddhism. See Abdul Momin Chowdry's *Dynastic History of Bengal* (154–85) for a full account of the Candra dynasty. The reign of Śrīcandra lasted from 930–975 C.E., the longest reigning monarch of the Candra dynasty. Undoubtedly, the political stability of the Candra dynasty in the ninth and tenth centuries contributed to the flourishing of Buddhism in Magadha as well as East India.
6. There is one text attributed to Cintā in the Tengyur: *Accomplishing the Truth That Clarifies Existence*, Dg.T. rgyud, *wi* (Toh. 2222).
7. Adam Krug (*Seven Siddhi Texts*, 336) opines that Cintā, the author of *Accomplishing the Truth That Clarifies Existence*, is Vilāsavajra, the disciple of Indrabhūti II, in the lineage of Koṭalipa's *Stages of the Inconceivable*. However, while it is possible that the yoginī Cintā mentioned in the above story is the same person as the yoginī Vilāsyavajra, the guru of Jalendra in the Saroruha Hevajra lineage, it is unlikely. It is plausible that she could be the Ācārya Vilāsavajra, who is a disciple of Indrabhūti II in the lineage of Koṭalipa's *Stages of the Inconceivable*.
8. *HT*, Dg.K., f. 20b, line 4.
9. *HT*, Dg.K., f. 25b, line 7.
10. *HT*, Dg.K., f. 12b, line 5.
11. The term *so so rang rig* (Skt. *svasaṃvedana*) defies ease of translation because there are two distinct ways it is understood. Smṛtijñānakīrti (*Explanation of the*

Commentary on Bodhicitta, Dg.T. rgyud, *ci* [Toh. 1802], f. 129a) glosses two lines of the *Commentary on Bodhicitta* (Nāgārjuna, *Commentary on Bodhicitta*, Dg.T. rgyud, *ngi* [Toh. 1801], f. 39b, line 3) as *so so rang rig spyod yul sems*. He defines *svasaṃvedana* as follows. "*Svasaṃ* (*so so rang*) is the thing (*dharmatā*) that cannot be shown or described to another, like the pleasure of girl. Apprehending and perceiving that [thing] is the meaning of 'The mind is the range of intrinsic cognizance.'" Following Nāgārjuna, Smṛtijñānakīrti then distinguishes this definition from the Yogacāra theory of reflexive cognition (*svasaṃvedana*). His refutation of the Yogacāra theory of reflective cognition is as follows: "Sensation (*tshor ba*, Skt. *vedana*) is the meaning of *svasaṃvedana*, as sensation is the activity of cognition. Since a sensation arises dependent on the mutual meeting of the triad [sense organ, object, and sense consciousness], there will be no sensation in absence of an object of sensation," and so on (*Explanation of the* Commentary on Bodhicitta, f. 130a, line 7–f. 130b, line 1). The difficulty in translating this term accurately in Vajrayāna texts is that when this term is used, it is often difficult to tell which meaning, Madhyamaka or Yogacāra, a given author is referencing. Here, and in the previous volume, I have settled on "intrinsic cognizance." See Jamgön Kongtrul, *Sakya: The Path with Its Result, Part One*, p. 561, note 7.

12. Maitreyanātha, Dg.T. sems tsam, *phi* (Toh. 4020), f. 19a, lines 5–7.
13. There is a lacuna in *D*: *nyi ma gnyis dang gsum pa la'ang spyan gsum gsal gdab pa'i tshul bsgom ste/ mdor na spyan gsum/ mdor na spyan gsum po gsal bar 'dod na gsal la/ med oar 'dod na med pa'i bar du dmigs pa brtan par bya ste.*
14. *HT*, Dg.K., f. 24a, line 1. In the passage, the first line has been moved from its original place following the second two lines in the text.
15. Unattested.
16. Because the nāḍīs are seen as deities.
17. sBal ston Dar ma dbyung gnas, possibly of the twelfth to thirteenth centuries.
18. *sLob dpon Pad ma ba dzra mdzad pa'i rdzogs rim mar me'i rtsol ta bu'i gdams ngag*. Identical with Saroruhavajra, *Resembling the Tip of a Lamp Flame*. Dg.T. rgyud, *nya* (Toh. 1220).
19. NOTE: Emptiness.
20. NOTE: The three explanations.
21. NOTE: As inexpressible.
22. Saroruhavajra, *Resembling the Tip of a Lamp Flame*. Dg.T. rgyud, *nya* (Toh. 1220), gives *bdag med rdo rje* for *DNZ* and *P*, *yan lag med pa rdor.*
23. NOTE: Through diet, and so on.
24. NOTE: If it is not good, then abstain from meditation for several days or months.
25. NOTE: It is said, in a place without people.
26. NOTE: At night, not during the day.
27. NOTE: If one's health is good.
28. NOTE: Without lice, according to the temperature.

29. NOTE: Do so in the spring, summer, and fall, but do not do so in the winter.
30. NOTE: Vajrāsana.
31. NOTE: Without a back support.
32. NOTE: Expel three times with strong and weak movements.
33. NOTE: Slightly relax lethargy and agitation.
34. NOTE: First, one gathers the eight goddesses into the eight faces up to here; one then meditates on only the completion stage, resembling the tip of a lamp flame.
35. NOTE: Nairātmyā.
36. NOTE: Appearances vanish like mist on a mirror.
37. NOTE: Recall that the object is the nature of the universe and the class of female beings.
38. NOTE: Seen in objects.
39. NOTE: The size of a chickpea.
40. NOTE: Who dissolves.
41. NOTE: If it is clear, [be satisfied] it is clear and stop. If it is not clear, [accept] it is not clear and stop. This is a key point that should be understood for all previous and following visualizations.
42. Saroruhavajra, *Resembling the Tip of a Lamp Flame* reads *skra rings. DNZ* and *P* read *sgra ris*.
43. NOTE: The five paths.
44. NOTE: On the nine deities.
45. NOTE: The five paths.
46. NOTE: Such as the image of the form, and so on.
47. NOTE: Of creation and completion.
48. NOTE: This was stated by Gayadhara's guru.

4. *Completing the Whole Path with Caṇḍālī*

1. *sLob dpon nag po spyod pas mdzad pa'i gtum mo lam rdzogs. DNZ*, pp. 43–53. *P*, 445–57.
2. Amezhap's *Illuminating the Extensive Doctrine* (pp. 272–74) says, "Cakrasaṃvara, the sixth division of tantras, the utterly unsurpassed mother tantra of the ultimate secret, is the highest of all tantras. Why is this ultimate secret especially profound, more profound than other tantras? Here, the position of Guru Phamtingpa is that the extensive root tantra, the *Khasama* [not extant], was taught to countless yogis and yoginīs of the tenth stage by Mahāvajradhara, and it was practiced by them. Thinking that it could not be utilized as a path by people in the future age of the five degenerations, they were unable to write the text in letters and the sound vanished into space; because it was sealed, it is held to be the sixth gate. The position of Dharikapa the Indian and Mahākarunika the Nepali (Śāntibhadra) is that the *Khasama* root tantra was written down in molten gold in a sapphire book in a temple in Oḍiviśa by the heroes and yoginīs.

Since it is present after it was sealed, this is asserted as the sixth gate. The meaning of both those accounts is that the practice of the heroes and ḍākinīs abiding on the tenth stage is only this division of tantra because the practice is more profound than that of other tantras. Even Ratnākaraśānti, the one with the twofold omniscience in the Kali Yuga, was unable to write a commentary on this tantra through his own power. Thus, it is held to be the sixth gate of tantra. Further, from the perspective of other dharmas, it is explained that the nirmāṇakāya is no longer present, having attained nirvana. However, it is asserted to be the sixth gate because the nirmāṇakāya teacher of this tantra and the gnosis heroes and yoginīs actually exist in the twenty-four lands of Jambudvipa, they swiftly bless the continuums of practitioners, and siddhis are nearby. [Qualm:] It may be thought those nirmāṇakāyas are also taught in the other Saṃvara tantras, like the *Union with All Buddhas Supplementary Tantra*, and so on, and thus, it is not a special feature of this one. [Reply:] While there is a similarity, the method of invoking profound blessings exists only in this tantra, and thus it is superior. It is more profound than other Saṃvara tantras because of the profound methods at the occasion of the creation stage; merging three messengers; and at the occasion of the completion stage the intimate instruction of the ornament of spring. [Qualm:] Now then, it may be thought that it might be superior from the point of view of method, but it cannot be superior through the presence of the nirmāṇakāya teacher. [Reply:] It is superior to other tantras through the door of method alone. That superiority to the other Saṃvara tantra is the key meaning."

3. It should be noted that the largest portion of Kunga Nyingpo's writings were on Cakrasaṃvara, including the first full-length commentary on the *Laghusaṃvara Tantra* composed by a Tibetan.
4. Amezhap, *Effortless Accomplishment of the Two Benefits*, pp. 452–53.
5. Kunga Nyingpo, *Chronicle of the Gurus of the Kṛṣṇa System of Cakrasaṃvara*, 11–22. Tāranātha's hyperbolic biography of Kṛṣṇācārya has been translated by David Templeman in *Tāranātha's Life of Kṛṣṇācārya/Kāṇha*.
6. Kunga Nyingpo identifies him as a tīrthika, or a non-Buddhist king. See chapter 3, note 4.
7. In the ultimate secret tradition of Naropa, one must leave the body alone for a full seven days as it is possible that the deceased's consciousness can return to the body during this period. Drakpa Gyaltsen states, "As such, if one puts the vāyu into the central nāḍī through either the path of yoga or the path of the messenger, there will be nirvana in this life. Since it is possible for the consciousness to return to this body after having transferred in an instant to Akaniṣṭha, it is said to be improper to cremate the body for a period of seven days after the practitioner of this meditation has died" (*Central Channel Instruction*, p. 163, lines 1–2).
8. The "thirty-seven" deities are the twenty-four couples, the eight directional gaurdians, and the five central deities of the Cakrasaṃvara maṇḍala.

9. *yi ge mgo gcad* or *yig mgo gcad.*
10. *Revision of Kṛṣṇa's Four Stages* (p. 85, line 2) defines *kha yed* as *hang gdangs,* literally, "hollow sound."
11. Reading *DNZ, rtsar,* for *P, rtsal.*
12. These are Vajrayāna pilgrimage places mentioned in such tantras as Cakrasaṃvara, Hevajra, and so on.

5. *Instruction for Straightening the Crooked*

1. *Nag po u tsi ta 'chi ba med pas mdzad pa yon po srong ba'i gdams pa. DNZ,* pp. 55–57. *P,* pp. 457–61.
2. Here, *'chi ba* (to die) is rendered according to its meaning of *zhig pa* (to perish), or *cyuti.* The Tibetan title gives this yogin's name as Nag po U tsi ṭa 'chi ba med pa, or Kṛṣṇa Acyuta.

6. *Obtained in Front of a Stupa*

1. *sLob dpon klu sgrub gyis mdzad pa'i mchod rten drung du thob. DNZ,* pp. 59–65. *P,* pp. 400–406.
2. King Dejö Zangpo (rGyal po bDe spyod bzang po) is identified in numerous sources in the Tengyur as the intended recipient of a number of texts authored by Nāgārjuna, most notably *Letter to a Friend.*
3. Sakyapa sources also credit Saraha with being the first human to receive the Laghusaṃvara Tantra from Vajrapāṇi. Amezhap recounts, in *Illuminating the Extensive Doctrine* (pp. 145–46), a history of Cakrasaṃvara: "Saraha was born in South India into the highest caste, the brahmin caste. He trained in the eighteen sciences, such as composition, and so on, and had complete knowledge of the four Vedas. When he reached seventeen years of age, he heard a voice from the sky say, 'Brahmin, what are you doing? Pursue mahāmudrā!' The moment he heard this, Saraha had a supreme realization. He abandoned the activities of a brahmin and left for Śrī Parvata, where Saraha was empowered into an emanated maṇḍala by Vajrapāṇi. Having received the transmission for all the tantras, Saraha obtained supreme siddhi and resided on Śrī Parvata for a few hundred years. His name was Saraha. *Sa* means 'with' and *raha* means 'joy.' Hence, he was called the Joyful One (dGa' dang bcas pa). In order to benefit sentient beings in that southern region, he adopted the accoutrements of a fletcher for a few hundred years and was known as Saraha. *Sara* means 'arrow' and *ha* means 'to pierce.' Hence, he was called the Archer. Following this, he was ordained in the Ārya Sthaviravāda order at Śrī Nālandā, taking the name Rāhulabhadra. Having adopted the garb of a paṇḍita, he remained there for a few hundred years acting as an abbot. After that he discarded the signs of ordination and took on the signs of being a great yogi, performing the benefit of

sentient beings for a few hundred years. When totaled, he lived in Jambudvipa for one thousand eight hundred years, after which he departed into the state of mahāmudrā. It is also said in another chronicle, that for the benefit of the pretas, after he abandoned his body, the purifying smoke of his cremation emptied the city of all pretas, who were reborn in the world of the devas."

4. For an account for how Saraha was received by Tibetans in general, and the Kagyu school specifically, see Kurtis Schaeffer, *Dreaming the Great Brahmin.*
5. In discussing Advayavajra's *Extensive Commentary*, Shaeffer (*Dreaming the Great Brahmin*, 113–15) notes that the Tibetan name of Saraha in the *Treasury of Couplets*, Danun (mDa' bsnun), has been rendered as Nyingpo (*snying po*, Skt. *sāraḥ*). Shaeffer speculates that the commentator chooses this name to emphasize a spiritual significance. He takes *snying po* to be a translation of "hṛdaya," failing to notice the similarity between Saraha and "sāraḥ." He clearly overreaches in his interpretation of the significance of this alternate translation of Saraha's name in Advayavajra's commentary.
6. This citation is commonly attributed to the *Guhyasamāja Tantra*, but the actual source of this citation is Nāgārjuna's *Guhyasamāja* sādhana, *Concise Sādhana*, Dg.T. rgyud, *ngi* (Toh. 1796), f. 2b, lines 3–4. The bodhicitta of Akṣobhya is found in *Guhyasamāja Tantra*, Dg.K. rgyud, *ca* (Toh. 442), f. 94b, lines 4–5: "These entities do not arise. Since phenomena and their nature do not exist and lack identity like space, this way of obtaining awakening is stable" (*dngos po 'di rnams ma skyes pa/ chos dang chos nyid med pa ste/ nam mkha' lta bur bdag med pa/ byang chub tshul 'di brtan pa'o*).
7. *Guhyasamāja*, Dg.K. rgyud, *ca* (Toh. 442), f. 94b, lines 2–3; *The Commentary on Bodhicitta* (D 1800), f. 38a, line 6; and *Commentary on Bodhicitta*, Dg.T. rgyud, *ngi*, f. 43b, lines 6–7.
8. *Treasury of Couplets*, Dg.T. rgyud, *zhi* (Toh. 2224), f. 73a, line 4.
9. Ibid., f. 76, line 7.
10. Ibid., f. 74b, line 5.
11. Ibid., f. 75b, line 2.
12. Nāgārjuna, *Commentary on Bodhicitta*, Dg.T. rgyud, *ngi* (Toh. 1801), f. 40a, lines 6–7.
13. *Nondual Uniformity Tantra*, Dg.T. rgyud, *cha* (Toh. 453), f. 131b. In early Sakya sources, this passage is ascribed to the *Union with All Buddhas Supplementary Tantra*, Dg.K. rgyud, *ka* (Toh. 366), but it is not found here. A nearly identical passage is found in the *Guhyagarbha Tantra*, rnying rgyud, *kha* (Toh. 832), f. 112a, lines 4–5.
14. *Treasury of Couplets*, Dg.T. rgyud, *zhi* (Toh. 2224), f. 71b, line 2.
15. Ibid., f. 74b, lines 3–4.
16. The three fruits are *Emblica officinalis*, *Terminalia bellerica*, and *Terminalia chebula*.
17. Reading *P*, *lus sems hur phyung* for *DNZ*, *lus hur phyung*.

7. *Mahāmudrā without Syllables*

1. *sLob dpon ngag dbang grags pas mdzad pa'i pjhyag rgya chen po yi ge med pa. DNZ*, pp. 67–79. *P*, pp. 406–19.
2. See Drakpa Gyaltsen, *Miscellaneous Notes on Individual Sādhanas*, p. 639.
3. Vāgīśvarakīrti is one of the main sources of the widely promulgated long-life practice, Sitatāra Cintacakra, which exists in all traditions of Tibetan Buddhism, and the author of the *Intimate Instruction on Cheating Death.*
4. *Compendium of the Gnosis Vajra*, Dg.K. rgyud, *cha* (Toh. 450), f. 34a, lines 5–6.
5. In Śraddhākaravarman, *Introduction to the Meaning of Unsurpassed Yoga Tantra*, Dg.T. rgyud, *tsu* (Toh. 3713), f. 109a, lines 4–5, though it is miscited as Vāgīśvarakīrti, *Illuminating the Precious Truth*. See also Vāgīśvarakīrti, *Seven Limbs*, Dg.T. rgyud, *pi* (Toh. 1888), f. 190a, line 7.
6. See Catherine Dalton, "Enacting Perfection," 278–82.
7. *Ancillary Tantra*, Dg.K. rgyud, *ca* (Toh. 443), f. 153a, lines 4–5.
8. Vāgīśvarakīrti, *Seven Limbs*, Dg.T. rgyud, *pi* (Toh. 1888), f. 190a, line 7.
9. Vāgīśvarakīrti's position is clearly held to be the normative position by the end of the eleventh century concerning the presence of the fourth empowerment in the *Ancillary Tantra*. No less a personage than Śraddhākaravarman, through whom the Jñānapāda tradition of Guhyasamāja passes, cites the first passage of the *Seven Limbs* given above verbatim in his *Introduction to the Meaning of Unsurpassed Yoga Tantra*. Vāgīśvarakīrti's arguments in chapter 2 include a rejection of subitist interpretations of mahāmudrā—the claim that mahāmudrā cannot be attained by meditating on the form of the deity, reciting mantras, and so on, and that it is only to be attained by meditating on emptiness and relying on a nonconceptual mind. These themes are echoed in later Sakya skepticism concerning such mahāmudrā traditions as sutra mahāmudrā, the so-called white panacea, and so on.
10. See also Amezhap's discussion of the presence of the fourth empowerment in the Jñānapāda system (*Amazing Storehouse of Jewels*, pp. 728–31) where he cites the *Seven Limbs*.
11. Referred to here as *bZhi pa snang par byed pa*. This title is a nickname taken from the first verse of the *Explanation of Illuminating the Precious Truth*: "The illumination of the fourth [empowerment] shall now be fully explained" (*bzhi pa'i snang par rab bshad bya*).
12. *'byung po'i nyi ma*, the twenty-ninth day of the lunar month, the fourteenth day after a full moon.
13. Unknown.
14. *ST*, f. 83b, line 5.
15. Ibid, f. 83b, lines 5–6. In the text the verse is altered from *rdo rje sems dpa' phyag 'tshal bstod* to *rdo rje'i gsung la phyag tshal bstod.*
16. Ibid., f. 83b, line 6. In the text the verse is altered from *byang chub sems la phyag 'tshal bstod* to *thabs chen mchog la phyag 'tshal bstod.*

17. *Uniform Nonduality Tantra*, Dg.T. rgyud, *cha* (Toh. 453), f. 299b, line 7; and Nāgārjuna, *Five Stages*, Dg.T. rgyud, *ngi* (Toh. 1802), f. 52a, line 5.
18. The resin of the tree, *Commiphora wightii*.
19. NOTE: Nāgabodhi indicates this refers to the passing away of Buddha.
20. Nāgārjuna, *Five Stages*, Dg.T. rgyud, *ngi* (Toh. 1802), f. 52a, line 4.
21. NOTE: This refers to an optical illusion where an image of the city of the Candra dynasty, Harikela, on the coast of modern day Bengal, was reflected from the surface of the Bay of Bengal into the sky.
22. This reading follows Advayavajra: "The realized do not dwell in forests or houses." *Extensive Commentary*, Dg.T. rgyud, *wi* (Toh. 3068), f. 261b, line 2: *rtogs pa nags dang khyim na gnas pa min*, while *DNZ* and *P* read *rtogs pa nags dang khyim na gnas pa khyad par med*. Saraha's *Treasury of Couplets* reads, "Having throughly understood, at that time, one should never go to the forest nor remain in a house but always abide continuously in awakening." See Dg.T. rgyud, *zhi* (Toh. 2224), f. 76b, line 3: *nags su ma 'gro khyim du ma 'dug par/ gang yang de ru yid kyis yongs shes nas/ ma lus rgyun du byang chub rtag par gnas.*
23. *ST*, f. 86a, lines 5–6.
24. Following *DNZ yang gong ltar*, for *P*, *yang gang ltar yang.*
25. NOTE: Bhāviveka states, "Ārya Vajrasena explains that the rūpakāya that is the support for the dharmakāya, which possesses the experiential domain of Akaniṣṭha, is the vipākakāya. Ārya Asaṅga explains it to be the sambhogakāya." TN: See *Precious Lamp*, Dg.T. dbu ma, *tsha*, (Toh. 3845), f. 286a, lines 3–4. Ārya Asaṅga's explanation is applied here.

8. Śrī Koṭalipa's *Instruction on the Inconceivable*

1. *dPal tog tse ba'i bsam mi khyab kyi gdams ngag. DNZ*, pp. 81–118. *P*, pp. 347–95.
2. Thanks are due to Karl Brunnhölzl for his contribution in helping me to standardize the Sanskrit names referred to in the text.
3. NOTE: The inconceivable nature in union with the empty essence is nondual emptiness.
4. NOTE: The three inconceivable methods are inconceivable.
5. NOTE: That is the homage of the confirmation or realization of all dharmas, the personally known gnosis that is seen perfectly, to which homage is paid here.
6. NOTE: The cause continuum.
7. NOTE: Perfectly relinquishing.
8. NOTE: Said to be the initial support.
9. This is a direct reference to *VT*, f. 44a, line 3: *ngan pa brtags pa'i rnam rtog gyis/ rin chen sems ni dri can bya*, "The jewel mind is tainted with concepts of false imputations."
10. Reading *rtogs* as *rtog* following Gö, f. 100b, line 3.
11. Reading Gö, *spangs*, for *P* and *DNZ*, *yang.*
12. NOTE: inner and outer.

13. A medieval Indian sect who worshipped the sun.
14. The Gö translation (Koṭalipa, *Stages of the Inconceivable*, Dg.T. rgyud, *wi* [Toh. 2228], 102b, line 1) gives a slightly different rendering and an extra line: *rjes su rnal 'byor rig pa'i mchog/ gnyis 'das shin tu rnal 'byor te/ gnyis med ye shes rnal 'byor che.*
15. The six flavors are sweet, sour, salty, hot, bitter, and astringent.
16. *byol song lam*; Gö glosses *byol song lam* as *lam mchog*, supreme path.
17. Gö glosses this as *'dzag pa*, dripping.
18. Reading Gö, *lta dang snom*; for *P* and *DNZ*, *lha dang sgom.*
19. Gö glosses this as *sa bon pad snol rnam pa mtshungs* ("The lotus uniformly embraces the seed").
20. Gö glosses this as the thirty-two nāḍis.
21. Reading Gö, *gsal ba*, for *P* and *DNZ*, *'dor ba.*
22. Omitted in *P* and *DNZ*, supplied by Gö, f. 104b, line 2, *nges pa'i lam yang gsal 'gyur ba.*
23. Drokmi Lotsāwa Śākya Yeshe.
24. Kun rik.
25. Chöbar.
26. Kunga Nyingpo.
27. Verses 94–95.
28. NOTE: According to the Pāramitāyāna, the object to be established is the aggregates, sense elements, and sense bases. Here, since the object to be established is the body, voice, and mind, the sufferings of samsara arise as experiences of body, voice, and mind. The arising of samādhi and the path arises for the body, voice, and mind. The siddhi of the result, the vajras of body, speech, and mind, transform those three [body, voice, and mind], which are said to be the support or the basis.
29. NOTE: Exhaling as the essence of *hūṃ*; inhaling, *oṃ*; and pausing, *aḥ.*
30. NOTE: Existing in all nāḍīs.
31. NOTE: The nature of the body and voice is supported on the mind; the circumstance of the mind is supported on the body and voice. For as long as the trio of body, voice, and mind are not parted, it is asserted they are a single entity.
32. NOTE: All mental experiences belong to the same genre in one cognition. Since there are no phenomena other than that, [the body and voice are established implicitly by establishing the mind].
33. NOTE: As an isolate.
34. NOTE: For one who does not realize the essence, the eight groups of concepts of the six realms of samsara are subsumed by the eight consciousnesses. TN: This passage is omitted in *DNZ.*
35. NOTE: Not mixed with different kinds of concepts.
36. NOTE: Through the power of the different ways of realizing the essence, there are the different paths and conclusions of the non-Buddhists and Buddhists.

37. NOTE: There are different modes of arising from one entity, which have diverse appearances.
38. NOTE: All siddhis are the same in essence; when the method is encountered, they arise.
39. NOTE: Though the power that generates those minds exists through the same entity, they will not arise if the method is not encountered.
40. NOTE: If the sesame seed does not meet the condition of the stick, and so on, its oil will not be produced; should the sesame seed meet the stick, the oil will be produced.
41. NOTE: In one mind everything appears: the cause, the path, and the result.
42. NOTE: Because those three [inconceivabilities] are ultimately empty of the trio: cause, intrinsic essence, and result.
43. NOTE: By any cause, result, and so on.
44. NOTE: Since a second dharma exists within one dharma, this seems like a contradiction, but this is not a contradiction.
45. NOTE: Since it cannot be found on investigation.
46. NOTE: Further, [union] is not like merging existence and nonexistence. [Union] is not like dividing one into two. [Union] is not the existence of one side and the nonexistence of the other side. [Union] is not like binding two things into one. In brief, if one searches with an idea of method, [union] wholly exists. If one searches with an idea of wisdom, [union] wholly does not exist. The mere nonassertion of duality is called "nonduality" or "union," as [union] is said to be beyond the range of all expressions.
47. NOTE: When focusing the mind there is no experience of the taste of śamatha or vipaśyana.
48. During the beginning of the demonstration of the third empowerment, the instruction of focusing the mind on space, and so on, the mind is focused.
49. NOTE: When the five inconceivabilities are realized.
50. NOTE: There is suffering in the body, nāḍīs, vāyus, and so on. For the voice, there are the karma vāyus. For the mind, concepts come and go.
51. NOTE: Like accomplishing the gold-transformation elixir, the body floats and is light, and there is heat and bliss; the voice speaks, laughs, and so on; and the mind is the samādhi of the method, the samādhi of wisdom, and the samādhi of union.
52. NOTE: Since the body appears like a rainbow, one can appear in many forms according to the inclinations of those to be tamed, one can teach in many languages, and one knows in an instant the quantity and nature of all objects of mind; [body, speech, and mind are subsumed under gnosis].
53. NOTE: The consciousness of relative truth evaluates experience.
54. NOTE: The characteristic, quality, and power.
55. NOTE: The cause, path, and result. TN: *snang ba* is missing in *DNZ*.
56. NOTE: Not found when investigated and examined.

57. NOTE: Since experience is unceasing.
58. NOTE: The tripiṭaka and the four divisions of tantra.
59. NOTE: The speech of the gurus from the first one, Paramāśva, down to one's own guru.
60. NOTE: After the equipoise of the experience of the method, wisdom, and union, subsequently one should have confidence in dharmatā because of recalling those three [method, wisdom, and union].
61. NOTE: Lord Kharchung said that the view should be explained first, and later the mind should be focused because it is easier to focus the mind when the view is understood. Lord Mugulung said that if the mind cannot be focused, even if the view is explained, it will not be understood. Therefore, first focus the mind, then explain the view later.
62. NOTE: Clinging to entities because of not realizing the essence.
63. NOTE: From among the two kinds of poison for a practitioner.
64. NOTE: The stream of ordinary conceptuality.
65. NOTE: Having protected the three places.
66. NOTE: Having sought the concentration of prāṇāyāma from the guru, next, put this into practice.
67. NOTE: Sitting straight up with knees to the chest or cross-legged.
68. NOTE: Exhale strongly three times.
69. NOTE: Rest naturally for a short while.
70. NOTE: The thought "I will attain the stage of total awakening and benefit all sentient beings."
71. NOTE: Generate intense devotion and then imagine the guru dissolves.
72. NOTE: Recite *hūṃ* and recall *hūṃ* in the mind.
73. NOTE: The same as Virūpa's.
74. NOTE: If one thinks that since the Ācārya did not explain the ultimate because it is free from all proliferation, there is no method of realizing this elsewhere; [in fact] there is the example in verse 83cd and 84ab of the root text.
75. NOTE: Both the samādhi of method and the samādhi of wisdom are faulty meditations. The samādhi of union is faultless.
76. NOTE: Face toward the eastern direction.
77. NOTE: Since this is not the same as the two below, [the experience of freedom from extremes] arises as bliss and emptiness.
78. NOTE: One is attached to one's seat as one does not want to move elsewhere.
79. NOTE: That returns even though it is launched.
80. NOTE: Above and below.
81. NOTE: Because of freedom from extremes.
82. NOTE: Because of not being established at all.
83. NOTE: Pervading all cognitions and objects of cognition.
84. NOTE: The thought that it cannot be destroyed by anything.
85. NOTE: Though a complete body has developed inside of a fertilized swan's egg,

if the outer shell has not broken, it will not be able to move. If it is broken, the body will be able to move.

86. NOTE: Though orpiment [*ba bla*, *bab bla*, *Arsenic trisulfide*, a toxic bright yellow mineral] is inside it, without breaking it open, it cannot be seen. If it is broken open, it can be seen.
87. NOTE: After a silkworm encases itself in its own silk, it is not visible. But as soon as that cocoon is removed, it is nakedly visible.
88. NOTE: Names are not established entities, but because there is attachment and aversion through clinging to entities, [the name is applied, etc].
89. NOTE: The one who has completed the limbs of concentration.
90. NOTE: Nothing arises from a named thing, since [names] are mere temporary designations.
91. NOTE: As such, even if one praises the name, there is no benefit; even if one describes its faults, there is no harm.
92. NOTE: Not obstructed by anything, since space dissolves into self.
93. NOTE: Citation unidentified.
94. NOTE: Omitted in the citation.
95. *Perfection of Wisdom in Eighteen Thousand Lines*, f. 261a, line 5. This citation incorrectly mentions Subhuti. The person being addressed in this series of quotes is Indra (a.k.a. Kauśika).
96. NOTE: Attachment, aversion, and so on are nonarising, but they are bonds because of attachment to entities.
97. NOTE: Of arising.
98. NOTE: Investigate what is the location of body, voice, and mind.
99. NOTE: Investigate what is the type: male, female, or genderless.
100. NOTE: Investigate what is its color, shape, and so on.
101. NOTE: Grasping to the object of meditation, the meditating consciousness, and the meditator as entities, which are not established.
102. NOTE: The consciousness merely looking inward.
103. NOTE: Whichever samādhi of the method arises for all of those, it should be maintained.
104. NOTE: Though attachment and aversion do not arise in equipoise, they can arise when conditions are met.
105. NOTE: Lord Mugulung holds that one trains on the first one; Lord Kharchung asserts it is easier to complete if one trains from sound; and Lord Gönpowa asserts that the practices should be applied according to the differences in the person.
106. NOTE: One does not look elsewhere apart from those.
107. NOTE: It is very important not to focus on anything.
108. NOTE: On the second day, and so on.
109. NOTE: In the end, train in looking as far as a shouting distance, a league, and so on.

110. NOTE: Attractive forms, unattractive forms, and ordinary forms and, likewise, for sound, and so on.
111. NOTE: Becoming bliss and emptiness.
112. NOTE: Since samādhi arises.
113. NOTE: Since it is not other than destroying the concept of self and not other than destroying [the concept of] entities of appearance.
114. NOTE: Since the yogi's (*dzo gi*) realization arises through the arising of attachment and aversion to the ordinary, at that moment faults do not arise even though one uses objects of desire.
115. NOTE: Without requiring other antidotes.
116. NOTE: A fault of concentration.
117. NOTE: Engage in many repetitions.
118. NOTE: So it is said.
119. NOTE: Add three cushions at once.
120. NOTE: A handful.
121. NOTE: Then meditate.
122. NOTE: Less for pitta and blood; more for kapha and vata.
123. NOTE: For those who are younger, less; for the elderly, more.
124. NOTE: Less during autumn and summer; more during the cold seasons.
125. NOTE: Said to be looking at the place of the devas.
126. NOTE: A concept sent to the end of space.
127. NOTE: Its ability to remove lethargy or not.
128. NOTE: First, that is dispelled into the empty space beyond oneself and the cushion. If it is not dispelled, imagine a transparent red dharmodaya in the anus.
129. NOTE: In the mind.
130. NOTE: With the balls of the feet.
131. NOTE: When the robe is shortened, one moves forward; when it is lengthened, one moves backward.
132. NOTE: The first early morning session should be tight and short, and so on.
133. NOTE: The first day has tight and short sessions. The second day has relaxed and long sessions, and so on.
134. NOTE: Do not eat before the first session and meditate; eat before the second session, and so on.
135. NOTE: Sometimes one meditates; sometimes one does not meditate.
136. NOTE: The mind does not wish to leave its focus, just like touching glue with one's hand.
137. NOTE: Since there is no other path traversed that is higher than this, this is said to be the profound path.
138. NOTE: The *Hevajra Tantra* states, "The yogin who has received permission/ will receive a prediction from the yoginīs,/ 'Take the mudra named so-and-so,/ and hold the vajra by benefiting sentient beings'" (f. 14b, line 7–f. 15a, line 1).
139. NOTE: Though one can rely on a young woman who is a siddha yoginī in the

beginning to familiarize oneself, here it is said that mainly it is a young woman who has been predicted.

140. An apsara is a kind of female divinity, often associated with gandharvas.
141. NOTE: For example, if one is a practitioner of the Akṣobhya family, the purified mudra is generated as Māmaki, and so on.
142. NOTE: All of the pure element of method is under the control of the lunar bindu. All of the pure element of wisdom is under control of solar blood.
143. NOTE: Where their nāḍīs meet.
144. NOTE: Like the lines on one's palm.
145. NOTE: The purified continuum of the method.
146. NOTE: The purified continuum of the wisdom.
147. NOTE: Transforming into light rays.
148. NOTE: Which purifies the vāyu.
149. NOTE: There is none higher.
150. Drakpa Gyaltsen here follows Gö, f. 104, line 1.
151. NOTE: The central channel of both method and wisdom.
152. NOTE: In the central nāḍī.
153. NOTE: When it is drawn up.
154. NOTE: Multicolored.
155. NOTE: In both method and wisdom.
156. NOTE: Mutually.
157. NOTE: Since all of samsara and nirvana are perceived as a single bindu.
158. These two last verses are unattested.
159. The root text reads *gnyis med rgya mtsho las byung ba*, but here the author chooses to present *gnyis med rgya mtsho dam pa nyid.*
160. Unattested in the root text. It suggests that the manuscript we have at present is missing passages.
161. NOTE: Since objects of desire are not abandoned on the path in either equipoise or post-equipoise or in either the creation stage and completion stage, in the result the appearance of objects of desire never ceases.
162. NOTE: Since one can always see which sentient beings are ready to be tamed and which are not ready to be tamed.
163. NOTE: Since the stream of sentient beings to benefit is uninterrupted, it is impossible not to benefit them.
164. NOTE: Since those to be tamed are uninterrupted, one benefits them.
165. NOTE: Strictly, so it is said.
166. NOTE: Since it arises for everyone over the mountain peak.
167. NOTE: The mind essence.
168. NOTE: Because everyone holds their own school and conclusion to be true.
169. NOTE: Generated by each person's treatise system.
170. NOTE: Unidentified.
171. NOTE: Since a cause is a substantial phenomena, it is not established in the mind.

172. NOTE: Since everything is free from extremes.
173. NOTE: All examples do not transcend the two extremes. The essence is free from extremes.
174. NOTE: Because the mind is partless.
175. NOTE: Nothing becomes good or bad because the essence is purified.
176. NOTE: There are no differences in the phenomena of samsara and nirvana.
177. NOTE: Through reification.
178. NOTE: There is destruction through the condition of lethargy and agitation; illustration with the example of reflection, and so on; and abandoning conceptuality and the arising of nonconceptuality. Progressing higher through enhancements, the diligent obtain the result in one lifetime, the mediocre obtain the result in the bardo, and the average obtain the result within seven lifetimes or within sixteen lifetimes.
179. NOTE: The experience, the third empowerment, and so on.
180. NOTE: Unchanged throughout the three times.
181. NOTE: Since the meaning is unmodified.
182. NOTE: Since it has always existed.
183. Reading *P*, *mngon du sgrub* for *DNZ*, *sngon du sgrub*.
184. NOTE: Because of pervading all of samsara and nirvana without good or bad.
185. NOTE: Because of the emanation of all samsara and nirvana.
186. NOTE: To be applied gradually to the realization of reality, and so on.
187. NOTE: Since this is the threshold of the path.
188. NOTE: The nominal enumeration of them all.
189. Reading *DNZ*, p. 283, *smyug dong ltar* for *P*, *hang dang du*.
190. NOTE: If there is diarrhea, it is said that it will stop by strongly contracting the lower vāyu.
191. *DNZ* ends here. The colophon has been added for the sake of completeness from *P*.

9. *Path Cycle of the Mudra*

1. *sLob dpon indra bhūti'i mdzad pa'i phyag lam skor. DNZ*, pp. 119–36. *P*, pp. 461–79.
2. In this text, the Tibetan spelling slips between *rta* (horse) and *brda* (symbol), but the passage on p. 124, line 6, dispels any doubt as to the proper spelling: "Just as one will quickly arrive at any desired place by mounting a horse, likewise since [reliance on a mudra] causes one to swiftly arrive at the stage of buddhahood, it is said, "[Devadatta] used a horse."
3. *Bola* and *kakkola* are Vajrayāna euphemisms for the penis and vagina, respectively.
4. This is a pun on *yoga*: "union" (*mnyam sbyor*) is *samayoga* in Sanskrit while "application" (*sbyor ba*) is *prayoga*.

5. The lotus, doe, conch, and variegated one, respectively.
6. *Union with All Buddhas Supplementary Tantra*, Dg.K. rgyud, *ka* (Toh. 366), f. 151a, line 3.
7. Green cardamom, black cardamom, nutmeg, clove, saffron, and bamboo pith.
8. Indrabhūti, *Accomplishing Gnosis*, Dg.T. rgyud, *wi* (Toh. 2219), f. 49b, lines 5–6. The passage as given in the canonical translation is *yang dag ye shes rig pa las/ khyab dang rdo rje'i sku nyid dang/ 'gyur ba med pa nyid dang ni/ kun mkhyen nyid ni de yis 'grub*. In this rendition, Drakpa Gyaltsen gives *khyab dang rdo rje'i sku nyid dang/ 'gyur ba med pa nyid dang ni/ yang dag ye shes grub pa dang/ kun mkhyen nyid ni de yis 'grub*. Drakpa Gyaltsen's *Precious Wish-Fulfilling Tree* (p. 270) gives a second version: *khyab dang rdo rje'i sku nyid dang/ 'gyur ba med pa nyid dang ni/ yang dag ye shes rig pa las/ kun mkhyen nyid ni de yis 'grub*. He explains there that this passage is identical in meaning to the passage in Maitreyanātha, *Unsurpassed Continuum*, Dg.T. sems tsam, *phi* (Toh. 4042), f. 55a, line 1: "Uncompounded, naturally perfected/ not to be realized through other conditions/ omniscient, loving, and powerful/ buddhahood possesses two benefits."
9. This part of the text is quite corrupted in *D*, from p. 125, line 2, to the middle of line 3; following *P*, p. 466, lines 4–6.
10. *ril ba zhabs 'tshags*.
11. *Piper nigrum*, *Piper longum*, and *Alpinia officinarum*.
12. Above the kidneys on the sides of the body.
13. This is a euphemism for first menses of a young women.
14. *tshwa rgod 'thung*.
15. NOTE: Also *kha liṅga* occurs.
16. Kambala, *Difficult Points of Cakrasaṃvara*, Dg.T rgyud, *ba* (Toh. 1401), f. 73b, lines 5–6.
17. *upamapāda*.
18. Indrabhūti III, *Amṛta of Reality*, f. 323b, lines 4–6.
19. Prajñākaragupta, *Precious Drop*, Dg.T. rgyud, *ta* (Toh. 1332), f. 294b, lines 1–2: "I obtained that in Oḍḍiyāna from the supreme lotus mouth of Palme (dPal me, Lakṣmī)."

Jamgön Kongtrul's Commentary on the Eight Ancillary Path Cycles: Introduction

1. See Jamgön Kongtrul, *A Gem of Many Colors*, 159–60. On p. 206, Kongtrul mentions that he finalized the last volumes of *The Treasury of Precious Instructions* and edited them toward the end of 1882 or beginning of 1883.

10. Medicinal Elixir of the Fortunate Bezoar

1. *Ḍom bi he ru ka'i lhan cig skye grub kyi khrid yig bkra shis gi vaṃ sman bcud ces bya ba. DNZ* 6, pp. 137–50. *L* 20, pp. 286–301.
2. This refers to Sachen Kunga Nyingpo and his two eldest sons, Lopön Sönam Tsemo and Jetsun Drakpa Gyaltsen.
3. This refers to Sakya Paṇḍita, the nephew of Sönam Tsemo and Drakpa Gyaltsen; and Chögyal Phakpa, the nephew of Sakya Paṇḍita.
4. This citation is taken from Ḍombi Heruka, *Accomplishing the Connate*, Dg.T. rgyud, *wi* (Toh. 2223), f. 70a, lines 6–7. However, it is is actually a citation from *HT*, f. 10, lines 6–7. Drakpa Gyaltsen, *Possessing Purity*, *SKB* 6, p. 518, lines 3–519, line 4, explains these two lines in the following way: "Now the nonreferential meditation on the connate nature is the passage, 'Why? If one does not meditate with the mind . . .' There are three topics here: how to actually meditate, explaining how that [connate nature] pervades everything, and avoiding criticism. First, that connate gnosis that is the nature of all entities is free from all extremes of proliferation, as was explained already in the chapter on reality. There is no benefit to mentally eliminating doubt; it is necessary to meditate. Because that meditation is a meditation that resembles [such a connate gnosis], it will not produce a dissimilar realization. *SP*, f. 85b, line 5, states, "Do not meditate on the empty,/ do not meditate on the nonempty;/ the practitioner who does not avoid the empty,/ does not avoid the nonempty./" Nāgārjuna, *Commentary on Bodhicitta*, Dg.T. rgyud, *ngi* (Toh. 1801), f. 40a, line 7, says, "Dwelling in the mind free of references/ is the characteristic of space;/ that meditation on space/ is asserted to be the meditation on emptiness./ Here, in accordance with Ācārya Nāgārjuna's instruction, a beginner should train in focusing the mind on space or recognizing gnosis in objects . . . if one meditates with four characteristics—with an unchanging support, without moving the body, without closing the eyes, and without grasping with the mind—nonconceptuality will arise. Then, one should switch to other supports, such as sound objects, and so on. Once śamatha has arisen, when one merges it with the view as explained previously and meditates, self-originated gnosis will arise. That being the case, since all migrating beings dissolve into that state, it is called meditation."
5. Ḍombi Heruka, *Accomplishing the Connate*, Dg.T. rgyud, *wi* (Toh. 2223), f. 70a, line 7.
6. Senmo (*bsen mo*) are a class of female spirits, typically depicted naked and disheveled.
7. Gyalgong (*rgyal 'gong*) are a class of male spirits, typically depicted wearing monastic garb.
8. Local guardians (*gnyan sa bdag*) are a class of spirits that spread serious contagious diseases.
9. Here, Kongtrul clearly reads *sad pa mi 'byed* in the original text as *sad par mi byed*, leading to the difference in renderings between these passages.

10. The words in italics make up the personal name of Jamgön Kongtrul: bLo gros mtha' yas.

11. Fortunate Mustard Seedpod

1. *Pad ma badzra'i zab pa'i tshul dgu'i khrid yig bkra shis yungs kar gong bu. DNZ*, pp. 151–80. *L*, pp. 301–32.
2. There is no extant copy of an Indian text by this name in the Tengyur. However, there is a text by this name arranged by Sönam Tsemo: *dPal kyai rdo rje'i dkyil chog nas gling ma, SKB* 3, pp. 534–82.
3. *HT*, f. 12b, line 5. In this text Kongtrul gives *'khor ba rnam par rtog pa la* instead of *'khor ba dang ni mya ngan 'das*. Kongtrul's *Word Commentary on the Two-Section King Tantra* explains the line on p. 328 as follows: "Following the experience of the gnosis of the wisdom consort in the third empowerment, the principle (*de kha no nyid*; Skt. *tattva*) of the example and its meaning will be correctly explained. Ultimately, there isn't the slightest difference between pure gnosis (free of the taint of the sign of concepts and possessing the form or nature of great bliss) and samsara (endowed with afflictions and the dualistic conceptuality for purifying those afflictions), because the essence is a uniform state of union, as everything lacks inherent existence."
4. *HT*, 20b5.
5. *HT*, 25b7–26a1.
6. This citation is an alternate translation of Nāgārjuna, *Sixty Verses*, Dg.T. dbu ma, *tsa* (Toh. 3825), 20a4.
7. *HT*, f. 24a, lines 4–6.
8. HT, f. 27b, line 7–f. 28a, line 1.
9. See p. 30.
10. Kongtrul left this section as it is because of the lacunae in the manuscript he had at his disposal. See chapter 3, note 13.
11. This short verse contains an epigram of Kongtrul's alternate name: *Pa dma gar gyi dbang phyug*.

12. Essence of Fortunate Curd

1. *Nag po u tsi ṭa 'chi ba med pa'i yon po srong ba'i khri yig bkra shis zho'i snyin po shes bya ba, D*, pp. 181–88. *L*, pp. 367–74.

13. Excellent Tree of Fortunate Bilva

1. *'Phags pa klu sgrub kyi mchod rten drung thob kyi khrid yig bkra shis bi lva'i ljong bzang. DNZ*, pp. 189–212. *L*, pp. 374–97. Bilva is the fruit of *Aegle marmelos*. It is a common medicinal substance used in Tibetan medicine and Ayurveda.

2. Kongtrul here gives the title as *dPal nam mkha' dang mnyam pa'i gsang 'dus rtsa rgyud.*
3. The *Commentary on Bodhicitta* provides *bsgribs pa*, "obscured," for *DNZ*, *brtags pa*, "imputed." Kongtrul explicates this passage in terms of imputations of various types but returns to the notion of obscuration at the conclusion of his argument.
4. Nāgārjuna, *Commentary on Bodhicitta*, Dg.T. rgyud, *ngi* (Toh. 1801), f. 38b, lines 3–4.
5. Ibid., f. 40a, lines 5–6.
6. Ibid., f. 40b, lines 2–3.
7. Ibid., f. 41a, line 1.
8. The five faults are laziness, inattentiveness, torpor, lethargy, and agitation. The eight factors are initiative, effort, faith, peacefulness, mindfulness, attention, intention, and equanimity.
9. Ibid., f. 40a, line 5.
10. Ibid., f. 42a.
11. See Karmay (*Arrow and the Spindle*, 247) for an explanation of the distinction between *phya* and *phywa*.
12. *srid pa'i bskos pa'i phya*. Gampo Tashi's *Brief Discussion* (p. 86) explains, "The origin of existence of inner inhabitants, the gods, humans, and sentient beings, is the account of the destiny of existence; that is, the explanation of the destiny or fate of all the things of the world" (*nang bcud kyi srid kyi srid pa ste lha mi sems can byung tshul/ srid pa'i bskos rabs te 'jig rten gyi dngos po kun gyi bskos thang gam bkod thang bshad pa*).
13. Saraha, *Treasury of Couplets*, Dg.T. rgyud, zhi (Toh. 2224), f. 71b, lines 1–2.
14. Mokṣākaragupta, *Difficult Points*, Dg.T. rgyud 'grel, *mi* (Toh. 2258), f. 276a, lines 4–5: "'The activity arising from mind' refers to all arising of concepts. 'That is the nature of the protector' refers to the fundamental luminosity arising as concepts, for example, like water and waves.' Advayavajra's *Extensive Commentary* (f. 249a, line 7–f. 249b, line 1) states, "The mind of the yogin appears as activity that arises from the mind. However long that may be, for that long they encounter the sublime guru protector. The nature that arises from that [meeting] is the truth that is not realized elsewhere. That being the case, though it seems like there is transformation from that innate nature, it is not so. For example, though the water and waves in the ocean cannot be estimated, there is nothing else that arises from the ocean. That being the case, since [water and waves] are not different entities, samsara and nirvana are pure by nature, like the nature of space."
15. Saraha, *Treasury of Couplets*, Dg.T. rgyud, zhi (Toh. 2224), f. 74b, line 7.
16. Nāgārjuna, *Commentary on Bodhicitta*, Dg.T. rgyud, *ngi* (Toh. 1801), f. 40a, lines 1–3.
17. Saraha, *Treasury of Couplets*, Dg.T. rgyud, zhi (Toh. 2224), f. 72b, line 6.
18. *Collected Verses on the Noble Perfection of Wisdom*, Dg.K. shes rab sna tshogs, *ka* (Toh. 13), f. 8b, lines 3–4.

19. Ibid., f. 12a, line 2.
20. This prayer, attributed to Sakya Paṇḍita, is known in Tibetan as *Gang gi mchod rdzas ma*. It is found in Lodrö Gyaltsen's *Offering the Maṇḍala*, *SKB* 13, pp. 389–91.
21. This verse is the second verse in the prayer commonly known in Sakya as the *Kun bzang dbang bzhi* composed by Losal Gyatso in his *Four Empowerments*. I am giving the full verse here for convenience.
22. Saraha, *Treasury of Couplets*, f. 73, line 4.
23. Ibid., f. 76, line 7.
24. Ibid., f. 75b, line 2.
25. *Perfection of Wisdom in Eight Thousand Lines*, Dg.K. brgyad stong (Toh. 12), f. 167b, line 5.
26. Saraha, *Inexhaustible Treasury*, Dg.T. rgyud, zhi (Toh. 2264), f. 33a, line 4. This doha's attribution to Saraha is generally contested in the Sakya school. See Kurtis Schaefer, *Dreaming the Great Brahmin*, 73–78.
27. *Sutra of Bhadrakarātrī*, Dg.K. mdo sde, *sa* (Toh. 313), f. 162b, lines 1–2.
28. *Grub snying skor*. According to Rangjung Dorje's *Catalog of Translated Treatises*, pp. 525–26, this a collective name for two cycles of texts, the siddha division (*grub pa'i sde*), and the essential cycle (*snying gi skor*). The siddha division includes the *Intimate Instructions on the Stages of the Inconceivable* and the root text of *Accomplishing the Connate*. The essential cycle contains a large number of texts by Advayavajra/Maitripa. To this is sometimes added Saraha's dohas and their commentaries (*do ha'i bskor*), as appears to be the case here.
29. These six are described in a treasure revelation of the Drukpa Kagyu master Tsangpa Gyare (gTsang pa rgya ras ye shes rdo rje, 1161–1211) titled *Tibu's Root Verses of the Sixfold Cycle of One Taste*, which the tradition holds was brought to Tibet by Rechungpa Dorje Drakpa (Ras chung pa rdo rje grags pa, 1085–1161) and then concealed as a treasure by him.
30. Gönpo Dorje, *Comprehensive Summary of One Taste*, 4:260, line 4.
31. Ibid.
32. Ibid.
33. The terms *'du ba* (Skt. *dhātu*) and *nyes pa* (Skt. *doṣa*) refer to the three humors, vata (*rlung*), pitta (*mkhris pa*), and kapha (*bad kan*), in their healthy and pathogenic states, respectively. When the term *'du ba* is used, it refers to the way in which the three humors function to support the body in its healthy state. When the term *nyes pa* is used, it refers to how the three humors come into conflict and harm the body.

14. Fortunate Shoot of Dūrva Grass

1. *Ngag dbang grags pa'i phyag rgya chen po yi ge med pa'i khrid yig bkra shis dūrva'i myu gu*. *DNZ*, pp. 213–229. *L*, pp. 397–415.
2. Padmavajra, *Secret Accomplishment*, Dg.T. rgyud, *wi* (Toh. D 2217), f. 14b, line 1.

3. Kālacakrapāda, *Padmani*, Dg.T. rgyud, *na* (Toh. 1350), f. 83b, lines 6–7.
4. *Garland of Vajras Tantra*, Dg.K. rgyud, *ca* (Toh. 445), f. 250b, lines 2–3.
5. Ibid., f. 250b, lines 3–4.
6. Ibid., f. 249a, lines 2–3.
7. *Sutra of Never Wavering from Dharmatā*, Dg.K. mdo sde, *da* (Toh. 128), f. 171, lines 1–2.
8. This sutra passage is not found in the Tibetan canon; it is found in Gampopa Sönam Rinchen's *Sunlight of Citations*, pp. 299–300.
9. This citation is drawn directly from the *Sunlight of Citations*, p. 297. It is also found in the *Host of Buddhas Sutra*, f. 88b, lines 5–6.
10. Saraha, *Treasury of Couplets*, Dg.T. rgyud, *zhi* (Toh. 2224), f. 75a, line 2.
11. *DNZ* and *L* both read *bcu gsum*, thirteen, but this is a mistake.
12. Atiśa Dīpaṃkaraśrījñāna, *Lamp of the Path of Awakening*, Dg.T. dbu ma, *ki* (Toh. 3947), f. 240b, lines 2–4. This passage is most commonly attributed to the *Mahāvairocanābhisambodhi*, sometimes referred to as the *Vairocanamāyājāla*, but it is not found in this text in any form. Atiśa seems to have drawn this citation from the *Great Illusion Tantra*, Dg.K. rgyud, *ja* (Toh. 466), f. 131a, lines 3–4. The difference between these two passages is that the word rendered *ma rig pa* by Atiśa was earlier rendered *rmongs pa* by Rinchen Zangpo.
13. Saraha, *Treasury of Couplets*, Dg.T. rgyud, *zhi* (Toh. 2224), f. 75b, lines 6–7. The final line is not present in the Derge block print. It is present in Mokṣākaragupta, *Difficult Points*, Dg.T. rgyud 'grel, *mi*. (Toh. 2258), f. 279b, line 7–280a, line 1: "'It is the syllable that is not a syllable' means it is a symbolic syllable, but if there is no syllable, the syllable *a* is known as empty form. Further, in 'For that long one has the best understanding of syllables,' a syllable is *akṣa*, understood to be unchanging bliss. What syllable? It says, 'It is the syllable that is not a syllable.' A syllable is a concept, and that concept does not exist. 'It is the syllable' refers to the bliss of nonconceptuality.'"
14. Termed *vipākakāya* in the root text.

15. Fortunate Pure Crystal Mirror

1. *Tog rtse pa'i bsam gyis mi khyab pa'i khrid yig bkra shis dvangs shel med long*. *DNZ*, pp. 231–54. *L*, pp. 263–87.
2. The poison of conceptual dualism is implied by grasping to entities and signs, but is not explicitly addressed here.
3. Kongtrul here is reading *ba rgya bral* (breaking free of a spider web) found in *DNZ*, for *P*, pp. 372, line 2, *bab rgya dbral* (to split open orpiment). Here *bab* is clearly defined in the marginalia of *P* as *bab bla* (*ba bla*, orpiment). It is translated here according to what he understood the text to mean.
4. Drakpa Gyaltsen, *Clarification of the Instruction*. *DNZ* 6, p. 105.
5. This incorrectly mentions Subhuti. The person being addressed in this series of quotes is Indra (a.k.a. Kauśika).

6. *Perfection of Wisdom in Eighteen Thousand Lines*, Dg.K. khri brgyad (Toh. 10), f. 261a, line 5.
7. Reading *DNZ*, *rgyu 'khrul* as an erroneous reading of *DNZ*, *rgyun lugs* (p. 109, line 5).
8. Here, a cup is about the amount that fits in one's palms.
9. A weak Tibetan alcoholic beverage made from fermented barley.
10. Erroneously enumerated as eight.

16. Fortunate Right-Turning White Conch

1. *Indra bhū ti'i phyag rgya'i lam khrid yig bkra shis dkar gyas 'khyil*. *DNZ*, pp. 255–69. *L*, pp. 333–50.
2. See chapter 9, note 2.
3. Green cardamom, black cardamom, nutmeg, clove, saffron, and bamboo pith.
4. *Union of All Buddhas Supplementary Tantra*, Dg.K. rgyud, *ka* (Toh. 366), f. 151a, line 3.
5. Nāgārjuna, *Five Stages*, Dg.T. rgyud, *ngi* (Toh. 1800), f. 49a, line 7–f. 50b, line 1. Though this whole passage is commonly attributed to the *Union of All Buddhas Supplementary Tantra*, the last two lines are not found there.
6. See chapter 9, pp. 131–34.
7. Published as Jamgön Kongtrul, *Jonang: The One Hundred and Eight Teaching Manuals* (Boulder: Shambhala, 2020).

17. Fortunate Vermilion Ornament

1. *Nag po pa'i gtum mo lam rdzogs kyi khrid yig bkra shis li khri'i thig le*. *DNZ*, pp. 271–87. *L*, pp. 350–67.
2. The text gives *spyod 'chang dbang po*. The title *spyod 'chang* (*caryadhāra*) for Kṛṣṇavajra (Nag po rdo rje; a.k.a. Kṛṣṇācārya, Nag po spyod pa) occurs in Amitābha, *Commentary on Śrī Kṛṣṇavajra's Treasury of Couplets*, Dg.T. rgyud, *zhi* (Toh. 2302).
3. Two of these texts, the *Condensed Essence* and the *Ornament of Mahāmudrā*, are no longer extant.
4. This is an addition to the lineage.
5. Here the syllable *ai* is given, but as it contradicts the root text, which gives *oṃ*, it must be an error of transcription.
6. Here, upward (*kha gyen*) is mistakenly given for downward (*kha thur*).
7. This instruction is at a clear variance with the root text, which mentions that the fire entering the tathāgatas enters the right nostril or calf.

18. *Dharma Connection with the Six Gatekeepers*

1. *'Drog mi lo tsā bas mkhas pa sgo drug la gsan pa'i sgo drug chos 'brel du grags pa'i khrid yig*. *DNZ*, pp. 269–303. *mKhas pa sgo drug la rje 'drog mi chos 'brel du zhus pa'i gdams ngag* in Kunga Zangpo, *Red Volume*, pp. 394–410.
2. Jamgön Kongtrul, *Jonang: The One Hundred and Eight Teaching Manuals*, ch. 9, guidebooks 52–57.
3. Amezhap, *Ocean That Gathers Excellent Explanations*, p. 477.
4. Ratnākaraśānti, *Endowed with Purity*, Dg.T. shes phyin, *ta* (Toh. 380).
5. Ratnākaraśānti.
6. NOTE: The desire realm, form realm, and formless realm.
7. NOTE: Those are called "nondual" from the beginning, but become cherished as a self.
8. NOTE: Though they appear, they do not cling. They are illusory bodies.
9. *HT*, f. 2b, line 6.
10. NOTE: There are three realms because of lacking knowledge in profound dependent origination.
11. NOTE: Permanence.
12. NOTE: Grasping to annihilation.
13. NOTE: They are not established as truly existing natures.
14. NOTE: Escapes from samsara's three realms as well as śrāvakas and pratyekabuddhas.
15. *Collected Verses on the Noble Perfection of Wisdom*, Dg.K. shes rab sna tshogs, *ka* (Toh. 13), f. 2b, lines 3–4.
16. NOTE: The light rays shine upward, presenting offerings to the noble ones, and then enter their hearts. The light rays return and the blessing of the nondual gnosis of their minds enters oneself. The light rays shine downward, the universe is purified into a celestial mansion, and all its inhabitants are purified into gods and goddesses. This is also said to be the meaning of "When the three worlds are transformed."
17. NOTE: Meditate on the deity either briefly or extensively. All appearances and emptiness are the maṇḍala of the body, all clarity and emptiness is the maṇḍala of speech, and all bliss and emptiness is the maṇḍala of mind, which are called the gnosis vajra of body, speech, and mind. This is also said to be the meaning of the tantra. These statements by Śantipa are said to have been set down as annotations by Drokmi.
18. Here, *bsgoms* is given for *bsams*.
19. *ST*, f. 74a, line 3.
20. *Collected Verses on the Noble Perfection of Wisdom*, Dg.K. shes rab sna tshogs, *ka* (Toh. 13), f. 11b, lines 1–2.
21. Ibid., f. 5a, lines 1–2.
22. *HT*, f. 12a, line 2.
23. *HT*, f. 27a, line 7.

24. *Collected Verses on the Noble Perfection of Wisdom*, Dg.K. shes rab sna tshogs, *ka* (Toh. 13), f. 14a, line 1.
25. NOTE: This is the meaning of the passage from the *Mayajala*, "Vajra hūṃ proclaims hūṃ." TN: *Chanting the True Names of Mañjuśrī*, Dg.K. rgyud, *ka* (Toh. 360), f. 8, lines 6–7. Derge Kangyur reads "Vajra hūṃ has the form of *hūṃ*" (*rdo rje hūṃ mdzad hūṃ gi gzugs*). The form found here (*rdo rje hūṃ ste hūṃ zhes sgrogs*) is found in several commentaries on this tantra in the Tengyur.
26. NOTE: If one is residing in a dangerous place.
27. NOTE: Male, female, and nāga spirits.
28. NOTE: "The Vajra King has great bliss." TN: *Chanting the True Names of Mañjuśrī*, Dg.K. rgyud, *ka* (Toh. 360), f. 4b, line 6.
29. NOTE: It is said that all illnesses arise from the desire to engage in many activities, like the desire for the activity of vāyu and mind.
30. NOTE: According to how it is idealized.
31. This syllable is missing in *DNZ*.
32. NOTE: Retain.
33. NOTE: The *hūṃ* and the guru do not spin; the vajra and the bindu spin.
34. NOTE: [*Phyag*] is translated as "grasping" from the word, *bhuja*, but here it is "nature," and so on.
35. NOTE: Since it is taken from the term mudrā, it means "do not go beyond," "indivisible," and "pervasive."
36. NOTE: There is not even a speck of an object, and there is no duration for even the length of a finger snap.
37. Ngawang Lozang Gyatso identifies Se as Shen Gom Se (gShen sgom se) and Rog as Gyergom Rokpo (Gyer sgom rog po), both circa eleventh century (*Appendix of Reading Transmission Lineages*, p. 393).
38. gNyos, c. eleventh century.
39. Yer pa sgom seng, c. eleventh to twelfth centuries.
40. Grub thog lha 'bar, c. twelfth to thirteenth centuries.
41. Kha rag sgom pa c. twelfth century.
42. bLa ma Lung phu ba, Nam mkha' bsod nams, c. twelfth to thirteenth centuries.
43. bKra shis lung pa c. thirteenth century.
44. gZhon nu grub c. thirteenth century.
45. *HT*, f. 14b, line 3.
46. *HT*, f. 10b, line 5.
47. *HT*, f. 10b, line 5.
48. *HT*, f. 10b, lines 5–6.
49. *HT*, f. 6a, line 7.
50. NOTE: It is also considered good to visualize the eleven wrathful deities at the eight joints, the crown, the heart, and the rectum.
51. Buddhalocana is usually given as the consort of Ratnasambhava.
52. NOTE: Vajrarūpa, Vajraśabda, Vajraghande, Vajrarasa, and Vajrasparśa. As such, the gods of the physical organs are seated cross-legged on moon seats. As such,

there are one hundred eighty deities. All are empty forms of the dharmadhātu arising as deities, meditated on like reflections in a mirror.

53. Yaśabhadra, *Compendium*, Dg.T. rgyud, *pha* (Toh. 1390), f. 20b, line 5.
54. dKon mchog rgyal po, 1034–1102.
55. Bla ma shangs pa, another name for Khyung po rnal 'byor, 1050–1127.
56. Kun dga' snying po, 1092–1158.
57. Grags pa rgyal mtshan, 1147–1215.
58. Unidentified.
59. Zhon nu grub.
60. NOTE: Instantly meditate on oneself as the deity and meditate on the guru on the crown of one's head. Having generated devotion, the guru dissolves into the deity, and one focuses the mind on that.
61. *dKar nag mtshams* is a descriptive term for the area between the two nipples.
62. Reading *L*, *phrin las*, for *DNZ*, sangs rgyas.
63. Reading *L*, *rlung srog rtsol*, for *DNZ*, *lus srog rtsol*.
64. Reading *L*, *kun gzhi*, for *DNZ*, *kun gyis*.

19. Lineage Supplication of *Parting from the Four Attachments*

1. *Zhan pa bzhi bral gyi brgyud 'debs. DNZ* 6, pp. 305–7.
2. Ngorchen Kunga Zangpo.
3. Jampa Kunga Tenzin (Byams pa kun dga' bstan dzin), 1776–1862.
4. dPal ldan lhun grub steng, the principal Sakya monastery in Derge, Eastern Tibet.

20. *Cycle of Parting from the Four Attachments*

1. *bLo sbyongs zhan pa bzhi bral. DNZ* 6, pp. 309–56. *G* 23, pp. 495–535.
2. See Jamgön Kongtrul, *Jonang: The One Hundred and Eight Teaching Manuals*, ch. 9, guidebook 1.
3. *The Instruction on Parting from the Four Attachments*, pp. 605–10.
4. Kun dga' snying po.
5. bZang po'i thabs, the same posture in which Maitreya is typically depicted.
6. NOTE: This is the offering and the commitment to explain.
7. NOTE: The meaning of the passage in Vasubandhu's *Treasury of Abhidharma*, "Abiding in discipline, endowed with hearing and reflection, always applies oneself to meditation" [f. 18b, line 7] is covered up to here. This explicitly demonstrates the distinction between the true and the false. It also implicitly demonstrates the method of meditating on the difficulty of attaining human birth, the certainty of death, and impermanence.
8. NOTE: Having explicitly explained the faults of samsara, rejecting and accepting karma and its results are implicitly explained.

9. NOTE: After implicitly meditating on the cause (love and compassion), the result (exchanging self and other) is explicitly demonstrated.
10. NOTE: Having relinquished the view of permanence and annihilation, the general means of placing the mind in nondual union is explained.
11. NOTE: These stages are shared in common with the bodhisattva Cittamātra adherents. Next, the uncommon Mahāyāna Madhyamaka will be explained.
12. NOTE: Having implicitly explained the meditation of śamatha, here the method of meditating on vipaśyana, the meditation of union free from proliferation, is explicitly explained through establishing apparent objects as mind and confirming that the mind lacks inherent existence, is dependently originated, and is inexpressible.
13. Nub Rig 'dzin grags, c. thirteenth century.
14. Drakpa Gyaltsen.
15. Kun dga' snying po.
16. Kun dga' legs pa'i rin chen, c. fifteenth century, disciple of Ngorchen Kunga Zangpo.
17. Ba ri lo tsā ba Rin chen grags (1040–1112), the second Sakya throne holder.
18. bSod nams rtse mo.
19. This passage is missing in *DNZ* (p. 319) but is supplied in *G* (p. 495).
20. NOTE: To practice, adopt vajrāsana or whatever posture is comfortable, go for refuge, and generate bodhicitta as the preliminaries.
21. Śāntideva, *Introduction to the Conduct of Awakening*, Dg.T. dbu ma, *la* (Toh. 3871), f. 1a, line 5–f. 1b, line 1.
22. Ibid., f. 8b, lines 6–7.
23. NOTE: To briefly recount these, the eight lacks of freedoms to be avoided are "These eight who lack freedom/ are hell beings, pretas, animals,/ long-lived devas, barbarians,/ those with wrong view, those who live when a buddha is absent,/ and mutes" [Prajñākaramati, *Difficult Points*, f. 45b, lines 4–5]. The ten endowments are the five personal endowments, "Born human, born in a central country, with complete faculties/ without negative actions, and faith in the foundation [vinaya]" and the five external endowments, "The teacher has arrived, taught the dharma,/ the doctrine is present,/ there are followers of that doctrine,/ and sincere appreciation due to others." Thus, combined with the ten endowments, the difficulty of acquiring a human body that possesses the eighteen freedoms and endowments should be explained in accordance with one's own and others' intelligence. [These two verses are traditional verses, likely composed on the basis of Kṛṣṇa Paṇḍitā's *Difficult Points*, f. 291b, lines 2–4.]
24. Aśvaghoṣa, *Removing Misery*, Dg.T. spring yig, *nge* (Toh. 4177), f. 33a, line 2.
25. *Sutra of the Extensive Play*, Dg.K. mdo sde, *kha* (Toh. 95), f. 88a, line 2.
26. Aśvaghoṣa, *Removing Misery*, Dg.T. spring yig, *nge* (Toh. 4177), f. 33b, line 3.
27. *DNZ* gives *thog med 'gro*, while the Tengyur edition gives *rgyang ring 'gro*, "travel far away."

28. Ibid., f. 33b, line 2.
29. Nāgārjuna, *Necklace of Gems*, Dg.T. spring yig, *ge* (Toh. 4158), f. 117b, line 1.
30. *Possession of the Root of Virtue Sūtra*, Dg.K. mdo sde, *nga* (Toh. 101), f. 145b, line 4: "I have seen the faults here in the desire realm, I have likewise seen the faults of the form realm, and I have also seen the faults of the formless realm. I have seen that the peace of nirvana is without fault" (*bdag gyis 'dod 'pa'i khams ni 'dir skyon mthong ste/ de bzhin gzugs kyi khams skyon dang bcas par mthong/ gzugs med khams kyang skyon dang bcas par mthong/ bdag gyis mya ngan 'das pa zhi skyon med mthong*). This passage is rendered following *DNZ*: *'dod 'pa'i khams ni skyon dang bcas pa ste/ de bzhin gzugs kyi khams skyon dang bcas/ gzugs med khams kyang skyon dang bcas pa tse/ mya ngan 'das pa 'ba' zhig skyon med mthong*.
31. *Sutra of the Close Application of Mindfulness of the Sublime Dharma*, Dg.K. mdo sde, *ya* (Toh. 287), 285b, line 7–286a, line 1. In the text of the sutra, these realms are given in reverse order.
32. Vasubandhu, *Treasury of Abhidharma*, f. 10a, line 3.
33. Huhuva, Hahava, and Aṭaṭa are onomatopoeia. Only the last one is translatable. The first two are the sounds one makes when extremely cold.
34. Here, *mnye ma* is an archaic spelling for *gnye ma*.
35. Vasubandhu, *Treasury of Abhidharma*, Dg.T. mgon pa, *ku* (Toh. 4089), f. 9b, line 7–f. 10, line 3.
36. The passage has been rendered in gender neutral terms.
37. On f. 153a, line 5, the text reads, "The cause is bodhicitta. The root is great compassion. The ultimate is the method" (*rgyu ni byang chub sems so/ rtsa ba ni snying rje chen po'o/ mthar thug pa ni thabs so*).
38. Nāgārjuna, *Letter to a Friend*, Dg.T. spring yig, *nge* (Toh. 4182), f.43b, line 7.
39. Unidentified.
40. This citation is erroneously attributed to Candra.
41. Buddhaśrījñāna, *Introduction to the Victor's Path*, Dg.T. dbu ma, *gi* (Toh. 3964), f. 214a, line 7.
42. Maitreyanātha, *Ornament of Mahāyāna Sutras*, Dg.T. sems tsam, *phi* (Toh. 4020), f. 26b, line 7–f.27a, line 1. Here, the second line is presented as *de sdug bsngal las yang dag skye*. However, the Derge Tengyur version reads "Happy when there is suffering . . ." (*de sdug bsngal nab de ba yis*).
43. This citation is erroneously attributed to Candra.
44. Buddhaśrījñāna, *Introduction to the Victor's Path*, Dg.T. dbu ma, *gi* (Toh. 3964), f. 214a, line 7.
45. Maitreyanātha, *Ornament of Mahāyāna Sutras*, Dg.T. sems tsam, *phi* (Toh. 4020), f. 4b. line 3.
46. Bhūripa, *Extensive Daily Confession of Śṛī Cakrasaṃvara*, Dg.T. rgyud, *za* (Toh. 1533), f. 95a, line 4.
47. Śāntideva, *Introduction to the Conduct of Awakening*, Dg.T. dbu ma, *la* (Toh. 3871), f. 23b, lines 1–2.

48. Following G, *sgra'i klag* co; for *DNZ, dgra'i gtsor glag*.
49. Maitreyanātha, *Ornament of Mahāyāna Sutras*, Dg.T. sems tsam, *phi* (Toh. 4042), f. 229a, lines 3–4.
50. gNas brtan Byang chub Bzang po, c. thirteenth century. He was a disciple of Chögyal Phakpa. None of his works have survived.
51. *Samādhirāja Sutra*, Dg.K. mdo sde, *da* (Toh. 127), f. 26b, line 1.
52. Nāgārjuna, *Sixty Verses*, Dg.T. dbu ma, *tsa* (Toh. 3825), f.22b, lines 3–4.
53. NOTE: In the future, it would be good to clearly write the sources of the citations.
54. Ngag dbang legs grub (b. 1811).
55. For a translation of this work, see Sakya Trizin, *Freeing the Heart and Mind*, 137.
56. bSod nam Seng ge (1429–1489), a famous Sakyapa madhyamaka scholar and the sixth abbot of Ngor Monastery. For a translation of this work, see Sakya Trizin, *Freeing the Heart and Mind*, 141.
57. Nam mkha' dPal bzang (1611–1672), the twenty-third abbot of Ngor Monastery. This work seems to be lost.
58. This verse dedication is taken from Nāgārjuna, *Sixty Verses*, Dg.T. dbu ma, *tsa* (Toh. 3825), f. 22b, lines 3–4.
59. This mantra is found in the *Inquiry of Sāgaramati Sūtra*, Dg.K. mdo sde, *pha* (Toh. 152), f. 111b, lines 1–3. [*tadyathā*] *śame śamavati śamitaśatru aṃkure maṃkure mārajite karāṭe keyūre tejovati ohokamati viśaṭha nirmalé malāvanaye okhare okharā grase khayāgrase grasate temukhī paramukhi amukhi śamitāni sarvagrahabhandhanāni nigraṃhiha sarvaparapravadina vimuktāmārapāśā sthāpitābuddhamudrā samudaghatitāḥ sarvamārā sucaritapadapariśuddhya gacchantu sarvamārakarmaṇi.*
60. This traditional Sakya verse is taken from Lodrö Gyaltsen, *Homage and Offering to the Lineage of the Path with Its Result, SKB* 13, p. 80, lines 7–8. It is provided here in full because the opening, "*rdzogs pa'i byang chub* . . ." ("Full awakening . . ."), is not readily recognizable to the average western Buddhist reader.
61. Lodrö Gyaltsen, *Offering the Maṇḍala and Supplication to the Guru*. This part of the text is typically known as the *Gang gi mchod rdzas ma*.
62. Lodrö Gyaltsen, *Homage and Offering to the Lineage of the Path with Its Result*. This is the traditional conclusion of the maṇḍala offering.
63. Reading *Garland of Incarnations, btud*, for *tu*.
64. Āryaśūra, *Garland of Incarnations*, Dg.T. skyes rab, *hu* (Toh. 4150), f. 125a, lines 1–2.
65. *Inconceivable Secret Sutra*, Dg.K. dkon brtsegs, *ka* (Toh. 47), f. 119a, line 7–f. 119b, line 1. The version given here is a common alternate translation.
66. This is stock phrase found in many sutras.
67. Vasubandhu, *Pedagogical Strategies*, Dg.T. sems tsam, *shi* (Toh. 4061), f. 65b, line 4.
68. Beginning on p. 313.
69. Prajñākaramati, *Difficult Points*, Dg.T. dbu ma, *la* (Toh. 3872), f. 45b, lines 4–5.

70. This verse and the following verse concerning the five external endowments are traditional verses, likely composed on the basis of Kṛṣṇa Paṇḍitā's *Difficult Points*, f. 291b, lines 2–4.
71. Śāntideva, *Compendium of Training*, Dg.T. dbu ma, *khi* (Toh. 3940), 3b, line 3.
72. This terminology of light and dark eons seems to be a Tibetan idiom. The names of the eons in which there is the advent of a buddha are taken from the concluding portion of the *Fortunate Eon Sūtra*, ff. 338b–339b. However, the number of eons given between each so-called light eon is quite different, and the order of the names of the light eons is also different. To paraphrase, following this Fortunate Eon, sixty-five eons pass where no buddha arrives. Then there is an eon called "Great Fame." After that, eighty eons pass in which no buddhas arrive. Then there is an eon called "Starlike." After that, three hundred eons pass in which no buddhas arrive. Then there is an eon called "Array of Qualities." So here, the number of dark eons is four hundred forty-five.
73. *Sūtra of Extensive Play*, Dg.K. mdo sde, *kha* (Toh. 95), 187b, lines 5–6.
74. *Na ya*, for Skt. Naya (Tshul)
75. Āryaśūra, *Garland of Incarnations*, Dg.T. skyes rab, *hu* (Toh. 4150), f. 29, lines 5–6.
76. Asaṅga, *Explanation of the Unsurpassed Continuum*, Dg.T. sems tsam, *phi* (Toh. 4025), f. 129, line 6.
77. Lodrö Gyaltsen, *Jeweled Rosary*, *SKB* 13, p. 236, lines 4–5.
78. *Aspiration of the Conduct of Samantabhadra*, Dk.K. gzungs 'dus, *waM* (Toh. 1095), f. 264a, lines 4–5.
79. *Maṅgalaśrījvālajambudvīpamaṇḍantu.*

21. Increasing the Two Accumulations

1. Kun dga' chos 'phel.
2. Drinking water and foot-washing water.
3. These (*sngon 'gro nyer spyod*) are the offerings of flowers, incense, light, scent, and food traditionally offered to welcome a guest to an Indian household after they have been presented with water for drinking and water for washing their feet before entering a house.
4. This paragraph is drawn from the opening of Lodrö Gyaltsen, *Homage and Offering to the Lineage of the Path with Its Result*, p. 72.
5. This verse is attributed to the Mahāsiddha Darikpa, who appended it to the opening of the *Continuous Practice of Yoginī*, Dg.K. rgyud, *ga* (Toh. 375), f. 34a, lines 1–2.
6. These verses are extracted from Sakya Paṇḍita Kunga Gyaltsen, *Uncommon Supplication*, pp. 401–3.
7. These verses are extracted from Sakya Paṇḍita Kunga Gyaltsen, *Common Supplication*, pp. 400–401.
8. Drokmi Lotsāwa.

9. dPal chen 'od po (1150–1203), the youngest son of Kunga Nyingpo and Sakya Paṇḍita's father.
10. Sakya Paṇḍita's personal name.
11. Sakya Paṇḍita Kunga Gyaltsen Palzangpo (Kun dga' rgyal mtshan dpal bzang po, 1182–1251).
12. Jo gdan pa bSod nams rgyal mtshan, thirteenth century.
13. Beginning from "Homage to all gurus . . ." to this line, the text is taken from Lodrö Gyaltsen, *Homage and Offering*, pp. 71–80.
14. This verse incorporates the ordination name of Chögyal Phakpa, Lodrö Gyaltsen Palzangpo (bLo 'gros rgyal mtshan dpal bzang po). The rest of these verses, likewise, incorporate the names of their subjects.
15. Zhangtön Könchok Pal (Zhang ston dKon mchog dpal, d. 1317).
16. Trakphukpa Sönam Pal (bSod nams dpal, 1277–1346).
17. Sönam Gyaltsen (bSod nams rgyal mtshan, 1312–1375), the fourteenth Sakya throne holder.
18. Palden Tsultrim (dPal ldan tshul khrims, 1333–1399).
19. Sharchen Yeshe Gyaltsen (Shar chen Ye shes rgyal mtshan, 1359–1406), one of the two main students of Palden Tsultrim.
20. Ngorchen Kunga Zangpo (Ngor chen Kun dga' bzang po, 1382–1456), the founder of Ngor monastery.
21. Könchok Gyaltsen (dKon mchog rgyal mtshan, 1388–1469/70), Ngor mkhan chen 2.
22. Jamyang Sherap Gyatso ('Jam dbyangs shes rab rgya mtsho, 1396–1474), Ngor mkhan chen 3.
23. Kunga Wangchuk (Kun dga' dbang phyug, 1424–1478), Ngor mkhan chen 4.
24. Palden Dorje (dPal ldan rdo rje, 1411–1482), Ngor mkhan chen 5.
25. Gorampa Sönam Senge (Go rams pa bSod nams seng ge, 1429–1489), Ngor mkhan chen 6.
26. Könchok Phelwa (dKon mchog 'phel ba, 1445–1514), Ngor mkhan chen 7.
27. Sangye Rinchen (Sangs rgyas rin chen, 1450–1524), Ngor mkhan chen 8.
28. Lhachok Senge (Lha mchog seng ge, 1468–1535), Ngor mkhan chen 9.
29. Könchok Lhundrup (dKon mchog lhun grub, 1497–1557), Ngor mkhan chen 10.
30. Sangye Senge (Sangs rgyas seng ge, 1504–1569), Ngor mkhan chen 11.
31. Könchok Palden (dKon mchog dpal ldan, 1526–1590), Ngor mkhan chen 12.
32. Namkha Palzang (Nam kha' dpal bzang, 1532–1602), Ngor mkhan chen 13.
33. Jampa Kunga Tashi (Byams pa kun dga' bkra shis, 1558–1603), Ngor mkhan chen 14.
34. Kunga Sönam Lhundrup (Kun dga' bsod nams lhun grub, 1571–1642), Ngor mkhan chen 15.
35. Palden Döndrup (dPal lda don grub, 1571–1642), Ngor mkhan chen 16.
36. Namkha Sangye (Nam mkha' sangs rgyas, 1500–1599), Ngor mkhan chen 17.
37. Sherap Jungne (Shes rab 'byung gnas, 1596–1663), Ngor mkhan chen 18.

38. Namkha Rinchen (Nam mkha' rin chen, 1612–1669), Ngor mkhan chen 19.
39. Sönam Gyatso (bSod nams rgya mtsho, 1617–1667), Ngor mkhan chen 21.
40. Palchok Gyaltsan (dPal mchog rgyal mtshan, 1599–1673), Ngor mkhan chen 22.
41. Namkha Palzang (Nam mkha' dpal bzang, 1611–1672), Ngor mkhan chen 23.
42. Lhundrup Palden (Lhun grub dpal ldan, 1624–1697), Ngor mkhan chen 24.
43. Sangye Phuntsok (Sangs gyas phun mtshog, 1649–1705), Ngor mkhan chen 25.
44. Sangye Tenzin (Sangs rgyas bstan 'dzin, 1667–1697), Ngor mkhan chen 26.
45. Sherap Zangpo (Shes rab bzang po, 1661–1714), Ngor mkhan chen 27.
46. Jampa Tsultrim Palzang (Byams pa tshul khrims dpal bzang, 1675–1710), Ngor mkhan chen 28.
47. Sönam Palden (bSod nams dpal ldan, 1669–1713), Ngor mkhan chen 29.
48. Jampa Sönam Zangpo (Byams pa bsod nams bzang po, 1689–1749), Ngor mkhan chen 30.
49. Tashi Lhundrup (bKra shis lhun grub, 1672–1739), Ngor mkhan chen 31.
50. Tsultrim Lhundrup (Tsul khrims lhun grub, 1676–1730), Ngor mkhan chen 32.
51. With this verse, citation resumes at p. 75, line 2 of Lodrö Gyaltsen, *Homage and Offering*, pp. 71–80.
52. This concludes the citation of Lodrö Gyaltsen, *Homage and Offering*, pp. 71–80.
53. From "all this abundant wealth . . . to the stage of the two kāyas."
54. This refers to Vajradhara.
55. This refers to arhats, and the enemy is the afflictions.
56. The source for the thirty-seven-heap maṇḍala and the concluding prayer, commonly known in the Sakya tradition as *Gang gi mchod rdzas ma*, is Lodrö Gyaltsen, *Offering the Maṇḍala*, in *SKB* 13, pp. 389–91.
57. These three and a half verses are adapted from Lodrö Gyaltsen, *Homage and Offering*, p. 76.
58. This verse contains the name of Kunga Gyaltsen Palzangpo, Sakya Paṇḍita.
59. This verse is based on Chögyal Phakpa's first name, Lodrö (bLo 'gros). The next verse is based on his second name, Gyaltsen (rGyal mtshan). The third verse after this is based on the first part of his last name, Pal (dPal). The fourth verse is based on the second part of his last name, Zangpo (bZang po).
60. Here, *rtogs pa dag pa khyad par can* is a variant reading of *rtogs pa dge ba* in Lodrö Gyaltsen, *Uncommon Supplication to the Root Guru*, p. 123, line 2.
61. This bulk of the supplication is taken from Lodrö Gyaltsen's *Uncommon Supplication to the Root Guru*, pp. 71–80.
62. This set of verses is found in Lodrö Gyaltsen, *Ocean of Hearing*, p. 108.
63. Ngorchen Kunga Zangpo.

22. Procedure for Preparing Barley Liquor

1. *dPal bde mchog sdom 'byung nas kyi chang gi cho ga*. *DNZ* 6, pp. 387–401.
2. Chos rje srad pa kun dga' blo gros (b. 1433/34).

3. *Source of Needs and Wants*, p. 506.
4. Reading *bzhi* as *gzhi*.
5. *bCud len*, medicinal substances for restoring youth and enhancing longevity.
6. Kunga Zangpo, *Letter to Benefit Disciples*. This text sets out to explain the faults of enjoying liquor, the faults of making a livelihood from eating meat, and the manner in which meat and liquor are rejected in Secret Mantra.
7. *bcos pa'i chang*.
8. *Saṃvarodaya Tantra*, Dg.K. rgyud, *kha* (Toh. 373), f. 274a, line 4.
9. Ibid., f. 274b, line 6.
10. *rigs ldan ma*.
11. Ibid., f. 282b, line 3.
12. Ibid., f. 282b, line 1.
13. Ibid., f. 297b, line 4.
14. Ibid., f. 307b, lines 6–7.
15. Ibid., f. 309a, line 5.
16. Ibid., f. 298b, line 4.
17. Ibid., f. 300b, lines 3–4. This passage is somewhat corrupted in the text, so I am following the passage as it is given in the Dg.K. edition.
18. Ibid., f. 298b, lines 4–7.
19. *Phyllanthus emblica* (*skyu ru ra*).
20. The author miscounted the number of lines, identifying them as ten.
21. Ratnarakṣita's *Padminī* (Dk.T, rgyud, *wa* [Toh. 1420], f. 84a, line 5) specifies that "substance" (*rdzas*) refers to *Phyllanthus emblica*, and "roots" (*rtsa ba*) refers to different kinds of medicines. "Trees" refers to mango, and so on.
22. Skt. *paiṣṭa*, no Tibetan equivalent is given.
23. Skt. *mādhavī*, no Tibetan equivalent is given.
24. *Saṃvarodaya Tantra*, Dg.K. rgyud, *kha* (Toh. 373), f. 299a, line 6–f. 299b, line 1. This passage is given here in full.
25. Ayurveda and Tibetan medicine commonly measure amounts by volume rather than weight. As the term *sho* is used for both weight and volume measurement, and since it is not clear what volume measurements this term refers to, it is being left in Tibetan transliteration.
26. *Moringa oleifera*, common names include drumstick tree, and so on.
27. Ibid, f. 299b, line 2–f. 300a, line 3.
28. *Woodfordia fruticosa*.
29. The margin note for this liquor states, "*Dhātaki*, a tree that grows red flowers, is definitely needed for this liquor, and has a sweet, excellent scent."
30. *Cinnamomum cassia*.
31. *khara* from *śarkaraka*.
32. The margin note for this substance questions if *śigru* is black pepper.
33. Ratnarakṣita's *Padminī* (f. 84a, line 5) indicates that *śobhañjana* is an alternate name for *śigru*. However, the margin note identifies this as so-called white pepper (*na le sham dkar po*). Gawe Dorje's *Stainless Crystal Mirror* (p. 137) identi-

fies "white pepper" as black pepper that has had its rind removed by soaking in water.

34. Reading *klu ma rnams* as *glum rnams*.
35. *Saṃvarodaya Tantra*, Dg.K. rgyud, *kha* (Toh. 373), f. 300a, lines 2–3.
36. Ratnarakṣita, *Padminī*, f. 84b, line 3.
37. *phabs*.
38. *Saṃvarodaya Tantra*, Dg.K. rgyud, *kha* (Toh. 373), f. 299b, line 1. The text erroneously gives Ananta rather than Nanda. This also renders suspect the mantra provided above. It originally must have been *oṃ aḥ vajra nandaya hūṃ svāha*.
39. Ratnarakṣita, *Padminī* (f. 83a, line 3–f. 83b, line 3) provides a detailed and interesting commentary on this passage: "'Mandāra' and the 'Ocean of Milk' (*kṣirasāgara*) are examples based on what is widely known in the world. These are other conventions for the gnosis vajra and the space dhātu. There are seven reasons for 'amṛta.' 'Emitted [reading *byung* as *phyung*] from Mandāra' is falling from Mandāra. 'All' means all. 'Becomes the river' refers to the five rivers. 'Flows through the center' refers to the one that flows through the middle, meaning the Ganges. The 'Ocean of Milk' is explained to be outside these. 'Imbibe the moon' has the nature of imbibing the moon. 'Form' (*sku*) refers to the Bhagavāti Vajravārāhi, who exists in the body (*lus*). If it is asked how she exists there, it is said the meaning is that she exists in the embrace of Bhagavān Heruka, melted through great passion. 'All heroes,' and so on, refer to 'all become one,' that is, inanimate and animate entities. 'All becomes one' also refers to all the nāḍīs. 'Amṛta' is freedom (*mokṣa*), the nature of which is connate joy. Since the Bhagavāti has no fear of the māras of affliction, and so on, she has a 'fearsome female form.' The liquor goddess has the form of liquor through the great joy generated by the bodhicitta that melts through the nature of great bliss (spreading through all the nāḍīs via the path of the avadhūti through their [Heruka and Vajravārāhī's] crowns) and through the Bhagavatī herself. Some say, "When the stream of white bindu descends in the day and the night, that is not liquor but rather Māmaki. Also, here it is not different from [*HT*, f. 10b, line 2:] 'The form of the semen is the Bhagavān./ The one who desires that bliss is called the mother.' Therefore, because of being bliss, in some tantras the nature of the bhagavān is explained as bliss and bodhicitta. In some contexts, bliss signifies the male; in others, the female; and when strictly looking at bliss alone, it is explained to be genderless. 'Plunders' refers to suffering. 'Acts' refers to rejoicing. 'Enjoys' refers to the nature of great bliss that is merely a mind that arises from the nature of the mind. Thus, 'therefore, it is the essential amṛta.' However, amṛta exists relatively in the body. It is also explained to exist externally, hence the mention of the hearth, and so on."
40. In this context, a female name.
41. Ibid., f. 298b, lines 1–3.
42. Ibid., f. 288a, line 5–f. 288b, line 1.
43. Ibid., f. 299b, lines 1–2.

44. Ibid., f. 299a, line 7.
45. Ibid., f. 300a, line 4.
46. Reading *phyun po* as an erroneous transcription of *chun po*.
47. Ratnarakṣita, *Padminī*, f. 84b, line 7–f. 85a, line 5.
48. Kunga Zangpo, *Play of Samantabhadra*.
49. *Saṃvarodaya Tantra*, Dg.K. rgyud, *kha* (Toh. 373), 298b7–299a1.
50. Ibid., f. 299a, lines 1–2.
51. Ibid., f. 299a, line 2.
52. Ibid.
53. Ratnarakṣita, *Padminī*, 83a6–84a3.
54. *Laghusaṃvara*, p. 4, line 3. This citation is taken from the *Laghusaṃvara* translation of Mal Lotsāwa Lodrö Drakpa (bLo 'gros grags pa), the recension regarded in the Sakya school as the most authoritative.
55. *Saṃvarodaya Tantra*, Dg.K. rgyud, *kha* (Toh. 373), f. 299a, lines 4–5.
56. *'dus pa*, Skt. *gaṇa*.
57. Ibid., f. 299a, lines 5–6.
58. Ibid., f. 298b, lines 3–4.
59. Ibid., f. 300a, line 3.
60. Ibid., f. 299a, lines 3–4.
61. Ibid., f. 299a, line 6.
62. Sangs rgyas dpal, dates unknown.

23. Blazing Brilliance and Strength

1. *dPal nag po chen po gur mgon lha brgyad kyi sgrub thabs rjes gnang dang bcas pa gzi brjid stobs 'bar. DNZ* 6, pp. 403–24.
2. *Ma mo*.
3. The source of this verse is Śraddhākaravarman, *Medium Rite*, Dg.T. rgyud, *tshu* (Toh. 3774).
4. These three verses are taken from Vararuci, *Mahākāla Sadhana*, Nar.T., rgyud 'grel, *zhu* (N 3688), f. 261a, line 7–f. 261b, line 1.
5. Taken from Lodrö Gyaltsen, *Bali Rite to the Siblings*, p. 148.
6. For this bali offering, see Jamgön Kongtrul, *Sakya: The Path with Its Result, Part One*, 183.
7. For the text of the daily confession, see Jamgön Kongtrul, *Sakya: The Path with Its Result, Part One*, 154.
8. Ibid., 154–55.
9. *Gangs can mtsho*, translated here as *sāgara*, is a common misspelling of *gang chen mtsho*, an alternate translation for the term *sāgara*, *rgya mtsho*. This equivalent may be found in Śūra's *Commentary on the Sūtra of Personal Liberation* (Dg.T. 'dul ba, *du* [Toh. 4104], 8a, line 4) as well as in Dānaśila's *Recalling the Verses of Personal Liberation* (Dg.T. 'dul ba, *mu* [Toh. 4109], f. 167a, line 7).
10. These mantras have been omitted.

11. Nor bu gling pa.
12. Rin chen bzang po, 958–1055.
13. bLo gros grags pa, c. eleventh century.
14. Kun dga' grags pa, 1230–1303.

Bibliography

1. The Present Texts

The Source Volume

Jamgön Kongtrul Lodrö Taye, comp. *The Treasury of Precious Instructions. gDams ngag rin po che'i mdzod.* vol. 6 (*cha*). Delhi: Shechen Publications, 1999. dnz.tsadra.org. BDRC W23605.

The Translated Texts

Drakpa Gyaltsen. *Ācārya Padmavajra's "Creation Stage Adorned with the Nine Profound Methods." sLob dpon pad ma ba dzra gyis mdzad pa'i bskyed rim zab pa'i tshul dgu brgyan pa. DNZ* 6, pp. 19–38; Second source: *P*, pp. 419–41.

———. *"Accomplishment of the Connate" Composed by Ḍombi Heruka. Ḍombi he ru ka mdzad pa'i lhan gcig skyes. DNZ* 6, pp. 8–17; Second source: *P*, pp. 387–400.

———. *"Completing the Whole Path with Caṇḍālī" Composed by Ācārya Kṛṣṇācārya. sLob dpon nag po spyod pas mdzad pa'i gtum mo lam rdzogs. DNZ* 6, 43–53; Second source: *P*, 445–57.

———. *Instruction for "Straightening the Crooked" by Kṛṣṇa Acyuta. Nag po u tsi ta 'chi ba med pas mdzad pa yon po srong ba'i gdams pa. DNZ* 6, pp. 55–57; Second source: *P*, pp. 457–61.

———. *"Mahāmudrā without Syllables" Composed by Ācārya Vāgīśvarakīrti. sLob dpon ngag dbang grags pas mdzad pa'i phyag rgya chen po yi ge med pa. DNZ* 6, pp. 67–79; Second source: *P*, pp. 406–19.

———. *"Obtained in Front of a Stupa" Composed by Ācārya Nāgārjuna. Lop dpon klu sgrub gyis mdzad pa'i mchod rten drung du thob. DNZ* 6, pp. 59–65; Second source: *P*, pp. 400–406.

———. *"The Path Cycle of the Mudra" Composed by Ācārya Indrabhūti. sLob dpon indra bhūti'i mdzad pa'i phyag lam skor. DNZ* 6, pp. 119–36; Second source: *P*, pp. 461–79.

———. *Śrī Koṭalipa's "Instruction on the Inconceivable." dPal tog tse ba'i bsam mi khyab kyi gdams ngag. DNZ* 6, pp. 81–118; Second source: *P*, pp. 347–95.

Jamgön Kongtrul ('Jam mgon kong sprul). *Blazing Brilliance and Strength: The*

Sādhana and Permission of the Eight-Deities of Śrī Vajramahākāla Pañjaranātha. dPal nag po chen po gur mgon lha brgyad kyi sgrub thabs rjes gnang dang bcas pa gzi brjid stobs 'bar. *DNZ* 6, pp. 403–24.

———. *Essence of Fortunate Curd: The Manual of "Straightening the Crooked" by Kṛṣṇa Acyuta. Nag po u tsi ṭa 'chi ba med pa'i yon po srong ba'i khri yig bkra shis zho'i snying po*. *DNZ* 6, pp. 181–88; Second source: *L* 20, pp. 367–74.

———. *Excellent Tree of Fortunate Bilva: Ārya Nāgārjuna's Manual "Obtained in Front of a Stupa." 'Phags pa klu sgrub kyi mchod rten drung thob kyi khrid yig bkra shis bi lva'i ljong bzang*. *DNZ* 6, pp. 189–212; Second source: *L*, pp. 374–97

———. *Fortunate Mustard Seedpod: The Manual of the "Nine Profound Methods" of Padmavajra. Pad ma badzra'i zab pa'i tshul dgu'i khrid yig bkra shis yungs kar gong bu*. *DNZ* 6, pp. 151–80; Second source: *L*, pp. 301–32.

———. *Fortunate Pure Crystal Mirror: The Instruction Manual of Śrī Koṭalipa's "Inconceivable." Tog rtse pa'i bsam gyis mi khyab pa'i khrid yig bkra shis dvangs shel med long*. *DNZ* 6, pp. 231–54; Second source: *L*, pp. 263–87.

———. *Fortunate Right-Turning White Conch*: *The Manual of Indrabhūti's "Path of the Mudra." Indra bhū ti'i phyag rgya'i lam khrid yig bkra shis dkar gyas 'khyil*. *DNZ* 6, pp. 255–69; Second source: *L*, pp. 333–50

———. *Fortunate Shoot of Dūrva Grass: The Manual of "Mahāmudrā without Syllables" Composed by Ācārya Vāgīśvarakīrti. Ngag dbang grags pa'i phyag rgya chen po yi ge med pa'i khrid yig bkra shis dūrva'i myu gu*. *DNZ* 6, pp. 213–229; Second source: *L*, 397–415.

———. *Fortunate Vermillion Ornament: Kṛṣṇācārya's Manual of "Completing the Whole Path with Caṇḍālī." Nag po pa'i gtum mo lam rdzogs kyi khrid yig bkra shis li khri'i thig le*. *DNZ* 6, pp. 271–87; Second source: *L*, 350–67.

———. *Medicinal Elixir of the Fortunate Bezoar: The Manual of Ḍombi Heruka's "Accomplishing the Connate." Ḍom bi he ru ka'i lhan cig skye grub kyi khrid yig bkra shis gi vaṃ sman bcud*; *DNZ* 6, pp. 137–50; Second source: *L*, pp. 286–301.

Kunga Chöphel (Kun dga' chos 'phel). *Increasing the Two Accumulations: A Systematic Arrangement of the Offering Rite to the Gurus of the Path with Its Result. Lam 'bras bla ma mchod pa'i cho ga khrigs chags su bkod pa tshogs gnyis rab rgyas*. *DNZ* 6, pp. 357–86.

Kunga Lodrö (Kun dga' blo gros). *Procedure for Preparing Barley Liquor from the "Śrī Samvarodaya Tantra." dPal bde mchog sdom 'byung nas kyi chang gi cho ga*. *DNZ* 6, pp. 387–401.

Kunga Nyingpo (Kun dga' snying po), et al. *The Mind Training Titled "The Cycle of Parting from the Four Attachments." bLo sbyong zhen pa bzhi bral gyi skor*. *DNZ* 6, pp. 309–56. Second source: *G*, vol. 23, pp. 481–535. Delhi: N. Lungtok & N. Gyaltsan, 1971–1972.

Kunga Zangpo (Kung dga' bZang po). *Lineage Supplication of "Parting from the Four Attachments." Zhan pa bzhi bral gyi brgyud 'debs*. *DNZ* 6, pp. 305–7.

———. *Supplication to the Lineage of the Eight Ancillary Path Cycles. Lam skor phyi ma brgyad kyi brgyud pa'i gsol 'debs ngor chen kun dga' bzang po mdzad pa. DNZ* 6, pp. 1–6.

Padmavajra. *Ācārya Padmavajra's "Completion Stage Instruction Resembling the Tip of a Lamp Flame." sLob dpon pad ma ba dzra mdzad pa'i rdzogs rim mar me'i rtse mo lta bu'i gdams ngag. DNZ* 6, pp. 38–41; Second source: *P*, pp. 441–45.

Zhönu Drup (gZhon nu grub), et. al. *The Manual Known as "The Dharma Connection with the Six Gatekeepers" Received by Drokmi Lotsāwa from the Six Paṇḍita Gatekeepers. 'Drog mi lo tsā bas mkhas pa sgo drug la gsan pa'i sgo drug chos 'brel du grags pa'i khrid yig. DNZ* 6, pp. 269–303; Second source: *mKhas pa sgo drug la rje 'drog mi chos 'brel du zhus pa'i gdams ngag.* In Kunga Zangpo, *Little Red Volume*, pp. 394–410.

2. Works Cited in the Texts

Kangyur (Scriptures)

Ākāśagarbha Sutra. Āryākāśagarbhanāmamahāyānasūtra. 'Phags pa nam mkha'i snying po zhes bya ba theg pa chen po'i mdo. Dg.K. mdo sde, *za* (Toh. 260).

Ancillary Tantra. rGyud phyi ma. Dg.K. rgyud, *ca* (Toh. 443).

Aspiration of the Conduct of Samantabhadra. Āryabhadracaryāpraṇidhānarāja. 'Phags pa bzang po spyod pa'i smon lam gyi rgyal po. Dg.K. gzungs 'dus, *waM* (Toh. 1095).

Caturpitha Tantra. Śrīcaturpīṭhavikhyātatantrarājanāma. Dpal gdan bzhi pa'i rnam par bshad pa'i rgyud kyi rgyal po zhes bya ba. Dg.K. rgyud, *nga* (Toh. 430).

Chanting the True Names of Mañjuśrī. Mañjuśrījñānasattvasyaparamārthanāmasaṃgīti. 'Jam dpal ye shes sems dpa'i don dam pa'i mtshan yang dag par brjod pa. Dg.K. rgyud, *ka* (Toh. 360).

Collected Verses on the Noble Perfection of Wisdom. Āryaprajñāpāramitāsañcayagāthā. 'Phags pa shes rab kyi pha rol tu phyin pa sdud pa tshigs su bcad pa. Dg.K. shes rab sna tshogs, *ka* (Toh. 13).

Compendium of the Gnosis Vajra. Śrījñānavajrasamuccaya. dPal ye shes rdo rje kun las bsdus pa. Dg.K. rgyud, *cha* (Toh. 450).

Continuous Practice of Yoginī. Yoginīsañcārya. rNal 'byor ma'i kun tu spyod pa. Dg.K. rgyud, *ga* (Toh. 375)

Direct Awakening of Mahāvairocana. Mahāvairocanābhisambodhivikurvatīadhiṣṭhānavaipulyasūtraindrarājānāmadharmaparyāya. rNam par snang mdzad chen po mngon par rdzogs par byang chub pa rnam par sprul pa byin gyis rlob pa shin tu rgyas pa mdo sde'i dbang po'i rgyal po zhes bya ba'i chos kyi rnam grangs. Dg.K. rgyud, *tha* (Toh. 494).

Essence of Gnosis Tantra. Śrījñānagarbhanāmayoginīmahātantrarājayatirāja. dPal ye shes snying po zhes bya ba rnal 'byor ma chen mo'i rgyud kyi rgyal po'i rgyal po. Dg.K. rgyud, *nga* (Toh. 421).

Fortunate Eon Sutra. Āryabhadrakalpikanāmamahāyānasūtra. 'Phags pa bskal pa bzang po pa zhes bya ba theg pa chen po'i mdo. Dg.K. mdo sde, *ka* (Toh. 94)

Garland of Vajras Tantra. Śrīvajramālābhidhānamahāyogatantrasarvatantrahridayarahasyavibhaṅgaiti. rNal 'byor chen po'i rgyud dpal rdo rje 'phreng ba mngon par brjod pa rgyud thams cad kyi snying po gsang ba rnam par phye ba. Dg.K. rgyud, *ca* (Toh. 445).

Great Illusion Tantra. Māyājālamahātantrarājanāma. rGyud kyi rgyal po chen po sgyu 'phrul dra ba zhes bya ba. Dg.K. rgyud, *ja* (Toh. 466).

Guhyagarbha Tantra. Śrīguhyagarbhatattvaviniścaya. gSang ba'i snying po de kho na nyid rnam par nges pa. Dg.K. rnying rgyud, *kha* (Toh. 832).

Guhyasamāja. Sarvatathāgatakāyavākcittarahasyoguhyasamājanāmamahākalparāja. De bzhin gshegs pa thams cad kyi sku gsung thugs kyi gsang chen gsang ba 'dus pa zhes bya ba brtag pa'i rgyal po chen po. Dg.K. rgyud, *ca* (Toh. 442).

Heart of the Perfection of Wisdom Sutra. Bhagavatīprajñāpāramitāhṛdaya. bCom ldan 'das ma shes rab kyi pha rol tu phyin pa'i snying po. Dg.K. shes rab sna tshogs, *ka* (Toh. 21).

Hevajra Tantra. Hevajratantrarājanāma. Kye'i rdo rje zhes bya ba rgyud kyi rgyal po. Dg.K. rgyud, *nga* (Toh. 417, 418).

Host of Buddhas Sutra. Buddhāvataṃsakanāmamahāvaipūlyasūtra. Sangs rgyas phal po che zhes bya ba shin tu rgyas pa chen po'i mdo. Dg.K. phal chen, *ka*, *kha*, *ga*, *a* (Toh. 44).

Inconceivable Secret Sutra. Āryatathāgatācintyaguhyanirdeśanāmamahāyānasūtra. 'Phags pa de bzhin gshegs pa'i gsang ba bsam gyis mi khyab pa bstan pa zhes bya ba theg pa chen po'i mdo. Dg.K. dkon brtsegs, *ka* (Toh. 47).

Inquiry of Ratnacūḍa Sutra. Āryaratnacūḍaparipṛcchānāmamahāyānasūtra. 'Phags pa gtsug na rin po ches zhus pa zhes bya ba theg pa chen po'i mdo. Dg.K. dkon brtsegs, *cha* (Toh. 91).

Inquiry of Sāgaramati Sutra. Āryasāgaramatiparipṛcchānāmamahāyānasūtra. 'Phags pa blo gros rgya mtshos zhus pa zhes bya ba theg pa chen po'i mdo. Dg.K. mdo sde, *pha* (Toh. 152).

Laghusavara Tantra. Tantrarājaśrīlaghusamvaranama. Ma'i ma bla na med pa rnal 'byor gsang mtha'i rgyud kyi rgyal po bde mchog nyung ngu. In rGyud sde khag gcig phyogs bsgrigs 2:7–93. Kathmandu: Sachen International, 2000. BDRC W1KG17191.

Nondual Uniformity Tantra. Śrīsarvatathāgataguhyatantrayogamahārājadvayasamatāvijayanāmavajraśrīparamamahākalpādi. dPal de bzhin gshegs pa thams cad kyi gsang ba rnal 'byor chen po rnam par rgyal ba zhes bya ba mnyam pa nyid gnyis su med pa'i rgyud kyi rgyal po rdo rje dpal mchog chen po brtag pa dang po. Dg.T. rgyud, *cha* (Toh. 453).

Ornament of Mahāmudrā. Śrīmahāmudrātilakaṃnāmayoginītantrarājaadhipati. Dpal phyag rgya chen po'i thig le zhes bya ba rnal 'byor ma chen mo'i rgyud kyi rgyal po'i mnga' bdag. Dg.K. rgyud, *nga* (Toh. 420).

Perfection of Wisdom in Eight Thousand Lines. Āryāṣṭāsāhasrikāprajñāpāramitānā. 'Phags pa shes rab kyi pha rol tu phyin pa brgyad stong pa. Dg.K. brgyad stong, (Toh. 12).

Perfection of Wisdom in Eighteen Thousand Lines. Āryāṣṭādaśasāhasrikāprajñāpāramitānāmamahāyānasūtra. 'Phags pa shes rab kyi pha rol tu phyin pa khri brgyad stong pa zhes bya ba theg pa chen po'i mdo. Dg.K. khri brgyad (Toh. 10).

Possession of the Root of Virtue Sutra. Āryakuśalamūlasaṃparigrahanāmamahāyānasūtra. 'Phags pa dge ba'i rtsa ba yongs su 'dzin pa zhes bya ba theg pa chen po'i mdo. Dg.K. mdo sde, *nga* (Toh. 101).

Realization of Mahāvairocana. Mahāvairocanābhisambodhivikurvatīadhiṣṭhānavaipulyasūtraindrarājānāmadharmaparyāya. rNampar snang mdzad chen po mngon par rdzogs par byang chub pa rnam par sprul pa byin gyis rlob pa shin tu rgyas pa mdo sde'i dbang po'i rgyal po zhes bya ba'i chos kyi rnam grangs. Dg.K. rgyud, *tha* (Toh. 494).

Samādhirāja Sutra. Āryasarvadharmasvabhāvasamatāvipañcitasamādhirājanāmamahāyānasūtra. 'Phags pa chos thams cad kyi rang bzhin mnyam pa nyid rnam par spros pa ting nge 'dzin gyi rgyal po zhes bya ba theg pa chen po'i mdo. Dg.K. mdo sde, *da* (Toh. 127).

Saṃpūṭa Tantra; Saṃpūṭanāmamahātantra. Yang dag par sbyor ba zhes bya ba'i rgyud chen po. Dg.K. rgyud, *ga* (Toh. 381).

*Saṃpūṭatilaka Tantra. *Mahātantrarājaśrīsaṃpūṭatilakanāmatantra. rGyud kyi rgyal po chen po dpal yang dag par sbyor ba'i thig le zhes bya ba.* Dg.K. rgyud, *ga* (Toh. 382).

Saṃvarodaya Tantra. Śrīmahāsaṃvarodayatantrarājanāma. dPal bde mchog 'byung ba zhes bya ba'i rgyud kyi rgyal po chen po. Dg.K. rgyud, *kha* (Toh. 373).

Sutra of Bhadrakarātrī. Āryabhadrakarātrīnāmasūtra. 'Phags pa mtshan mo bzang po zhes bya ba'i mdo. Dg.K. mdo sde, *sa* (Toh. 313).

Sutra of Entry into Laṅka. Āryalaṅkāvatāramahāyānasūtra. 'Phags pa lang kar gshegs pa'i theg pa chen po'i mdo. Dg.K. mdo sde, *ca* (Toh. 107).

Sutra of the Close Application of Mindfulness of the Sublime Dharma. Āryasaddharmasmṛtyupasthāna. 'Phags pa dam pa'i chos dran pa nye bar gzhag pa. Dg.K. mdo sde, *ya* (Toh. 287).

Sutra of the Extensive Play. Āryalalitavistaranāmamahāyānasūtra. 'Phags pa rgya cher rol pa zhes bya ba theg pa chen po'i mdo. Dg.K. mdo sde, *kha* (Toh. 95).

Sutra of Never Wavering from Dharmatā. Āryadharmatāsvabhāvaśūnyatācalapratisarvālokasūtra. 'Phags pa chos nyid rang gi ngo bo stong pa nyid las mi g.yo bar tha dad par thams cad la snang ba'i mdo. Dg.K. mdo sde, *da* (Toh. 128).

Union with All Buddhas Supplementary Tantra. Śrīsarvabuddhasamayogaḍākinījālasaṃbaranāmauttaratantra. dPal sangs rgyas thams cad dang mnyam par sbyor ba mkha' 'gro ma sgyu ma bde ba'i mchog ces bya ba'i rgyud phyi ma. Dg.K. rgyud, *ka* (Toh. 366).

Vajraḍāka Tantra. Śrīvajraḍākanāmamahātantrarāja. rGyud kyi rgyal po chen po dpal rdo rje mkha' 'gro zhes bya ba. Dg.K. rgyud, *kha* (Toh. 370).

Vajrapañjara Tantra. Āryaḍākinīvajrapañjaramahātantrarājakalpanāma. 'Phags pa mkha' 'gro ma rdo rje gur zhes bya ba'i rgyud kyi rgyal po chen po'i brtag pa. Dg.K. rgyud, *nga* (Toh. 419).

Tengyur (Treatises)

Abhayadatta. *Chronicle of the Eighty-Four Mahāsiddhas. *Caturaśītisiddhapravṛtti. Grub thob brgyad cu rtsa bzhi'i rnam thar.* Nar.T. rgyud, *lu* (N 3095).

Advayavajra. *Extensive Commentary Illuminating the Innate Principle of the Song of the Inexhaustible Full Treasury. Dohanidhikoṣaparipūrṇagītināmanijatattvaprakāśaṭīkā. Mi zad ba'i gter mdzod yongs su gang ba'i glu zhes bya ba gnyug ma'i de nyid rab tu ston pa'i rgya cher bshad pa.* Dg.T. rgyud, *wi* (Toh. 2257).

Amitābha. *Commentary on Śrī Kṛṣṇavajra's Treasury of Couplets. Śrīkṛṣṇavajrapādadohakoṣaṭīkā. dPal nag po rdo rje zhabs kyi do ha mdzod kyi rgya cher 'grel pa,* Dg.T. rgyud, *zhi* (Toh. 2302).

Amoghavajra. *Karmamudrāparīkṣopadeśa. Las kyi phyag rgya brtag pa'i man ngag* (Toh. 1746).

Āryaśūra. *Garland of Incarnations. Jātakamāla. sKyes pa'i rabs kyi rgyud.* Dg.T. skyes rab, *hu* (Toh. 4150).

Asaṅga. *Explanation of the Unsurpassed Continuum. Mahāyānottaratantraśāstravyākhyā. Theg pa chen po rgyud bla ma'i bstan bcos rnam par bshad pa.* Dg.T. sems tsam, *phi* (Toh. 4025).

Aśvaghoṣa. *Removing Misery. Śokavinodana. Mya ngan bsal ba.* Dg.T. spring yig, *nge* (Toh. 4177).

Ātīśa Dīpaṃkaraśrījñāna. *Lamp of the Path of Awakening. Bodhipathapradīpa. Byang chub lam gyi sgron ma.* Dg.T. dbu ma, *ki* (Toh. 3947).

Bhāviveka. *Blaze of Dialectics: A Commentary on the Heart of Madhyamaka. Madhyamakahṛdayavṛttitarkajvālā. dBu ma'i snying po'i 'grel pa rtog ge 'bar ba.* Dg.T. dbu ma, *dza* (Toh. 3856).

———. *Heart of Madhyamaka. Madhyamakahṛdayakārikā. dBu ma'i snying po'i tshig le'ur byas pa.* Dg.T. dbu ma, *dza* (Toh. 3855).

———. *Precious Lamp of Madhyamaka. Madhyamakaratnapradīpanāma. dBu ma rin po che'i sgron ma zhes bya ba.* Dg.T. dbu ma, *tsha* (Toh. 3845).

Bhūripa. *Extensive Daily Confession of Śrī Cakrasaṃvara. dPal 'khor lo bde mchog gi rgyun bshags rgyas pa.* Dg.T. rgyud, *za* (Toh. 1533).

Buddhaśrījñānapāda. *Introduction to the Victor's Path. Jinamārgāvatāra. rGyal ba'i lam la 'jug pa.* Dg.T. dbu ma, *gi* (Toh. 3964).

———. *Ornament of Liberation. Muktilakanāma. Grol ba'i thig ke shes bya ba.* Dg.T. rgyud, *di* (Toh. 1859).

Cintā. *Accomplishing the Truth That Clarifies Existence. Vyaktabhāvānugatatattvasiddhi. dNgos po gsal ba'i rjes su 'gro ba'i de kho na nyid grub pa.* Dg.T. rgyud, *wi* (Toh. 2222).

Dānaśīla. *Recalling the Verses of Personal Liberation. Prātimokṣapadābhismarṇa. So sor thar ba'i tshig gi brjed byang.* Dg.T. 'dul ba, *mu* (Toh. 4109).

Ḍombi Heruka. *Accomplishing the Connate. Śrīsahajasiddhināma. dPal lhan cig skyes pa grub pa zhes bya ba.* Dg.T. rgyud, *wi* (Toh. 2223).

Kambala. *Difficult Points of Cakrasaṃvara. Sādhananidānanāmaśrīcakrasaṃvara-*

pañjikā. dPal 'khor lo sdom pa'i dka' 'grel sgrub pa'i thabs kyi gleng gzhi zhes bya ba. Dg.T rgyud, *ba* (Toh. 1401).

Koṭalipa. *Stages of the Inconceivable. Acintyakramopadeśanama. bSam gyis mi khyab pa'i rim pa'i man ngag ces bya ba.* Dg.T. rgyud, *wi* (Toh. 2228).

Kṛṣṇā Paṇḍitā. *Difficult Points in the Explanation of the Introduction to the Conduct of Bodhisattvas. Byang chub sems dpa'i spyod pa la 'jug pa'i rnam par bshad pa'i dka' 'grel.* Dg.T. dbu ma, *la* (Toh. 3873).

Kṛṣṇācārya (Kṛṣṇavajra). *Illuminating the Secret Principle. Guhyatattvaprakāśanāma. gSang ba'i de kho na nyid rab tu gsal ba zhes bya ba.* Dg.T. rgyud, *wa* (Toh. 1450).

———. *Explanation of Vows. Saṃvaravyākhyā. sDom pa bshad pa.* Dg.T. rgyud, *zha* (Toh. 1460).

———. *Four Stages. Rim pa bzhi pa bzhugs.* Dg.T. rgyud, *wa* (Toh. 1451).

———. *Ornament of Spring. Vasantatilakanāma. dPyid kyi thig le zhes bya ba.* Dg.T. rgyud, *wa* (Toh. 1448).

Indrabhūti II (Vajrabodhirāja). *Accomplishing Gnosis. Jñānasiddhināmasādhanopāyikā. Ye shes grub pa zhes bya ba'i sgrub pa'i thabs.* Dg.T. rgyud, *wi* (Toh. 2219).

Indrabhūti III. *Amṛta of Reality Intimate Instruction. Śrītattvāmṛtopadeśa. dPal de kho na nyid kyi bdud rtsi'i man ngag.* Dg.T. rgyud, *ta* (Toh. 1337).

Kālacakrapāda. *Padmani Commentary. PadmaninĀmapañjikā. Padma can zhes bya ba'i dka' 'grel.* Dg.T. rgyud, *na* (Toh. 1350).

Maitreyanātha. *Ornament of Mahāyāna Sutras. Mahāyānasūtrālaṃkārakārikā. Theg pa chen po mdo sde'i rgyan zhes bya ba'i tshig le'ur byas pa.* Dg.T. sems tsam, *phi* (Toh. 4020).

———. *Unsurpassed Continuum. Mahāyānottaratantraśāstraratnagotravibhāga. Theg pa chen po rgyud bla ma'i bstan bcos.* Dg.T. sems tsam, *phi* (Toh. 4042).

Mokṣākaragupta. *Difficult Points of the Inexhaustible Treasury. Dohakoṣapañjikānāma. Do ha mdzod kyi dka' 'grel zhes bya ba.* Dg.T. rgyud 'grel, *mi* (Toh. 2258).

Nāgabodhi. *Clarification of the Five Stages. Pañcakramārthabhāskaraṇanāma. Rim pa lnga'i don gsal bar byed pa zhes bya ba.* Dg.T. rgyud, *ci* (Toh. 1833).

Nāgārjuna. *Commentary on Bodhicitta. Bodhicittavivaraṇa. Byang chub sems kyi 'grel pa zhes bya ba.* Dg.T. rgyud, *ngi* (Toh. 1800 and 1801).

———. *Concise Sādhana. Piṇḍīkṛtasādhana. sGrub pa'i thabs mdor byas pa.* Dg.T. rgyud, *ngi* (Toh. 1796).

———. *Five Stages. Pañcakrama. Rim pa lnga pa.* Dg.T. rgyud, *ngi* (Toh. 1802).

———. *Letter to a Friend. Suhṛllekha. bShes pa'i spring yig.* Dg.T. spring yig, *nge* (Toh. 4182).

———. *Necklace of Gems. Rājaparikathāratnāvali. rGyal po la gtam bya ba rin po che'i phreng ba.* Dg.T. spring yig, *ge* (Toh. 4158).

———. *Praise to the Incomparable. Nirupamastava. dPe med par bstod pa.* Dg.T. bstod tshogs, *ka* (Toh. 1119).

———. *Sixty Verses on Reasoning. Yuktiṣaṣṭikākārikā. Rigs pa drug cu pa'i tshig le'ur byas pa zhes bya ba.* Dg.T. dbu ma, *tsa* (Toh. 3825).

Padmavajra. *Secret Accomplishment. Sakalatantrasambhavasaṃcodanīśrīguhyasiddhināma. rGyud ma lus pa'i don nges par skul bar byed pa dpal gsang ba grub pa zhes bya ba.* Dg.T. rgyud, *wi* (Toh. D 2217).

Pawo Ösal (dPa' bo 'od gsal). *Essence of the Realization of the Eighty-Four Siddhas. Caturaśītisiddhasambodhihṛdayanāma. Grub thob brgyad cu rtsa bzhi'i rtogs pa'i snying po zhes bya ba.* Dg.T. rgyud, *zhi* (Toh. 2292).

Prajñākaragupta. *Precious Drop. Śrīratnabindunāmasādhanopāyikā. dPal rin chen thigs pa zhes bya ba'i sgrub pa'i thabs.* Dg.T. rgyud, *ta* (Toh. 1332).

Prajñākaramati. *Difficult Points of the Introduction to the Conduct of Awakening. Bodhicaryāvatārapañjikā. Byang chub kyi spyod pa la 'jug pa'i dka' 'grel.* Dg.T. dbu ma, *la* (Toh. 3872).

Ratnākaraśānti. *Endowed with Purity. Abhisamayālaṃkārakārikāvṛttiśuddhamatīnāma. mNgon par rtogs pa'i rgyan gyi tshig le'ur byas pa'i 'grel pa dag ldan zhes bya ba.* Dg.T. shes phyin, *ta* (Toh. 380).

———. *Establishing the Middle Way. Madhyamakālaṃkāravṛttimadhyamapratipadāsiddhināma. dBu ma rgyan gyi 'grel pa dbu ma'i lam grub pa zhes bya ba.* Dg.T. sems tsam, *hi* (Toh. 4072).

———. *Garland of Jewels. Piṇḍīkṛtasādhanopāyikāvṛttiratnāvalīnāma. mDor bsdus pa'i sgrub thabs kyi 'grel pa rin chen phreng ba zhes bya ba.* Dg.T rgyud, *ci* (Toh. 1826).

———. *Intimate Instruction on the Ornament of the Madhyamaka. Madhyamkaālaṃkāropadeśa. dBu ma rgyan gyi man ngag.* Dg.T. sems tsam, *hi* (Toh. 4085).

Ratnarakṣita. *Padminī Commentary on Difficult Points. Śrīsaṃvarodayamahātantrarājasyapadminīnāmapañjikā. dPal sdom pa 'byung ba'i rgyud kyi rgyal po chen po'i dka' 'grel padma can zhes bya ba.* Dk.T, rgyud, *wa* (Toh. 1420).

Śāntideva. *Compendium of Training. Śikṣāsamuccaya. bsLab pa kun las btus pa.* Dg.T. dbu ma, *khi* (Toh. 3940).

———. *Introduction to the Conduct of Awakening. Bodhicaryāvatāra. Byang chub sems dpa'i spyod pa la 'jug pa.* Dg.T. dbu ma, *la* (Toh. 3871).

Saraha. *Inexhaustible Treasury. Dohakoṣopadeśagītināma. Mi zad pa'i gter mdzod man ngag gi glu zhes bya ba.* Dg.T. rgyud, *zhi* (Toh. 2264).

———. *Treasury of Couplets. Dohakoṣagīti. Do ha mdzod kyi glu.* Dg.T. rgyud, *zhi* (Toh. 2224).

———. *Resembling the Tip of a Lamp Flame. Śrīhevajrapradīpaśūlopamāvavādakanāma. dPal kye rdo rje'i mar me'i rtse mo lta bu'i gdams pa zhes bya ba.* Dg.T. rgyud, *nya* (Toh. 1220).

Smṛtijñānakīrti. *Explanation of the Commentary on Bodhicitta. Bodhicittavivaraṇatīkā. Byang chub sems kyi 'grel pa'i rnam par bshad pa.* Dg.T. rgyud, *ci* (Toh. 1802).

Śraddhākaravarman. *Medium Rite in Three Parts. Cha gsum 'bring po'i cho ga.* Dg.T. rgyud, *tshu* (Toh. 3774).

———. *Introduction to the Meaning of Tantra. Yogānuttaratantrāthāvatārasaṃgrah-*

anāma. rNal 'byor bla na med pa'i rgyud kyi don la 'jug pa bsdus pa zhes bya ba. Dg.T. rgyud, *tsu* (Toh. 3713).

Śūra. *Commentary on the Sutra of Personal Liberation. Prātimokṣasūtrapaddhati. So sor thar ba'i mdo'i gzhung 'grel.* Dg.T. 'dul ba, *du, nu* (Toh. 4104).

Vāgīśvarakīrti. *Explanation of Illuminating the Precious Truth. Tattvaratnāloka-vyākhyāna. De kho na nyid rin po che snang ba'i rnam par bshad pa.* Dg.T. rgyud, *pi* (Toh. 1890).

———. *Illuminating the Precious Truth (Illuminating the Fourth). Tattvaratnāloka. De kho na nyid rin po che snang ba.* Dg.T. rgyud, *pi* (Toh. 1889).

———. *Intimate Instruction on Cheating Death. Mṛtyuvañcanopadeśa. 'Chi ba bslu ba'i man ngag.* Dg.T. *sha* (Toh. 1748).

———. *Seven Limbs. Saptāṅga. Yan lag bdun pa.* Dg.T. rgyud, *pi* (Toh. 1888).

Vajragarbha. *Hevajrapiṇḍārthaṭīkā. Kye'i rdo rje bsdus pa'i don gyi rgya cher 'grel pa.* Dg.T. rgyud, *ka* (Toh. 1180).

Vajrāsana. *Supplication to the Eighty-Four Siddhas. Grub thob brgyad cu rtsa bzhi'i gsol 'debs.* Dg.T. rgyud, *tshu* (Toh. 3758).

Vanaratna. *dPyid kyi thig le rgya cher 'grel pa zhes bya.* Dg.T. rgyud, *wa* (Toh. 1449).

Vararuci. *Mahākāla Sādhana. dPal nag po chen po'i bsgrub thabs.* Nar.T. rgyud 'grel, *zhu* (N 3688).

Vasubandhu. *Explanation of the Ornament of Sutras. Sūtrālaṃkārabhāṣya. mDo sde'i rgyan gyi bshad pa.* Dg.T. sems tsam, *phi* (Toh. 4026).

———. *Explanation of the Treasury of Abhidharma. Abhidharmakośabhāṣya. Chos mngon pa'i mdzod kyi bshad pa.* Dg.T. mngon pa, *ku* (Toh. 4090).

———. *Pedagogical Strategies. Vyākhyāyukti. rNam par bshad pa'i rigs pa.* Dg.T. sems tsam, *shi* (Toh. 4061).

———. *Treasury of Abhidharma. Abhidharmakośakārikā. Chos mngon pa'i mdzod kyi tshig le'ur byas pa.* Dg.T. mgon pa, *ku* (Toh. 4089).

Yaśobhadra. *Compendium of Essential Vajra Verses. Vajrapadagarbhasaṃgrahanāma. rDo rje'i tshig gi snying po bsdus pa zhes bya ba.* Dg.T. rgyud, *pha* (Toh. 1390).

Tibetan Works

Collections

Collected Works of Sakya. Sa skya bka' 'bum. 15 vols. Dehra Dun: Sakya Center, 1992–1993. BDRC W22271.

Jamgön Kongtrul Lodrö Taye. *Great Treasury of Precious Treasures. Rin chen gter mdzod chen mo.* 111 vols. Paro: Ngodrup and Sherab Drimay, 1976–1980. BDRC W20578.

Kunga Nyingpo (Kun dga' snying po), et al. *Instructions on Parting from the Four Attachments. Zhen pa bzhi bral gyi gdams ngag.* Dharamsala: Library of Tibetan Works & Archives, 2017. BDRC W8LS34504.

Loter Wangpo (bLo gter dbang po), ed. *Collection of All Tantras. rGyud sde kun btus.*

30 vols. Delhi: N. Lungtok & N. Gyaltsan, 1971–1972. Second source: 43 vols. Kathmandu: Sachen International, 2004. BDRC W21295.

———. *Lam 'bras slob bshad.* 21 vols. Dehra Dun: Sakya Centre, 1983–1985. BDRC W23649.

Tibetan Authors

Amezhap (Ngag dbang kun dga' bsod nams). *Amazing Storehouse of Jewels. dPal gsang ba 'dus pa'i dam pa'i chos byung ba'i tshul legs par bshad pa ngo mtshar rin po che'i bang mdzod.* In Collected Works of Ngawang Kunga Zonam, vol. 11, pp. 481–797. Kathmandu: Sa skya rgyal yongs gsung rab slob gnyer khang, 2000. BDRC W29307.

———. *Effortless Accomplishment of the Two Benefits. Bod yul bstan pa'i mnga' bdag rje btsun sa skya pa'i yab chos lam skor phyi ma brgyad kyi khrid yig sngags 'chang chos kyi rgyal po'i gsung rtsom 'phro can gyi kha bskang pa don gnyis lhun grub.* In Collected Works of Ngawang Kunga Zonam, vol. 22, pp. 429–86. Kathmandu: Sa skya rgyal yongs gsung rab slob gnyer khang, 2000. BDRC W29307.

——. *Illuminating the Extensive Doctrine. dPal 'khor lo sdom pa'i rtsa ba'i rgyud kyi don 'grel khog phub legs par bshad pa bde mchog rgyud bshad bstan pa rgyas pa'i nyin byed.* In Collected Works of Ngawang Kunga Zonam, vol. 17, pp. 273–594. Kathmandu: Sa skya rgyal yongs gsung rab slob gnyer khang, 2000. BDRC W29307.

———. *Ocean that Gathers Excellent Explanations. Yongs rdzogs bstan pa rin po che'i nyams len gyi man ngag gsung ngag rin po che'i byon tshul khog phub dang bcas pa rgyas par bshad pa legs bshad 'dus pa'i rgya mtsho.* In Collected Works of Ngawang Kunga Zonam, vol. 21, pp. 339–700. Kathmandu: Sa skya rgyal yongs gsung rab slob gnyer khang, 2000. BDRC W29307.

———. *Revision of Kṛṣṇa's Four Stages. Nag po rim bzhi'i zur 'debs chos rje rin po che sangs rgyas dpal bas mdzad pa'i dpe ma dag pa'i zhu dag sa skya pa ngag dbang kun dga' bsod nams kyis gsung bzhin bgyis pa.* In Collected Words of Ngawang Kunga Zonam, vol. 22, pp. 429–86. Kathmandu: Sa skya rgyal yongs gsung rab slob gnyer khang, 2000. BDRC W29307.

———. *Source of Needs and Wants. 'Khor lo bde mchog gi dam pa'i chos byung ba'i tshul legs par bshad pa yid bzhin rin po che'i phreng ba dgos 'dod kun 'byung.* In Collected Words of Ngawang Kunga Zonam, vol. 16, pp. 289–618. Kathmandu: Sa skya rgyal yongs gsung rab slob gnyer khang, 2000. BDRC W29307.

———. *Word-by-Word Commentary on the Root Tantra. Tshul bzhi sngon du 'gro ba dang bcas pa'i dpal kyai rdo rje'i rtsa rgyud brtag pa gnyis pa'i tshig 'grel rgyud bshad bstan pa rgyas pa'i nyin byed.* In Collected Works of Ngawang Kunga Zonam, vol. 20, pp. 7–522. Kathmandu: Sa skya rgyal yongs gsung rab slob gnyer khang, 2000. BDRC W29307.

Anonymous. *Doha Chronicle. Phyag rgya chen po do ha'i lo rgyus (dbu med bris ma).* In Bod kyi lo rgyus rnam thar phyogs bsgrigs (3160), vol. 12, pp. 133–46. Zi ling: mTsho sngon mi rigs dpe skrun khang, 2011.

Drakpa Gyaltsen (Grags pa rgyal mtshan). *Central Channel Instruction. rTsa dbu ma'i khrid yig.* In *SKB* 8, pp. 155–81.

———. *Chronicle of the Indian Gurus. Bla ma rgya gar ba'i lo rgyus.* In *SKB* 6, pp. 691–707.

———. *The Instruction on Parting from the Four Attachments.* In *SKB* 9, pp. 605–10.

———. *Miscellaneous Notes on Individual Sādhanas. sGrub thabs so so'i yig sna.* In *SKB* 8, pp. 597–685.

———. *Possessing Purity. brTag pa gnyis pa'i rnam par bshad pa ma dag pa rnams 'joms par byed pa'i rnam 'grel dag ldan.* In *SKB* 6, pp. 395–660.

———. *Precious Wishfulling Tree. Gyud kyi mngon par rtogs pa rin po che'i ljon shing.* In *SKB* 6, pp. 9–286.

Gönpo Dorje (mGon po rdo rje). *Comprehensive Summary of One Taste. mNyam med rgod tshang pa'i zhal gdams ro snyoms sgang dril.* In Collected Works of Gönpo Dorje. vol. 4, pp. 261–305. Thimphu, Bhutan: Tango Monastic Community, 1981. BDRC W23661.

Hagiography of the Teacher of Nyan. Gnyan ston pa'i rnam thar. In bKa' brgyud pa'i bla ma brgyud pa'i rnam thar khag cig dang khrid yig sogs, pp. 152–73. BDRC W1KG1286.

Jamgön Kongtrul Lodrö Taye ('Jam mgon kong sprul blo gros mtha' yas). *Word Commentary on the Two-Section King Tantra. rGyud kyi rgyal po brtag pa gnyis pa'i tshig 'grel.* BDRC W1KG13831. Inderpuri, New Delhi: Shechen Publications, 2005.

Kunga Gyaltsen, Sakya Paṇḍita (Sa skya paṇḍita kun dga' rgyal mtshan). *Common Supplication to the Guru. bLa ma la sol ba 'debs pa thun mong ba.* In *SKB* 12, pp. 400–401.

———. *Uncommon Supplication to the Sublime Guru. bLa ma dam pa la thun mong ma yin pa'i sgo nas gsol ba 'debs pa.* In *SKB* 12, pp. 401–403.

Kunga Nyingpo, Sachen (Sa chen Kun dga' snying po). *Chronicle of Ācārya Saroruha. sLob dpon mtsho skyes kyi lo rgyus.* In *SKB* 2, pp. 685–89.

———. *Chronicle of the Gurus of the Kṛṣṇa System of Cakrasaṃvara. bDe mchog nag po pa'i lugs kyi bla ma brgyud pa'i lo rgyus.* In *SKB* 2, pp. 11–22.

Kunga Zangpo, Ngorchen (Ngor chen Kun dga' bzang po). *Letter to Benefit Disciples. sPring yig slob ma la phan pa.* In Collected Works of Kunga Zangpo, vol. 4, pp. 621–62. Dehra Dun: Sakya Centre, 199?. BDRC W11577.

———. *Little Red Volume. Lam 'bras pu sti dmar chung dkar chag ltar gsung thor bu tshar du dngar ba tshangs 'grigs.* In *L* 13, pp. 1–469. Dehra Dun: Sakya Centre, 1983–1985.

———. *Play of Samantabhadra. Tshogs kyi 'khor lo'i cho ga kun bzang rnam rol.* In Collected Works of Kunga Zangpo, vol. 3, pp. 287–304. Dehra Dun: Sakya Centre, 199?. BDRC W11577.

———. *Sunlight That Increases the Doctrine. Lam 'bras kyi man ngag gi byung tshul bstan pa rgyas pa'i nyi 'od.* In Collected Works of Kunga Zangpo, vol. 1, pp. 437–510. BDRC W11577.

Lodrö Gyaltsen (bLo gros rgyal mtshan). *Bali Rite to the Siblings. lCam dral gyi gtor chog. SKB* 15, pp. 164–70. Dehra Dun: Sakya Center, 1992–1993.

———. *Homage and Offering to the Lineage of the Path with Its Result. Lam 'bras brgyud pa'i phyag mchod.* In *SKB* 13, pp. 71–80.

———. *Jeweled Rosary: The Praise to Mañjughoṣa at the Five Peaked Mountain. 'Jam dbyangs la ri bo rtse lngar bstod pa nor bu'i phreng ba.* In *SKB* 13, pp. 226–37.

———. *Ocean of Hearing. Thos pa'i rgya mtsho.* In *SKB* 13, p. 108.

———. *Offering the Maṇḍala and Supplication to the Guru. bLa ma la maṇḍala 'bul zhing gsol ba 'debs pa.* In *SKB* 13, pp. 389–91.

———. *Protector Sādhana Text. mGon po'i sgrub yig.* In *SKB* 15, pp. 120–38.

———. *Uncommon Supplication to the Root Guru. rTsa ba'i bla ma thun mong ma yin pa'i sgo nas gsol ba 'debs pa.* In *SKB* 13, pp. 134–36.

Losal Gyatso (Blo gsal rgya mtsho). *Supplication to the Guru that Combines Three Lineages of the Precious Oral Instructions and the Aspiration of the Stage of the Path. gSung ngag rin po che rgyud gsum 'dus kyi bla ma gsol ba 'debs pa lam rim smon lam dang bcas pa.* In *L* 14, pp. 235–48.

Loter Wangpo (bLo gter dbang po). *Great Sīta River of Amṛta that Benefits Others. dPal gsang ba 'dus pa 'jam pa'i rdo rje'i dkyil 'khor du slob ma dbang bskur ba'i cho ga gzhan phan bdud rtsi sI ta'i klung chen.* In *G*, pp. 667–744.

Ngawang Lozang Gyatso (Ngag dbang blo bzang rgya mtsho). *Appendix of Reading Transmission Lineages. Zur gyi rtags yod pa'i lung brgyud.* In Collected Works of Ngawang Lozang Gyatso, vol. 1, pp. 390–418. Pe cing: Krung go'i bod rig pa dpe skrun khang, 2009. BDRC W1PD107937.

Pema Karpo (Pad+ma dkar po). *rJe btsun na ro pa'i phyag rgya lam rdzogs kyi khrid.* In Collected Works of Pema Karpo, vol. 19, pp. 449–76. Darjeeling: Kargyud Sungrab Nyamso Khang, 1973–1974. BDRC W10736.

———. *Tibu's Root Verses of the Sixfold Cycle of One Taste. Ti bus mdzad pa ro snyoms skor drug gi rtsa tshig.* In Collected Works of Pema Karpo, vol. 24, pp. 31–38. Darjeeling: Kargyud Sungrab Nyamso Khang, 1973–1974. BDRC W10736.

Rangjung Dorje (Rang byung rdo rje). *Catalogue of Translated Treatises. Thugs dam bstan 'gyur gyi dkar chag.* In Collected Works of Rangjung Dorje, vol. 4, pp. 427–606. Zi ling: mTshur phu mkhan po lo yag bkra shis, 2006. BDRC W30541.

Sheja Kunrik (Shes bya kun rig). *Byang chub sems kyi 'grel bshad nyi ma'i 'od zer.* In Collected Works of Sheja Kunrik, vol. 1, pp. 565–607. Skye dgu mdo: Gangs ljongs rig rgyan gsung rab par khang, 2004. BDRC W28942.

Sönam Rinchen (bSod nams rin chen). *Sunlight of Citations. bsTan bcos lung gi nyi 'od.* In Collected Works of the Throne of Holders of Gampo, vol. 4, pp. 277–328. Pe cin: Krung go'i bod rig pa dpe skrun khang, 2013. BDRC W1AC309.

Tokme Zangpo Pal (Thogs med bzang po dpal). *Theg pa chen po mdo sde'i rgyan gyi 'grel pa rin po che'i phreng ba.* Gangtok: Gonpo Tsetan, 1979. BDRC W13914.

3. Reference Bibilography

Abhayadatta. *Buddha's Lions: The Lives of the Eighty-Four Siddhas.* Translated by J.B. Robinson. Berkeley, CA: Dharma Publishing, 1979.

Chowdry, Abdul Momin. *Dynastic History of Bengal: c. 750—1200 A.D.* Dacca: Asiatic Society of Pakistan, 1968.

Dalton, Catherine. "Enacting Perfection: Buddhajñānapāda's Vision of a Tantric Buddhist World." PhD diss., University of California, Berkeley, 2019.

Drakpa Gyaltsen, et al. *Instructions on Parting from the Four Attachments. Zhen pa bzhi bral gyi gdams ngag.* Dharamsala: Library of Tibetan Works & Archives, 2017. BDRC W8LS34504.

Gampo Tashi (sGam po bkra shis). *A Brief Discussion of the Ritual Terms of the Rites of the Original Religious Tradition of Tibet. Bod kyi gdod ma'i chos lugs kyi chos ga'i gyer tshig gi skor che long tsam gleng ba.* In gTsos mi rigs dge 'os mtho rim ched sbyong slob grwa'i dpyad rtsom phyogs bsgrigs, 80–99. Pe cin: Mi rigs dpe skrun khang, 2006. BDRC W00KG07630.

Gawe Dorje (dGa' ba'i rdo rje). *Stainless Crystal Mirror. 'Khrungs dpe dri med shel gyi me long.* Pe cin: Mi rigs dpe skrun khang, 2002. BDRC W20069.

Krug, Adam. *The Seven Siddhi Texts: The Oḍiyāna Mahāmudrā Lineage in Its Indic and Tibetan Contexts.* PhD. diss., University of California–Santa Barbara, 2018.

Kunga Nyingpo (Kun dga' snying po). *Concise Topics of the Saroruha Sādhana. sGrub thabs mtsho skyes kyi bsdus don.* In *SKB* 2, pp. 689–93.

———. *General Presentation of the Six Treatises. gZhung drug spyi'i rnam gzhag.* In *SKB* 2, pp. 22–23.

———. *Outline of Olapati. O la ba ti'i sa bcad.* In *SKB* 2, pp. 32–34.

———. *Outline of the Ornament of Spring. dPyid kyi thig le'i sa bcad.* In *SKB* 2, pp. 34–35.

———. *Outline of the Truth of the Secret. Gsang ba'i de kho na nyid gsal ba'i sa bcad.* In *SKB* 2, pp. 27–32.

———. *Vase of Verses. mNgon rtogs tshig gi bum pa.* In *SKB* 2, pp. 693–713.

Jamgön Kongtrul Lodrö Taye ('Jam mgon kong sprul blo gros mtha' yas). *A Gem of Many Colors: The Autobiography of Jamgön Kongtrul.* Translated by Richard Baron. Ithaca, NY: Snow Lion, 2003.

———. *Jonang: The One Hundred and Eight Teaching Manuals.* The Treasury of Precious Instructions, vol. 18. Translated by Gyurme Dorje. Boulder: Shambhala, 2020.

———. *Sakya: The Path with Its Result, Part One.* The Treasury of Precious Instructions, vol. 5. Translated by Malcolm Smith. Boulder: Snow Lion, 2022.

Sa skya Paṇḍita. "Illuminating the Sages Intent." In Dölpa, Gampopa, and Sakya Paṇḍita, *Stages of the Buddha's Teachings: Three Key Texts,* translated by Ulrike Roesler, Ken Holmes, and David Paul Jackson, pp. 385–602. Somerville, MA: Wisdom. 2015.

Sakya Trizin, His Holiness. *Freeing the Heart and Mind, Part One: Introduction to the Buddhist Path.* Edited by Gyaltsen and Chodron. Boston, MA: Wisdom, 2011.

Samten Karmay. *The Arrow and the Spindle.* Kathmandu: Maṇḍala Book Point, 1998.

Saroruhavajra. *Saroruha Sādhana. sGrub thabs mtsho skyes.* BDRC W8LS17963.

Schaeffer, Kurtis R. *Dreaming the Great Brahmin: Tibetan Traditions of the Poet-Saint Saraha.* New York: Oxford University Press, 2005.

Schmidt, Toni. *The Eighty-Five Siddhas.* Stockholm: Statens Ethnografiska Museum, 1958.

Sönam Tsemo (bSod nams rtse mo). *Four-Limb Direct Realization of Śrī Hevajra. dPal kyai rdo rje'i mngon par rtogs pa yan lag bzhi pa.* In *SKB* 5, pp. 7–74.

Tarānātha. *Life of Kṛṣṇācārya/Kāṇha.* Translated by David Templeman. Dharamsala: Library of Tibetan Works and Archives, 1989

Thubten Jinpa. *Mind Training: The Great Collection.* Somerville, MA: Wisdom, 2006.

Yeshe Tsogyal. *Life of the Lotus Born: The Life Story of Padmasambhava.* Translated by Eric Pema Kunzang. Hong Kong: Rangjung Yeshe, 1998.

Index

Abhayadattaśrī, *Hagiography of the Eighty-Four Siddhas*, 83
abiding, three experiences of, 198–99
Acala, 313
Accomplishing Gnosis (Indrabhūti II), 121, 125, 133–34, 209, 246, 255
Accomplishment of the Connate (Ḍombi Heruka), 11, 12, 153, 223
  influence of, xix–xx
  lineage, 4, 141–42
  on meditation, 144–45, 448n4
  sources, 141–42
  See also ascetic path; infant path
accumulation field, 28, 34–35, 174, 196–197
Advayavajra, *Extensive Commentary*, 437n5, 439n22, 450n14
affirmations, six necessary, 118, 446nn177–81
afflictions, 115, 289, 304
  and delusions, three times of, 78, 217
  and examples of illusion, merging, 79, 219
  investigating, 111, 232, 443nn96–100
  latent, antidote to, 80, 221
  as path, 177
  temporary, antidote to, 80
aggregates, 62, 188, 189, 190, 210, 279, 358, 440n28
aging, 58, 101, 182
agitation, 434n33, 446n178, 450n8
  controlling, 198–99
  in near placement, 171
  removing, 43, 66, 113–14, 203–4
  three types, 113
Akaniṣṭha, 197, 406, 439n25
Ākāśagarbha, 288, 358
Ākāśagarbha Sutra, 335
Akṣobhya, 96, 219, 399
  bodhicitta of, 62, 187, 437n6
  family of, 445n141
  visualizations, 79, 161, 167, 287, 399, 404
  yoga of, 239
Akṣobhya Guhyasamāja, 223
alcohol, 115, 127, 130, 234, 250. *See also* liquor
all-basis, 293, 381
Amezhap Ngawang Kunga Sönam, xix
  Amazing Storehouse of Jewels, 61, 62
  Illuminating the Extensive Doctrine, 434n2, 436n3
  Ocean That Gathers Excellent Explanations, 273–74
  See also *Effortless Accomplishment of the Two Benefits*
Amitābha, 79, 167, 219, 287, 336, 399
Amitayus, 96
Amoghasiddhi, 79, 96, 219, 287, 400
Amoghavajra, xvii, 5, 71, 207
amṛta, 99, 101
  bindu of, 42
  in caṇḍālī, 51, 263, 264
  five types, 131, 254, 400
  of gnosis, 48, 395, 397
  offering, 371, 392
  as poison, 399
  relying on, 115, 237
  seven reasons for, 395, 464n39
Amṛta of Reality Intimate Instructions (Indrabhūti III), 134–35

analogies and examples
bee collecting pollen, 74
boat, disabled, 110, 230, 442n79
bonfire, 234
container, three faults of, 342
crow flying from ship, 64, 199
dreams, 63, 194
elephant's mind, 66, 202
enemy's child, feeding, 307
forest fire, 221
gold, 26, 158, 198
illusions, 192, 309, 310, 337
lamps, 65, 199
loosening cord, 198
mirages, 307, 316, 325
mirror, 97
moon in water, 74
ox, 64, 199
prisoner, 198
rope as snake, 205
sea turtle and yoke, 317
seed and conditions, 332
sesame oil, 108, 225–26, 441n40
star in daytime, 347
sun, 108, 225
twelve of illusion, 77, 79, 216, 219, 220
vulture's tail, 71
water poured into water, 26, 54, 80, 158, 220, 338
waves and water, 194
wish-fulfilling gem, 91, 114, 225, 235
Anaṅga II, 134
Anaṅgavajra, 6, 22, 23, 41, 155, 156. *See also* Jalendra (a.k.a. Anaṅgavajra); Padmavajra (a.k.a. Saroruha)
Ananta, 394, 397
Ancillary Tantra, 70, 438n9
anger, 111, 217, 232
animals, 317
rebirth as, 329, 344
suffering of, 320, 326–27
annihilation, 310, 335, 457n10
antidotes, five kinds, 119–20
appearances
beneficial, 112, 234, 444n112
deluded, transforming, 309, 310–11
directly ascertaining, 211
and emptiness, inseparability of, 66, 74, 108, 191, 202, 283, 289
of gnosis, 117, 445n161
as great bliss, 246
as illusory, 190, 278, 306
immaculate aspects, 91
mind and, 63, 79, 282–83
as one's teacher, 221
poison of, 292
recalled, 78, 217
apsaras, 116, 239, 445n140
armor, donning/binding, 29, 30, 36, 166, 167, 176
Āryadeva, 4, 61, 188
Āryaśūra, *Garland of Incarnations*, 341, 347–48
Asaṅga, 345, 348, 439n25
ascetic path, 12, 429n8
bodhicitta on, 143
body method, 147–48
preparation, 146–47
result of, 430n39
shared instructions, 14, 142, 149–50
vows of, 13, 143
Aspiration of the Conduct of Samantabhadra, 348
asuras, 67, 327
Aśvaghoṣa, *Removing Misery*, 318, 319
attachment. See *Parting from the Four Attachments* cycle
avadhūti. *See* central nāḍī
Avadhūtipa, 361
Avalokiteśvara, 288, 358
Avīci hell, 310, 323

bali offerings, 105, 391, 394, 395
for blessings, 71–72
in Mahākāla sādhana, 403–4, 407–12, 420
neglecting, 130, 251
in post-session yoga, 43
Balton Darma Jungne, 40
bardo, 15, 151, 430n38
Bari Lotsāwa, 313, 457n17
Barzinpa, 6
Beautiful Ornament of the Three Tantras, 387

Bee in the Lotus, 134
Bhadrapāda, 102, 104
  instructions of, 85, 86, 87, 88, 97
  lineages, 3, 98, 224
Bhāviveka, 439n25
Bhusanapa, 3, 105, 107, 224
bindus, 164–65, 282, 292, 431–32n87
  of amṛta, 42
  of bliss, 53
  of bodhicitta, 28, 51, 107
  body and, 18, 53, 244, 253–54, 431n72
  clarity of, 265–66
  crooked, 58, 182
  descent, 127, 148, 247
  dissolution of, 173, 415
  drawing up, 11, 148, 248–49, 265–66
  of light, 29, 31–32, 34, 170, 173
  multicolored, 27, 160
  preserving, 129–31, 249–51
  retaining, 11, 12, 127, 128, 143, 248
  single, 37, 116, 177, 239, 445n157
  solar and lunar, 99, 116, 239, 445n142
  spreading, 19, 128, 148, 149, 249, 431–32n87
  stabilizing and transforming, 253–55
  transformation into syllables, 35, 42, 174
  and vajra, spinning, 282, 455n33
birth, causes of, 97
birthplaces, 95
  coiled, 100
  four, 27–28, 156, 159–60
  of knowledge consorts, 123, 252
blazing and dripping, 51, 264, 285–86
blessing lineage, 122, 244
blessings
  descent of, 278, 292
  equality of, 126, 247, 253
  impaired, bindu loss through, 130, 251
  ritual for, 71–73
bliss
  arising of, 14
  attaining, 306
  in caṇḍālī, 51–54
  contaminated, 116, 211, 283
  and emptiness, inseparability of, 54, 82, 125, 167, 211, 246, 268, 283, 289
  experience of, 212, 292
  fainting from, 149
  nonconceptual, 86
  retention and meditation, 127–28, 248
  source of, 92
  See also great bliss
boat, disabled, 110, 442n79
bodhicitta, 13, 85–86, 143, 292, 332
  accomplishing, 122
  aspirational, 193, 197, 212, 315
  in caṇḍālī, 263, 264
  cultivating, 196, 315, 334–35, 442n70
  descending, 52
  dripping, two types, 288
  of eight parts of body, 132
  engaged, 193, 212, 315
  in fourth empowerment, 116
  fundamental, 289
  irreversible, 314
  meditations, 146, 189, 197, 229
  nine elements, 239–40
  offering, 371
  recalling, 309, 310
  relative, 193, 197, 335
  in removing obstacles, 114, 235–36, 444n128
  retention, three methods, 127–28, 248
  reversing, 248–49
  single stream, 177
  spreading, 128, 249
  supplication, 313
  ultimate, 192, 196, 197
bodhisattva stages. *See* twelve stages
body, 15
  branch of, 112
  as deity, 176
  developing, 18, 431n72
  features of, 145
  free from proliferation, 158
  frugality of, 12–13, 143
  giving away, 78, 218
  as great bliss, 246
  increasing tissues, 127
  key points for concentration, 198, 229
  pain in, 119–20, 204–5, 237–38, 246
  purifying, 101, 147, 166, 389
  rainbow appearance, 73, 227, 441n52
  in removing obstacles, 203–4

body (*continued*)
as support, 107–8, 225, 440n28, 440n31
times for recognizing, 108, 441nn50–52
twenty-four places in, 131
and voice, equality of, 126, 253
See also postures
Brahma, 96, 98–99, 134, 162, 193, 310, 346
Brahma aperture, 114, 204, 235, 421
breath, 293
in completion stage, 41, 434n32
exhalation, 14, 109, 150, 261, 442n68
gentle, 266
inhalation, 13–14, 18, 149, 429nn15–16, 429nn19–21, 431n71, 431n87
Buddha Śākyamuni, 97, 98, 295, 336, 346, 439n19
buddhafields, 132, 159, 175, 219
buddhahood, 59, 92, 249
aspiration for, 183
deeds of, 193
inconceivability of, 88
as nonduality, 87, 93–94, 95
realizing, 47, 66, 203, 254, 255
seed of, 304
and sentient beings, merger of, 26, 159
time in attaining, 178
Buddhajñānapāda tradition, 223, 274, 428n3 (Introduction)
Buddhalocana, 287, 358, 455n51
Buddhaśrī, Mahāsiddha, 3, 4, 5, 6, 7, 8, 365
Buddhaśrījñāna, *Introduction to the Victor's Path*, 333, 334

cakras, 100
in caṇḍālī, 49, 166
four joys and, 131–33, 264–65
six, 49–50, 285–87
sixteen joys and, 254–55
three maṇḍalas and, 48, 258, 260–61
See also individual cakras
Cakrasaṃvara, 207, 223
emanation of, 46
in guru yoga, 260
making liquor and, 394, 397
Saraha and, 436n3
secrecy of, 434n2
systems of, 45
thirteen-deity maṇḍala, 394
thirty-seven-deity maṇḍala, 48, 435n8
Cakrasaṃvara Tantra, 47, 257
Caṇḍālī (goddess), 34, 164, 167, 172
caṇḍālī yoga, 29, 167
caṇḍālī, meaning of, 268
lineage supplication, 6–7
meeting of tips of mothers, 262–63, 264
self-empowerment and, 166
in two stage meditation, 288
visualization, 50–51
See also *Completing the Whole Path with Caṇḍālī* (Kṛṣṇācārya)
Caṇḍikā, 11, 428n3 (ch. 2)
Candra dynasty, 22, 46, 432n5, 439n21
Candrakīrti, 4, 63, 188
Candratilaka. *See* Padmavajra (a.k.a. Saroruha)
Caurī, 34, 164, 165, 167, 172
celestial mansion, 26
all appearances as, 158
in completion stage, 173
in guru yoga, 260
instant, 175
pure universe as, 289
recollecting, 146, 172, 184
visualizations, 28, 162, 356–57
central nāḍī (*avadhūti*)
in caṇḍālī, 49, 51, 261, 263, 264
characteristics of, 431n82
controlling, 15, 150
fourth joy in, 116
of mudras, 123, 125, 149, 252, 447n5
cessation, 16, 110, 178, 195, 231
Chanting the True Names of Mañjuśrī, 291, 455n25
charnel grounds, 103, 134–35, 392, 404
eight, 28, 162, 168, 414–15
recalling, 34, 172
Chime Tenzin Nyima, 297, 343
Chögyal Phakpa. *See* Lodrö Gyaltsen Palzangpo (Chögyal Phakpa)
Chökyi Gyalpo, 343
Cintā, 22, 23, 432nn6–7
Cittavajrā, 166
clairvoyance, 16, 35, 48
arising of, 117, 152

in dreams, 115, 174, 238
five kinds, 54, 59, 131, 185, 255, 268
clarity, 199
in caṇḍālī, 52
and emptiness, inseparability of, 54, 63, 66, 125, 144, 202, 246, 268, 282, 289
experience of, 212, 231
identifying/introducing, 65, 199–200
of mind, 195, 292
Clear Mindfulness of the Innate (Vāgīśvarakīrti), 281
four empowerments, 285–86
lineage, 289
meditation on two stages, 286–89
cocoon, removing, 110, 232–33, 443n87
cognizance, 292
and emptiness, inseparability of, 54, 66, 74, 125, 202, 246, 268, 289
recognizing, 199–200
See also intrinsic cognizance
Collected Verses on the Noble Perfection of Wisdom, 195, 196, 277, 278–79, 454nn10–14
Commentary on Bodhicitta (Nāgārjuna), 190, 192
on bodhicitta, 189, 193
on emptiness, 191
instructions (see *Obtained in Front of a Stupa*)
on meditation, 65, 200, 210–11, 448n4
on mind, 194–95
sources, 61, 62, 188
commitment beings, 28, 165, 418, 423
commitment deities
in bardo, 151
blessings of, 122
divine pride of, 126
inviting, 78
meditation on, 198, 205–6
offerings to, 63, 196
recalling, 58, 75, 183
self-visualization, 212
compassion
arising of, 193
cultivating, 334
great bliss and, 87
impartial, 338
inconceivable, 85
meditation on, 457n9
nondual, 95, 98
nonreferential, 81, 222, 278
Compendium of the Gnosis Vajra, 69
Completing the Whole Path with Caṇḍālī (Kṛṣṇācārya), 45–46
composition of, 55
concise explanation, 47–48, 258–59
gnosis stage, 51–53, 264–66
lineage, 55, 257–58
mantra stage, 50–51, 262–64
nonduality stage, 54–55, 268–69
secret stage, 53–54, 266–67
sources, 47
tantra stage, 48–50, 259–61
title, meaning of, 268
completion stage, 34, 35, 102
beginners, 173
buddhahood and, 97
caṇḍālī as name of, 268
in eight ancillary path cycles, xix, 223
empowerment for, 167
exhaustion by, 390
inseparability of samsara and nirvana in, 158
Kṛṣṇa's six summaries, 47, 257–58
place and time for, 41, 433n26, 434n29
sessions of, 43
three purities in, 31–32
three secret dharma maṇḍalas of, 27, 160
See also two stages
Completion Stage Instruction Resembling the Tip of a Lamp Flame (Padmavajra), xvii, 21–22, 41–43, 155
complexion, 14, 15, 148, 151, 429nn22–23, 431n87
concentration
poison of, extracting, 31, 169, 170
sixfold preliminaries (limbs), 109, 229–30, 442n73
concepts, 108, 198, 199, 211, 221, 227, 441n47
conceptuality, 76, 88, 93
absence of, 90, 91
as blockage, 118

conceptuality (*continued*)
controlling, 213, 214
dualism in, 452n2
employing on path, 202–3, 451n29
as great ignorance, 215, 452n12
spirits as, 205
suffering of, 157
as "syllables," 78
Condensed Essence (Kṛṣṇācārya), 47, 258
conduct, 38, 178
bindu loss through, 130, 250
of bodhisattvas, 335
culmination of, 177
cultivating all, 112, 233–34
of listening to Dharma, 341–43
madman's, 206
of mahāmudrā, 81, 211–12, 221
and realization, connecting, 66, 116–17, 140, 239–40
in removing obstacles, 113, 235
secret, 15–16, 151–52, 430n39
of strict discipline, 16, 59, 66, 152, 430nn41–42
of total freedom, 59, 185
confession, 28, 414
confidence, 37, 65–66, 115, 201–2, 216, 228, 238
connate joy, 11, 12, 29, 428n6
of cause, 13, 145, 150, 429n11
of connate, 48, 259, 265–66
of method/path, 13–15
nonarising reality, 144–45, 448n4
of result, 15–16, 150–53, 429n32
"connate by nature," 12, 142, 144, 428n7
consciousness
five gnoses and, 95
mistaken, 190
and objects, merging, 54–55
in removing cocoon, 232–33
as samādhi, 14–15, 149, 150
See also eight consciousnesses; six consciousnesses
creation stage, 122
approach to, xx
beginners, 162–68
in Buddhajñānapāda system, 274
culmination of, 29
dispensing with, 36, 176
empowerments for, 166, 244
five limbs, 27
inseparability of samsara and nirvana in, 158
nine stages of śamatha and, 21
purification by, 260
reducing components of, 174
sessions of, 33–34
ultimate level, 166
view, 26–27
See also two stages
Creation Stage Adorned with the Nine Profound Methods (Padmavajra), xx, 21, 223
brief explanation, 25, 156
on four types of persons, 27–28, 34–37, 159–60
on nine profound methods, 37–39
nine stages of śamatha, 30–33
sessions, 33–34
seven limbs of three kāyas, 40
source lineage, 155–56
view, 26–27, 157–59
visualization, 28–30
creators, 63, 118, 193–94, 306, 337
cremation, 46–47, 434n7
crown cakra (*mahāsukhacakra*)
burning, 51, 263, 288
in creation stage, 167
deity meditation in, 287
free from syllables, 49, 261
joy in, 52, 131, 266
in removing obstacles, 114, 235
Cycle of Siddhas, 202, 451n28

ḍākinīs
blessings of, 54, 130–31, 208, 254, 267
flesh-eating, 405
gnosis, 224
offerings to, 12
predictions of, 116, 239, 444nn138–39
reversing obstacles of, 36, 175
Ḍamarupa, 361
Dampa Kunga Drakpa, 420, 423
death, 309
certainty of, 318–19, 456n7

destroying, 101
dharma at, 319–20
freedom from, 58, 182
signs at, 15, 151, 430n35
suffering of, 305
time, uncertainty of, 307, 319, 320, 347
dedication prayers, 338, 340
deities
in completion stage, 174
forms as reflection of buddha, 90–91
instant self-visualization, 292, 456n60
manifold forms of, 100
purity of, 168, 170
recollection of, 146, 288
self-visualizations, 286–88, 455n50
Dejö Zangpo, 61, 67, 436n2 (ch. 6)
delusion
as gnosis, 309, 310–11
three times of, 77, 78, 216, 217
dependent origination, 39, 122, 178, 190–92, 244, 260, 306, 457n12
Deshek Dupa residence, 424
desire
bodhicitta and, 249
equality of, 126, 247, 253
objects of, 177, 178, 234, 445n161
as path, 14, 126, 149, 247
desire realm, 323
destiny of existence, 194, 450n14
Devākaracandra, 5, 71, 207
devas, 320, 323, 327, 344
Devīkoṭa, 46
devotion
conduct of, 341
in four stages, 268
to lineage, 75
of mudras, 252
in offerings, 378
to root guru, 58, 63, 64, 73, 183–84, 196–97, 198, 213, 229, 286
to Sakya Paṇḍita, 364
for secret mantra practice, 124
Dewe Nyugu, 83
Dharikapa, 434n2
Dharma
becoming dharma, 309
of inconceivability, 90
listening to, 341–43
rarity of, 346–47
at time of death, 319–20
Dharma Connection with the Six Gatekeepers, xx, 273
dharmacakra. *See* heart cakra
dharmadhātu, 90, 108, 228, 278, 282
Dharmakarṇapa, 3
dharmakāya, 26, 100, 212
as equality of desire, 126
inseparability of samsara and nirvana of, 159, 278
nonarising wisdom of, 289
as nondual dhātu and gnosis, 29, 164
seed of, 304
suffering of formations and, 292
support for, 439n25
See also seven limbs of three kāyas
Dharmapāda, 88, 98
Dharmapāla, 141
Dharmasena, 3, 104, 224
dharmatā, 202
affirming, 118, 446n180
grasping, 306
mahāmudrā and, 209
mere designation and, 111
one taste in, 158
space-like, 195
dharmodaya, 99, 247, 400, 444n128
blessings and, 126
in removing obstacles, 114, 235–36
visualizations, 162
Dhātviśvarī, 288
diet, 178, 185
bindu loss through, 130, 250
in increasing tissues, 127
for infant path, 148
in removing obstacles, 114, 234, 235, 444nn122–24
yoga of eating and drinking, 399
Direct Awakening of Mahāvairocana, 332, 458n37
discursiveness, 77, 80, 170–71, 198–99, 201, 216
Doha Chronicle, 155
Ḍombi Heruka
identity of, 12, 428n2 (ch. 1)

Ḍombi Heruka (*continued*)
Light of Amṛta, 71, 207
lineages, 4, 134, 141
tradition, xix
with Virūpa, 11–12
See also *Accomplishment of the Connate*
Ḍombinī (goddess), 34, 164, 167, 168, 172
Drakpa Gyaltsen, xvii, 256, 448nn2–3
Chronicle of the Indian Gurus, 11
Clarification of the Instruction, 231
Clarification of the Stages of the Inconceivable, 139
on cremation, 434n7
homage, 362
lineages, 67, 289, 456n57
Miscellaneous Notes on Individual Sādhanas, 69
on parting from the four attachments, 309–11
Possessing Purity, 448n4
dreams
as analogy, 309, 310, 337
bindu loss in, 129–30, 250
bliss arising in, 149
clairvoyant, 35, 174, 238
clarity in, 150
delusion in, 77
recognizing, 216, 292
signs in, 14, 15, 115, 151
Drogön Chögyal Phakpa, 314
Drokmi Lotsāwa Śākya Yeshe, xix, 233, 440n23
lineages of, 105, 142, 156, 182, 208, 224, 243, 289
supplications, 3, 4, 5, 6, 7, 8, 362
teachers of, 69
translations by, 43, 83, 102
transmissions received, xvii, 71
at Vikramaśīla, 273–74, 277, 281, 291
Drukpa Kagyu, 140, 451n29
dullness, course and subtle, 203
Durjayacandra, 4, 142
Dveśavajrā, 165–66

Effortless Accomplishment of the Two Benefits (Amezhap), xvii, 11, 12
on Kṛṣṇācārya system, 45
on *Obtained in Front of a Stupa*, 61
on Padmavajra's system, 21
on *Path Cycle of the Mudra* authorship, 121
on *Stages of the Inconceivable*, 83
eggshell, breaking, 110, 231, 442n85
eight ancillary path cycles
commentaries on, xvii–xviii
empowerments required, xix
lineage supplication, 3–9
order of, xviii
transmission and sources, xvii, 223, 256
eight consciousnesses, 289, 440n34
eight factors and five faults, 192, 450n8
eight freedoms, 318, 344–45, 457n23
eight relativities, 97
eight worldly dharmas, 80, 115, 221, 238, 304, 344
Eight-Deity Mahākāla sādhana, xxi
body permission, 416
conclusion, 420–22
entrustment and praises, 407–12
invocations, 406–7
master's conclusion, 422–23
mind permission, 419
permission preliminaries, 412, 413–15
praise, very concise, 411
preparation, 401–4
reading transmission/permission, 418, 421
speech permission, 417–19
visualization, 404–6
Ekajāti, 404–6, 415
elements
five, 96
nine, 107, 116, 225, 239–40, 440n30
obstacles of, 66, 204
pacifying, 59, 185
ten, 37, 176–77
empowerments, xix, 18
controversy over, 70, 438n9
creation stage and, 28, 29–30
for making liquor, 394
role of, 196
supreme great bliss, 167
See also individual empowerments
emptiness, 108, 162, 230

conduct and, 212
experiencing, 110, 442n82
four, 253
free from all extremes of proliferation, 338
grasping and attachment to, 190, 310
meditation, 65, 192, 200, 211, 278, 448n4
possessing core of compassion, 279
possessing supreme of all aspects, 212
potential of, 292
sixteen, 96–97
See also under bliss; clarity; cognizance
enhancement, eight kinds, 115
enjoyments, 12, 78, 142, 218
Entryway to Dharma (Sönam Tsemo), 353
eons, light and dark, 345–46, 460n72
equipoise, 74, 145
in creation stage, 162–68
preliminaries, 161–62
profundity of, 39
remaining in, 289
signs in, 34, 80–81
space-like, 192
three methods, 198, 199–200
See also under post-equipoise
error correction, 237–38
Essence of Gnosis Tantra, 210
Essential Texts, 202, 451n28
Evaṃ Chöden, 353, 401
Evaṃ Tartse Khenchens, 353
exchanging self and other, 335, 457n9
Explanation of the Path with Its Result for Disciples, 121
Explanation of the Unsurpassed Continuum (Asaṅga), 348
eyes, branch of, 112, 443n106

faith, 341, 342, 345, 383, 385, 421, 450n8, 457n23
fear
of death, 15, 151, 385
emptiness and, 212
liberation from, 197, 331
as mind's appearance, 190, 216, 218
pacifying, 205
in suffering of change, 327
in visualization, 73, 214
See also hope and fear
fearlessness, 123, 252, 330, 360, 374
feet, soles of, 204
five gnoses, 95, 96, 163, 164
five inconceivabilities, 83–84, 108, 118, 225–26, 440nn35–36, 441nn37–46
chronicle of, 103–5
enhancements, 115
realization of, 441n49
sessions, 115, 444nn132–35
signs, 115, 444n136
five limbs of three kāyas, 121, 133–34, 255
five paths, 122, 134, 245. *See also individual paths*
five poisons, 112, 221, 234, 444n114
forgetfulness, 65, 170, 199, 238
Fortunate Eon Sutra, 460n72
Fortunate Right-Turning White Conch (Kongtrul), xviii, 121
four immeasurables, 28, 161–62, 165, 193
four joys, 131, 147
at empowerment, 177
in fourth empowerment, 116, 239–40, 445n142
in gnosis stage, 52, 264–65
signs of, 254–55
stabilizing, 148
three yānas and, 38
four kāyas, 81, 222
four limbs
accomplishment, 28, 29, 160, 166, 176
approach limb, 28, 29, 160, 165
great accomplishment, 28, 29, 176
near-accomplishment, 28, 29, 160, 165, 176
three purities and, 168
four lineages, 122, 134, 244
four means of gathering disciples, 335
four types of persons, 27–28
Four Vajra Seats Tantra, 412
fourfold assembly, 345
fourth empowerment, 430n45
in creation stage, 30, 167–68
mahāmudrā and, 208
path of, 116–17, 239, 286, 289, 444n137
freedom and endowments, 316–18, 344–47
freshness, 198

Gampo Tashi, *Brief Discussion*, 450n12
gaṇacakras (feasts), 260, 390, 397
Ganges River, reversing, 11
Garbharipa, 4, 142
Garland of Vajras Tantra, 209–10
Gaurī, 33, 36, 164, 165–66, 167, 172
Gayadhara, xvii, 6, 43, 55, 156, 182, 258, 361–62
gazing, 170, 203, 233, 278
Ghantapāda system, 45
Ghasmarī, 34, 164, 165, 167, 172
gnosis, 48, 85, 176, 246
  appearance of, 117, 445n161
  connate, 38, 164, 178, 249
  of connate nature, 118, 446n184
  gathering, 162, 168, 174
  inconceivable, 86, 108, 227, 441n49
  liquor and, 391
  mingled example and meaning, 212
  nonconceptual, 195, 202
  nondual, 86–90, 93–94, 97, 98, 111, 112, 232
  of self-liberation, 289
  of transformation, 26, 159
  vajra, 124–25, 292
  See also five gnoses
gnosis beings, 28, 160, 165, 167, 418, 423
gnosis of prajñā empowerment. *See* wisdom consort empowerment
gnosis vajra, 246, 454n17, 464n39
Gö Khukpa Lhetse, 83
goddess of liquor, 394–96, 397, 464n39
Gönpo Dorje, *Comprehensive Summary of One Taste*, 140
Gönpowa, 63, 71, 105, 188, 208, 443n105
Gorampa Sönam Senge, 296, 340, 459n56, 461n25
grasping, 80, 112, 220
  in four attachments, 301, 306, 310, 335–38, 351–52
  offering, 78
  to self and other, 194
  to two identities, 189–90
great bliss, 54, 145, 268
  arising of, 92, 99
  attaining, 176, 177
  compassion and, 87
  connate gnosis of, 164
  empowerment of, 167
  nonconceptual, 209
  nondual, 88, 90, 98
  of three kāyas, 55
great compassion, 90, 149, 279, 332
gugul, 73, 439n18
Guhyapati Vajrapāṇi, 243, 392
Guhyaprajñā, 8
Guhyasamāja, 223, 243
Guhyasamāja Tantra, 61–62, 71, 187–88, 437n6
Guhyasamāja Tantra cycle, 69, 70, 438n9
Guṇḍerī, 98, 104, 224
Gundhiri, 3
guru yoga, xxi, 260, 355
gurus
  meditations on, 109, 146, 196–97, 198, 205–6, 213, 229, 292, 442n71, 456n60
  pleasing, 397
  qualifications of, xix
  refuge in, 259
  supplication verse, 72
  See also vajra masters
gyalgongs, 145, 448n7
Gyalwa Drakphupa, 314
Gyergom Rokpo (Rok), 283, 455n37

hatred, 14, 78, 149
health, 41, 43, 433mm23–24
hearing, reflection, meditation, 102, 303, 304, 316, 456n7
heart cakra (dharmacakra), 100
  burning, 263
  in creation stage, 167
  deity meditation in, 287
  joy in, 52, 131, 265
  in removing obstacles, 114, 235
  syllables, 49, 261, 278
Heart Maṇḍala of the Ḍākinī, 71
Heart of the Perfection of Wisdom Sutra, 340
hell realms, 317
  cold, 321–22, 458n33
  hot, 322–23
  peripheral, 324–25
  rebirth in, 330, 344, 400
  suffering of, 78, 218, 320

Heruka, 46, 259, 268, 400, 401, 415, 416, 417–18
Hevajra, 156
empowerments, xix
homage, 355
master visualized as, 414–15
meditation on, changes in, 35, 174
nine-deity maṇḍala, 21, 26, 30, 161, 165, 172, 414–15
practices related to, 223, 275
sādhana, 21
self-visualizations, 41–42, 146–47, 161, 184, 213, 404
Hevajra Tantra, 47, 71, 257, 285, 286, 444n138
on connate, 12, 142
creation stage visualization in, 167–68
on great bliss, 158
on poṣadha vows, 279
on samsara and nirvana, inseparability of, 25, 26, 27, 156, 157
on tantra topics, 277, 454nn6–8
on union, 36
Hevajra Tantra cycle, 69
hope and fear, 118, 142, 203–4, 205, 211, 226, 230
Host of Buddhas Sutra, 211
hūṃ recitation, 281–82, 455n25
human birth, 320, 327, 341, 456n7. *See also* freedom and endowments
humors, 145, 204, 235, 451n33

identity, two absences of, 189, 190–91
ignorance
conceptuality as, 215, 452n12
connate, 189, 191
dispelling, 304
illness and, 204
as path, 15, 150
poison of, 109, 228, 442n63
seal of, 217
illness and disease, 204
bindu loss through, 129, 250
from bodhicitta, 249
curing, 15, 46, 53, 149, 150, 282, 455n29
postures according with, 229
self-liberating, 16, 152
three connate, 13, 14–15, 145, 429–30n32
illusory bodies, 454n8
immortality, 59, 185
impermanence, 191
meditating on, 309, 318–20, 347, 456n7
and permanence, distinction between, 86
Inconceivable lineage, 3–4
Inconceivable Secret Sutra, 341
Increasing the Two Accumulations (Kunga Chöphel)
aspiration prayer, 380–84
blessings, requesting, 376–77
concluding rites, 384–86
condensed visualization, 387–88
lineage supplication, 357–70
offerings, 371–76
preliminaries, 355–57
seven limbs, 378–79
sources, 355, 460nn4–7, 461n13, 462nn56–57
Indra, 162
Indrabhūti I, 3, 6, 8, 98, 103, 135, 156, 224, 243
Indrabhūti II, 121, 135. See also *Accomplishing Gnosis*; *Path Cycle of the Mudra*
Indrabhūti III, 22–23, 83, 103, 134–35, 243
Indrabhūti short lineage, 8
Inexhaustible Treasury, attribution, 451n26
infant path, 12, 148–49, 429n9, 430n47
bodhicitta on, 143
consorts on, 14, 17, 19, 431n81
preliminaries, 147
shared instructions, 14, 142, 149–50
vows of, 13, 143
Intimate Instruction of Preventing Obstacles in Samādhi and the Mind (Ratnavajra), 281, 282–83
Intimate Instruction on Cheating Death, The, 69
intrinsic cognizance, 145, 209–10
purity of, 30, 31, 32, 168, 170
term, translation of, 432n11
Īrṣyavajrā, 166
Īśvara, 193

Jains, 91, 98
Jālandhara, 46, 47, 55, 57, 181, 257, 258
Jalendra (a.k.a. Anaṅgavajra), 6, 22–23
Jamgön Kongtrul
  commentaries of, xvii–xviii, xix, xx, 139–40
  epigrams of, 153, 179, 449n10 (ch. 10), 449n11
  names of, 256
  Word Commentary on the Two-Section King Tantra, 449n3
  See also *Treasury of Precious Instructions*
Jamgön Nesarwa, 343
Jampa Kunga Tashi, 461n33
Jampa Kunga Tenzin, 456n3 (ch. 19)
Jampa Ngawang Lhundrup, 343
Jampa Sönam Zangpo, 462n48
Jampa Tsultrim Palzang, 462n46
Jampal Zhönu Dorje Rinchen, 297
Jamyang Khöntön Ngawang Dorje Rinchen, 343
Jamyang Khyentse Wangpo, xviii, 139, 222
  homages, 141, 155, 181, 187, 207, 223, 243, 257
  lineages, 156, 182, 188, 208, 224, 244, 256, 258
Jamyang Sherap Gyatso, 461n22
Jayaśrī, 142
Jinpa, Thubten, *Mind Training*, xx
Jñānabhūtirāja, 134
Jñānaḍākinī, 3, 103
Jñānapāda tradition, 69, 70, 438n9
Jñānaśrīmitra, 273, 274, 281, 282

Kālacakra Tantra commentary, 208
Kālayakṣa, 405–6, 415, 416
Kālayakṣī, 405–6, 415, 416
Kāmadhātviśvari, 409–10, 415
Kāṇha, 11, 361
karma
  appearances and, 194
  illness and, 204
  neutral, 331
  reflecting on, 320
  results of, 329–30, 456n8
  suffering of change and, 327
  unvirtuous, 328–30
  virtuous, 330–31
karmanāthas, 406, 407–12, 416, 418
Karṇapa, 105, 107, 224
Kauśika, 111, 231, 443n95, 452n5 (ch. 15). *See also* Indra
Kāyavajrā, 166
Kharak Gompa, 283, 455n41
Kharchung, 105, 442n61, 443n105
Khasama root tantra, 434–35n2
Khecari realm, 103, 382
Khön Könchok Gyalpo, 289, 456n54
Kyungpo Naljor (a.k.a. Lama Shangpa), 275, 289, 456n55
knowledge consorts, 101, 147, 148, 245, 249, 250. *See also* pure-knowledge consorts
knowledge obscurations, 189, 280
Könchok Gyaltsen, 135, 296, 461n21
Könchok Gyatso, 343
Könchok Lhundrup, 343, 461n29
Könchok Pal, 3, 4, 5, 6, 7, 8, 295, 461n31
Könchok Yeshe, 67
Koṭalipa, 3, 83, 104, 107, 224. See also *Stages of the Inconceivable*
Kṛṣṇa Acyuta, 57–58, 181, 182, 436n2 (ch. 5)
Kṛṣṇācārya
  Cakrasaṃvara system of, 45
  Explanation of Vows, 47, 258
  Four Stages, 47, 258, 264
  with Kṛṣṇa Acyuta, 57–58, 181–82
  life of, 45–46
  lineages, 55, 182, 258
  six completion stage summaries, 47, 257–58
  supplications, 6, 7, 257
  title, 453n2 (ch. 17)
  See also *Completing the Whole Path with Caṇḍālī*
Kṛṣṇapāda, 4, 63, 156, 188
Kṣitigarbha, 288, 358
Kubera, 163
Kunga Chödrak, 297
Kunga Chöphel. See *Increasing the Two Accumulations*
Kunga Drölchok, 8, 273. See also *One Hundred and Eight Manuals of Jonang*

Kunga Gyaltsen, Sakya Paṇḍita, 299, 340, 387, 448n3
  lineages, 67, 314
  supplications to, 3, 4, 5, 6, 7, 8, 295, 357–60, 363–64, 461n10, 462n58
  supplications written by, 355
Kunga Lekdrup, 297
Kunga Lekpa, 338, 340
Kunga Lekrin, 338
Kunga Lodrö, 297
Kunga Namgyal, 297
Kunga Nyingpo, Sachen, xvii, 8, 299, 440n26, 448n2
  Cakrasaṃvara commentary of, 435n3
  Chronicle of Ācārya Saroruha, 22
  homage, 362
  on Kṛṣṇācārya, 45, 46
  lineages, 55, 63, 67, 71, 105, 188, 224, 289, 295
  visions of, 299, 301, 313–14
Kunga Sönam Lhundrup, 461n34
Kunga Wangchuk, 343, 461n23
Kunzang Chöjor, 9
Kūrmapāda, 6, 55, 258
Kuśalanātha, 46
Kyenrap Tenzing Zangpo, 343

Ladrang Phende Kunkhyap Ling, 297
Laghusaṃvara Tantra, 61, 435n3, 436n3, 465n54
Lakṣmī, 23, 98, 99, 103, 135, 156, 224, 447n19
lalanā (left nāḍī), 429n27
  controlling, 14, 149
  in four-cakra visualization, 49, 260, 261
  of knowledge consort, 125, 253
  as mother of sleep, 50–51, 262–63, 264
Lalitavajra, 3
laziness, 115, 238, 450n8
lethargy, 43, 66, 113–14, 199, 203, 234–35, 434n33, 446n178, 450n8
levitation, 14, 150
Lhabar, 283, 455n40
Lhachok Senge, 461n28
Lhundrup Palden, 462n42
Lhawang Drak, 8
liquor
  benefits of, 401
  blessing, 398
  chang, 235, 453n9
  divisions of, 392–93
  drinking properly, 397–400
  faults of, 390, 400
  five families and, 400
  necessity of, 390–92
  procedures for making, 393–97
Locana, 37, 177
Lodrö Gyaltsen Palzangpo (Chögyal Phakpa), 61n14, 348, 424, 448n3, 462n59
  lineage, 314
  supplications by, 355
  supplications to, 3, 4, 5, 6, 7, 8, 365
Lodrö Tenpa, 82
Lord Brothers, 3, 4, 5, 6, 7, 8. *See also* Sakya lords
Lord Sakyapa Chenpo. *See* Kunga Nyingpo, Sachen
Losal Sangak Tenzin, 256
Losel Tenkyong, 9
love, cultivating, 332–33, 457n9
Lozang Thuthop Je, 9
lucidity, 64, 198
Luipa, 45
luminosity, 92, 101, 195, 225, 292
Lungphuwa, 283, 289, 455n42

Madhyamaka school, 457n11
Mahākālī, 406, 411, 419, 420
Mahākarunika the Nepali, 434n2
mahāmudrā
  in creation stage, 167
  in eight ancillary path cycles, xix
  emptiness of, 286, 289
  four aspects of essence, 209
  as fourth empowerment, 70, 438n9
  introduction to reality without syllables, 73–74
  Kongtrul's commentaries on, 139–40
  meaning of term, 81, 208–9, 283
  nondistraction from, 220
  as nondual gnosis, 90
  obstacles and, 282

mahāmudrā (*continued*)
realization, view of, 66, 202, 209–10
in Sakya school, xx, 61, 438n9
of view, meditation, conduct, experience, 81–82, 210–12
without syllables, meaning of, 78, 217, 452n13
without syllables, spontaneous realization of, 219
Mahāmudrā That Removes the Three Sufferings (Nāropa), 275, 281, 291–93
Mahāmudrā without Syllables (Vāgīśvarakīrti), 140, 223
blessing ritual, 71–75, 83, 213
lineage, 5–6, 207–8
on *mahāmudrā*, meaning of, 208–9
mind, focusing, 75–76, 213–15
mind, placing, 77–81, 216–20
mind, taming, 76–77, 215–16
result, 81, 212, 221–22
signs of accomplishment, 74, 80–81, 220–21
transmission, 69, 71, 82
Vāgīśvarakīrti's instruction and, 275
view/cause, meditation, conduct, experience, 81–82, 209–12
mahāsukhacakra. *See* crown cakra
Mahāvairocana. *See* Vairocana
Mahāvajradhara. *See* Vajradhara
Mahāyāna, 229, 352, 357
mahāyoga tantra, 47, 257
Maheśvara, 7, 182
Maitreya, 358, 456n5
Maitreyanātha. See *Ornament of Mahāyāna Sutras*
Mal Lotsāwa Lodrö Drakpa, 45, 420
Māmaki, 239, 287, 445n141, 464n39
maṇḍala offerings, 196–97, 292, 341, 352, 356
in permissions, 413–14, 423
seven-heap, 377
thirty-seven-heap, 196, 341, 377, 462n56
maṇḍalacakra, 91, 160
dependent origination of, 39, 178
dissolution, 26
path of, 122, 244
signs and, 35
in tantra state, 48–49
maṇḍalas
bhaga, 27, 37, 160, 176, 177
bodhicitta, 27, 37, 160, 176–77
body, 36–37, 159, 176
Cakrasaṃvara thirteen-deity, 394
Cakrasaṃvara thirty-seven-deity, 48, 435n8
commitment, 36, 176
fire, 49, 50, 261, 262
four elemental, 162, 163, 286–87
gnosis, 29, 36, 165, 176
Guhyasamāja, 243
Hevajra nine-deity, 21, 26, 30, 161, 165, 172, 183, 414–15
vajra, 36, 175
Mandāra, Mount, 395, 464n39
Mangkhar Mugulung. *See* Drokmi Lotsāwa Śākya Yeshe
Mañjughoṣa Arapacana, 313
Mañjuśrī, 362
emanation of, 69
at sense organ, 358
supplicating, 295, 339
visions of, 299, 301, 313–14
Manu, 98
Māra, 348, 363–64, 381, 385
māras, 205–6
of death, 16, 152, 205
external, 59, 66, 185
four, 33, 146, 162, 172, 184
mantra to eliminate, 340, 459n59
massage, 58, 182
Mātsaryavajrā, 166
Mayajala, 455n25
meaning lineage, 122
meditation
at death, 151
entities and nonentities in, 87, 91
merging sutra and tantra, 278, 454nn16–17
as nondistraction from view, 191–92, 210–11
objects of, 62, 187–88
without meditator nor object, 90, 111, 286, 443n101
memory, 65, 115, 200, 238
merit, 63, 161, 174, 193, 306, 336, 352. *See also* two accumulations

Meru, Mount, 58, 182
messenger, relying on, 18
method and wisdom, 279
  evaluating, 108, 227–28
  as father and mother inseparable, 287–88
  in five inconceivables, 226
  as generator and support, 94
  nonduality of, 108
  order of, 278
  purifying, 116–17, 445nn145–46, 445nn151–55
  union of, 95, 97, 116, 445n142
mind
  activity from, 194, 450n14
  branch of, 112, 443n107
  in completion stage, 41, 42, 434n33
  conceptual taints of, 86, 439n9
  as connate nonarising of entities, 13, 429n13
  emptiness of, 62, 188
  examining, 194–95
  features of, 145
  focusing, 75–76, 109–10
  free from proliferation, 158
  frugality of, 13, 143
  giving away, 78, 218
  as illusory, 337
  innately pure, 282
  in mahāmudrā, 63, 64, 75–81
  placing, 77–81, 110–11
  purifying, 166, 389
  recalling in heart, 114
  in removing obstacles, 203–4
  samsara and nirvana as nature of, 156
  settling, key point of, 229
  space and, 65, 192, 195, 211
  stabilizing, 16
  support and supported for, 107–8, 225, 440n28, 440nn30–32
  times for recognizing, 108, 441nn50–52
Mind Only school (Cittamātra), 189, 190, 274, 457n11
mind training texts, xx–xxi, 299
mindfulness, 450n8
  abiding with, 214
  in controlling obstacles, 201, 204, 213, 215, 216
  in equipoise and post-equipoise, 202
  in recognizing illusion, 219
  recognizing original purity, 289
  undistracted, 198–99
  of view, 191–92
Mohavajrā, 165–66
Mokṣākaragupta, *Difficult Points*, 450n14, 452n13
Mönbu Bhatas, 405–6, 411
Mönbu Putras, 405–6, 411, 415, 416
mothers, cultivating love toward, 332–33
mudra siddhi, 122, 131, 245, 254
mudras, 445n141
  actual and gnosis, instructions on, 121, 125, 245, 248
  age and suitability, 123–24, 252
  arising of, 55
  citriṇī, 17–18, 123, 148, 431n74, 431nn58–61
  dharma, 167, 283
  divisions of, 210
  four, 210, 282–83
  gnosis, 208
  hariṇī, 123, 252
  hastinī, 18, 148, 431nn62–67
  karma, 147, 167, 208, 248, 251–53, 283
  as mental object, 127
  padminī, 17, 123, 148, 149, 177, 239, 252, 430nn48–53
  path, empowerment for, 166
  predictions of, 239, 268
  relying on, 14, 29, 37, 38, 47, 48, 177, 178, 431n87
  samaya, 167, 282, 407
  śaṅkhinī, 17, 123, 148, 252, 430nn54–56
  twelve, 17–18, 430n46
  See also infant path; knowledge consorts; *Path Cycle of the Mudra* (Indrabhūti II); wisdom consorts
Mugulungpa, 63, 188, 442n61, 443n105

nāda, 42
nāḍīs
  buddhahood in, 101
  in caṇḍālī, 49–50
  crooked, 58
  five concealed, 254

nāḍīs (*continued*)
four types of persons and, 27
purifying, 239–40
seeking, 18, 431n69, 431n74
thirty-two, 440n20
training, 147–48
See also central nāḍī; lalanā (left nāḍī); rasanā (right nāḍī)
nāga class of spirits, 13, 15, 145, 150, 162, 394, 397, 410
nāga kings, 394, 395, 397
Nāgabodhi, 439n19
Nāgārjuna
Concise Sādhana, 437n6
Letter to a Friend, 332
life of, 61–62, 67
lineages, 63, 188
Necklace of Gems, 319, 335, 350, 351
Sixty Verses, 159
supplications, 4, 187
See also *Commentary on Bodhicitta*; *Obtained in Front of a Stupa*
Nāgārjuna lineage supplication, 4–5
Nairātmyā, 41, 69, 434n35
emanation of, 22
lineage, 141
sādhana, 71, 207
in *Stages of the Inconceivable*, 83
supplications, 4, 361
symbol of, 146–47, 184
visualizations, 163, 414–15
Nairātmyayoginī, 166
Naktrö, 4, 142
Nālandā University, 436n3
names, 110, 194, 231, 443n88, 443nn90–91
Namkha Palzang (Ngor mkhan chen 13), 461n32
Namkha Palzang (Ngor mkhan chen 23), 340, 459n57, 462n41
Namkha Rinchen, 462n38
Namkha Sangye, 461n36
Namkha Wangchuk, 297
Nanda, 395
Nāropa
ultimate secret system of, 45, 434n2, 434n7
at Vikramaśīla, 273, 274, 291
See also *Mahāmudrā That Removes the Three Sufferings*
navel cakra (*nirmāṇacakra*), 100
Aparagodānīya in, 133
blazing *aṃ* in, 50–51, 258, 262–64, 285, 288
in correcting errors, 237–38
in creation stage, 167
deity meditation in, 287
joy in, 52, 131, 264–65
syllables, 49, 261
Necklace of Ketaka Gems (Ngawang Lekdrup), xx–xxi
negation, six points, 118, 445n171, 446nn172–76
Nesarwa, 297
Neten Chang Zang, 336, 459n50
Ngawang Choklek Dorje, 343
Ngawang Kunga Lhundrup (a.k.a. Morchen), 297, 343
Ngawang Lekdrup, 299, 353
Ngawang Lhundrup, 297
Ngawang Nampargyal, 9
Ngorchen Dorjechang, 8
Ngorchen Jampeyang Könchok Lhundrup, 353
Ngorchen Kunga Zangpo, 338, 389, 401, 461n20, 462n63
gaṇacakra rite of, 397
Letter to Benefit Disciples, 390, 463n6
lineages, 314, 343
on Saroruha, 23
supplications by, 3–8, 139, 295–96
supplications to, 9, 369
nine profound methods, 21, 25
certainty in, 177–78
list of, 37–39
sequence of, 39
source lineage, 155–56
nine stages of śamatha, 21, 25
instructions for, 30–33, 168–71
sessions of, 172
nirmāṇacakra. *See* navel cakra
nirmāṇakāya, 100
buddhafields of, 36
in Cakrasaṃvara tantras, 434–35n2

in creation stage, 30, 167
as equality of body and speech, 126
suffering of suffering and, 292
See also seven limbs of three kāyas
nirvana, 310
accomplishing, 305
as mind, 79
nirmāṇakāyas and, 152–53
and samsara, inseparability, 21, 25, 26–27, 116–17, 157–59, 177, 239, 278, 445n157
Nivāraṇaviṣkambhin, 288, 358
nonarising, 65, 201, 231, 293
inconceivable, 110–11, 232, 442n85
by nature, 158
of three experiences, 212
nonconceptuality, 150, 209
bliss of, 452n13
in caṇḍālī, 52
and conceptuality, distinguishing, 87
experience of, 212, 231
increasing, 254
recognizing, 54
resting in, 213, 264, 267
Nondual Uniformity Tantra, 65
nonduality, 48, 91, 95, 98, 226, 306, 457n10
beginningless, 101
of dhātu and gnosis, 117
and duality, relationship of, 89
inconceivable, 87, 102
as mere name, 88, 110–11, 231
self-originating, 85
stage of, 54–55, 268–69
as union, 441n46
nonmeditation, 36, 145, 176, 233, 448n4
nonvirtues, 317, 328–29, 345
Norbu Lingpa, 420
Nupa Rikzin Drak, 299, 340
Nyanton, 67
Nyima Chöphel, 9
Nyingpo Tayezhap, 9
Nyö, 283, 455n38

objects
conditions of, 112, 444nn110–11
gnosis, recognizing in, 233–34
of knowledge, 125, 133–34, 227–28, 230, 246, 255
mind escaping toward, 215
of proliferation, 201
obstacles, 260
for connate dharmas of cause, 13, 145
in mahāmudrā, 66, 203–6
self-liberating, 152
in "straightening the crooked," 59, 185
Obtained in Front of a Stupa (Nāgārjuna), 223
accumulations, 63, 196–97
alternate titles, 187
conduct and realization, connecting, 66, 202–6
influence of, xix–xx
introduction to reality, 64–66, 199–202
Kongtrul's commentary on, 139–40
lineage, 63, 67, 187–88
mind control, 64, 197–99
result, 66, 206
sources, 61, 62
view, 63, 189–96
Oḍḍiyāna, 22, 62, 83, 103, 104, 155, 224, 243
Oḍiviśa, 22, 434n2
offerings, 91, 439n12
to ḍākinīs, 71–73
of enjoyments, 12, 142, 218
to gurus, importance of, 360
inner, 71, 408, 422
mental, 12
for merit accumulation, 63
neglecting, 251
outer, 407, 422
secret, 92
sense offerings, 374–75
torma, 397
water, 355, 371, 460n2
welcoming, 355, 372, 460n3
See also bali offerings; maṇḍala offerings
One Hundred and Eight Manuals of Jonang (Kunga Drölchok), xvii, xviii, xx, 256, 299
One Hundred and Eight Teaching Manuals of Jonang, 256
one taste, 80, 94, 234, 292, 338

original face, 292, 293
Ornament of Mahāmudrā (Kṛṣṇācārya), 47, 258
Ornament of Mahāmudrā Tantra, 208
Ornament of Mahāyāna Sutras (Maitreyanātha), 21, 32–33, 168, 336
Ornament of Spring (Kṛṣṇācārya), 47, 257–58
orpiment ore, breaking, 110, 443n86, 452n3 (ch. 15). *See also* spider web, breaking free

Padmācārya, 98
Padmanarteśvara, 400
Padmani Commentary (Kālacakrapāda), 208–9
Padmavajra (a.k.a. Saroruha)
  life of, 22–23
  lineages, 134, 155, 156
  Secret Accomplishment, 208
  supplications, 3, 6, 155
  See also *Completion Stage Instruction Resembling the Tip of a Lamp Flame*; *Creation Stage Adorned with the Nine Profound Methods*
Padmavajra II, 104, 155, 224
Padmavajra lineage, 6, 21
pain
  antidotes for, 119–20, 204–5, 237–38, 246
  at death, 151
  vāyus and, 53–54, 267
Pal Sakyapa Ngawang Kunga Lodrö Sangye Tenpe Gyaltsen Palzangpo, 343
Palchen Öpo, 363, 461n9
Palchok Gyaltsan, 462n40
Palden Döndrup, 461n35
Palden Dorje, 8, 461n24
Palden Gyalwa, 67
Palden Lhundrup Teng, 297, 456n4 (ch. 19)
Palden Sakyapa, 3, 4, 5, 6, 7, 8
Palden Tsultrim Zhap, 3, 4, 5, 6, 7, 8, 295, 314, 461n18
Pāṇḍaravāsinī, 287
Paramāśva, 3, 98, 103, 107, 224, 228, 442n59
parent sentient beings, 146, 183, 205, 306
Parting from the Four Attachments cycle, xx–xxi, 299
  concluding verses, 347–48
  on current life, 301, 303–4, 309–10, 316–20, 344–49, 457n20
  four antidotes, 309–11
  on grasping, arising of, 301, 306, 310, 335–38, 351–52
  importance of, 299
  lineage, 295–97, 313–14, 343
  Mañjuśrī's verse, 301, 303, 314
  on personal benefit, 301, 306, 307, 310, 331–35, 350–51
  preliminaries, 314–15, 340–43
  purpose of, 307
  retreat instructions, 347–48, 349–50, 351–52
  on three realms, 301, 305–6, 307, 310, 320–31, 349–50
Path Cycle of the Mudra, The (Indrabhūti II)
  belt taken to its place, 128, 248–49
  on bindu preservation, 129–31
  breath, releasing, 128, 248
  commentary, 139, 243
  Devadatta used a horse, 122–25, 247, 251–53
  on four joys, 131–33
  for gates opened with nāga, 125–26, 253
  hold desire by pulling bow, 127, 248
  lineages, 122, 134–35, 243–44
  pace of tortoise, 127–28, 248
  progressing in, 253–55
  relying on one's own body, 245–51
  result, 133–34, 255
  summary verse, 122, 245
  two explanations of, 121
path of accumulation, 122, 245, 280
  beginners, 161–73
  completion stage and, 41
  culmination of, 27, 54, 159, 160, 173, 268
path of application, 122, 245, 280
  arrival at, 35
  in completion stage, 41
  culmination of, 27, 54, 159, 160, 268
  heat level, 174

highest mundane level, 36
patience level, 36, 175
peak level, 35, 175
second type of person, 174–76
supreme mundane level, 176
path of attaining perfection, 37, 42, 177
path of cultivation, 37, 122, 245, 280
in completion stage, 42
culmination of, 27, 160
entering, 37
four persons on, 176–77
path of seeing, 122, 245, 280
in completion stage, 42
culmination of, 27, 159
entering, 37
four persons on, 176
Path with Its Result
guardians of, 423–24
offering ritual (see *Increasing the Two Accumulations* (Kunga Chöphel))
perfection of wisdom, 200, 209
Perfection of Wisdom in Eight Thousand Lines, 46, 200
Perfection of Wisdom in Eighteen Thousand Lines, 111, 231
Perfection of Wisdom in Twenty-Five Thousand Lines commentary, 274
permanence, 110, 230, 310, 335, 442n84, 457n10
pervasiveness, 110, 230, 246, 442n83
Phakpa Rinpoche, 295
Phakpe Lha, 120
Phamtingpa, 434n2
phenomena
arising of, 193–94, 210
emptiness of, 191
in equipoise and post-equipoise, 201–2
as free from proliferation, 307
illusory nature of, 216, 220
investigating, 226, 336
lack of identity, 62, 188
mahāmudrā view of, 65
mind and, 125, 144–45, 158, 246, 306
selflessness of, recalling, 309, 310
as single maṇḍala, 177
pilgrimage places, 121, 436n12. *See also* thirty-two lands
Piṇḍapa, 4
pithas, 48, 55, 436n12
Possession of the Root of Virtue Sutra, 320, 458n30
post-equipoise, 39, 43
appearances in, 192–93
and equipoise, differentiated, 220
and equipoise, merging, 36, 65–66, 201–2, 221
instructions, 173
recalling equipoise in, 280
signs in, 34, 80–81
postures
ardhaparyaṅka (deity), 163
of ascetic path, 13, 429n14
for caṇḍālī, 50, 262
for completion stage, 41, 434nn30–31
for concentration, 347
crouching dwarf, 404
for enhancing focus, 214
for inconceivables, 109, 442n67
for mahāmudrā practice, 64, 197, 212
for mental consort practice, 245–46
for mudras, 124
for "straightening the crooked," 58–59, 185
Vairocana seven-point, 286, 293
vajra, 336
Prajñākaragupta, xvii, 135, 243
Intimate Instruction of Preventing Obstacles by External Spirits, 281–82
Precious Drop, 135, 447n19
at Vikramaśīla, 273, 274
prāṇa vāyu, 48, 259, 265–66, 293
prāṇāyāma, forceful, 57
pratyekabuddhas, 177, 308, 310, 330, 332, 351
Precious Oral Intimate Instructions, xix, 223
pretas, 317, 436–37n3
rebirth as, 330, 344
suffering of, 320, 325–26
pride
accomplishing, 304
of commitment deity, 126
of deity, 109, 169, 173, 394, 395, 399, 442n72
in Dharma, 342
of father and mother deities, 247

profound, twofold meaning of, 39
protection cakra, 28, 31
  in completion stage, 173
  in guru yoga, 260
  instant, 175
  recollecting, 146, 172, 184
  visualizations, 162
Pukkasī, 34, 164, 167, 172
punishment, training in manner of, 109, 110, 229–30
pure-knowledge consorts, 123–26
  qualities from birth, 123–24, 251–52
  qualities from training, 124–26, 253
purity, natural/original, 278, 282, 289
Putra brothers and sister. *See* Mönbu Putras

Rāgavajrā, 166
Rāhula, 61
Rāhulabhadra. *See* Saraha (a.k.a. Rāhulabhadra)
rasanā (right nāḍī), 429n27
  controlling, 150
  in four-cakra visualization, 49, 260, 261
  of knowledge consort, 125, 253
  as mother of fire, 50–51, 262–63, 264
rasāyana. *See* rejuvenator (*bcud len*; Skt. *rasāyana*)
Ratnākaraśānti (a.k.a. Śāntibhadra), 434–35n2
  Merging Sutra and Tantra, 274, 277
  Padminī, 389, 397, 398–99, 464n39
  at Vikramaśīla, 273
Ratnasambhava, 79, 96, 167, 219, 287, 400
Ratnatārā, 287
Ratnavajra, 9, 83, 102, 135, 243, 273, 274. See also *Intimate Instruction of Preventing Obstacles in Samādhi and the Mind*
rebirth, 304, 307–8, 320, 325
Rechungpa Dorje Drakpa, *Root Verses of the Sixfold Cycle of One Taste*, 140, 451n29
reflexive cognition, refutation of, 432–33n11
refuge, 75, 259, 292
  liturgy, 356
  Mahāyāna, 314–15
  in Three Jewels, 58, 197, 212, 356
  uncommon, 183, 259
rejuvenator (*bcud len*; Skt. *rasāyana*), 66, 204, 390, 391, 437n16, 463n5
relative truth, 108, 157, 191, 227–28, 441n53
relaxation, application of, 115, 292
reversal, power over, 176
rewards, training in manner of, 109, 110, 229–30
Rinchen Gyatso, 9
Rinchen Zangpo, 420
root of virtue, 161, 196, 279, 338
Rootless Path with Its Result, 430n45
Rudra, 162
rūpakāya, 26, 100, 159, 212, 289, 439n25

sādhanas
  Hevajra, 21
  Mahākāla, four types, 421
  Nairātmyā, 71, 207
  See also Eight-Deity Mahākāla sādhana
Śaivas, 91, 98
Śakra, 305
Sakya lords, 142, 156, 182, 187, 207, 223, 244, 257, 258, 412, 420, 448n2
Sakya Monastery, 59, 66, 296, 306
Sakya school
  Cakrasaṃvara in, 45
  mahāmudrā in, xx, 61, 438n9
  Parting from the Four Attachments in, 299
  primary translators, 428n1 (Introduction)
  seven limbs of union in, importance of, 69
  Stages of the Inconceivable in, 83
  uncommon refuge in, 183
Samādhirāja Sutra, 336, 337
samādhis, 37, 87, 260
  as amṛta, 101
  binding, freedom from, 111
  of bliss, clarity, nonconceptuality, 264, 265, 429n32
  of bliss and emptiness, 211, 233, 248, 249
  body, voice, mind in, 108, 441n51
  of clarity and emptiness, 59, 185
  complexion and, 429n22
  faulty and faultless, 230, 442n75

of "great desire," 14, 429n26
inconceivable, 108, 227, 441n48
of method and wisdom, union of, 227
in ninth placement method, 32–33
obstacles to, preventing, 282–83
"pervaded by great bliss," 149
"three doors of liberation," 231
Samantabhadra, 91, 288, 358, 359
śamatha, 441n47, 457n12
faulty, 199, 215
grasping, 80
instructions on, 336
and mahāmudrā meditation, distinctions in, 76
overpowering, 77
predominance of, 54, 216, 267
as remedy to grasping, 335
as sign with effort, 80, 220–21
as support, 192
vipaśyana and, 192, 338
See also nine stages of śamatha
samayas
accepting, 423
damaged, bindu loss through, 130–31, 251
of eating, 390
as foundation, 389–90
freedom from, 36, 176
liquor and, 391, 397
protecting, 421
Samayatārā, 287
sambhogacakra. *See* throat cakra
sambhogakāya, 28, 100, 126, 164, 222, 292, 439n25, 452n14. *See also* seven limbs of three kāyas
Saṃpūṭa Tantra, 79, 219–20, 278
Saṃpūṭatilaka Tantra, 47, 257, 268
samsara
gnosis and, 157, 449n3
investigating, 307
as mind, 79
recalling faults of, 305–6, 309–10, 320–28
root cause of, 215
See also under nirvana
Saṃvarodaya Tantra, xxi, 268, 389, 390–92, 393, 397–98, 399–400
Sangye Pal, 401
Sangye Rinchen, 297, 461n27
Sangye Senge, 461n30
Sangye Tenzin, 462n44
Śāntibhadra. *See* Ratnākaraśānti (a.k.a. Śāntibhadra)
Śāntideva
Compendium of Training, 335, 345
Introduction to the Conduct of Awakening, 316, 317, 335, 340
Saraha (a.k.a. Rāhulabhadra), 140, 187, 202
life of, 61–62, 67, 436n3, 437n5
lineages, 63, 188
See also *Treasury of Couplets*
Sarasvatī, 99
Saroruha Sādhana, 21, 155
Saroruhavajra, identity of, 23
Sauras, 91, 98, 440n13
Śavarī, 34, 164, 167
Se Kharchung/Sekhar Chung, 63, 71, 188, 208
secrecy, 399–400, 421
secret empowerment, 29, 122, 166, 167, 244, 285, 288
secret place
blessing, 28
deity meditation in, 287
fire in, 285
joy in, 133, 254, 265
in retention, 128, 248
stabilizing, 124, 131, 246
Secret Principle (Kṛṣṇācārya), 47, 258
self, 89, 189–91, 194, 203, 204–5
self-empowerment, 29, 122, 166, 244
sending and taking, 205
senmos, 145, 448n6
sense bases/organs, 157
absence of, 62, 188, 210
blessing of, 166
in Pāramitāyāna, 440n28
relaxing, 111
views of, 189, 190
in visualizations, 285, 288, 358, 455n52
sense consciousnesses, 111, 166
sense elements, 29, 62, 164, 188, 189, 190, 210, 440n28
sense objects, 95, 166, 285

sentient beings
abiding as cause, 108, 109, 227
buddhahood and, 26, 159
compassion toward., 279, 334
inconceivable kinds, 317
love toward, 333
nature of, 26
as nine deities, 158
Sepa Kunga Lodrö, 389
Setön Kunrik, xvii, 3, 4, 5, 6, 7, 8, 156, 224, 362
seven limbs of three kāyas, xx, 21, 25, 134, 255, 428n3 (Introduction)
from caṇḍālī, 55, 269
from inconceivables, 117–18, 240
from mahāmudrā, 66, 81, 206, 221–22, 439n25
source, 69
from "straightening the crooked," 59, 185–86
from two stages, 37, 40, 178–79
seven limbs of union. *See* seven limbs of three kāyas
Shakya Yeshe, 102
Shangpa Kagyu, 275
Shen Gom Se, 283, 455n37
Sherap Jungne, 461n37
Sherap Zangpo, 462n45
Siddhavajrā, 134
siddhis, 39, 91, 145, 178. *See also* mudra siddhi
signs, 34
of bardo, 15, 151, 430n38
of bindu retention, 128, 248
in caṇḍālī, 50, 51, 54, 262, 264, 266
in current life, 151
in empowerments, 29–30
of experience, 238
of faulty śamatha, 199
of heat, 115, 239, 444n136
in mahāmudrā, 74, 80–81, 220–21
of mind's focus, 214
of mudra's suitability, 123–24
of thirteen stages, 132, 133, 254–55
of three experiences, arising, 15, 16, 150–51
of two stages, 43, 173, 434n47
of vipaśyana, 200
single taste, 86, 89, 90
Śiva, 57, 58, 92, 96, 98–99
six consciousnesses, 29, 285
six excellent substances, 124, 246, 447n7, 453n3 (ch. 16)
six flavors, 95, 440n15
six kinds of existence and nonexistence, 226–27
six ornaments, 16, 152, 167, 430n41
six perfections, 196, 279, 335, 342–43
six realms/six classes of being, 26, 36, 158, 218, 221, 317, 345
sixteen joys, 128, 134
in caṇḍālī, 52–53, 265–66
in reversing bodhicitta, 248–49
in twelve stages, 131–33, 254–55
skillful means, 332. *See also* method and wisdom
sleeping, 15, 115, 150
Smṛtijñānakīrti, 432n11
Sönam Gyaltsen, 3, 4, 5, 6, 7, 8, 295, 364, 365, 461n17
Sönam Gyaltsen Palzangpo, 314
Sönam Gyatso, 462n39
Sönam Palden, 3, 4, 5, 6, 7, 8, 462n47
Sönam Tsemo (Lopön Rinpoche), xvii, 295, 314, 353, 362, 448nn2–3
song of reality, 73–74
space, 110, 182, 443n92
abiding in, 291
dhātu, 464n39
as example, 230, 231
experiencing, 110, 442n81
meditations, 65, 192, 200, 211, 441n48
nonduality and, 85, 229
realization and, 96
spider web, breaking free, 231, 232, 452n3 (ch. 15)
spirits
bindu loss through, 129–30, 250
freedom from, 149, 150
obstacles of, 205–6
protection from, 281–82, 455n25
self-liberating, 152
three kinds, 13, 14–15, 16, 145, 429–30n32, 455n27
See also nāga class of spirits

Śraddhākaravarman, 420, 438n9
śrāvakas, 76, 177
  attaining stage of, 332
  awakening of, 330
  deviation into, 351
  mudras and, 128, 249
  rebirth as, 308
  views of, 189, 194
Śrī Gunavat, 67
Śrī Parvata, 61, 67, 436n3
Śrīcandra, 46, 432n5, 435n6
Śrīdevī Kāmadhātviśvari, 134, 405, 410, 415, 416, 417–18, 421
Śrīdhara, 4, 6, 7, 55, 63, 156, 182, 188, 258
Śrīnātha Mahākālaya, 409
Stages of the Inconceivable (Koṭalipa), xvii, 83
  conduct, 112, 233–34
  conduct connected with result, 116, 239–40
  enhancements, 115, 236–37
  errors, correcting, 237–38
  lineage, 3–4, 224
  mind focus, 109–10, 229–30
  mind placing, 110–11, 230–33
  obstructions, 234–36
  path, 94–101, 228
  result, 24, 101–2, 117–18
  view, 85–94, 107–9, 118, 224–28, 440n28, 442n61, 445n171, 446nn172–76
stages of the path (*lam rim*), 299
"straightening the crooked," 57, 139
  lineage, 7–8, 60, 182
  main practice, 184–85
  main practice and result, 58–59
  preliminaries, 58, 183–84
  result, 185–86
suchness, 118, 168, 170, 226–27, 446n180
suffering
  abandoning, 38, 178
  of change, 292, 305, 327
  compassion and, 334
  of formations, 292, 305, 328
  of others, 15, 335
  as path, 291
  of suffering, 292, 305, 321–27
Sukhaśrī. *See* Indrabhūti I
Sukhāvatī, 102
Sumeru, 286, 375
supplication prayers, 315
  for bodhicitta, 313
  eight ancillary path cycles lineage, 3–9
  Parting from the Four Attachments lineage, 295–97
  to Vajradhara, 183, 184, 197
suppression, 114–15, 236
Sutra of Bhadrakarātrī, 201
Sutra of Never Wavering from Dharmatā, 210
Sutra of the Close Application of Mindfulness of the Sublime Dharma, 320
Sutra of the Extensive Play, 318, 346
Sutra of the Space-like Samādhi, 211
svabhāvakāya, 81, 222, 289, 292
syllables
  blazing, 50, 262–63
  consonants, 42, 49, 99, 163, 261
  decapitating, 51, 264
  in mahāmudrā without meaning, 78, 217, 452n13
  nāḍī, 37, 160, 176, 263
  three, 107, 225, 239
  vowels, 42, 49, 99, 163, 261
symbolic lineage, 122, 244

tantra
  four divisions of, 177, 228, 442n58
  and sutra, inseparability of, 277
Tārā, 5, 69, 71, 75, 82, 207, 212, 289
Tashi Lhundrup, 462n49
Tashi Lungpa, 283, 289, 455n43
ten endowments, 318, 345, 457n23
ten nonvirtues, 328–29
ten virtues, 330
Tenzin Zangpo, 297
thirteenth stage, 102, 116–17, 133
thirty-two lands, 131–33, 254
three authorities, 108, 228, 442nn58–60
three doors
  nine features, 145
  relaxing, 286
  as supports, 107–8, 225, 440n28, 440n31
  time for recognizing, 108, 227

three frugalities, 431n70
of body, 12–13, 143
of enjoyments, 12, 142
of mind, 13, 143
three fruits, 66, 204, 437n16
three gates of liberation, 110–11. 231
emptiness, 15, 150, 429n31
signlessness, 14, 150, 429n30
without aspiration, 14, 149, 429n28
Three Jewels, 12, 58, 75, 197, 212, 214, 356, 357
three kāyas, 121, 126, 247, 292. *See also* seven limbs of three kāyas
three poisons, 13, 16, 145, 157, 330, 429n12
three purities, 30, 31–32, 167–68, 170
three realms, 454n10
attachment to, 301, 305–6, 307, 310, 320–31, 349–50
as buddhafields, 159
cause of, 157
deviating into, 212
impermanence of, 318
transforming, 26, 277, 454n6, 454n16
three spheres, 352
three vows, 12–13, 122, 124, 134, 143, 244, 253
throat cakra (*sambhogacakra*), 100
burning, 51, 263
in creation stage, 167
deity meditation in, 287
joy in, 52–53, 131, 266
syllables, 49, 261
traces, 86, 92, 93, 194, 280
training
in examples, 77, 216, 229–30
long-distance, 110, 230
looking further and further, 112, 443n109
in meaning, 77–79, 217–19
short-distance, 109, 229–30
Trakphukpa Sönam Pal, 295, 365, 461n16
traveling in sky, 59
Trayastriṃśa heaven, 323
Treasury of Couplets (Saraha), 194, 199
on clarity, 65
on liberation, 198
on mind, 64, 66, 195, 211
on realization, 79, 439n22
sources, 61, 62, 187
on syllables, 217
Treasury of Precious Instructions (Kongtrul), 139, 424, 447n1
Trinle Kyi, 275, 293
tripiṭaka, 228, 442n58
Tsadra Rinchen Drak, 256
Tsangpa Gyare, *Tibu's Root Verses of the Sixfold Cycle of One Taste*, 451n29
Tsewang Norbu, 9
Tsultrim Lhundrup, 462n50
Tuṣita heaven, 323
twelve bases of instruction, 228
twelve stages, 121, 134, 269
first, 203
signs of, 131–33
twelfth, 116, 239
two accumulations, 28, 35, 36, 142, 175, 229
two benefits, 186, 193, 269, 332
two extremes, 65, 76, 80, 110, 191, 200–201, 214, 230, 442n77, 446nn172–73
two stages, 26, 92–93
conceptuality and, 86
culmination of, 178–79
five signs in, 173
inseparable, meditation of, 286–89, 455n50
objects of desire in, 445n161
in single session, 178
two truths, 158

Ucita, 7
ultimate path, 122, 160, 245, 280
ultimate truth, 108, 228
Uma (goddess), 58, 182
union, 212
of bola and kakkola, 122, 245, 446n3
of clarity and emptiness, 144
with ḍākinīs, 175
of father and mother, 29
inconceivable, 108, 226, 228, 441n46
of spring and its ornament (*dpyid thig*, Skt. *vasantatilaka*), 264
three perceptions and, 147
of two truths, 158

Union of All Buddhas Supplementary Tantra, 253, 453n5 (ch. 16)
Union with All Buddhas Tantra, 124, 201
unsurpassed yoga tantra, xviii, 223, 403, 404
upapithas, 55, 436n12
Upendra, 162
uṣṇīṣa, 32, 33, 171, 172, 287

Vagendrakīrti, 5
Vāgīśvarakīrti, 69, 82, 207, 438n3
  Explanation of Illuminating the Precious Truth, 71, 207, 438n11
  lineage, 289
  Seven Limbs, xx, 69, 70, 71, 207, 428n3 (Introduction)
  at Vikramaśīla, 273, 274
  See also *Clear Mindfulness of the Innate*; *Mahāmudrā without Syllables*
Vairocana, 96, 219, 399
  bodhicitta of, 62, 188
  symbol of, 398
  visualizations, 79, 167, 287, 406
Vairocana Sāgara, 416, 417–18
Vaiṣṇavas, 91
vajra masters
  authority of, 108, 442n59
  empowerment, 29, 166
Vajrabhūtirāja/Vajrabhodhirāja. *See* Indrabhūti II
Vajraḍāka Tantra, 47, 257, 268
Vajradhara, 87
  in completion stage, 42
  instructions of, 103, 434n2
  lineages, 63, 122, 156, 182, 188, 224, 244, 258
  in maṇḍala offering, 196
  result, 12, 430n39
  as root guru, 146, 198, 357
  samayas of, 420
  Śiva and, 57, 58, 182
  stage of, 99, 240, 386
  supplications, 3, 4, 5, 6, 7, 8, 197, 359, 361
  visualizations, 29, 34, 35, 163–68, 174, 183, 287, 387
Vajradhātviśvarī, 287
Vajraghantapāda, 6, 55, 258
vajrakāya, 125, 133, 246, 255, 447n8
Vajramahākāla Pañjaranātha, 404–6, 407, 414–15, 417–18, 419, 420, 421. *See also* Eight-Deity Mahākāla sādhana
Vajrapānī, 4, 63, 135, 188, 288, 358, 404, 436n3. *See also* Guhyapati Vajrapāṇi
Vajrapañjara Tantra, 403, 412
Vajrāsana, 406, 416
Vajrasattva, 85, 209, 259–60, 292
Vajrasena, 439n25
Vajravairocanā, 395, 464n40
Vajravārāhī, 46, 49, 260, 394, 397
Vajrayāna, 47, 257
Vajrayoginī, 45, 55, 258, 268, 400
Vakvajrā, 166
Vararuci, 412, 420
Varuṇa, 394, 395, 397
vase empowerment, 122, 167, 244, 285, 288
Vasubandhu, 168
  Pedagogical Strategies, 342
  Treasury of Abhidharma, 316, 321, 323, 456n7
Vāsuki, 394, 395, 397
vāyus, 150, 249
  in ascetic path, 147
  āyama, 293
  in caṇḍālī, 50, 53, 262–63, 264
  conceptual grasping and, 205
  controlled by wrathful form, 58, 182, 184–85
  crooked, 58
  dissolution, 133, 254
  downward-voiding, 14, 53, 124, 128, 149–50, 246, 267
  of eight parts of body, 132
  in error correction, 237–38
  expelling, 101
  faults of, removing, 53–54, 267
  holding a vase, 265
  karma, 132, 204, 205, 441n50
  life-sustaining, 53, 266, 267
  metabolic, 54, 267
  methods of, 18, 431–32n87, 431nn76–81
  pervading, 54, 267
  purifying, 116, 445nn147–48

vāyus (*continued*)
uniting upper and lower, 288
upward-moving, 14, 53–54, 267
See also prāṇa vāyu
Vedas, 91
verbal lineage, 122
Vetalī, 34, 164, 165, 167, 172
vidyādharas, 15, 430n35
views
of dharmatā as free from proliferation, 191
four characteristic in, 246
"gnosis vajra," 124–25
inseparability of samsara and nirvana, 21, 25, 26–27, 157–59
on nonexistence, 190
and path, order of explaining, 442n61
personality, 190
"suchness of bodhicitta without beginning or end and liberated from the four extremes," 47, 258
and vāyu training, simultaneous, 247
Vikramaśīla, xx, 61, 69, 70, 207, 273–74
Vilāsyavajra, 6, 22, 98, 103–4, 156, 224, 432n7
Vīṇapāda, 3, 98, 103, 224
vipākakāya, 81, 222, 439n25, 452n14
vipaśyana, 200, 441n47, 457n12
cultivating, instructions on, 337
purpose, 336
as remedy to grasping, 335
śamatha and, 192, 338
as sign without effort, 80, 221
as supported, 192
Vīravajra, xvii, 3, 4, 63, 105, 107, 142, 188, 224
Virūpa, 4, 11–12, 37, 141, 177, 361, 429n27
Viṣṇu, 92, 96, 98–99, 193
visualization techniques
on clarity, 31, 434n41
clear appearance, time in attaining, 261
deity appearances transforming, 35, 174
for enhancing focus, 214–15
in mahāmudrā, 78–79
with recitation, 169–70
stability, 33
Visukalpa, 62
vital force (*phya*), 193–94
voice, 145, 229
benefitting others, 15, 430n33
and body, equality of, 126, 253
control of resting vāyu, 15
exhalation, 14, 109, 442n68
inhalations, 13–14, 18, 429nn15–16, 429nn19–21, 431n71, 431n87
as support, 107–8, 225, 440nn28–29, 440nn31–32
times for recognizing, 108, 441nn50–52
vows of five families, 414

Whatever Offering Substances, 196, 451n20
White Tārā, 69
wisdom consort empowerment, 29, 122, 244, 394
in creation stage, 166, 167
focusing mind in, 227, 441n48
path, 286, 288
seal of, 176
wisdom consorts, 92, 99–100
word lineage, 244

Yama, 163
yantras, 59, 185
Yerpa Gomseng, 283, 455n39
Yeshe Gyaltsen, 295, 314, 343, 461n19
yoga
conceptual, 84, 86
of eating and drinking, 399
inconceivable, 88, 97
of method and wisdom, 89
Yogacāra, 432–33n11
Yoginī, Lady, 6
yoginīs, seven types, 123

Zhangtön Chöbar, xvii, 3, 4, 5, 6, 7, 8, 156, 224, 362
Zhangtön Könchok Pal, 314, 365, 461n15
Zhönu Drup (a.k.a. Khedrup Chöje), 275, 289, 455n44